A Pira environmental guide

Noise Control

Bob Peters

Published by
Pira International
Randalls Road
Leatherhead
Surrey
KT22 7RU
UK
Tel: +44 (0)1372 802080
Fax: +44 (0)1372 802079
email: publications@pira.co.uk
http://www.pira.co.uk

Pira environmental guide series
Series editor: Professor Andrew Porteous

ISBN 1 85802 140 5

Typeset in the UK by Lewis Marshall, Epsom Surrey
Printed in the UK by TJ International Ltd, Padstow, Cornwall

Contents

	List of figures	vii
	List of tables	xi
	Preface	xiii
	Acknowledgements	xv
Chapter 1	**Basic concepts and terminology**	**1**
	Introduction	1
	Basic concepts — what is sound and how is it measured?	1
	The decibel scale	15
	Frequency analysis	31
	Time-varying noise: L_{Aeq} and L_{AN}	36
	Summary	49
Chapter 2	**The effects of noise on people in the workplace and in the community**	**53**
	Introduction	53
	The ear and hearing	53
	Noise in the workplace	65
	Other (non-hearing loss) effects of noise	72
	Noise in the community	79
	Summary	85
Chapter 3	**Sound generation, radiation and propagation**	**87**
	Introduction	87
	The behaviour of sound waves	88
	The radiation of sound from noise sources	94
	Outdoor sound propagation	105
	Propagation of sound indoors	113
	The prediction of noise levels — conclusion	130
	Summary	133

Chapter 4 **Principles of noise generation and control** **135**
Introduction 135
Good planning, management and housekeeping 135
The mechanisms of noise generation 136
Noise control during sound transmission 138
Noise control at source 161
Active noise control 182
Specification of machinery noise 183
Diagnosis of noise sources, paths and mechanisms 185
Hearing conservation policies 188
Personal ear protectors 190
Summary 201

Chapter 5 **Case studies** **205**
Introduction 205
1 The control of noise in a paper mill 206
2 The acoustic design of a new paper board machine KM8 at Stora Billerud mill in Skoghall, Sweden 215
3 Active control of noise from vacuum pumps 217
4 Examples of noise control at source 221
5 Noise control in the corrugated board industry 228
6 Noise control in the production of sheet plastic film 233
7 Noise exposure assessment at a small print works 236
8 Noise exposure assessment in a large printing press 241
9 Control of noise from newspaper presses using acoustic enclosures, havens and partitions 246
10 Noise nuisance from a printing works 252
11 Protecting the hearing using industrial audiometry 256

Chapter 6	**Control of industrial noise by application of the law, standards and codes of practice**	**267**
	Introduction	267
	Noise in the environment	268
	Noise at work	289
	European Commission regulations	298
	Summary	303
Chapter 7	**Measurement and instrumentation**	**307**
	Introduction	307
	Instrumentation and equipment	307
	Other equipment	312
	Measurement and the use of equipment	318
	Summary	345
Appendix 1	**Glossary**	**349**
Appendix 2	**Additional information**	**359**
	Further reading	359
	Organizations	365
	Standards	366
	Index	**371**

List of figures

1.1	Generation of sound waves in a tube	2
1.2	Variation of sound pressure with time for a pure tone	4
1.3	Frequency and wavelength of everyday sound	5
1.4	Synthesis of a harmonic waveform, showing how a square wave can be built up from a series of sine waves (only the first three are shown)	10
1.5	Some different types of waveform and their frequency spectra	12
1.6	Illustrating peak and root mean square (RMS) values of a sound pressure signal	14
1.7	Equal loudness contours	23
1.8	International standard (A, B and C) weighting curves for sound level meters	24
1.9	Noise criteria (NC) curves (after Beranek)	35
1.10	Showing variation of sound level with time	37
1.11	Illustrating the calculation of continuous equivalent noise level	39
1.12	Nomogram for calculation of $L_{Ep,d}$	41
2.1	The main components of the outer, middle and inner ear	54
2.2	Section of cochlea (left) and basilar membrane with Organ of Corti	56
2.3	Audiograms showing presbycusis	58
2.4	Typical noise-induced threshold shift progressing with years of exposure	61
2.5	Number of people in Great Britain qualified for disablement benefit because of noise-induced hearing loss at work	67
2.6	Model of factors influencing the achievement of a successful hearing conservation programme	73
3.1	Reflection of sound	90
3.2	Constructive (a) and destructive (b) interference	92

3.3	Graph of sound level against distance (log) for a point source, illustrating the 6 dB per doubling of distance rule	99
3.4	Cylindrically shaped waves from a line source	101
3.5	Showing the variation of sound level with distance from a plane sound source	102
3.6	Illustrating near and far fields for a real noise source	103
3.7	The refraction of sound in the atmosphere due to sound velocity gradients	109
3.8	The method of calculating sound attenuation due to noise barrier	111
3.9	Typical variation of sound absorption coefficient with frequency for porous material	117
3.10	Typical variation of sound absorption coefficient with frequency for a cavity and panel resonators	120
3.11	Typical variation of sound pressure level with distance from a noise source in a room	124
3.12	Sound transmission between rooms	128
4.1	Simple source-path-receiver models of sound transmission	138
4.2	(a) Transmission of noise by different paths (b) Methods of noise control	140
4.3	The mass law for predicting the sound reduction (R) of a single-leaf partition	142
4.4	Typical variation of sound reduction index with frequency for a single-leaf panel	143
4.5	Design features of a double-leaf construction necessary to achieve good sound insulation	145
4.6	The isolation of vibration from a machine using anti-vibration mounts	147
4.7	Typical variation of transmissibility with frequency for a machine mounted on vibration rollers	148
4.8	Typical features of a noise enclosure	151
4.9	Typical construction and sound attenuation performance of (a) absorptive or dissipative silencers (b) reactive silencers	153
4.10	Damping of vibrating panels	157

4.11 Close shielding or acoustic cladding (or lagging) of noise-radiating panels 159
4.12 The structure and important features of a jet 167
4.13 Examples of the pneumatic exhaust silencer 169
4.14 Examples of the 'induced flow' jet nozzle 171
4.15 Typical noise sources on a press, and some forms of treatment combined with a safety guard 172
4.16 Press hall: typical sound levels running 32 pages at 32000 cph 175
4.17 Folder noise spectra showing change relative to speed 175
4.18 Estimated costs of noise control assuming treatment to existing press 177
4.19 Typical variation of noise level with position in press hall and reel room 178
4.20 Sound level variation across press hall and reel stand room 179
4.21 Press room noise dose reductions for different noise control measures 180
4.22 Reel room noise dose reductions from automation and soundproofing 180
4.23 The range of noise levels at operator positions at web-fed presses 181
4.24 Active noise control applied to fan noise in a duct 183
5.1 Active noise control components are shown on an 18″ discharge pipe between vacuum pumps and an exhaust stack 218
5.2 Narrowband plot of vacuum pump noise reduction measured at the exhaust stack 219
5.3 A narrowband spectrum of the noise measured close to the stack discharge 220
5.4 A 52″ diameter exhaust stack 220
5.5 RDK printing press noise reduction 222
5.6 Graph showing the effect of a technique to reduce whistle generated by flow-induced acoustic resonance 223

5.7 Graph showing the effect of a technique to reduce noise emitted by centrifugal fans with dominant component of 490 Hz 225
5.8 Drier oven burner noise reduction 227
5.9 Factory layout showing different noise reduction measures 234
5.10 Noise map showing dB(A) contours resulting from measurements for another part of the factory 235
5.11 Site plan showing noise levels in print works 237
5.12 Noise levels for casual operator No. 2 taken from data logging dosemeters 239
5.13 A plan view showing typical operator and noise monitoring positons on a large printing press 242
5.14 Examples of noise control treatments 248
5.15 Various sound insulation arrangements for both the press hall and the reel room 249
5.16 Type of audiometer commonly used in industrial audiometric programmes 263
5.17 An audiometric booth 264
6.1 Possible variation of residual noise and specific noise with time (re. BS4142) 282
7.1 Angles of incidence of sound striking a microphone 311
7.2 Components of a sound level meter 316
7.3 The function of the microphone in a sound level meter 316
7.4 Sample measurement checklist/report form 321

List of tables

1.1 The decibel scale 19
1.2 Some typical sound levels 25
1.3 Combining decibels 26
1.4 Examples of decibel combination 26
1.5 Factors to be applied to a measured noise level in order to correct for the presence of background noise 29
1.6 Increase in noise level with number of sources 29
1.7 Calculation of dB(A) from octave bands sound pressure levels 31
1.8 Typical recommendations for maximum various indoor environments 36
2.1 Number of people in every 100 likely to suffer 50dB hearing loss after various levels of noise exposure 62
2.2 Percentage of people showing annoyance to different noise types 80
2.3 Percentage of people showing annoyance to noise types in the UK 81
3.1 Octave band barrier attenuations 112
3.2 Typical values of sound absorption coefficient for some common materials 119
4.1 Typical values of sound reduction index in dB for some common building elements 144
4.2 Calculation of hearing protection 194
6.1 Noise levels corresponding to the noise exposure categories for new dwellings 276
6.2 BS4142 assessment for Example 1 285
6.3 BS4142 assessment for Example 2 286
6.4 Summary of Noise at Work Regulations. 292

Preface

Excessive noise from industrial processes, which often indicates poorly maintained machinery and inefficient working conditions, can lead to claims for compensation for hearing damage from employees, increased levels of absenteeism, high turnover of staff, and difficulty in recruitment. It also leads to reduced levels of productivity, complaints from neighbours, and prosecutions under environmental and occupational legislation, rejection of planning applications and to loss of sales if the company's product is noisier than its competitors'.

This book is intended to be a guide for those within an organization who have responsibility for managing the problems caused by the emission of noise by the organization's activities or by its products, and affecting either the company's own employees or those of its customers, or the community in the surrounding neighbourhood. It is intended as an introduction for those with little or no prior knowledge of the subject of noise, whilst at the same time attempting to be reasonably comprehensive in its coverage.

There seems little point, however, in providing more than an introduction to areas of the subject which are already well covered in other sources. There are already many detailed and excellent publications on noise, including some covering noise in the printing, publishing and papermaking industry. A list of these works and a guide to their usefulness are given at the end of the book.

The book is not specific to the printing, packaging and papermaking industries, but this is because the problems of noise and the way in which they can be handled are not particularly industry specific. The chapter comprising case studies does provide examples related to these industries.

Since the book is intended for managers who may not have a technical background, the amount of technical detail, theory and mathematics has been kept to a minimum, but a certain amount has been included in the belief that the manager will benefit from at least an introductory knowledge and awareness of terminology, concepts and theories, even if he/she is not directly involved in this level of detail.

It is inevitable that any such text will occasionally frustrate, either by providing too little information in some areas or by being too detailed or technical in others. It is hoped that these difficulties may be minimized by the provision of a detailed contents list and index, end-of-chapter summaries, a glossary, list of standards and bibliography.

The book contains case studies specific to the printing, packaging and paper making industries, but, of course, the problems of noise and the way in which they can be handled are not particularly industry specific.

It is hoped, overall, that the book will help the reader to make a contribution to reducing the effects of noise either in the workplace or in the community.

Acknowledgements

The author wishes to thank the many people who have provided material and given help and advice in the production of this work.

Thanks are due to the following for the provision of the material in the case studies in Chapter 5: David Bull of dB Acoustics, John Charman of Antisonics and the Noise Control Centre, R Hobbs of Noise Reduction Ltd, B Jaffrey of Industrial Acoustics Company, Dr S J Karmy of SJK Scientifics Ltd, Lars Landstrom of Ingemannson Technology, Dr H G Leventhall, Digisonix Nelson Industries Inc, A Somerville of Edinburgh District Council, A Timms of James Cropper plc, A Watson of Acoustic Consultancy Services, Peter Wilson of Industrial Noise and Vibration Control.

Thanks are also due to the following who have provided much general help and advice: L Beirne, K Broughton and the late H Lester of the Health and Safety Executive, Professor Andrew Porteous of the Open University (series editor), Ian Sharland of Ian Sharland Acoustics, Stephanie Owen, Colin Cobbing, and to the following for granting permission to include the material in various Figures: John Charman of Antisonics and the Noise Control Centre, The Health and Safety Executive, A Fry of the Salex Group Limited, Bilsom International.

He also wishes to thank Ingmar Folkmans of Pira International, Gail Murray and Lewis Marshall, formerly of Pira International, to Joan, Mark and Megan for their patience, support and encouragement, and to Rory Nolan for invaluable help in producing the diagrams.

1

Basic concepts and terminology

Introduction

The aim of this chapter is to provide the manager in industry with sufficient understanding of basic principles to be able to communicate effectively with machinery suppliers, noise control consultants, factory inspectors or environmental health officers, and to make decisions about noise control measures and noise policy. The chapter will cover the nature of noise and its description and assessment: frequency, sound pressure and sound pressure level, the decibel scale, dB(A), octave, one-third octave and narrow-band frequency analyses, NR (noise rating) and NC (noise criteria) curves, methods for describing time-varying noise, such as L_{AN} and L_{Aeq}.

Basic concepts — what is sound and how is it measured?

A simple definition of noise is that it is sound that is unwanted by the receiver. Hence, the basic concepts these are those relating to sound waves.

Sound waves in air

Sound is the sensation produced in the ear as a result of fluctuations in air pressure at the ear drum. To appreciate more fully how sound is propagated, consider the effect of a plane vibrating surface (a piston) on the air in a tube (Figure 1.1). As the piston moves forward it pushes forward the layer of air next to it, thus causing the air particles to crowd together and thereby a slight increase in air pressure (a compression) in front of the piston. During the second half of the cycle the piston moves away from its starting position, thus creating a slight reduction in pressure (called a rarefaction). The adjacent air layer is sucked backwards towards the piston into this region of lower pressure. Thus the oscillating motion of the piston produces oscillatory movement in the air particles next to it. Because air is an elastic medium having mass and stiffness, the oscillations of the air layer are transmitted to neighbouring air layers. The sound wave can thus be thought of as a succession of pressure increases (compressions) and pressure decreases (rarefactions) moving down the tube.

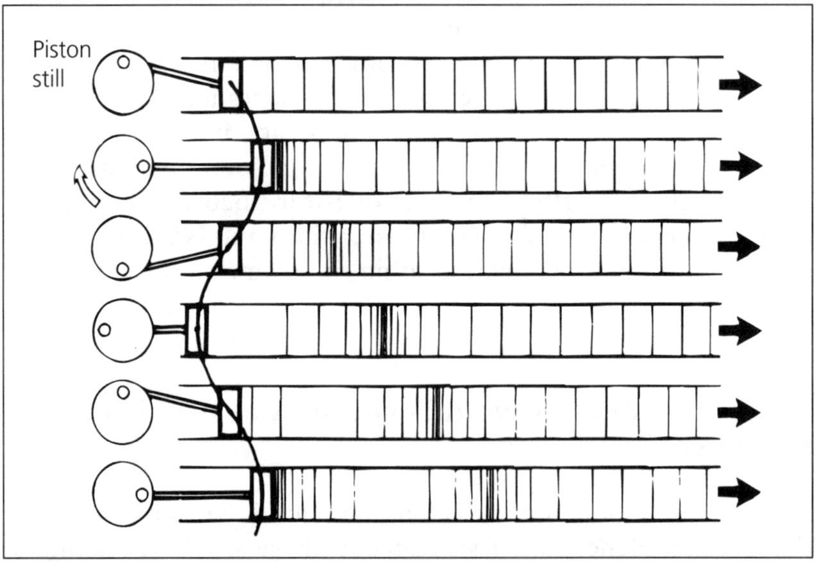

Figure 1.1 Generation of sound waves in a tube
Source: reproduced courtesy of the Sound Research Laboratories Ltd

Sound pressure (acoustic pressure)

In still air the pressure on the air is the atmospheric pressure produced by the weight of the layers of air above the earth's surface. Acoustic pressure, or sound pressure, is the fluctuation or variation in this atmospheric pressure produced by the passage of the sound wave.

Units of pressure

Pressure is measured in units of newtons per square metre (N/m^2 or Nm^{-2}), which is also given the special name pascal (Pa). Before considering the magnitude of typical sound pressures, it is worth refreshing our memory about this basic unit of pressure. The newton is the force required to produce an acceleration of $1\,ms^{-2}$ in a mass of 1 kg. The force of gravity with which the earth pulls on a mass of 1 kg (known as its weight) is approximately 10 newtons, since the acceleration produced in a falling object by the earth is $9.8\,ms^{-2}$. One newton therefore is a force equal to the weight of one-tenth of a kilogramme — let us say about the weight of an average-sized eating apple. If we now crush the apple and spread it evenly over a table of dimensions 1×1 m we produce a pressure of $1\,Nm^{-2}$ (or 1 Pa) on the table. Obviously, one pascal is only a very small pressure, in everyday terms. Atmospheric pressure is about 100 000 Pa.

The pure tone — sound pressure, frequency and wavelength

The simplest of all sounds to describe is the pure tone, in which the sound pressure varies sinusoidally with time, as shown in Figure 1.2. The frequency of the tone is the number of sound pressure cycles occurring each second, and is measured in hertz (Hz). The Greenwich mean time signal pips, for example, are short bursts of tone of 1000 Hz frequency (or 1 kHz).

Most noises are much more complex than pure tones, but can be thought of as being made up of a mixture of tones of different frequency. Sometimes broadband noises, as they are called, also have a tonal component. Such tones often give rise to descriptions such as a whistle, whine, hum, drone, and are important subjectively since it is generally accepted that the presence of such a feature causes the noise to be more annoying. This is reflected in some of the methods for assessing environmental noise, such as

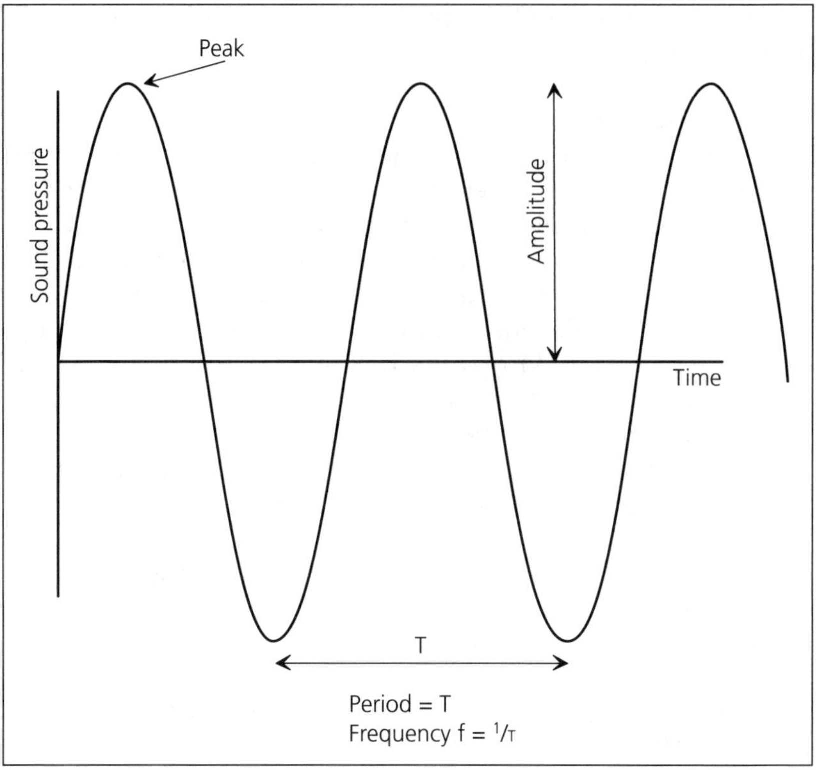

Figure 1.2 Variation of sound pressure with time for a pure tone

BS4142 and BS7445, described in Chapter 6, which include an adjustment to the measured noise level because of the tonality.

The audio-frequency range

The average human ear can hear acoustic waves in the frequency range 20–20000 Hz (20 kHz), although the exact range varies from one individual to another and it depends on the age of the person as well. The audio range is illustrated by Figure 1.3 which gives the frequencies of some well known sounds.

Acoustic waves can be produced at frequencies both above and below the audio range, although since our ears are not adapted to respond to them perhaps we should not call them sounds.

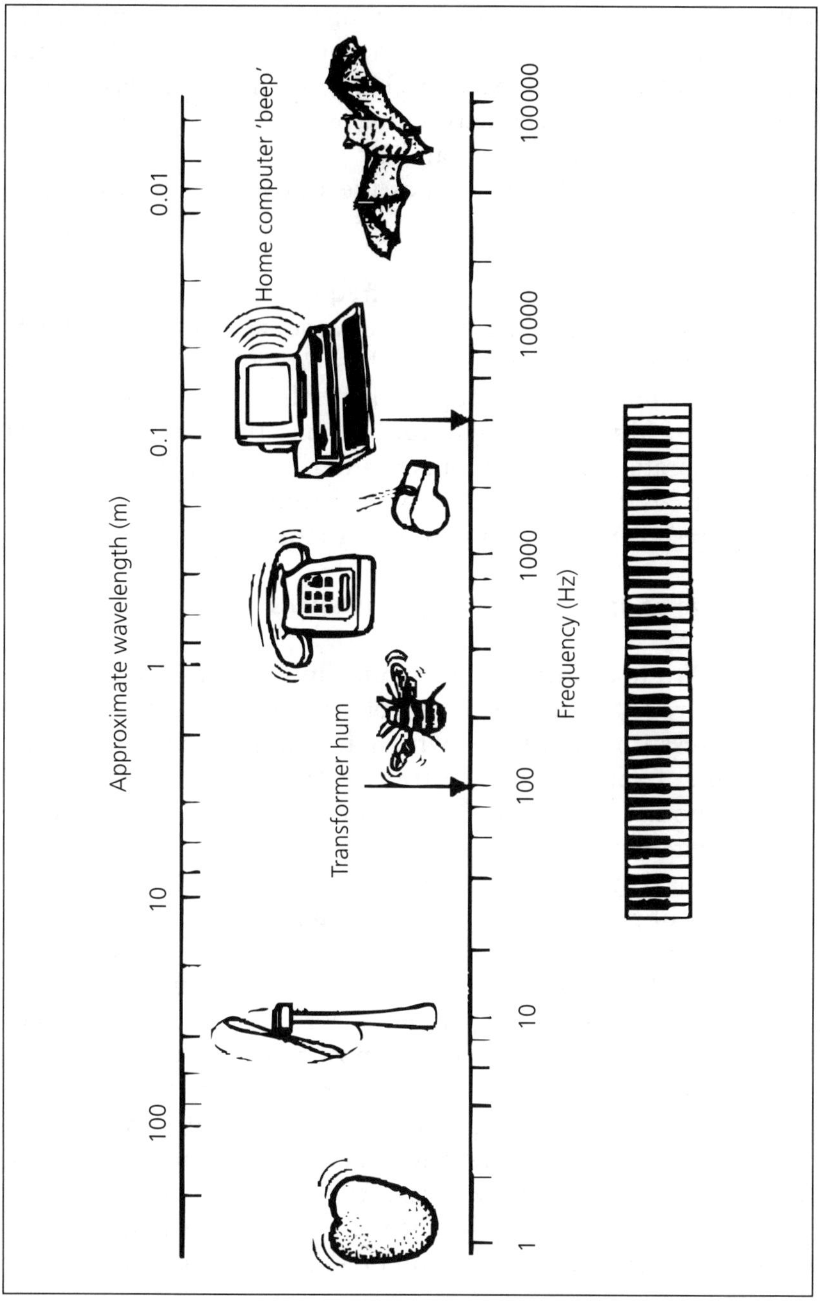

Figure 1.3 Frequency and wavelength of everyday sound
Source: reproduced courtesy of Sound Research Laboratories Ltd

Ultrasonic waves, above the audio range in frequency, are widely used in industry for a variety of purposes including ultrasonic cleaning and degreasing baths, welding and detecting flaws (such as cracks) in metal specimens. Ultrasonic waves are used by bats for echolocation purposes, and by ships fitted with sonar to detect underwater objects such as the seabed, shoals of fish and other ships.

Infrasonic waves, below the audio frequency range, may be produced in tall buildings by the effect of wind, and also by machines such as diesel engines and large boilers. At high amplitudes infrasonic waves may produce unpleasant feelings of sickness, headaches and giddiness in people, because they are capable of causing vibration of certain organs and parts of the body such as the chest cavity, the head and the stomach. They can also produce resonant vibration in some structures.

The range of audible acoustic pressures

The amplitude of the tone is the maximum excursion of sound pressure from the steady, atmospheric pressure The range of sound pressure amplitudes which are audible extends from a minimum of approximately 2.0×10^{-5} Pa (the threshold of hearing) to about 100 Pa (the threshold of pain). These figures are astonishing in two ways. First of all, the minuteness of these pressures is amazing. We have just seen that the pascal itself is only a small unit of pressure — about one hundred thousandth of an atmosphere. The smallest audible sound pressure detectable by the ear is only twenty millionths of one of these units. Even the most intense sound, at the pain level, corresponds to pressures of only about one-thousandth of an atmosphere. The ear must obviously be an extremely delicate instrument in order to detect such very small pressures. Next consider the extraordinary range of pressures to which our ears can respond. The ratio between the highest and lowest audible pressures is about 5 million to one. This very large range is one of the reasons for using a logarithmic, decibel scale for measuring sound pressures, because such a scale has the effect of condensing the audible range into a smaller range of decibel levels.

Wavelength

Figure 1.2 shows the way in which the sound pressure of a pure tone varies from moment to moment, at a particular point, for example, at the location of a microphone or at the receiver's ear drum. A similar variation will occur at an adjacent point, but with the two sine waves slightly out of step, or out of phase. The difference in phase increases with the separation of the two points, until eventually the two sound pressure cycles move back into phase again, when the separation becomes equal to one wavelength of the sound.

The frequency, f, and wavelength, λ of the tone are related by the speed of sound, c, in the medium by the equation:

$$c = f \cdot \lambda$$

The speed of sound in air varies with temperature, from about $330\,ms^{-1}$ at 0°C to about $340\,ms^{-1}$ at 20°C. The speed of sound in air does not vary with frequency, and so the wavelength decreases as the frequency increases. Hence low frequency sound has a long wavelength and high frequency sound a short wavelength. Taking the latter figure the above equation gives a wavelength of 0.34m at 1000Hz, increasing to 3.4m at 100Hz and reducing to 0.034m (or 3.4cm) at 10kHz.

The significance of frequency and wavelength

The velocity of sound depends only on the medium in which the sound is propagating, for example, air or water or some building material such as brick or concrete. The frequency of the sound depends entirely on the sound source. A sound wave may be transmitted from air via brickwork into water and then back into air again — and its frequency would remain unchanged as it moved from one medium to another, even though the wavelength would change.

It is important to know the frequency content of sounds because almost all acoustic parameters and properties associated with noise measurement and control vary with frequency, including the sensitivity of human hearing, the sound-absorbing and sound-insulating properties of materials, and the performance of noise sources. Thus, for example, the effectiveness of various noise control measures such as attenuators and silencers, acoustic tiles, partitions, enclosures, barriers and antivibration mounts varies with frequency. Usually it is easier to achieve noise reductions for high frequencies than for lower frequencies. The subjective impression created by the sound will also depend very much on its frequency content. The frequency of a tone also determines the subjective measure of its pitch.

Wavelength is important in determining how sound travels, i.e. how it is reflected by surfaces, scattered by obstacles and the extent to which it bends around barriers. The wavelength of a sound has a profound effect on the way it interacts with obstacles in its path. Thus, for example, the effectiveness of a noise barrier in shielding noise depends on its size compared with the sound wavelength, and so the barrier will be more effective at some frequencies than at others, as we shall see in Chapter 4. The pattern of sound radiation from a noise source (for example, a loudspeaker) will depend very much on the size of the noise source relative to the sound wavelength. For a given loudspeaker, the sound pattern will change with frequency, becoming more directional with increasing frequency. The same is true for the noise radiated from machinery. This has practical implications for the noise control engineer who can sometimes reduce the effect of high frequency noise by shielding, or by directing the sound away from the the receiver.

More complex sound waveforms

The pure tone is the simplest sort of sound. It is produced, for example, by a tuning fork or by a loudspeaker fed with a sinusoidal voltage signal. The pure tone is a single-frequency sound. Most sounds have a waveform that is more complicated than the simple sine wave and they can be considered to contain more than one frequency.

The next simplest type of sound is that produced by a musical instrument playing one single note. The waveform is harmonic, that is, it repeats itself but in a more complicated way than the sine wave of the pure tone waveform. The French mathematician Fourier showed that such a waveform could be built up or synthesized by combining a number of simple sinusoidal waveforms. The frequencies of these components are the fundamental frequency (the repeating frequency of the complex waveform) and multiples of it, called harmonics. Figure 1.4 shows a harmonic waveform and illustrates how it may be produced from a fundamental and two harmonics.

The reverse process to Fourier synthesis is Fourier analysis. This means the breaking down or analysing of complex waveforms into their component frequencies. Mathematical techniques can be used to do this theoretically for relatively simple repeating waveforms such as in Figure 1.4, and more complicated waveforms can also be analysed numerically using computers. The analysis can also be performed using frequency analysis instrumentation attached to the sound-measuring equipment. This consists of a series of electronic filters that allow only sounds within a particular range of frequencies to be measured. This is described more fully in Chapter 7.

The frequency spectrum of sounds

A frequency analysis may be displayed on a graph called the frequency spectrum showing the amplitude of the different frequencies (or frequency bands). The frequency spectrum and the waveform can be considered as alternative ways of describing a sound. For a pure tone, the frequency spectrum is exceedingly simple: it consists of a single line indicating the amplitude of the single frequency. A harmonic waveform also has a relatively simple spectrum, consisting of a line spectrum of the fundamental and the harmonics. The spectrum shows the relative amplitudes

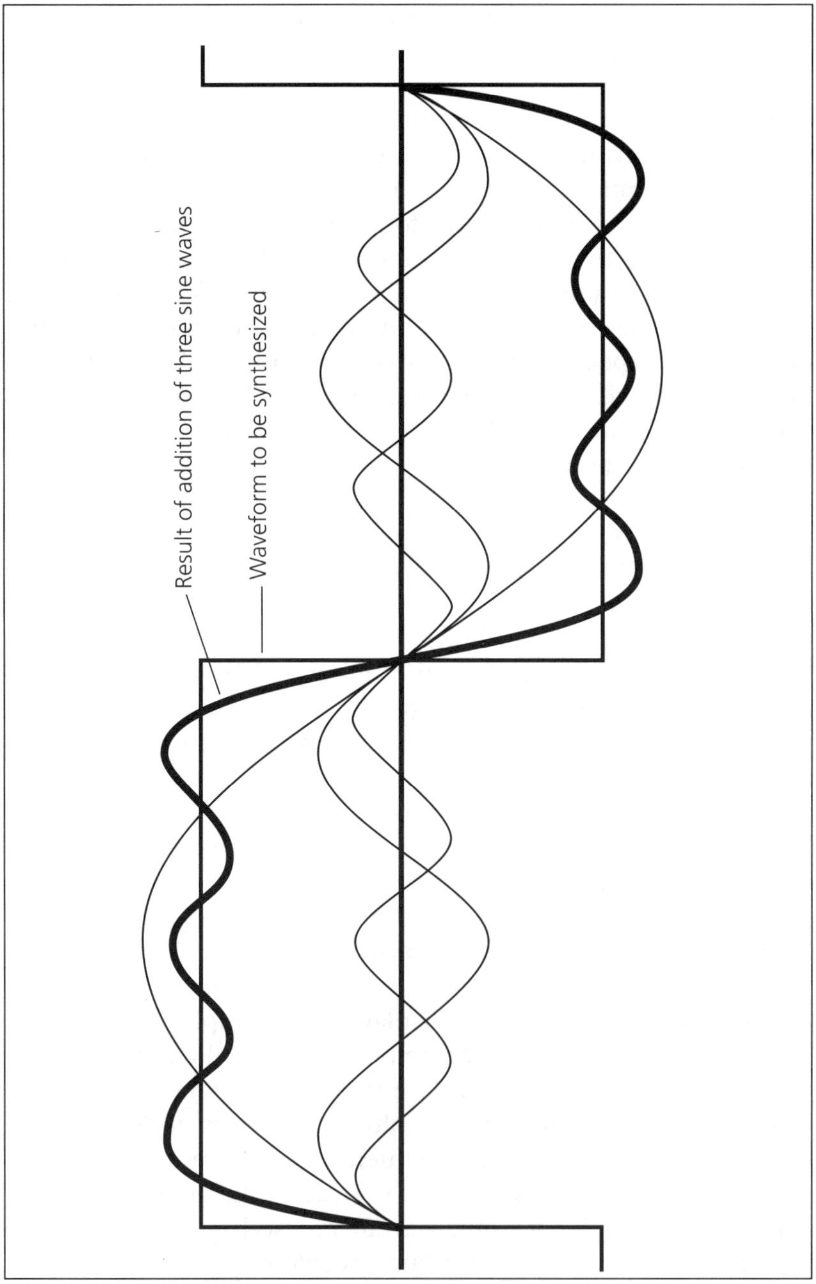

Figure 1.4 Synthesis of a harmonic waveform, showing how a square wave can be built up from a series of sine waves (only the first three are shown)

of the different harmonics and the fundamental, and thus the spectra of the same note played on two different musical instruments would be different.

It is worth mentioning two more types of waveform. Random waveforms describe sounds caused by processes which are random, and so never exactly repeat themselves. Hence the waveform is not repetitive. Examples are noise produced by traffic, by wind and by many sorts of machine. Even when it seems that the noise is produced by some repeating event such as the rotation of an engine, or of gear teeth, the noise often has a random component since the machine process never repeats exactly from cycle to cycle owing to slight changes in speed, load and other conditions.

Transient waveforms die away to zero after a period of time. They arise from a source which provides only a short transient burst of acoustic energy such as a plucked violin string, or the impact of a hammer blow on a rivet. The sound energy is dissipated by frictional processes. The simplest transient waveform resembles a sine wave but with an amplitude which decays with time. Examples are the noise produced by impulses such as those from punches, presses, hammering and mechanical handling of goods.

Frequency spectra can be assigned to transient and random sounds, but they are more complicated than periodic sounds. A random noise contains a little of all frequencies and so its frequency spectrum is a continuous curve. The frequency spectra of transient sounds are also complicated. In the case of the plucked violin string the spectrum will contain the fundamental frequency and its harmonics. In the case of a repeated transient, such as the impacts between teeth in a gear mechanism, the repetition rate of the impacts and its harmonics will also be important. Figure 1.5 shows some examples of different types of waveform and their frequency spectra.

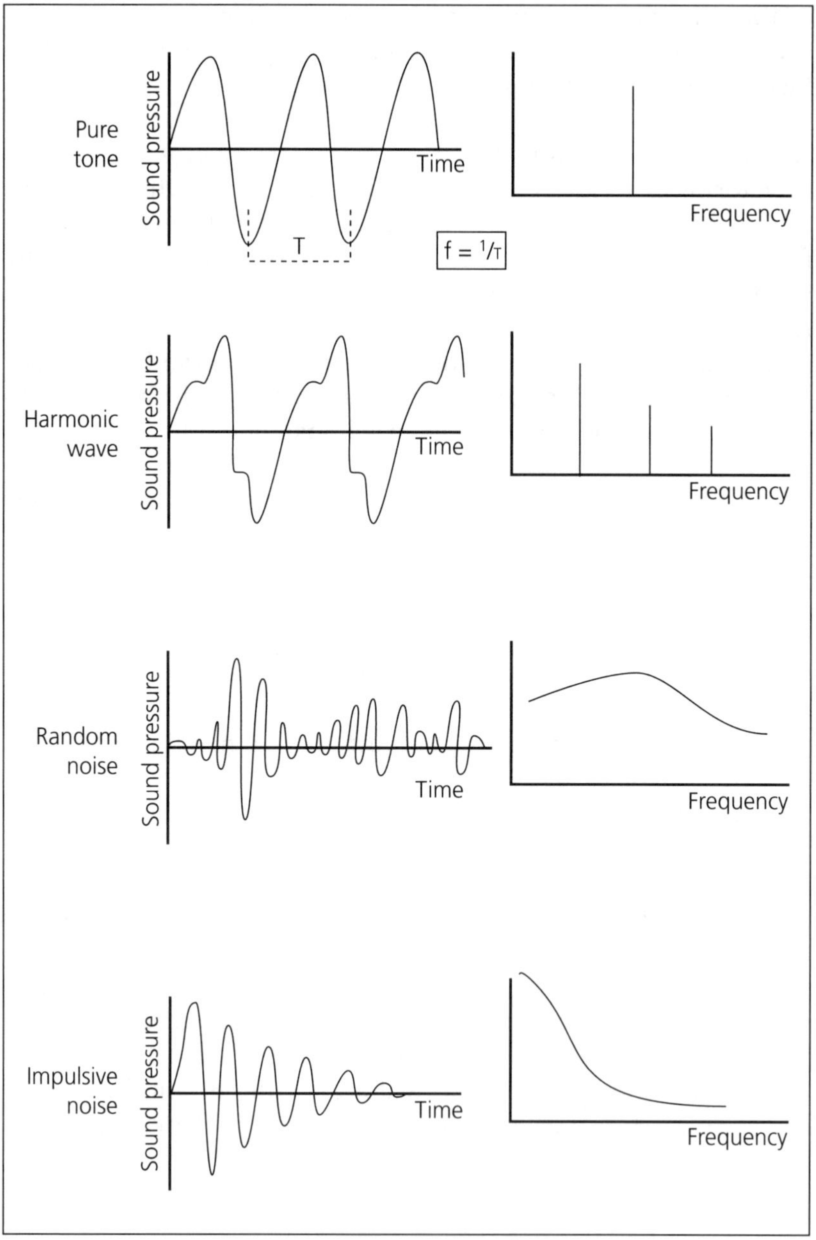

Figure 1.5 Some different types of waveform and their frequency spectra

The magnitude of sound pressures — RMS and peak values

If a pure tone were being played over the radio and the volume was turned up, the amplitude of the sound pressure would be increased — the sound would become louder. The amplitude is thus a convenient measure of the magnitude of the sound and can be related to its intensity and loudness, terms that are discussed later.

With a more complicated waveform (Figure 1.6), however, it is not so easy. One might think that the magnitude of the peak pressure of the waveform would be the value that would be most useful. However, the sound pressure might be near to the peak value for only a small fraction of the duration of the sound, and might not be closely related to the subjective impression of the sound. Perhaps an 'average' sound pressure would be a better measure of the 'size' of a sound? However, if we look at the waveform of Figure 1.2 for a pure tone, we see that, taken over a complete cycle, the average sound pressure, including rarefactions and compressions, is zero. This is true for all waveforms, not just a pure tone. We need an 'average' that takes into account the magnitude of the sound pressure fluctuations but not their direction (positive and negative) so that the compressions and rarefactions do not average out. There are various possible ways of obtaining a non-zero average sound pressure, but the one most commonly used is the root mean square (or RMS) sound pressure. This can best be described by looking at the waveform of Figure 1.6. In effect the sound level meter first squares the signal, that is multiplies it by itself. This has the effect of producing a pressure squared waveform which is always positive. (Remember that in algebra, $-1 \times -1 = +1$). The next stage is to take the average (or mean value) of this pressure squared waveform — called the mean pressure squared. Finally, by taking the square root of this value, we get back to a pressure — the root mean square pressure (strictly the square root of the mean pressure squared).

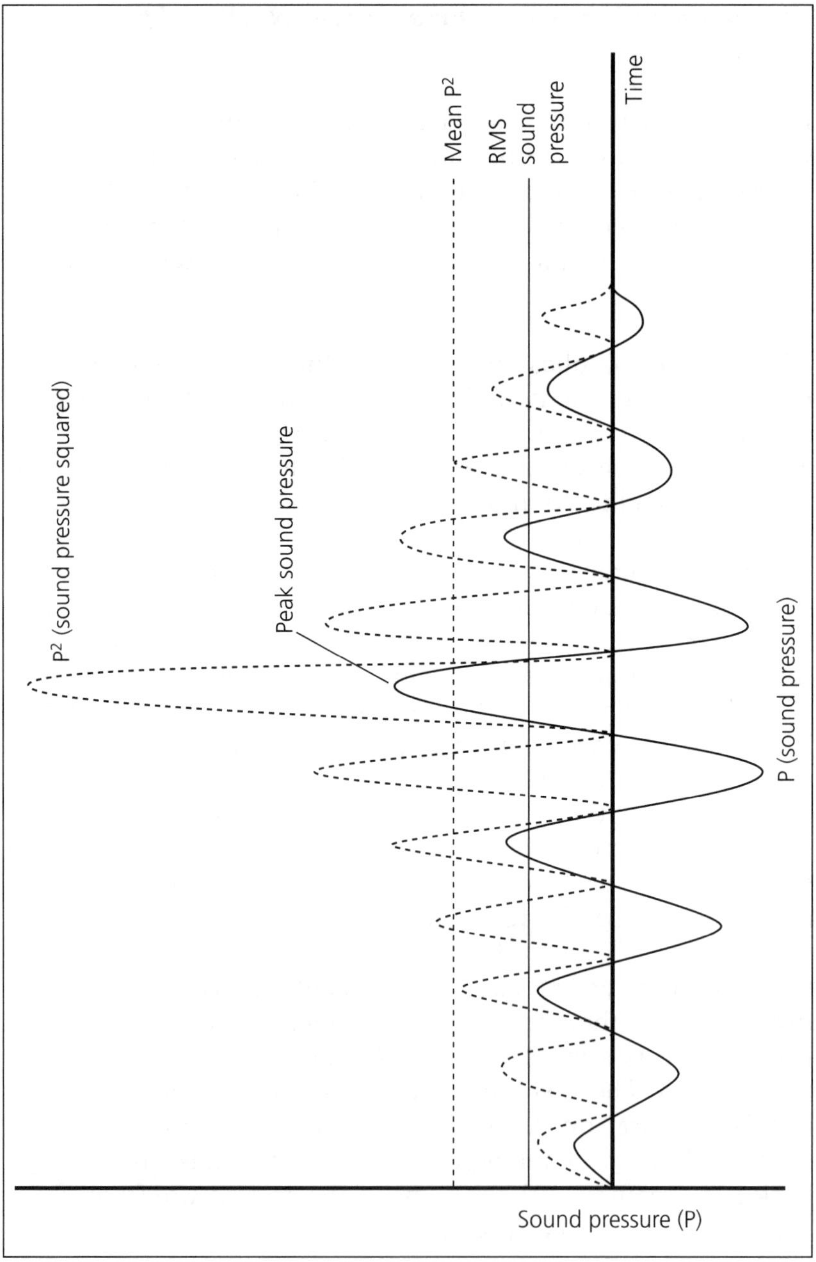

Figure 1.6 Illustrating peak and root mean square (RMS) values of a sound pressure signal

Most sound level meters have electronic circuits that convert the microphone signal into an RMS value corresponding to the RMS sound pressure. The RMS pressure is used because it can be related to the average intensity of the sound and to the loudness of the sound.

For a pure tone it can be shown that the peak pressure and the RMS pressure are simply related:

$$
\begin{aligned}
p_{\mathrm{RMS}} &= \frac{p_{\mathrm{Peak}}}{\sqrt{2}} \\
&= 0.707 \times p_{\mathrm{Peak}}
\end{aligned}
$$

For more complex signals there is no simple relationship between the two.

Despite what has been said here, there are occasions when it is important to measure the peak value of a complex sound waveform, or the peak-to-peak value. Examples could be the sound produced by impulsive noise, such as gunfire, explosions or punch presses. Some specialist impulse sound level meters can measure peak as well as RMS sound pressures.

In decibel terms (to be explained below), the peak level of a pure tone is 3dB higher than the RMS value, but the difference is higher for impulsive noise.

The decibel scale

The decibel scale is used for comparing and measuring powers (electrical as well as acoustic), and related quantities such as sound intensity and sound pressure, so it is necessary to explain the relationships between these quantities.

Acoustic energy, power and intensity

One of the features of all waves is that they transport energy — and sound is no exception. An important property of any sound source is the rate at which it radiates sound energy. This is called the sound power of the source, and is measured in watts (W).

Sound sources have a tremendous range of sound powers, varying from about 10^{-9} W for the human voice when whispering, to millions of watts radiated by a space rocket during launching. The human voice radiates about 20×10^{-6} W during conversation, and this could increase to about 10^{-3} W when shouting. A pneumatic drill used for road breaking radiates about 1W, and a typical figure for the noise output of a jet airliner is about 50 000 W.

Sound power is a basic property of a sound source and is used as a measure to rate and compare different sources, in the same way that we might compare different electric fires, or boilers or engines by their power rating. The actual amount of sound energy radiated by the source during a period of time may be obtained simply by multiplying the power in watts by the duration in seconds, but the figures in the last paragraph indicate that for most noise sources the quantity is very small, in energy consumption terms, even though the noise may affect a large number of people.

The sound power leaving a noise source, such as a burglar alarm, is spread more thinly as the sound waves travel outwards from the source. This is the main reason that the level of the noise decreases with distance from the source. The intensity of a sound is a measure of how thinly the sound power has been spread at a particular point. The intensity (I) of a sound is the power passing through unit area perpendicular to the direction in which the sound energy is travelling. It is measured in watts per square metre (W/m^2 or Wm^{-2}).

$$I = \frac{W}{S}$$

where W is the power in watts and S is the area in metres squared.

Example

Sound is passing from inside a room through an open window of area 5 m^2 to the outside. The intensity of the sound at the open window is $3.0 \times 10^{-4} Wm^{-2}$. Calculate the acoustic power W radiated through the window.

$$I = \frac{W}{S}$$

$$\therefore W = I \times S$$

$$= 3.0 \times 10^{-4} \times 5$$

$$\text{Acoustic power} = 1.5 \times 10^{-3} \text{ watts}$$

Audible sounds can have a very wide range of intensities, from $10^{-12} Wm^{-2}$ i.e. one-millionth of a millionth of a watt per square metre (the threshold of hearing for the average person) to more than 100 Wm^{-2} (approaching the threshold of pain) — a range of more than one million million to one. Sound intensity is a useful quantity because it can be related to the sound power of the noise source, and is one of the important factors in the subjectively assessed 'loudness' of the sound.

Although sound intensity is important as the basis of many prediction calculations (to be discussed in Chapter 3), sound pressure is a more useful quantity in practical terms, and is the quantity which is always measured using the microphone of the sound level meter. The intensity (I) of sound at a point is proportional to the square of the sound pressure (p) at that point:

$$I \propto p^2$$

Thus, for example, if the sound pressure is doubled then the sound intensity increases fourfold. It is because of this important relationship that the RMS value of pressure is often measured, since the average value of p^2 will be proportional to the mean or average intensity of the sound over the measurement period.

The decibel scale

The decibel scale is a logarithmic scale for measuring or comparing energies or powers, or related quantities such as sound intensity.

If two sounds have intensities I_1 and I_2 then, on a decibel scale, I_2 may be said to be N dBs above I_1, where:

$$N = 10\log\left(\frac{I_2}{I_1}\right)$$

A similar scale may be used to compare the sound power outputs (W_2 and W_1) from two noise sources, i.e. $N = 10\log(W_2/W_1)$.

Sound pressure is related to the sound intensity as discussed above, and so two sounds with sound pressures p_1 and p_2 may also be compared on the decibel scale:

$$N = 10\log\left(\frac{p_2}{p_1}\right)^2 = 20\log\left(\frac{p_2}{p_1}\right)$$

Table 1.1 gives some examples of how the scale works.

From the table a 20 dB noise reduction, typically achieved by a single-glazed window for example, corresponds to one-hundred-fold reduction in sound intensity, and the 50 dB sound insulation that is typically achieved by a masonry wall means that the wall transmits only one part in 100000 of the sound energy incident upon it.

The corresponding sound pressure ratios are the square root of those for intensity, so that a 20 dB reduction is equivalent to a pressure ratio of 10: 1 (= $\sqrt{100}$). Table 1.1 may be extended by adding or subtracting values from the right-hand column and multipyling or dividing the corresponding values from the left-hand column, or vice versa. Thus a decibel reduction of 26 dB

Table 1.1 The decibel scale

Intensity ratio I_2/I_1	Decibel difference NdB
1	0
2	3
3	4.8 i.e. approx. 5 dB
4	6
5	7
6	7.8 i.e. approx. 8 dB
7	8.5
8	9
9	9.5
$10 = 10^1$	10
$100 = 10^2$	20
$1000 = 10^3$	30
$10000 = 10^4$	40
$100000 = 10^5$	50
$1000000 = 10^6$	60

(= 20 + 6) corresponds to a sound intensity ratio of 400 (= 100 × 4) and a sound pressure ratio of 20 (= $\sqrt{400}$).

Reasons for using the decibel scale

The first reason is one of convenience, because by using a logarithmic scale the very large range of audible sound pressures (5 million to one, corresponding to an even larger range of sound intensities of 25 million million to one) is compressed into a much more manageable range of about 120 dB). The second reason is that the human response to sound is also logarithmic, with each tenfold increase (i.e. 10 dB) in sound intensity being judged, on average, to double the loudness of the sound, so that a one-hundred-fold increase, i.e. 20 dB, would produce a fourfold increase in loudness and a one-thousand-fold increase (30 dB) will increase the loudness by a factor of 8. A 3 dB increase, which corresponds to a doubling of sound intensity, produces a small but noticeable subjective increase of loudness in typical situations, but a 1 dB increase is only just noticeable under the most favourable listening conditions. The third reason is again one of convenience, for it is easier to deal with decibel values that are added or subtracted from each other (e.g. 20 dB + 30 dB = 50 dB) rather than with very small ratios that would have to be multiplied or divided together (e.g. 0.01 × 0.001= 0.00001).

Reference values: sound pressure level, sound intensity level and sound power level

The statement that machine A produces a noise level which is 10 dB higher than machine B uses the decibel scale in a relative way, without assigning an absolute value to either of the two levels. The use of internationally agreed reference levels gives an absolute value to quantities measured on a decibel scale. The reference value of sound pressure, $p_{0,}$ is 2×10^{-5} Pa, or 20×10^{-6} or 20 micropascals (μPa), which represents the threshold of hearing for the average young person with normal hearing and corresponds to 0 dB. Values measured on a decibel scale relative to this value are called sound pressure levels, and denoted by the symbols SPL or L_p. The reference value, W_0, for the sound power level scale (L_W) is 10^{-12} W, and for sound intensity level scale (L_I) the reference value (I_0) is 10^{-12} Wm^{-2}. Thus:

$$L_p = 20\log\left(\frac{p}{p_0}\right)$$

$$L_I = 10\log\left(\frac{I}{I_0}\right)$$

$$L_W = 10\log\left(\frac{W}{W_0}\right)$$

These three different scales represent three different physical quantities (sound pressure, power and intensity) although in each case the measure is in decibels. Which of the three is being referred to should be made clear by the context, but occasionally this may be made specific, or given emphasis by quoting the reference value, for example, 120 dB re. 10^{-12}W, which makes it clear that this is a sound power level.

The reference value for sound intensity has been chosen so that for certain sounds (the so-called plane wave approximation) the sound intensity level has the same numerical value as the sound pressure level, but sound level meters used to measure noise respond primarily to sound pressure and cannot give any indication of the direction of flow of sound energy. There are specialist sound intensity meters that can do this. These are discussed in Chapter 7.

The relationship between sound pressure level and sound power level is the basis of the method for predicting how noise levels vary with the distance from the noise source, discussed in detail in Chapter 3.

A-weighted decibels, dB(A)

The vast majority of noise measurements are of A-weighted decibels, dB(A). The A-weighting is an electronic frequency weighting network which attempts to build the human response to different frequencies into the reading indicated by a sound level meter, so that it will relate to the loudness of the noise.

Loudness is a measure of the subjective impression of the magnitude of a sound. It is related not only to the intensity of the sound but also to its frequency. Intensity and frequency are measures of the physical characteristics of the noise, independent of human response, whereas loudness is a measure of human response. Frequency weighting networks were first introduced into sound level meters in the 1950s in an attempt to simulate the equal loudness contours which show how the loudness of pure tones is related to sound pressure level and frequency (Figure 1.7). The contours were developed from the results of experiments in which listeners were asked to judge between the loudness of a reference tone at 1000 Hz, set at a constant level (for example, 60 dB for the 60 dB contour), and a test tone at another frequency. The level of the test tone is adjusted until the subject judges that the two tones are equally loud. The level and frequency are then plotted, as one point on the contour, and the experiment is then repeated at another frequency. The contours show that human hearing is most sensitive to frequencies in the 1–4 kHz range, with a reduced response at the low and very high frequency ends of the spectrum. Thus, for example, a pure tone of say 60 dB at 1 kHz will sound less loud than a tone of the same level at, say, 100 Hz, a measure of the difference being the increase in level of the lower frequency tone needed for it to sound equally as loud as the 1 kHz note (approximately 9 dB in this case).

The shape of the equal loudness contours indicates that human frequency response to sound varies with the sound level, with contours of higher level being 'flatter' than lower ones. Therefore three frequency weightings, A, B and C, were devised for use with sounds of low, medium and high levels, with a fourth weighting, D, being added later, specifically for use with aircraft noise.

Although the correlation of dB(A) with loudness is only approximate, and there are more accurate methods of determining loudness, the A-weighted SPL has, despite some limitations, become universally accepted as the simplest way of measuring a noise which does give some correlation with human response. The B- and D-weighting networks are no longer commonly used, but the C-weighting is sometimes used, as explained below. The value of the frequency weightings are specified by British and international standards (BS 5969 and IEC 651) and are shown graphically in Figure 1.8.

Low frequency noise

The value of the weighting is largest at low frequencies, and one of the most common criticisms of the use of dB(A) is that it may undervalue the disturbing effects of low frequency noise, such as that from commercial and industrial fans, which sometimes only becomes noticeable at nighttime when other sources of noise have ceased to operate. A good indication of the low frequency content

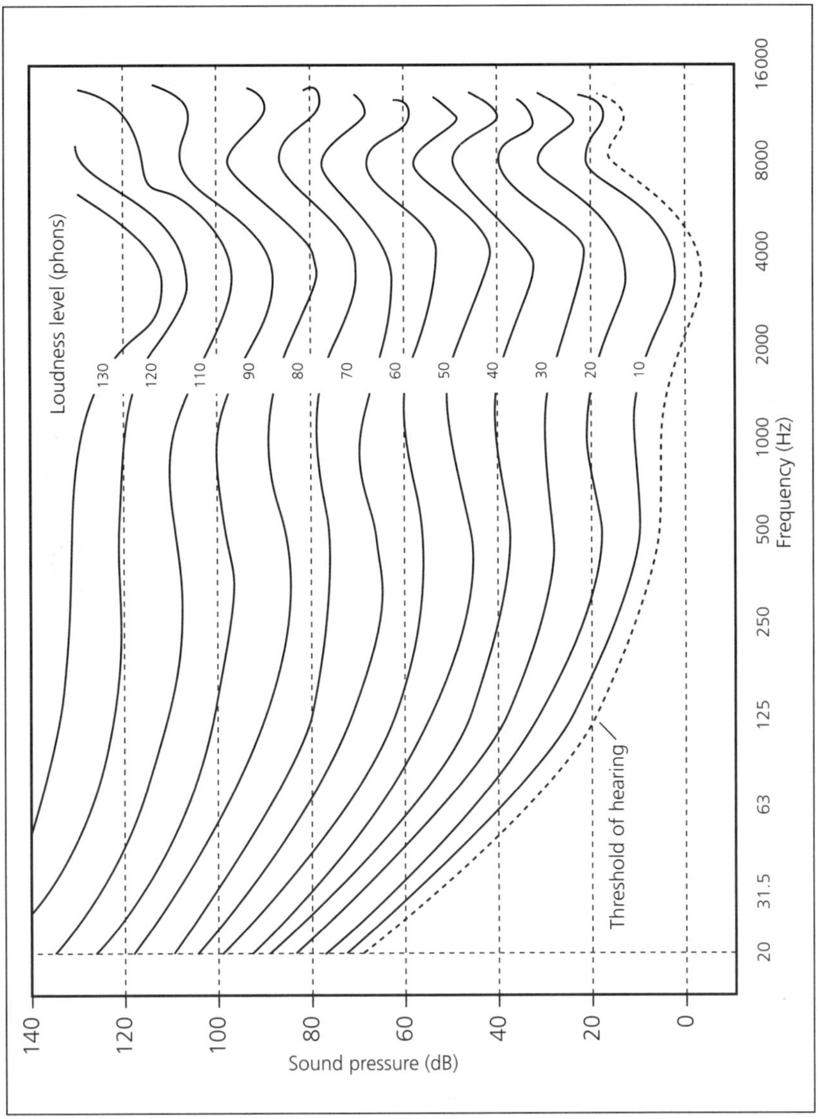

Figure 1.7 Equal loudness contours

in a noise may be obtained by comparing the A-weighted and the unweighted values of sound pressure level. If the difference between these is small then the sound contains mainly medium and high frequencies, whereas a low frequency noise will have a

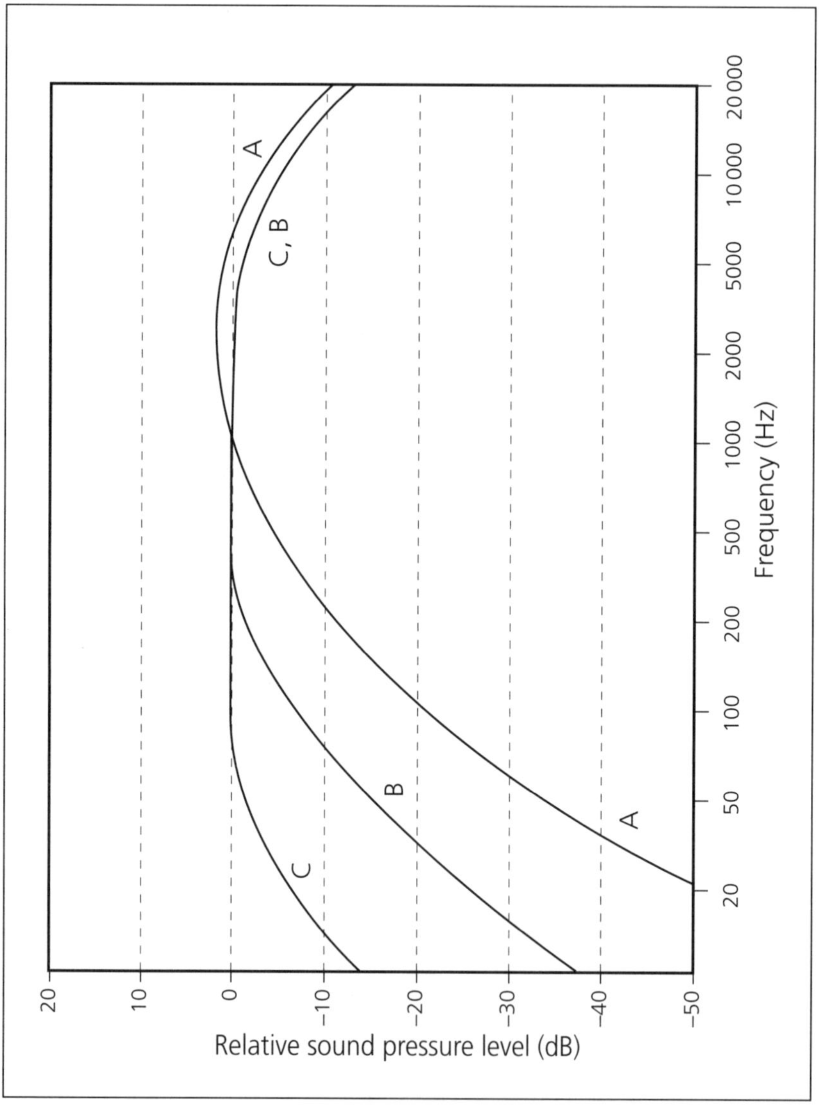

Figure 1.8 International standard (A, B and C) weighting curves for sound level meters

dB(A) value which is well below the unweighted value. The C-weighting is the 'flattest' of the weightings and so dB(C) is sometimes used as an approximation to the unweighted SPL, and the difference between dB(A) and dB(C) used as an indication of the low frequency content of a noise. The C-weighting is also increasingly used for measuring the peak sound pressure of impacts and impulsive noise, for which the A-weighting is inappropriate because of its effect on the low frequency components of the noise.

The A-weighted sound pressure level may also be written as L_{pA}. Table 1.2 gives typical examples of L_{pA} for some common sounds.

Table 1.2 Some typical sound levels

dB(A)	Examples
140	Threshold of pain
120	Jet aircraft at 100m
100	Road drill, loud disco
90	DIY drill (close to ear), lorry roadside
80	Traffic at a busy roadside
70	Hairdryer
60	Washing machine
50	TV in lounge
40	Quiet office
30	Bedroom at night
20	Broadcasting studio (background noise level)
0	Threshold of hearing

Combining sound pressure levels

When more than one noise source is operating simultaneously it becomes necessary to consider how the individual sound pressure levels combine. Since the decibel values are based on logarithms we should not expect them to obey the rules of ordinary arithmetic. We learnt earlier that a doubling of sound energy, power or intensity corresponds to an increase of 3dB. Hence if two machines each individually produces a level of, say, 90dB at a certain point, then when both are operating together we should expect the combined sound pressure level to increase to 93dB, but certainly not to 180dB.

Table 1.3 gives a method for combining levels in pairs, based on adding to the higher level a correction which depends upon the difference between the two levels. Although this is only an approximate method it should give results which are accurate to the nearest decibel, which is satisfactory for most purposes.

Table 1.3 Combining decibels

Difference between levels	Add to the higher level
0	3
1	3
2	2
3	2
4	1
5	1
6	1
7	1
8	1
9	1
10	0

As an example of the use of Table 1.3, consider the combining of four decibel levels: 82 dB, 84 dB, 86 dB, and 88 dB. The procedure may be laid out as shown in Table 1.4

Table 1.4 Examples of decibel combination

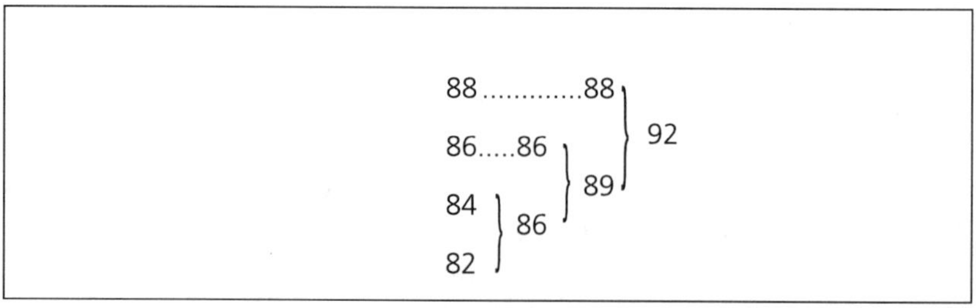

The levels are combined in pairs using Table 1.3. The first two levels in the series, 82 and 84, are combined to give 86 dB. This 'running total' is then combined with the next in the list, 86 dB, to give a new running total of 89 dB, which is then combined with the final value, 88 dB, to give a total combined level of 92 dB.

Note that according to the table, differences of 10 dB or more are negligible, so that the lower of the two levels may be ignored. Although the levels may be taken in any order, it is convenient to take them in ascending order, as in this example, so that lower values can be combined first, and so may make a significant contribution when combined with the higher levels.

The combined value, L_T, of several levels, L_1, L_2, L_3, ..., L_N may also be calculated, accurately, using the formula:

$$L_T = 10\log\left[10^{\frac{L_1}{10}} + 10^{\frac{L_2}{10}} + 10^{\frac{L_3}{10}} + \ldots + 10^{\frac{L_N}{10}}\right]$$

ı the above example:

$$L_T = 10 \log [10^{8.2} + 10^{8.4} + 10^{8.6} + 10^{8.8}]$$
$$= 91.6, \text{ or } 92\,\text{dB to the nearest decibel}$$

In the above formula each of the decibel levels is, in effect, converted back to an intensity, $10^{Lx/10}$. These intensities are added together and the total intensity converted back into a decibel value.

Some consequences of decibel arithmetic — background levels, multiple sources

Effect of background noise on sound level measurements

It can be seen from the decibel addition table (Table 1.3) that a decibel level which is more than 10 dB below other levels makes a negligible contribution (less than 0.5 dB) to the total level. When measuring the sound level from a particular noise source the microphone will also be affected by other noises, i.e. by the background noise. The total level indicated by the sound level meter will be the total sound pressure level, including the contribution from the background.

It follows that if the background noise level is not to produce a significant effect on the accuracy of measurements then the measured sound levels must be at least 10 dB higher than the background level. Putting it another way: background noise levels should ideally always be at least 10 dB below the noise level it is wished to measure.

Example
The noise level at 1 metre from a machine in a workshop is 92 dB(A). When the machine is switched off the background level is 88 dB(A). What would be the 'true' noise level from the machine, i.e. in the absence of the high background level?

The background level, L_B, has to be 'subtracted' from the measured level, L_M, to find the true level, L_T according to the following formula, which follows from the approach adopted in the preceding examples:

$$L_T = 10 \log \left[10^{\frac{L_M}{10}} - 10^{\frac{L_B}{10}} \right]$$

$$= 10 \log [10^{9.2} - 10^{8.8}]$$

$$= 89.8$$

$$\text{i.e. true level} = 89.8 \text{ dB, or } 90 \text{ dB}$$

In this example the background level is only 4 dB below the measured level, and this results in a reading which is just over 2 dB too high. A correction to the measurement can be calculated, as above, (alternatively a 'decibel subtraction' table as in Table 1.5 may be used) but it would be much better to try to remeasure the noise from the machine more accurately when background levels are much lower, maybe at lunchtime in the workshop, or in the evening or at the weekend.

Multiple noise sources
In many situations the total noise level arises from contributions from several noise sources and careful consideration of the

Table 1.5 Factors to be applied to a measured noise level in order to correct for the presence of background noise

Difference between measured noise level and background level (dB(A))	Amount to be subtracted from measured noise level (dB(A))
3	3
4–5	2
6–9	1
10 or more	0

relative importance of the contribution of each source to the total is necessary in order to develop an appropriate strategy for noise control. As an example let us consider the simplest situation where there are ten identical machines each producing a level of 80 dB at the receiver. If only one source is operating, i.e. with all the others switched off, the total level L_T will be 80 dB. Switching on another source doubles the sound intensity and so increases the level to 83 dB. The effect of operating a third source may be found by using Table 1.3 for combining decibels: combining 80 dB and 83 dB produces a total level of 85 dB. The result of continuing this process until all ten machine are switched on is shown in Table 1.6.

Table 1.6 Increase in noise level with number of sources

Number of machines switched on	Combined or total level L_T
1	80
2	83
3	85
4	86
5	87
6	88
7	88.5
8	89
9	89.5
10	90

As an alternative to using the combining decibels table the following formula could be used:

$$L_T = L + 10\log n \quad \text{(where } n \text{ is the number of sources)}$$

As each source is switched on the noise level increases, but by less and less each time. Ten identical sources combine to produce an extra 10 dB(A). In this situation the only way to produce an appreciable noise reduction is to pay equal attention to reducing noise levels from each source in the 'chorus'. For example, a noise reduction of, say, 4 dB from each of the ten machines will produce a total noise reduction of 4 dB(A), whereas a complete silencing (more than 30 dB noise reduction, let us say) of only two of the ten machines will achieve only a 1 dB(A) reduction in the 90 dB(A) level, since eight sources remain and produce a total of 89 dB(A).

Implications for noise control

The above example illustrates an important point about strategies for diagnosing the relative importance of the different noise sources. The only effective way to find out which is the most important contributor to the total noise is to switch all the sources off and then to switch each one on in turn. The alternative strategy, of switching the sources off one at a time, will be completely ineffective.

If one noise source is several decibels higher than all the others then the noise control strategy changes. Attention must then be paid, as a first priority, to reducing the noise from this one source, before it is worth considering noise control measures for the other sources. If, for example, an eleventh source producing a level of 90 dB(A) on its own is added to the chorus of ten in the above discussion, then it will be useless to consider noise reductions for these ten until the eleventh is silenced by at least 10 dB.

In practice it will be more complicated, and it will be necessary to conduct a noise control programme in several stages, assessing the changing priorities for noise reduction at each stage.

Frequency analysis

Although a single figure value such as the dB(A) is useful for assessing the effect of a noise, a more detailed knowledge of the frequency content of the noise is sometimes required, for example, when it is necessary to specify noise control measures. The sound pressure level is measured in a series of frequency bands and plotted as a graph of sound pressure level against frequency, called a frequency spectrum. The most commonly used method is octave band analysis, but one-third octave band and narrow-band analyses are also used. Instrumentation for carrying out frequency analysis is described in Chapter 7.

Octave band analysis

The sound pressure level is measured in a series of frequency bands, with centre band frequencies one octave (a doubling of frequency) apart: 31.5 Hz, 63 Hz, 125 Hz, 250 Hz, 500 Hz, 1000 Hz, 2000 Hz, 4000 Hz and 8000 Hz. Table 1.7 shows the octave band spectrum for the noise measured from two different machines, an electric drill, and a compressor.

Table 1.7 Calculation of dB(A) from octave bands sound pressure levels

(1)	(2)	(3)	(4)	(5)	(6)
Octave band	Drill	Compressor	A-weighting	A-weighted drill	A-weighted compressor
63	45	85	−26	19	59
125	58	89	−16	42	73
250	67	91	−9	58	82
500	74	80	−3	71	77
1000	79	81	0	79	81
2000	82	75	+1	83	76
4000	81	70	+1	82	71
8000	77	68	−1	76	67

The octave band values for the drill are listed in column 2 and show that the drill is a source of mainly high frequency noise, with the highest octave bands being at 1, 2 and 4 kHz. The corresponding data for the compressor are shown in column 3. They show that, in contrast, the compressor is predominantly a low frequency source, with highest sound pressure levels in the 125, 250 and 500 Hz bands. Column 4 gives the values of the A-weighting, rounded to the nearest decibel, and columns 5 and 6 the values of the A-weighted octave band levels for the drill and compressor respectively, obtained by adding the correction of column 4 to the levels in columns 2 and 3.

Combining the decibel values in column 5, using the methods shown in the previous section (i.e. table or formula), gives the overall dB(A) value for the drill. A sound level meter switched to dB(A) does this automatically, but only by measuring the octave bands and tabulating as shown can we see which bands have greatest influence in determining the dB(A) value. Both sets of data give the same dB(A) value, 87 dB(A), even though they have such differently shaped frequency spectra, and they sound different to the ear.

Combining the unweighted decibel values in column 2 gives the overall unweighted level (sometimes called the linear value, dB(Lin)) of 86 dB for the drill, and a similar exercise, using column 3, gives 94 dB for the compressor. It can be seen that for the low frequency noise from the compressor the unweighted value is 8 dB higher than the A-weighted value, demonstrating the discrimination of the A-weighting against low frequencies, whereas for the drill the two values are within 1 dB, because the noise from the drill is mostly high frequency.

The dB(C) values for the two spectra are 86 dB and 94 dB, i.e. the same, to the nearest decibel, as the unweighted values.

Specification of noise reduction

The noise reductions achieved by devices such as silencers, acoustic enclosures, screens and barriers should always be specified in octave bands. In fact it would be impossible to specify an overall noise reduction, in dB(A), for such a device because it will vary, depending on the frequency spectrum of the particular noise source. This is discussed in more detail in Chapter 4.

One-third octave and narrowband frequency analysis

Octave band analysis is adequate for and widely used for specifying noise control in industry, including for the selection of ear protectors (see Chapter 4). A more detailed description of the spectrum may be obtained using one-third octave band analysis, which gives three times as many frequency points in the spectrum since there are three one-third octave bands in each octave band. One-third octave analysis is widely used in building acoustics for the measurement of airborne and impact sound insulation.

Any more detailed breakdown of the spectrum is called narrowband analysis. It is usually carried out either to provide objective evidence of the existence of one or more tones in the noise or to provide accurate measurement of the frequency of the tone, in order to help diagnose the source or cause of the noise. Examples of the use of narrowband analysis are given in Case Studies 3 and 4 of Chapter 5.

Some narrowband analysers use filters with a bandwidth which is a constant percentage of the frequency of the centre of the band, so that, for example, the bandwidth of the 1000 Hz band is ten times the width of the 100 Hz band. This is the case with the octave and one-third octave band series, and one-sixth, one-twelfth and one-twenty-fourth octave band filters are also available. Other narrowband frequency analysers, such as fast Fourier transform (FFT) analysers, operate on a constant bandwidth basis, for example, a constant bandwidth of say 100, 50 or 20 Hz across the entire spectrum. Further information is given in Chapter 7.

Other frequency-based noise indices — NC, NR, SIL, PNdB, PHONS

Noise criteria (NC) curves were devised in the USA in order to assess annoyance caused by noise in offices; they are now widely used for specifying background noise levels in the indoor environment particularly from heating, ventilating and air conditioning sytems. A graph of the octave band spectrum of the background noise in the room is plotted against a family of NC curves as shown in Figure 1.9. In order to meet a particular target (such as NC40, which is a typical requirement for a general office), each octave band value must lie on or below the specified NC curve value. To express this in a different way, the NC rating of the noise in the room is the value of the highest NC curve met by any of the octave band levels in the noise spectrum. The spectrum plotted in Figure 1.9 fails to meet NC40 but would satisfy NC45. In many cases the NC value is often about five below the dB(A) value, so that an NC value of 45 often corresponds to a level of about 50 dB(A).

Noise rating (NR) curves were developed in Europe and were intended to have a wider range of applicability than the NC system. They operate in a similar way to the NC system and it is often a matter of custom and practice as to which is specified. There are many variations. A list of typical criteria for different types of internal space is given in Table 1.8. Although the dB(A) method is the simplest criterion to use, and does not require octave band measurement, the NR/NC system has the advantage that if noise reduction is necessary it is immediately apparent from the graphs how many decibels of reduction are required, and in which bands.

The speech interference level (SIL) is a measure related to the degree with which background noise interferes with communications. It is the arithmetic mean of the three octave bands which are most prominent in speech, 500 Hz, 1000 Hz and 2000 Hz. Other more complex measures which may be derived from octave or one-third octave band measurements are the loudness level of the sound in PHONS, or the perceived noise level, PNdB, but these are beyond the scope of this text, and are rarely used now.

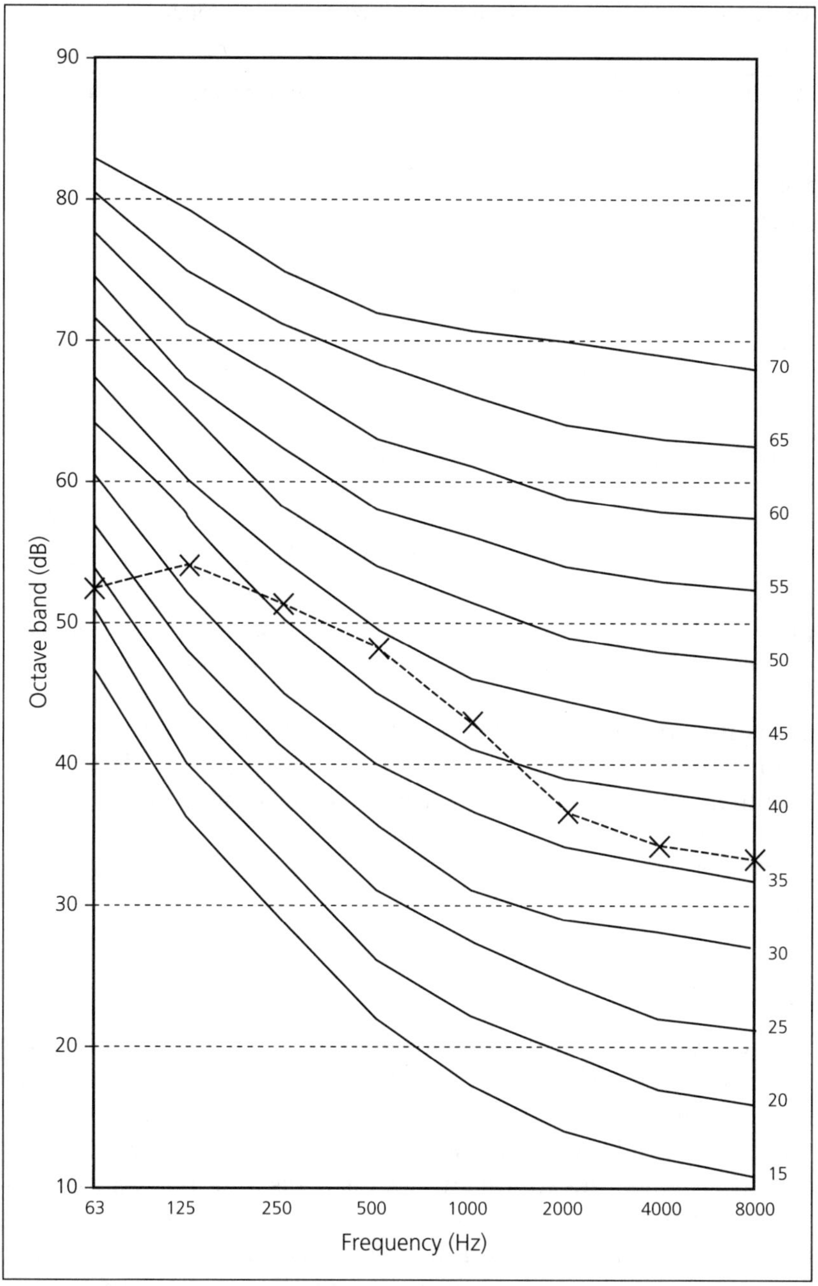

Figure 1.9 Noise criteria (NC) curves (after Beranek)

Table 1.8 Typical recommendations for maximum various indoor environments

Indoor environment	**Recommended maximum background noise level**
Broadcasting and recording studios, concert halls	NC 20–25
Theatres, lecture and conference rooms	NC 25–30
Cinemas, private offices, libraries	NC 30–35
General offices, restaurants, department stores	NC 35–45
Canteens, supermarkets, kitchens, gymnasia	NC 45–50

Time-varying noise: L_{Aeq} and L_{AN}

A noise which appears steady or constant to the ear may, when measured, show a variation of a few decibels, but provided that these fluctuations are no more than say ±4 dB the average sound pressure level may be a satisfactory measure. However, the level of noise in both the workplace and in the environment may sometimes vary over wide ranges of 30 or 40 dB or more, and in these cases it is necessary to use a different measure, of either the equivalent continuous level or the statistical percentile level. A graphical indication of the variation of level with time (Figure 1.10) is also useful in order to pinpoint the time of occurrence of certain noise events, and because certain types of event may sometimes be recognized by their 'level versus time' profile.

The equivalent continuous noise level, $L_{Aeq,T}$

The continuous equivalent noise level, L_{Aeq} of a time-varying noise is the level of a steady, continuous noise that over the period of time under consideration contains the same amount of A-weighted sound energy as the time-varying noise. The period of time over which the equivalent level is measured may vary from a few seconds to several hours, and is usually specified, and often indicated by the value of T in the symbol $L_{Aeq,T}$, for example, $L_{Aeq,1h}$ indicating a period of one hour. The equivalent level is

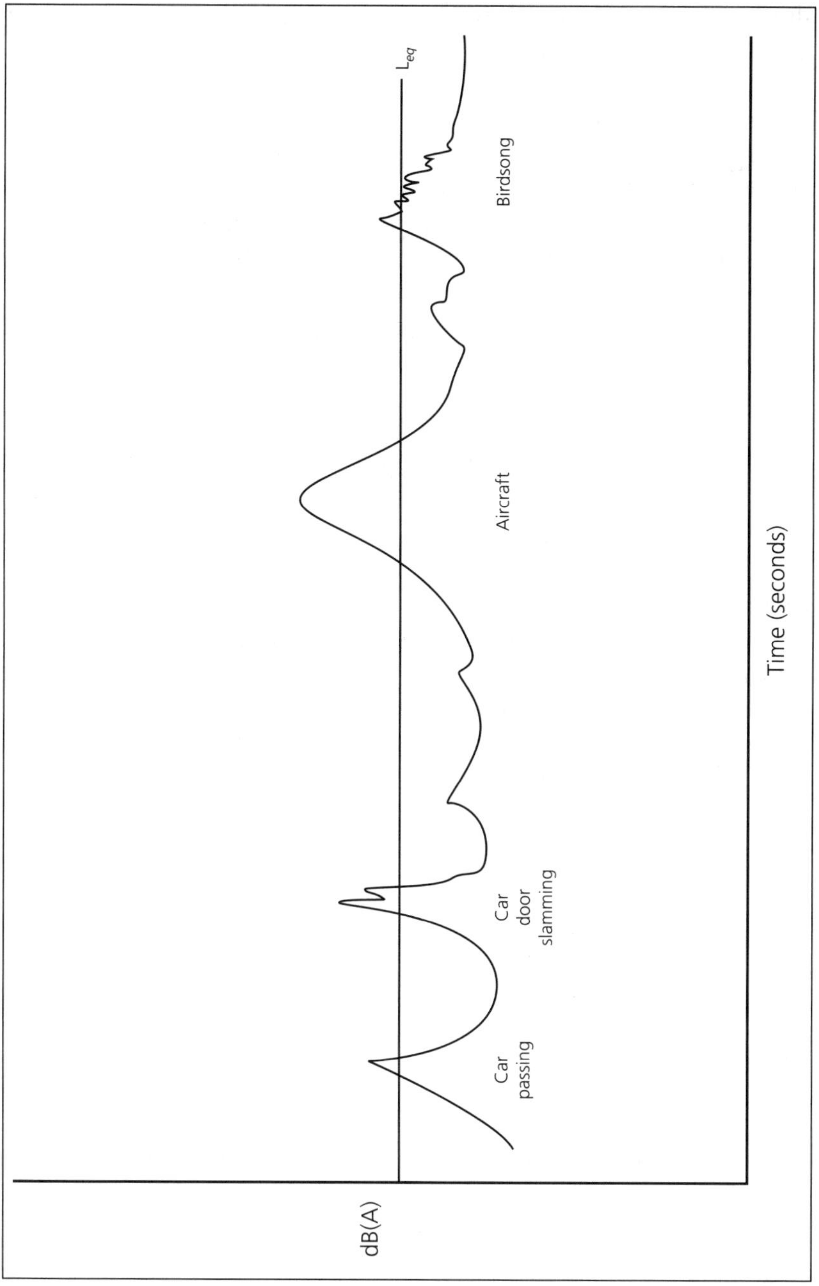

Figure 1.10 Showing variation of sound level with time

almost always measured in dB(A), but it is possible to measure L_{eq} in octave or one-third octaves.

If the level of noise is continually varying, as in Figure 1.10, then the L_{Aeq} can only be determined using an integrating sound level meter. If the variation is one of a number of periods of differing steady levels, as indicated in Figure 1.11, then it is possible to calculate the L_{Aeq} over the total period using the formula:

$$L_{AeqT} = 10 \log \left[\frac{t_1 \times 10^{\frac{L_1}{10}} + t_2 \times 10^{\frac{L_2}{10}} + \ldots + t_N \times 10^{\frac{L_N}{10}}}{T} \right]$$

where t_1 is the time for which the sound level is L_1 dB, t_2 is the time for which the sound level is L_2 dB and so on, and T is the total time over which L_{AeqT} is to be determined.

Example

A print worker spends most of his time working in relatively quiet conditions, outside an enclosure around the press, but has to spend some time each day making adjustments to the press, inside the enclosure. A typical noise exposure pattern for a 12 hour working shift is as follows:

Inside the enclosure:

At position A	93 dB(A) for 30 minutes (0.5 hours)
At position B	98 dB(A) for 15 minutes (0.25 hours)
At position C	93 dB(A) for 15 minutes (0.25 hours)

Outside the enclosure:

At control console, position D	78 dB(A) for 5.5 hours
At print output, position E	83 dB(A) for 5.5 hours

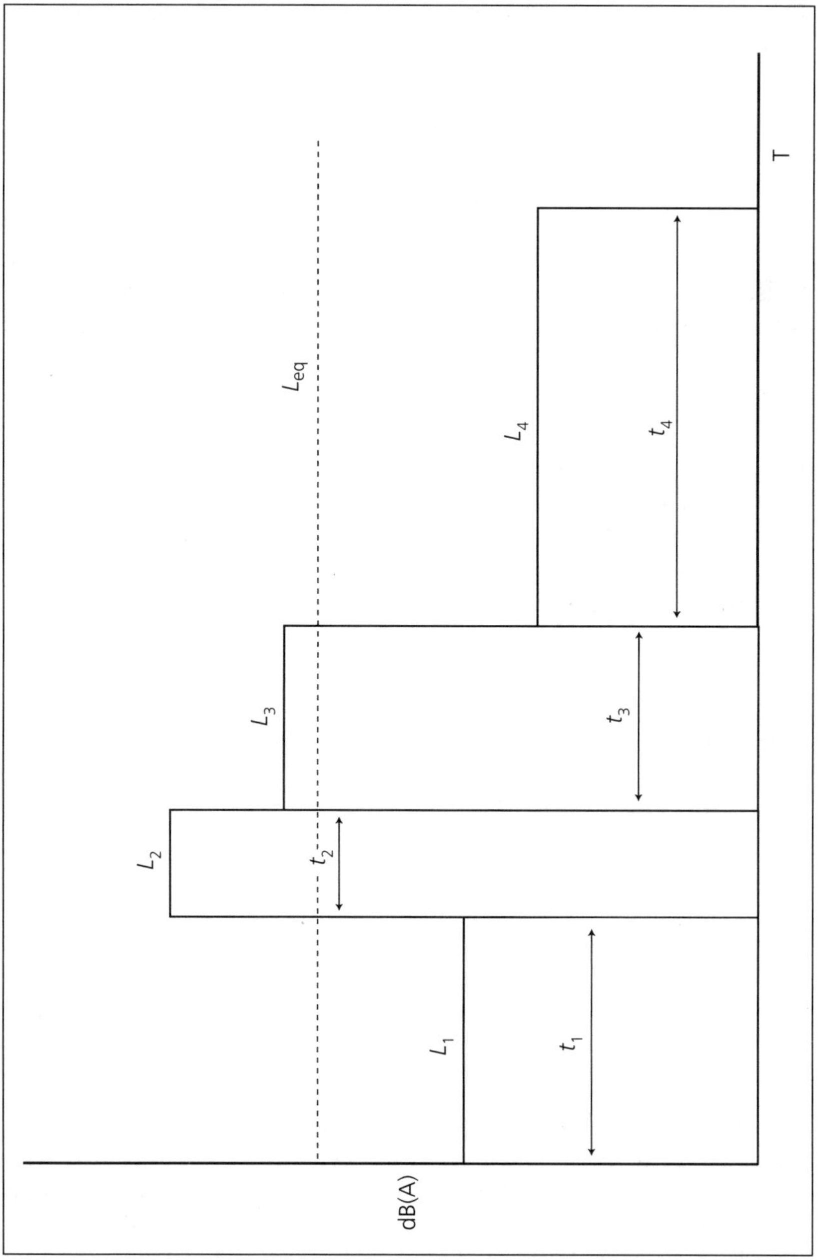

Figure 1.11 Illustrating the calculation of continuous equivalent noise level

The $L_{Aeq,T}$ over the 12 hour shift may be calculated using this formula thus:

$$L_{AeqT} = 10 \log \left[\frac{0.5 \times 10^{9.3} + 0.25 \times 10^{9.8} + 0.25 \times 10^{9.3} + 5.5 \times 10^{7.8} + 5.5 \times 10^{8.3}}{12} \right]$$

$$= 85.8, \text{ or } 86\,\text{dB(A) to the nearest dB}$$

The personal daily noise exposure level, or $L_{Ep,d}$, defined in the Noise at Work Regulations, is the $L_{Aeq,8h}$, i.e. the value of L_{Aeq} calculated over 8 hours. It is calculated by putting a value of 8 instead of 12 for T in the above formula, leading to a value of 87.5 dB(A), or 88 dB(A) to the nearest dB.

The value of $L_{Ep,d}$ may also be estimated using the nomogram shown in Figure 1.12 from the Guidance Notes to the Regulations. A fractional dose, *f*, is obtained from the nomogram for each component of the exposure. The fractional doses are added together and the total is converted, using the nomogram, into the $L_{Ep,d}$ value.

In the above example the fractional doses obtained from the nomogram are:

At position A $f = 0.13$
At position B $f = 0.\ 2$
At position C $f = 0.065$
At position D $f = 0$ (exposure at levels below 80 dB negligible)
At position E $f = 0.16$

The total value of *f* is thus 0.13 + 0.2 + 0.065 + 0.16 = 0.555, which gives an $L_{Ep,d}$ of 87.5 dB(A).

The Noise at Work Regulations define Action Levels corresponding to $L_{Ep,d}$ values of 85 dB(A) (First Action Level) and 90 dB(A) (Second Action Level). Because noise exposure is defined on an equal energy basis, it will remain the same if the value of the sound intensity is doubled (i.e. sound pressure level increased by

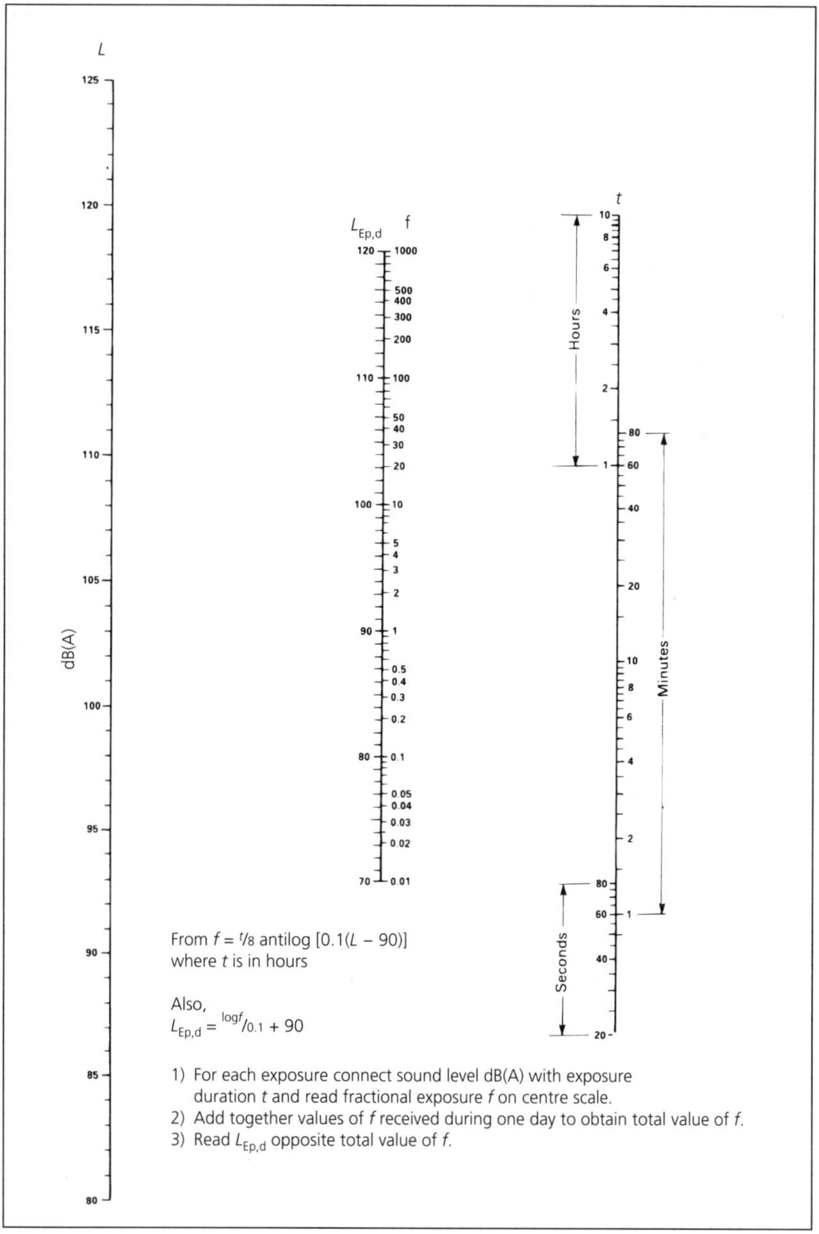

Figure 1.12 Nomogram for calculation of $L_{Ep,d}$
Source: reproduced courtesy of the Health and Safety Executive. Crown copyright is reproduced with the permission of the Controller of Her Majesty's Stationery Office

3 dB) but the duration is halved. Thus an exposure of 90 dB(A) for an 8 hour period is equivalent to:

93 dB(A) for 4 hours
96 dB(A) for 2 hours
99 dB(A) for 1 hours
102 dB(A) for 30 minutes
105 dB(A) for 15 minutes
108 dB(A) for 7.5 minutes, and so on.

This shows that exposure to very high noise levels, of 100 dB(A) or more, for only a few minutes a day will put employees' hearing at risk, and exceed the Action Levels of the Noise at Work Regulations. It also illustrates the importance of *always* wearing ear protectors.

The nomogram can be used in reverse, to estimate the maximum exposure time to a certain noise level corresponding to a given level of exposure. Thus we might wish to know the maximum time that the employee in the above example could work inside the enclosure, at position B, where the noise level is 98 dB(A), before his exposure exceeded the Second Action Level. Using the equal energy principle, as shown above, this time will be in excess of 1 hour, but less than 2 hours. Using the nomogram a more precise estimate, of about 70 minutes, is obtained. If the First Action Level is not to be exceeded, the time will be reduced to about 25 minutes. In practice the employee should be wearing ear protectors inside the enclosure. These time estimates have assumed no exposure to noise other than entering the enclosure. They would be reduced if there were other periods of significant exposure — setting up the machine before a print run, for example.

The above example shows that if the time over which the $L_{\mathrm{Aeq,T}}$ is calculated is changed (from 12 to 8 hours) for the same amount of sound energy received, i.e. for the same dose, the value increases, by 2 dB (or, more accurately, by $10\log(12/8) = 1.8$ dB). Similarly, if the noise exposure of an employee over a four hour period is, say, 90 dB, and he receives no significant sound exposure during the remainder of the day, then his exposure over an

8 hour period, which is always the basis of $L_{Ep,d}$, would reduce by 3dB (= 10log(4/8)) to 87dB. On this basis, noise exposure levels may be reduced by controlling exposure times, for example, by job rotation, but it can be seen that the benefits are limited to a 3dB reduction for a halving of exposure time.

More generally, the value of $L_{Aeq,T}$ over a time T_1 may be calculated from the value over time T_2, assuming the same noise dose (amount of energy received) using the formula:

$$L_{Aeq,T_2}(\text{over time } T_2) = L_{Aeq,T_1}(\text{over time } T_1) - 10\log\left(\frac{T_2}{T_1}\right)$$

This formula could be used, more precisely than the nomogram to calculate the maximum exposure times inside the print machine enclosure in the above example: 76 minutes for the First Action Level, 24 minutes for the Second.

As another example, suppose a particularly noisy activity, such as using a hand-held grinder, produces a noise level at the operator's ear of 118dB, but the operation lasts for only one minute. Then:

$$L_{Aeq,T_2}(\text{over 8 hours, from one burst of grinding})$$

$$= 115 - 10\log\left(8 \times \frac{60}{1}\right)$$

$$= 88\,\text{dB(A)}$$

(Note that both times must be expressed in the same units, in this case in minutes.)

One burst of grinding would exceed the First Action Level, and two bursts, giving an increase of 3dB to 91dB(A), would exceed the Second.

The continuous equivalent level, $L_{Aeq,T}$ is also widely used for the measurement and assessment of environmental noise. The Department of the Environment Planning Guidance Note

PPG 24 recommends the use of the 16 hour period from 07.00 to 23.00 hours for assessment of environmental noise for plannning purposes.

Example

A factory operates from 07.00 to 19.00 hours each weekday. The noise emitted from the factory premises is greatest at the start and end of the working day. The noise levels outside nearby premises were monitored, and the results are shown below. Estimate the $L_{\text{Aeq,T}}$ over the 12 hour operating period, and over the 16 hour period from 07.00 to 23.00 hours:

L_{Aeq} = 63 dB(A) between 07.00 and 09.00 hours
L_{Aeq} = 53 dB(A) between 09.00 and 17.00 hours
L_{Aeq} = 57 dB(A) between 17.00 and 19.00 hours

Over 12 hours: $L_{\text{Aeq,12h}} = 10 \log \left[\dfrac{2 \times 10^{6.3} + 8 \times 10^{5.3} + 2 \times 10^{5.7}}{12} \right]$

$= 57.4$, or 57 dB to the nearest dB

Over 16 hours: $L_{\text{Aeq,16h}} = 10 \log \left[\dfrac{2 \times 10^{6.3} + 8 \times 10^{5.3} + 2 \times 10^{5.7}}{16} \right]$

$= 56.1$ or 56 dB to the nearest dB

Alternatively: $L_{\text{Aeq,16h}} = L_{\text{Aeq,12h}} - 10 \log\left(\dfrac{16}{12}\right)$
$= 57.4 - 1.2$
$= 56$ dB, as before

Further details of PPG 24 are given in Chapter 6.

The British standard BS4142 uses L_{Aeq} values over periods of 1 hour in the daytime, and 5 minutes at night as the basis of its procedure for estimating the likelihood of complaints from industrial noise.

Example

A factory that operates continuously over 24 hours emits bursts of noise for 6 minutes every hour. The L_{Aeq} over each 6 minute period is measured outside a nearby house and is 65 dB(A). Calculate the value of L_{Aeq} over 1 hour, and over a 5 minute period.

Assuming that the noise level from the factory outside the house is negligible for the other 54 minutes each hour, the L_{Aeq} over 1 hour, is given by:

$$L_{Aeq,1h} = 10 \log\left[\frac{6 \times 10^{6.5}}{60}\right]$$

$$= 55\,\text{dB}$$

This is the value that would be relevant for a daytime assessment using BS4142.

Note: An approximate estimate could have been obtained by using the '3 dB reduction/increase per doubling/halving of time' rule, i.e. 65 dB for 6 minutes = 62 dB for 12 minutes = 59 dB for 24 minutes = 56 dB for 48 minutes = 53 dB for 96 minutes and so on, so that the answer, for 60 minutes, lies between 53 and 56 dB.

For a 5 minute period within the 6 minute 'on-time' the L_{Aeq} over 5 minutes, $L_{Aeq,5min}$, is simply 65 dB. This is the value which would be relevant for a nighttime assessment using BS4142.

If the duration of the bursts was reduced during the nighttime to 2 minutes each hour, in order to reduce disturbance to neighbours, the L_{Aeq} over 5 minutes would become:

$$L_{Aeq,5min} = 10 \log\left(2 \times 10^{\frac{6.5}{5}}\right)$$

$$= 61\,\text{dB}$$

i.e. the $L_{Aeq,5min}$ has been reduced by 4 dB (= $10 \log\left(\frac{5}{2}\right)$).

Further details of BS4142 are given in Chapter 6.

The noise exposure level SEL or L_{AE}

The previous examples indicate that noise is sometimes emitted in bursts, rather than continuously, and it may be more convenient to count the number of such bursts, rather than the total 'on-time', in order to estimate exposures, and to control exposure by limiting the number of bursts in a given time period. There may be different types of 'noise event', which produce bursts of noise, with different levels and durations, and so it would be useful to have a method for comparing these different noise events on a common basis.

The noise exposure level of a noise event is defined as the constant level that over a period of one second would contain as much A-weighted noise energy as the noise event. It is also known as the single event exposure level and represented by the symbols SEL, or L_{AE}.

Example
A particular sequence of operations involving drilling and cutting is performed repetitively by a sheet metal worker. The sequence takes, on average, 1.5 minutes to perform, during which the L_{Aeq} measured at the worker's ear is 92 dB(A). A second sequence involves using an air-jet to clean the workpiece for which the L_{Aeq} over a period of 40 seconds is 99 dB(A), again measured at the ear. Between performing these operations the noise level is 75 dB(A). Compare the noise exposure from the two different events, and calculate the personal daily noise exposure level, $L_{\mathrm{Ep,d}}$, of the worker if both operations are performed 5 times an hour during a 6 hour shift.

One way to compare the two different operations is to calculate the SEL for each, using the formula:

$$\text{SEL for event} = L_{\mathrm{Aeq,T}} + 10\log T$$

where T is measured in seconds.

For the drilling, and cutting event:

$$\text{SEL} = 92 + 10\log(90) = 112\,\text{dB}$$

For the air jet cleaning event:

$$\text{SEL} = 99 + 10\log(40) = 115\,\text{dB}$$

Thus it can be seen that each air-jet operation produces twice as much sound energy (i.e. a 3 dB difference) as each drilling and cutting operation.

Some integrating sound level meters which measure L_{Aeq} can also measure SEL, and this can be a convenient way of measuring bursts of noise from events, but the above example shows that the SEL can always be calculated from the L_{Aeq} value provided that the measurement time is also known.

The $L_{\text{Aeq,T}}$ produced by N events over time T (in seconds) is given by:

$$L_{\text{Aeq,T}} = \text{SEL} + 10\log N - 10\log T$$

When the $L_{\text{Ep,d}}$ is required T is 8 hours, or $8 \times 60 \times 60$ seconds, and $10\log T$ is $10\log(8 \times 60 \times 60) = 45\,\text{dB}$, to the nearest dB, and:

$$L_{\text{Ep,d}} = \text{SEL} + 10\log N - 45$$

For the cutting and drilling operations ($N = 5 \times 6 = 30$):

$$\begin{aligned} L_{\text{Ep,d}} &= 112 + 10\log(30) - 45 \\ &= 82\,\text{dB(A)} \end{aligned}$$

For the air-jet cleaning:

$$\begin{aligned} L_{\text{Ep,d}} &= 115 + 10\log(30) - 45 \\ &= 85\,\text{dB(A)} \end{aligned}$$

The total exposure level, obtained by combining the values of 82 and 85 dB(A) from both sets of operations is 87 dB(A), to the nearest dB. The continuous background noise level of 75 dB(A) makes a negligible contribution and may be ignored.

SEL values are widely used in the calculation of environmental noise, where a train passing by or an aircraft passing overhead are dealt with as individual noise events.

Example

A high-pressure steam release valve in a factory produces a burst of noise lasting a few seconds once every hour. The average SEL value of the burst of noise is measured outside the nearest house, and is 80 dB(A). Calculate the L_{Aeq} due to the bursts of noise over (a) a period of 1 hour, and (b) a period of 5 minutes.

$$L_{Aeq,1h} = SEL + 10\log N - 10\log T$$

(a) $N = 1$ event per hour, so that $10\log 1 = 0$, and $T = 3600$.

Hence:

$$L_{Aeq,1h} = 80 + 0 - 36$$
$$= 44\,dB(A)$$

This is the value that would be relevant for a daytime assessment using BS4142.

(b) $N = 1$ event per hour, so that $10\log 1 = 0$, and $T = 300$

Hence:

$$L_{Aeq,1h} = 80 + 0 - 25 = 55\,dB(A)$$

This is the value which would be relevant for a nighttime assessment using BS4142.

Statistical percentile levels, $L_{AN,T}$

The noise percentile level, L_N, is the level exceeded for N% of the time. It is usually measured in dB(A) over a specified period of time, T, hence $L_{AN,T}$. The most frequently used values of the percentile level are L_{A10} and L_{A90}, although in principle N may have any integer value between 1 and 99. The value of the tenth percentile, L_{A10}, i.e. the level exceeded for 10% of the time, is widely used for the measurement of traffic noise, usually over the 18 hour period between 06.00 and 24.00 hours, i.e. $L_{AN,18h}$.

The value of L_{A90} is the noise level exceeded for 90% of the time. This also means that the noise level falls below this L_{A90} value for only 10% of the time. The L_{A90} is widely used as a measure of the background noise level at a site because it gives an indication of the overall level of noise which underlies short term variations caused by transient events such as occasional traffic, trains or bursts of industrial noise. The value of L_{A99} has also been used as a measure of the long-term background noise, and L_{A1} as an indication of the highest level of short term bursts of noise, although L_{Amax}, the maximum level within a period of time, is more commonly used.

Summary

1 Noise has been defined as unwanted sound. Sounds are caused by minute pressure fluctuations in the air, which travel, in the form of waves, from the source to receiver.

2 The human ear is able to detect a very wide range of sound pressures, with even the most intense sound representing only a very small fluctuation in atmospheric pressure. Because of this the energies involved in noise are minimal even when those sounds produce major effects on listeners.

3 The simplest of all sounds, the pure tone, may be described in terms of its amplitude, frequency (f) and wavelength (λ). These last two terms are related by the equation $C = f$, where C is the velocity of sound in the medium.

4 Frequency is measured in hertz (Hz). The audible range of frequencies extends from 20 Hz to 20 000 Hz approximately.

5 Since the velocity of sound in air varies under normal conditions between 330 and 340 ms^{-1}, depending on the air tem-

perature, sound wavelengths vary from a few centimetres at high frequencies (3.3 cm at 10 000 Hz) to several metres at low frequencies (3.3 m at 100 Hz).

6 More complex sounds may be considered to consist of a mixture of pure tones of different frequencies. These include harmonic sounds, and random and transient noise. These sounds may be described in two possible ways: (a) by a waveform showing sound pressure fluctuations with time; (b) by a frequency spectrum (i.e. a graph of acoustic pressure or intensity versus frequency).

7 It is important to know the frequency content of sounds because almost all acoustic parameters and properties associated with noise measurement and control vary with frequency, including the sensitivity of human hearing, the sound-absorbing and sound-insulating properties of materials, and the performance of noise sources.

8 The effectiveness of various noise control measures such as attenuators and silencers, acoustic tiles, partitions, enclosures, barriers and antivibration mounts varies with frequency. Usually it is easier to achieve noise reductions at high frequencies than at lower frequencies.

9 The frequency of a tone determines the subjective measure of pitch. The subjective impression created by a noise will also very much depend on its frequency content.

10 Wavelength is important in determining how sound travels, i.e. is reflected by surfaces, scattered by obstacles and the extent to which it bends around barriers. The wavelength of a sound has a profound effect on the way it interacts with obstacles in its path.

11 Since, over a period of time, the positive and negative fluctuations in a sound (i.e. compressions and rarefactions) will average out to zero, the 'volume' or magnitude of a sound is

usually measured in terms of the root mean square, or RMS, sound pressure, although the peak and peak-to-peak pressures are sometimes also used.

12 The decibel scale is a logarithmic scale for comparing the ratios of two powers. Since sound intensity and sound pressure are related to sound power they also may be measured on a decibel scale.

13 Decibels are used for convenience in order to compress the enormous range of audible sound pressures into a manageable scale and to simplify sound transmission calculations, not only because multiply and divide processes become add and subtract processes when using decibels, but also because the human response to the stimulus of sound is logarithmic in nature.

14 Decibels may be used to compare two quantities in a relative manner, (e.g. machine X is 10dB noisier than machine Y) or, by introducing reference levels, they may be used to express quantities in absolute terms.

15 Because they are based on logarithms, decibel levels cannot be added together or averaged like ordinary numbers. The combination of sound pressure levels may be carried out either by calculation (hand-held calculator) or using special charts or nomograms. Two identical levels will combine to produce an additional 3dB and ten identical levels will produce an extra 10dB.

16 Subjectively, an increase of 3dB is noticeable and a 10dB increase represents a doubling of loudness.

17 In order that background noise should not have a significant effect on the accuracy of measurements the measured sound level must be at least 10dB above the background level.

18 A consideration of how sound levels from multiple noise sources combine is necessary in order to decide priorities for noise control.

19 The A-weighted sound pressure level, dB(A), is the most commonly used method of measuring noise. It includes the contributions of all the frequencies in a single figure value in a way which attempts to take into account the way in which the sensitivity of human hearing varies with frequency, so that the measured dB(A) value will relate to the average human perception of the magnitude of the noise.

20 When the noise is fairly constant in level it may be assessed or rated using NC (noise criteria) or NR (noise rating) curves. Both of these methods are based on an octave band analysis of the noise. Various guideline recommendations are available for maximum noise levels suitable for different types of room such as office, conference rooms and so on.

21 The equivalent continuous noise level of a time-varying noise is that constant noise level which, over the period of time under consideration, would contain the same amount of A-weighted sound energy as the time-varying noise. It may be calculated if the noise level exposure pattern is made up of a number of time intervals during each of which the level remains reasonably steady.

22 If the noise exposure consists of a series of individual noise events such as passing trains, or aircraft or bursts of industrial noise, then the concept of a single event noise exposure level is helpful in calculating L_{Aeq} values.

23 Time-varying noise may be described in statistical terms. L_{AN} is the level exceeded for N% of the time. Common measures are L_{A10} and L_{A90}. L_{A10} is used for measuring traffic noise and L_{A90} for measuring background noise.

2
The effects of noise on people in the workplace and in the community

Introduction

This chapter provides background information to enable the manager to understand the significance of noise in society and the basis on which noise level limits are decided. A brief description of the hearing mechanism is given, followed by an account of the effects of noise on people. Some information is then provided about the magnitude of the problem, in the form of estimates of the numbers of people exposed to different levels of noise both for employees in the workplace and for people in the community in general. Finally some attempts to assess the costs of noise and the benefits of its control are discussed, and of attitudes of employers and employees towards noise at work and its control.

The ear and hearing

The ear and how it works

The hearing mechanism consists of three parts; the outer, middle and inner ear (Figure 2.1). The outer ear collects the airborne sound waves and directs them down the ear canal to the ear drum, which is a thin membrane or diaphragm, which, acting rather like a drum-skin, is set into vibration by the sound. The middle ear consists of three little bones — the hammer, anvil and stirrup (often referred to by their Latin names: malleus, incus and stapes) — and collectively known as the ossicles.

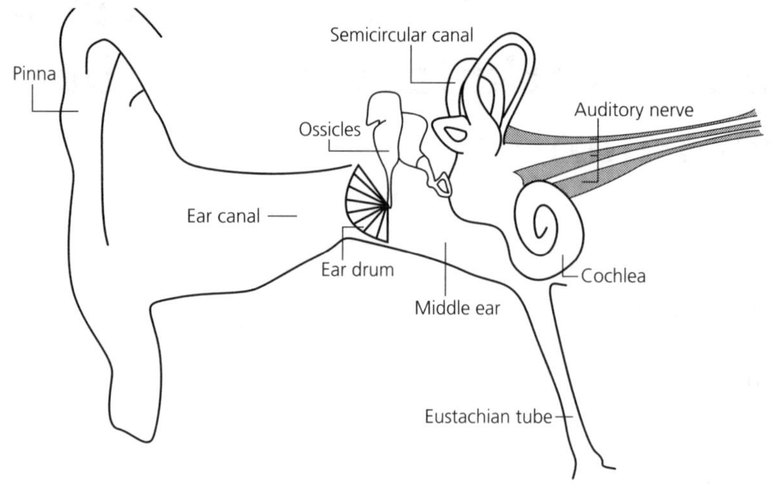

Figure 2.1 The main components of the outer, middle and inner ear

The ossicles, which are connected together, vibrate to and fro. Their function is to transmit the vibration of the ear drum to the inner ear, which is a fluid-filled tube, called the cochlea, embedded in a cavity in the skull. The malleus is connected to the ear drum and the stapes to the cochlea.

The ossicles themselves are surrounded by air and situated at the head of the Eustachian tube which connects to the back of the throat, so that both sides of the ear drum are always open to the atmosphere. This ensures that the ear drum is not affected by changes to atmospheric pressure, which are much larger than the very small pressure fluctuations caused by the sound waves which the ear is required to detect. It is the temporary failure of the Eustachian tube to equalize the pressure across the ear drum, remedied by swallowing or by sucking a boiled sweet, that we sometimes experience as a pressure on our ears during a change of altitude (for example take-off during an airflight or going underground into a tunnel). The Eustachian tube may also become blocked by the effects of a cold or other infections. Also part of the middle ear is a set of small muscles, called the stapediary reflex, connected to the ossicles and which comes into operation very quickly to try to protect the delicate hearing mechanism from the effects of sudden intense sounds such as gunfire or explosions.

An important function of the ossicles is to act as a bridge between the air in the ear canal, in which the vibrating air particles may have a relatively large amplitude of movement but do not exert much force or pressure, and the fluid in the cochlea where the movement of the fluid particles may be much less but causes much larger pressure changes. Without the buffering effect of the middle ear most of the sound energy striking the ear drum would be reflected rather than being transmitted into the cochlea, as required, rather like the way in which sound reflects off the surface of water in a swimming pool.

The stapes is connected to another diaphragm called the oval window that transmits the vibration to the inner ear. The cochlea is a fluid-filled tube coiled rather like a snail shell, and about the size of a pea. Running through its entire length is a complex structure of membranes and nerve cells that divides the cross-section of the cochlea into two parts (Figure 2.2), including the basilar membranes and the Organ of Corti. It is in the cochlea that the vibration in the cochlear fluid, caused by the sound waves at the ear drum, is converted, through the action of thousands of tiny 'hair cells' that are stimulated by the vibration into nerve impulses. It is damage to these hair cells caused by excessive exposure to noise that is the cause of noise-induced hearing loss.

The cochlea is also connected to a structure of three semicircular canals which controls the sense of balance, and which explains why certain disorders of the ear can affect balance. The nerve impulses generated by the hair cells in the cochlea are transmitted via the auditory nerve, connected to the cochlea, to the brain where they produce the sensation of hearing. The vibration that

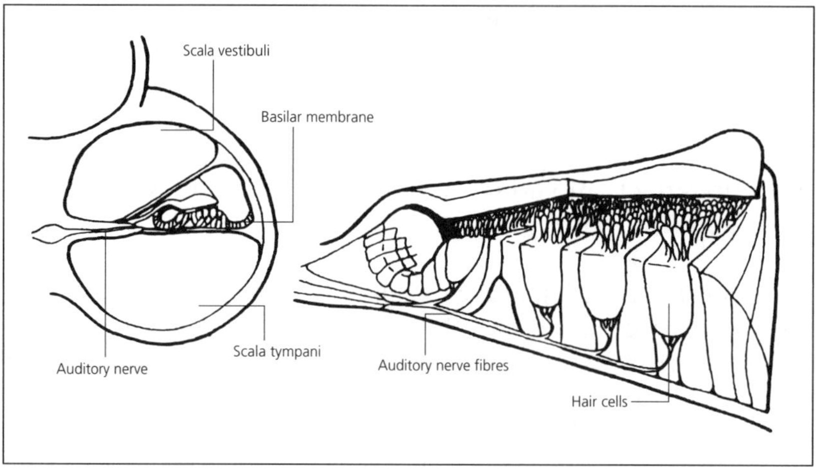

Figure 2.2 Section of cochlea (left) and basilar membrane with Organ of Corti
Source: reproduced courtesy of Bilsom International Ltd

enters the cochlea via the oval window travels as a wave along the length of the cochlea to its tip, and back through the second part of the cross-section to another membrane, called the round window, at its base, that communicates with the Eustachian tube and so acts as a pressure release device.

Some sound energy is also transmitted to the cochlea by 'bone conduction', directly via the skull, as well as via the middle ear.

Audiometry — the measurement of hearing

Audiometry is the science of the measurement of hearing sensitivity. The quantity which is measured is a person's threshold of hearing, i.e. the minimum sound pressure level which is just audible to that person under defined listening conditions. This varies with the frequency of the sound, and is indicative of the condition of the person's hearing. The baseline against which such measurements are compared is a standardized normal hearing threshold (defined in ISO 8253, 1989), derived from threshold measurements of samples of 'otologically normal' young people between the ages of 18 and 25 years.

There are a number of audiometric test methods but one of the most commonly used is pure-tone audiometry in which the subject is presented with pure tones, at frequencies of 500 Hz, 1, 2, 3, 4 and 6 kHz, of known sound pressure level, via a standardized and calibrated headset. The results of such a hearing test are presented as an audiogram which is a graph of hearing level against frequency, one for each ear, the hearing level being the difference in decibels between the measured hearing threshold of the person and the normal threshold at the same frequency. Thus a hearing level of –30 dB means a threshold of hearing 30 dB higher than the normalized threshold, indicating a hearing sensitivity which is 30 dB lower or less sensitive than that represented by standard threshold. The term 'hearing loss' is also used instead of hearing level although, strictly, hearing loss usually refers to a particular change in hearing level caused by an impairment, or to a deterioration in hearing threshold of a particular individual.

Factors affecting hearing levels

The sensitivity of hearing decreases with age, a phenomenon called presbycusis. The process starts with a slight loss of hearing at the higher frequencies, and with increasing age this increases and also spreads to lower and lower frequencies, as indicated by the typical audiograms shown in Figure 2.3.

The other various conditions affecting hearing loss may be characterized according to whether the condition affects the conductive part of the hearing mechanism — i.e. the outer and middle ear, or the inner ear — or the auditory nerve and the brain. The different conditions have different frequency dependencies, and so will produce differing effects on the shape of the audiogram of the subject.

Conductive deafness can be caused by the build-up of wax causing blockage of the ear canal, or by damage to the ear drum or to the ossicles, which can become fused together so that they are no longer able to vibrate effectively. All of these conditions can be remedied, the blockage simply by removing the wax and the other

Figure 2.3 Audiograms showing presbycusis

two conditions by surgery. Infections of the inner ear also affect hearing sensitivity, including the condition of 'glue ear', prevalent among children.

Hearing loss arising from damage to the cochlea is called sensorineural deafness and cannot be remedied. This includes the effects of exposure to noise, and presbycusis. All other forms of hearing loss, observed as the consequences of all types of medical abnormalities or pathology, are frequently called nosocusis.

Noise-induced hearing loss

Several hours' exposure to high levels of noise usually cause an immediate and noticeable temporary loss of hearing, which can be measured as an increase in hearing threshold, and is called a temporary threshold shift. After a period of relief from the noise exposure the hearing recovers, but continued repetition of the exposure causes the recovery time to increase and the recovery to be less complete, resulting eventually in a noise-induced permanent threshold shift (NIPTS). Recovery times vary, but although substantial recovery can sometimes occur within hours the process can continue over weeks, depending upon the level, duration and previous history of the exposure, and upon the individual's susceptibility to noise-induced hearing loss. An important practical consequence of this pattern of events is that routine audiometric monitoring of employees at work should ideally be carried out several hours after the last period of noise exposure at work (a minimum of 16 hours is recommended), i.e. at the beginning of the working shift, in order to avoid the audiogram including the effects of temporary threshold shift.

There is evidence to show that these effects are due to damage caused to the hair cells and nerve endings in the cochlea. It would seem that the pattern of exposure is significant, with some recovery of the hair cells taking place when exposure ceases, but with permanent damage eventually occurring after repeated prolonged exposure. The hair cells, once damaged beyond recovery, cannot be regenerated by the cochlea, nor can they be replaced by surgery. The damage to hearing is thus permanent and progressive. It is also cumulative, with the effects of noise-induced hearing loss combining with those of presbycusis, which is also due to loss of hair cells with age. Noise-induced hearing loss often produces a characteristic shape of audiogram, similar to that shown in Figure 2.4. A common feature is a dip in the audiogram, showing most hearing loss occurring at 4kHz, with this dip increasing in depth and also widening to other frequencies with increasing duration of exposure. Several explanations for this dip, which does not always occur, have been given, but one plausible one is that the spectrum of much industrial noise arising from noise from machinery often shows the highest levels in the 4kHz octave band.

Extremely high levels of noise, even of short duration, such as the noise arising from gunfire or from explosions can cause immediate and permanent damage called acoustic trauma. It is for this reason that the Noise at Work Regulations include a Peak Action Level of 200Pa which should not be exceeded.

Tinnitus is a condition in which noises that are heard by the sufferer are generated in his/her ear rather than originating from any external cause. It is a condition which is experienced by many people in a mild form on an occasional and temporary basis, in connection with a head cold for example, but which some people experience on a severe and permanent basis. There are a number of different causes of tinnitus, unconnected with noise exposure, but it is also often associated with noise-induced hearing loss — more than 20% of people who suffer from noise-induced hearing loss will also suffer tinnitus.

Loudness recruitment is another condition associated with noise-induced hearing damage, in which there is abnormal loudness perception above the elevated hearing threshold because the rate of growth of loudness with sound intensity is more rapid than for those with normal hearing.

The fact that excessive exposure to noise at work causes deafness has been known for several hundred years, since the Industrial

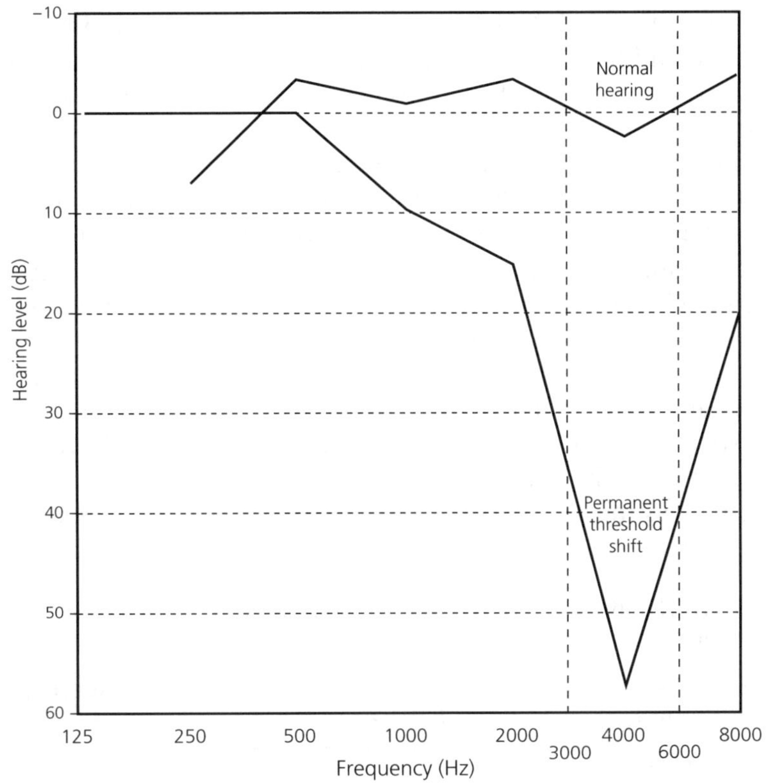

Figure 2.4 Typical noise-induced threshold shift progressing with years of exposure

Revolution. However, it was only in the 1960s that epidemiological studies established a quantitative link between the amount of noise exposure and the level of hearing loss, i.e. a so-called dose–response relationship. The link, identified by Burns and Robinson in the UK, was that it is the amount of A-weighted noise energy received by the ear that is best related to the amount of damage produced, and led to the development of the concept of an continuous equivalent noise level, L_{Aeq}, in order to deal with the difficulty of assessing the effects of noise levels that vary throughout the day. This work also led to the publication, in 1972, of a Department of Employment Code of Practice *Reducing the Exposure of Employed Persons to Noise.* This contained a guideline limit for noise exposure at work of an 8 hour L_{Aeq}, later to become the $L_{Ep,d}$ of 90 dB(A) of the 1989 Noise at Work Regulations. The work of Burns and Robinson and others has been used to compile Damage Risk Criteria published as ISO 1999: *Acoustics — Determination of occupational noise exposure and estimation of noise-induced hearing impairment*. The standard includes all types of noise (steady state, intermittent and impulsive) and the noise exposure is characterized by the noise exposure level, L_{EX}. The standard contains tables which enable an estimate to be made of the probability of a certain degree of NIPTS occurring as a result of an individual being exposed to various levels of noise (from 75 dB(A) to 100 dB(A)) for various periods of exposure (up to 40 years in employment). Such tables are used in claims for compensation for hearing loss. The statistical nature of the dose–response relationship, reflecting the fact that individuals differ in their susceptibility to noise-induced hearing loss means that there is still a risk of hearing loss even at exposure levels of 90 dB(A) and below, as shown in Table 2.1.

Table 2.1 Number of people in every 100 likely to suffer 50 dB hearing loss after various levels of noise exposure

Level of exposure (8 hour L_{Aeq})	Lifetime exposure (40 years)	10 years exposure
100	32	17
90	11	5
80	3	1

Source: reproduced courtesy of the Health and Safety Executive, Draft Code of Practice and Guidance Notes (1981). Crown copyright is reproduced with the permission of the Controller of Her Majesty's Stationery Office

It is generally considered that the risk becomes negligible below an exposure level of 75 dB(A).

The HSE estimates have assumed that hearing loss is due to the combined effect of aging and of occupational noise exposure alone, and do not take into account losses due to other types of hearing loss (nosocusis), or the effects of loss due to noise exposure whilst not at work (sociocusis). An $L_{Ep,d}$ of 75 dB(A) is equivalent to an L_{Aeq} over 24 hours of about 70 dB(A), and so the effects of leisure activities such as shooting, motor sports, DIY (the use of hand-held power tools), and listening to loud music can sometimes add significantly to the effects of noise exposure at work.

The combined effects of noise-induced hearing loss and presbycusis are to affect hearing levels of high frequencies more than lower frequencies. The main social problems resulting from this are to do with understanding speech. This is because much of the information content in speech is carried by the consonants that contain more of the higher frequencies in speech, particularly sibilants such as 's' and 't' and 'p', whereas the vowels, that contribute to the character and quality of the speech, contain more of the lower frequencies. Thus the listener may have difficulty in distinguishing between words with the same vowel sounds but beginning or ending with different consonants, such as 'car', 'cart', 'carp', and such as 'thought', 'taught', 'sought' and 'bought'. Therefore the effect of the damage to the hair cells is not simply to reduce the level of the sound that is heard, which would be rather like turning down the volume on the radio, and which could possibly be assisted using hearing aids to boost the volume again, but to remove information (i.e. the high frequencies) from the speech signal as well as lowering its volume, and this cannot be satisfactorily remedied by hearing aids. The result is the very frustrating one that even though the sufferer can hear the speech it appears muffled and indistinct (rather like seeing through frosted glass). The frustration may be aggravated by the effects of tinnitus.

The effects of noise-induced hearing loss are all the more insidious because they occur gradually, and at first may be undetected until considerable irreparable damage has occurred. The sufferer may learn to adapt, sometimes without realizing it, by turning up the volume of TV or radio, by sitting closer to the speaker in an audience and by paying more attention, and always turning to face the speaker and watching his or her lips during face-to-face conversations. The most serious problems occur when trying to participate in group conversations, when the sufferer does not always have direct face-to-face contact with the speaker, and when the conversation is taking place against a background of noise, such as those in pubs and at parties, and when using the telephone. When listening to radio or TV as part of a group the sufferer may not be able to hear at levels selected by the majority of the group, and may risk becoming unpopular if constantly requesting the volume to be increased. Conversations with the very young or with strangers, who do not have either the patience or the understanding to make allowance for the effects of the sufferer's condition, may become difficult.

In extreme cases these effects can lead to feelings of inadequacy, rejection, loneliness and isolation, and may be compounded by worries that the hearing loss may lead to inability by the sufferer to perform his/her job effectively and hence to further anxiety about job security.

Oto-acoustic emission

The ability of the ear to distinguish between different frequencies was first explained by a theory of cochlear mechanics proposed by Bekesy in 1960. Certain difficulties with this theory have prompted research in the past few years which has led to new understanding of the workings of the inner ear, which may lead to new ways of detecting and measuring noise-induced hearing loss.

The difficulties relate to the ability of the ear to detect and discriminate between different frequencies in a sound. According to the 'place theory' of Bekesy, sounds of different frequency produce maximum amplitudes of vibration, and therefore maximum stimulation of the hair cells at different positions along the length of the cochlea. Experiments on human frequency selectivity indicate that the cochlea can, in effect, be thought of as being divided into critical frequency bands, roughly corresponding to one-third octave bands, each having its own location along the cochlea. Bekesy's theory proposed that the place effect could be explained in terms of the mechanical vibration of the basilar membrane in the cochlea, and its frequency response. However, experiments in which cochleas from dead animals were subjected to vibration failed to produce the necessary degree of frequency selectivity, because the cochlea material is too well damped. This led to revised theories of cochlea vibration in which the basilar membrane is part of an active vibration system involving feedback from the hair cells, rather like the servo-mechanisms in engineering control systems, and which could only work in a living cochlea, controlled by the brain. These ideas led to experiments in which signals emitted by the cochlea in response to sound striking the ear drum were detected by sensitive miniature microphones placed very close to the ear drum of the test subject. Although these signals, or oto-acoustic emissions, have sometimes been called cochlear echoes they are really the active signals emitted by the cochlea in response to sound stimuli.

This new understanding of cochlear dynamics has already found practical application in the testing for deafness in babies and young children through the monitoring of oto-acoustic emissions. It is possible that in the future similar methods could be used as an alternative or supplement to audiometric testing in the diagnosis and monitoring of noise-induced hearing loss.

Noise in the workplace

The extent of noise exposure in the workplace

It has been estimated that 15–20% or more of the working population of Europe is affected by sound pressure levels of between 75 and 85 dB(A). In the UK, various bodies (such as the HSE, TUC, *The Lancet*) have estimated that somewhere between 0.75 and 2 million employees are exposed to levels of noise in excess of the First Action Level of the Noise at Work Regulations, 1989. In 1993 an HSE report on attitudes towards noise as an occupational hazard (Contract Research Report 54/1993) estimated that 1.7 million employees were exposed above 85 dB(A), and that 630 000 were exposed above 90 dB(A).

Another HSE report (Contract Research Report 116/1996), in 1996, estimated that the noise level is at least 85 dB(A) in one in ten, or about 88000, workplaces. Noise is far more of a problem in the production and engineering sectors (where the level exceeds 85 dB(A) in 20–25% of workplaces) than in the service sector (about 7%).

Between 1983 and 1990 almost 10000 people in Britain qualified for disablement benefit because of noise-induced hearing loss sustained at work (Figure 2.5).

In 1992 a Labour Force Survey suggested that around 100000 people considered that they had some measure of hearing loss potentially caused by their work. It has been claimed that, after backache, noise-induced hearing loss is the most common industrial health problem.

Insurance claims for noise-induced hearing loss are continuing to rise despite the move away from heavier, noisier industries over the past two decades. They currently represent about 80% of all occupational disease claims and about 50% of the value of all such awards.

The costs and benefits of noise in the workplace

The International Institute for Noise Control Engineering final working party report *Upper Limits for Noise Levels in the Workplace* (1997) states that:

> In the 1990s it has become widely recognised that the economic and social costs of high levels of noise in the workplace require significant action to reduce the exposure of workers to noise. Such costs include not only the financial compensation or damages that must be paid, and the reduced enjoyment of everyday life for those with a hearing loss, but also less quantifiable factors such as reduced productivity, increased stress, disturbed speech communication and risks of accidents for a large number of workers.

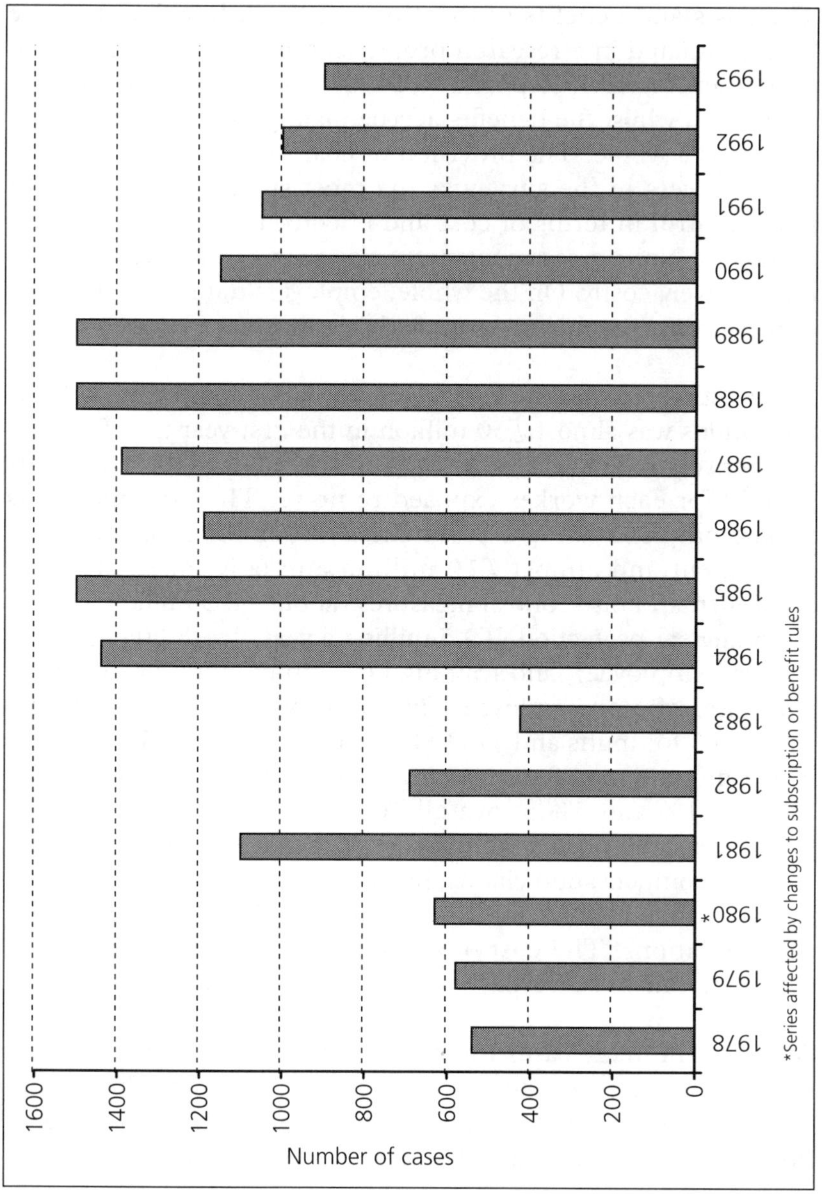

Figure 2.5 Number of people in Great Britain qualified for disablement benefit because of noise-induced hearing loss at work
Source: reproduced courtesy of the Health and Safety Executive. Crown copyright is reproduced with the permission of the Controller of Her Majesty's Stationery Office

The costs and benefits of the Noise at Work Regulations have been estimated in a research project commissioned by the HSE (Contract Research Report 116/1993). The costs fall mainly on employers, whilst the benefits accrue mainly to employees and to society as a whole. The provision of hearing protectors was seen by employers in the survey as the most significant element of noise control in terms of cost and effectiveness in terms of risk reduction. Noise assessments were also seen as effective measures but relatively costly. On the whole, employers did not see the cost of noise control as being particularly significant.

It was estimated that the cost to employers of complying with the regulations was almost £50 million in the first year and £37 million per year in following years. On an annual basis this represents £35.60 for each worker exposed to noise. The principal costs arose from conducting assessments (£21 million for the initial assessment and almost £10 million annually for subsequent assessments), noise control measures (about £8.5 million a year), providing ear protection (£9.5 million a year, or £8.60 per noise-exposed employee), and training (£7.3 million a year, or £5.60 per noise-exposed employee). The average cost of ear protectors was £9.65 for muffs and £0.39 for plugs. The cost of buying quieter plant or of modifying existing plant to reduce noise levels was between 1% and 5% of overall budget. Other significant costs which were identified were the cost of management time in dealing with compensation claims, higher insurance premiums resulting from such claims, and time spent ensuring compliance with the regulations. The cost of audiometry, undertaken by about 25% of the firms surveyed, was about £8 per employee.

Although in many cases the main reason for introducing noise control measures was found to be compliance with the regulations, i.e. the avoidance of a penalty, the following possible benefits to employers were also identified:

- improved efficiency, i.e. a perception that a quieter workplace was more efficient;

- reduced stress and improved morale;
- increased productivity;
- reduced absenteeism;
- reduced management time spent dealing with deafness compensation claims;
- reduced insurance premiums;
- reduced turnover of staff;
- raising the profile of health and safety in the workplace;
- demonstrating a professional approach to clients;
- demonstrating commitment to quality management processes, such as TQM;
- demonstrating a caring culture within the organization.

The benefits of audiometry were seen as:

- a defence against unwarranted claims for compensation;
- a means of checking on the effectiveness of noise control measures;
- a means of screening employees potentially at risk;
- reassurance of employees.

It is difficult to estimate the benefits to employers, in financial terms. Some of these potential benefits, such as improved morale and reduced stress, are qualitative. It is also difficult to isolate the possible beneficial effects of noise control from the effect of many other factors, and it may take several years to assess the effect of other possible benefits such as savings on employers' liability claims for industrial deafness. Nevertheless, it was estimated that the benefits to employers were about 25% of the costs. Four out of five of the employers who used noise control measures thought that there was a benefit, but most of them thought that it was limited.

The costs and benefits to society are even more difficult to quantify. The benefits to individual employees, of reduced loss of hearing, are obvious, but there are also benefits to society as a whole, in terms of health care and benefit payments. The costs to society, such as those falling on enforcement authorities, are small compared with those which fall on employers. It is estimated that the benefits to society of providing ear protectors are at least as great as the costs to the employers of providing them.

The most important reason for implementing noise control measures given by employers was the pursuit of good practice, with the desire to comply with health and safety and environmental law as the next most important. Pressure from employees, trade unions, HSE and insurers were seen as less important than these first two reasons.

Attitudes of employers and employees to the control of noise at work

An HSE report, published in 1993, investigated attitudes to noise as an occupational hazard among the workforce and management of 48 organizations in a variety of industries (*Attitudes Towards Noise as an Occupational Hazard*, Contract Research Report 54/1993). The aim of the study was to determine the level of awareness of noise and the factors that influence application of noise control measures and their effectiveness. It was found that the attitudes and commitment of senior management in companies were crucial in determining the success of noise control policy. Senior management was concerned with public relations and with the public image of the company, and was influenced by education and training on matters relating to health, safety and the environment. Middle managers in companies, who will usually be responsible for the day-to-day operation of noise control measures, take their lead and their motivation from targets set by senior managers, who should allocate resources and give responsibilities to named individuals for developing and achieving a successful hearing conservation programme with measurable goals, a structured plan of action and a system of audits and reviews.

Two of the three main findings of the report relate to the wearing of ear protectors by employees. Firstly, it was found that individual psychological factors are less important than management rules and peer norms in achieving a high level of hearing-protector wearing among the workforce. Secondly, workforces accept management rules about wearing hearing protectors provided that these rules are reinforced by training and by an obvious management commitment to hearing conservation.

The predominant workforce attitude was that noise control was a management responsibility, and that management should take responsibility and enforce the rules about ear protection. Factors that were found to be important to employees in deciding whether to wear ear protectors were:

- the enforcement of rules by supervisors;
- the wearing of protectors by managers;
- training — many employees said that training had changed their attitudes and behaviour;
- audiometric monitoring programmes;
- personal experience of noise-induced hearing loss (e.g. father, mother or other relative).

The third conclusion of the report is that an effective hearing conservation programme requires three management attributes: senior management commitment, the ability of middle management (particularly in production and engineering) to put hearing conservation measures into practice, and specialist technical knowledge of noise and of the legislation. Figure 2.6 shows a model of the factors influencing the achievement of a successful hearing conservation programme.

The HSE Research Paper 36: *Assessment of Compliance with the Noise at Work Regulations* (1996) describes the findings of a survey of employers, aimed at assessing the level of understanding and compliance with the Noise at Work Regulations. It concludes that although much has been done by industry to understand and comply with the requirements of the regulations there is a noticeable gap between knowledge and action, particularly in small firms.

Nearly three-quarters of employers were reported to have carried out a preliminary noise survey to decide if and where more detailed noise exposure assessments were needed; and where assessments were carried out, 79% of them were judged to be adequate. The assessments were seen to be a key factor in the hearing conservation programme because they give rise to the action plan that provided the motivation for management to take further measures to reduce noise exposure. Although over 80% of employers were reported to issue ear protection to employees the level of training given to employees, and management supervision to ensure that the protector were used effectively, was poor.

Other (non-hearing loss) effects of noise

Interference with speech communication

It is well known that bursts of high levels of noise can sometimes make it impossible to listen to the radio, television or some other audible signal or to continue a conversation. This is because of the phenomenon of masking, according to which the presence of one sound reduces the audibility, or masks, other sounds. The masking sound causes the threshold of hearing for other sounds to be raised, so that unless the signal level, i.e. the listening level, is increased above the raised threshold it will not be heard. Masking

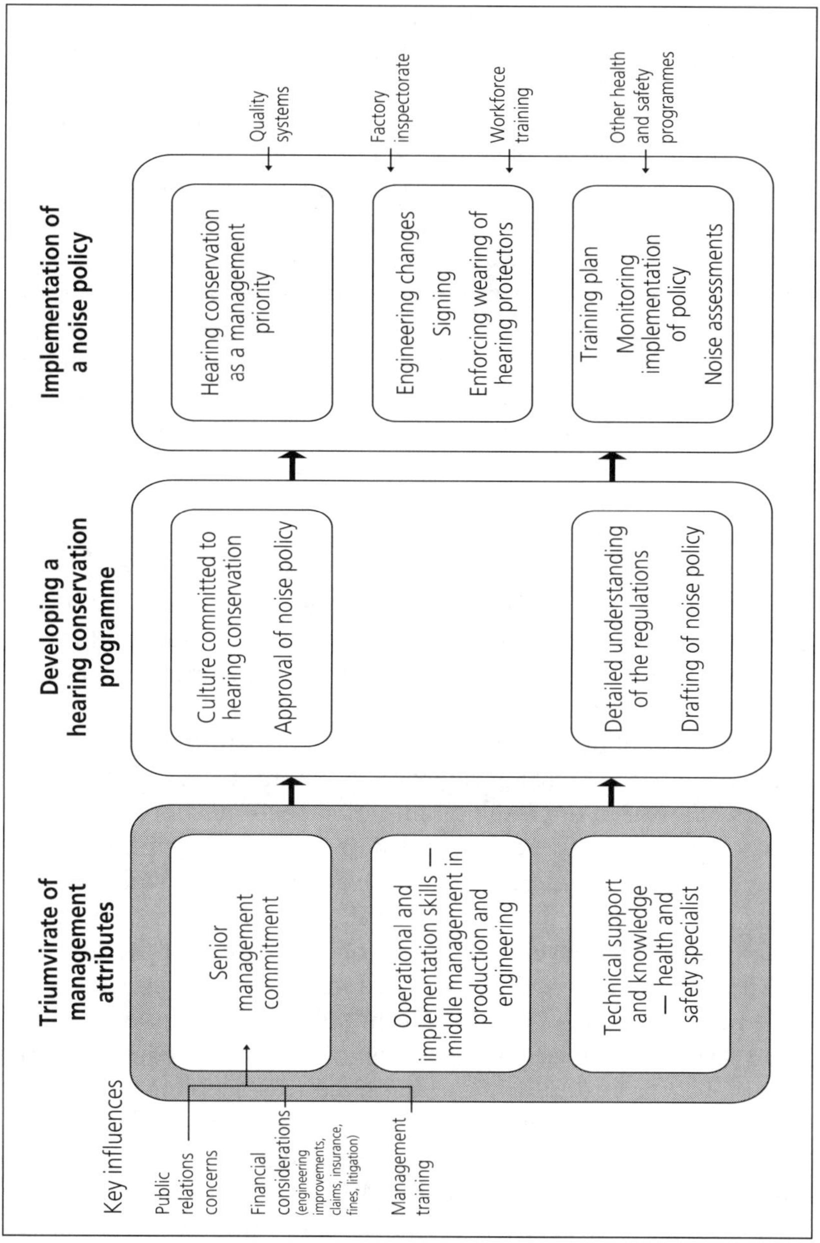

Figure 2.6 Model of factors influencing the achievement of a successful hearing conservation programme
Source: reproduced courtesy of the Health and Safety Executive. Crown copyright is reproduced with the permission of the Controller of Her Majesty's Stationery Office

can sometimes be turned to good use, for example when background noise can be used to increase privacy by masking conversations transmitted between offices. Masking sounds are also sometimes used by sufferers to alleviate the effects of their tinnitus. However, for many people the most undesirable effect of noise is to interfere with conversation in their homes, and their enjoyment of TV or radio. At work in the office, noise can interfere with communication, can cause annoyance and lead to inefficiencies and mistakes; in a factory environment it can lead to accidents, if, for example warning and alarm signals cannot be heard. The intelligibility of public address systems in noisy backgrounds in public places has assumed much greater importance in recent years since the publication of the recommendations of the Taylor Report following the Hillsborough football stadium disaster.

A noise is most effective at masking sounds of its own frequency, but is more effective at masking sounds that are above than below this frequency. Most of the sound energy in speech is in the frequency range 300–6000 Hz. It follows that sounds in this frequency range, or below, i.e. low and medium frequencies, are most effective at masking speech. Unfortunately it is this component of external noise which tends to be transmitted most effectively through the building envelope into homes and offices. Many factors determine the intelligibility of speech in a room, in addition to the level of background noise, including the distance between speaker and listener, the enunciation and voice level of the speaker and the familiarity of the listener with the speaker's voice, the hearing level and degree of motivation of the listener, and the reverberation time of the room. To ensure speech comprehension the level of the speech should always be at least as high as the level of the noise, and for situations requiring good listening conditions, for example in classrooms, or for telephone conversations, or where listeners have impaired hearing, it should be at least 10 dB above the noise level. A general guideline is that noise levels indoors should not exceed 40–45 dB(A) in order not to interfere with conversation in homes, and much lower for classrooms, rooms where meetings are held and homes for the elderly.

External noise levels of 70 dB(A) and above cause people to close windows in order to avoid interference with listening to speech.

These same considerations apply equally to the workplace, and noise levels in offices should also be below 45 dB(A).

Sleep disturbance

Noise can interfere with sleep in a number of ways. It can affect the time it takes to fall asleep, and cause awakening. Various levels of sleep have been identified, and exposure to noise whilst asleep can lead to changes in sleep patterns, from a deeper to a less deep level of sleep. Noise-disturbed sleep can lead to lowering of mood the following day and to other symptoms such as feelings of annoyance and headaches. These effects can be brought about both by continuous noise and by bursts of short duration from individual events such as an aircraft overhead or a passing train or lorry. The groups of people who are most sensitive to these effects are the ill, the elderly and shift workers.

Sleep disturbance starts at noise levels of 30 dB(A) for steady continuous noise at the sleeper's ear. However, the noise from single noise events such as trains, lorries and aircraft can also cause disturbance, and in order to ensure undisturbed sleep the maximum sound pressure level from such events, measured indoors, should not exceed 45 dB(A).

Annoyance

Annoyance is one of the most common and widespread effects of noise. Noise-related annoyance has been defined as a feeling of resentment, displeasure, discomfort, dissatisfaction or offence that occurs when noise interferes with someone's thoughts, feelings or activities. An important feature of noise-related annoyance is that it depends on a number of nonacoustical factors, as well as on the physical characteristics of the noise. These latter factors include the level of the noise, its frequency content and temporal characteristics, such as the time of day when the noise occurs, its duration, the frequency with which it is repeated, if intermittent, and the onset time in the case of sudden noises such as low-flying military aircraft, where the startle effects cause increased annoyance. The characteristics of the climate of background noise against which the intrusive noise takes place can also be important. Nonacoustical factors relating to annoyance include: the degree of control that the listener has over the noise, feelings about the necessity of the noise and the degree to which it could be controlled by others, the attitudes of the listener generally towards the source of the noise, e.g. fear of accidents etc. and the individual sensitivity of the listener to noise, and what he/she is doing whilst being exposed to the noise.

Noise-related annoyance is characterized by great variation in the response of individuals, and even in the response of any one individual on different occasions. Using social survey techniques, it is possible to predict the average value of the response of a population to a noise, but not the response of any one individual in that population. The social survey questionnaire is designed to measure the integrated long-term response of the individual to the noise, rather than a particular incident, and is plotted on a graph against the measured value of the noise to which the respondent is exposed. Unfortunately there is also a great variability in the design of questionnaires, which makes it difficult to compare the results of different surveys. Some surveys use complex procedures to construct scales of annoyance, whereas others will ask a simple, direct question. The results are often stated in terms of the percentage of respondents expressing differing degrees of disturbance or dissatisfaction.

The threshold for annoyance for steady continuous noise is an external L_{Aeq} of 50 dB(A), with few people becoming seriously annoyed for exposures less than 55 dB(A). The number of people seriously annoyed increases between 55 and 60 dB(A), and increases rapidly between 60 and 65 dB(A). Exposure levels at or above 65 dB(A) are generally considered to be unacceptable because most people will be seriously annoyed in the daytime, and there will be severe disturbance to sleep at night. The OECD has labelled locations where levels of community noise exposure exceed 65 dB(A) L_{Aeq} as 'black spot' areas, and those where the level is between 55 and 65 dB(A) as 'grey spot' areas. It has highlighted such areas as targets for improvement.

Another way of measuring public response is to measure community reaction to noise. At the lowest level this response might be complaints, or at the other extreme it might involve legal or political action against the source of noise. However, not every one who is annoyed will complain, and only a few may take more serious action, therefore although measures of community reaction may be closely related to annoyance, they are not the same as the measures of annoyance obtained from social surveys. Community reaction to noise tends to be relative, i.e. be related to the difference between the disturbing noise and the general level of background noise in the area.

The factors determining annoyance of employees at work, in addition to the level of the noise and the individual susceptibility of the employee, include: the nature and demands of the task being performed, the nature of the disturbing noise including its predictability, controllability, avoidability, and its information content. It has been estimated that 35–40% of office workers are severely annoyed above levels of 55–60 dB(A), and that in industrial situations 35–40% of employees are severely annoyed above 85 dB(A), and that absenteeism starts to occur above 75 dB(A).

Effect of noise on the performance of tasks

It is a matter of common experience that most people prefer to perform tasks that require intense concentration (sitting examinations, for example) in a quiet environment, whereas for other, more routine tasks, such as household chores, a background of speech or music is preferred. Such indications of preference do not, however, demonstrate that task performance will be affected by the level of noise. The effect of noise on task performance is a complex one, involving many factors. Most of the studies have been either laboratory based or from workplace situations. Noise can distract attention from the task, particularly for complex tasks involving multiple stages and requiring the use of short-term memory, but in other situations can increase arousal and performance. The performance of tasks which are dependent on receiving auditory cues may be adversely affected if these are masked by the noise, but monotonous tasks, and those involving mainly motor activity may not be affected by noise. In addition to the nature of the task, the effects of noise will also depend upon various characteristics of the noise, in addition to its level, including its irregularity, intermittency, information content and its familiarity to the listener.

It has been established that the learning of young children in schools is adversely affected by noise, a fact which has implications for the location of schools and nursery centres. The noise causes interference with communication, distraction and annoyance, in addition to any possible effect of noise on the performance of the task of learning.

Non-auditory noise-induced stress-related health effects

Many studies have shown that blood pressure is higher in workers exposed to noise and also in populations living in noisy areas around airports and on noisy streets than in control populations where no such effect was observed. The overall evidence indicates a weak association between long-term noise exposure and blood pressure elevation, or hypertension. The presence of such a correlation does not prove a direct causal link, and the effect is attributed not to any physical effects of the noise but to the fact that noise can lead to stress, perhaps because of annoyance, or interference with communications or with sleep. Increased blood pressure and hypertension are stress-related symptoms. It has also been suggested that noise-induced stress can cause biochemical effects involving changes to the composition of the blood, which can lead to ischaemic heart disease, and to effects on the immune system. These effects have been observed in residential areas where the noise levels from aircraft or road traffic (or both) exceed 70 dB(A) outside dwellings. Groups of people who are particularly susceptible include:

- those exposed to both high levels of noise at work and high levels of traffic noise at home;
- pregnant women exposed to occupational noise;
- those who suffer from noise-induced sleep disturbance;
- patients in hospitals.

It has been shown that the noise exposure of people resulting from their leisure activities can be as high as 70 dB(A) (24 hour L_{Aeq}) and can exceed that from the unwanted environmental noise. This is further evidence that it is not the physical characteristics of the noise that are important in determining these effects, but the undesirability of the disturbing or intruding noise that determines any potentially harmful health effects. This makes it difficult to relate the level of noise to the effect on health because the attitude of the listener towards the noise will be such an important factor.

Effects on social behaviour

There is evidence that noise levels above 80 dB(A) can cause reduced helping behaviour, that loud noise can also lead to an increase in aggressive behaviour, and that continuous exposure to high levels of noise may contribute to susceptibility to helplessness in schoolchildren. For most people, however, the most important effect of community noise is interference with rest, recreation and watching TV.

Noise in the community

The extent of noise exposure in the community

Much evidence has been gathered in recent years to indicate that many people in the developed world are exposed to high levels of community noise, and that this exposure is likely to increase. Traffic noise is the major source, followed by railway and aircraft noise and industrial noise. Much of the information in this section is based on a report carried out for the Commission of the European Communities in 1994 (**Lambert J** and **Vallet M**, Study related to the preparation of a communication on the future EC noise policy, INRETS, LEN report no. 9420). It has been estimated that in 1994 about 80 million citizens of the European Union, about 20% of the population, live in what the OECD calls black spot areas, where the continuous equivalent noise level (L_{Aeq}) from road traffic, measured outside dwellings, exceeds 65 dB(A). This is a level which most people in social surveys judge to be unacceptable. Approximately double this number i.e. 170 million people, about 40% of the population, live in grey spot areas where the continuous equivalent noise level from road traffic, measured outside dwellings, is between 55 and 65 dB(A). The corresponding figures for railway noise are 2% (black spot areas) and 8% (grey spot areas), and for airports about 1% (black spot areas). About 30% of the population, 100 million people, are exposed to noise at night exceeding 55 dB(A) L_{Aeq}, which is a level which is disturbing to sleep. Noise has been judged in a 1993 survey of EU residents as the fifth most important area of complaint about their local environment (after traffic, air pollution, landscape and waste) but the only one of these five for which concern was shown to be increasing in a repeat survey two years later.

The percentages of people annoyed by different types of noise are given in Table 2.2.

Table 2.2 Percentage of people showing annoyance to different noise types

EU member state	Indicator	Road	Rail	Aircraft	Industry
Germany (1986)	Severely affected	25.0	3.9	16.5	3.2
France (1989)	Annoyed	21.0	1.8	1.7	–
Great Britain (1991)	Annoyed	15.0	1.0	5.0	–
	Affected	28.0	4.0	16.0	2.0
Netherlands (1987)	Very affected	20.0	1.5	15.0	4.5

Source: **Lambert J, Vallet M** INRETS, LEN report 9420

It has been estimated that, in 1990, 56% of the UK population were exposed to a daytime L_{Aeq} exceeding 55 dB(A) and 63%

were exposed to a nighttime L_{Aeq} exceeding 45 dB(A), these being the World Health Organisation (WHO) guideline limits. The main noise sources outside dwellings recorded in this survey were: road traffic 66%, rail 1%, aircraft 3%, public works 1%, industry 1%, neighbourhood 17%, others 11%. The results of a survey carried out in 1991 as shown in table 2.3.

Table 2.3 Percentage of people showing annoyance to noise types in the UK

	% affected by noise	**% annoyed**
Road traffic	28	15
Rail traffic	4	1
Air traffic	16	5
Industry	2	–
Construction	3	–
Neighbours	22	12

Source: **Lambert J, Vallet M** INRETS, LEN report 9420

The problem of environmental noise is not restricted to the developed world, and there is evidence that it is increasing. A report of the United Nations Environmental Programme stated, in 1992, that 'noise has become a more significant problem than it was thought to be a decade ago. The problem is growing in particular in many urban centres in developing countries. Noise is a major problem in Manila, Bangkok, Cairo and many other cities.'

The OECD in 1991 identified the following four factors as being important in determining community noise exposure in the future:

- use of increasingly numerous and powerful sources of noise;
- wider geographical dispersion of noise sources, together with greater individual mobility and spread of leisure activities;
- increasing spread of noise over time, particularly in early morning, evenings and weekends;
- increasing public expectations which are closely linked to increasing incomes and education levels.

Public plans and programmes to reduce community noise

The environmental policies of many nations are governed by the concept of 'sustainable development' formulated at the International Conference on the Environment in Rio de Janeiro in 1993. There is sometimes argument as to whether noise policy should be covered by the sustainability idea, because noise does not have a lasting effect on the environment in the same way as other environmental effects such as air pollution or the greenhouse effect. There are many definitions of sustainable development, and one of them is: 'Development that meets the needs of the present without compromising the ability of future generations to meet their own needs.' According to this definition noise issues certainly should be included within any framework of policies based on the concept of sustainability, because any major new development which will produce noise in the community, such as a new motorway, has implications for future generations.

The Fifth Environmental Action Programme of the European Community, entitled *Towards Sustainability*, has the objective that 'No person should be exposed to noise levels which endanger health and the quality of life'. In order to meet this objective the following targets have been proposed, to be met by the year 2000:

- that nobody should be exposed to noise levels outside their dwellings of above 65 dB(A) L_{Aeq} at nighttime;
- that there should be no increase in exposure for those exposed between 55 and 65 dB(A);
- that the exposure for those currently exposed at levels below 55 dB(A) should not increase above 55 dB(A).

Proposals for meeting these targets were published in a European Green Paper in November 1996. Eight general categories of noise sources are identified as being significant in Europe: road, rail, aircraft, industry, civil engineering, building site activities, recreational activities and outdoor equipment (for example lawnmowers). Road traffic accounts for 90% of EU exposure levels. European policy on noise has previously concentrated on regulating emissions from noise sources such as vehicles and machinery, but in future this approach is to be supplemented by initiatives relating to noise exposure in the community. A common framework for the assessment of community noise exposure levels throughout Europe is proposed, involving harmonization of prediction, measurement and assessment methods and a programme of noise mapping to assess noise climate and noise exposure on a geographical basis. There is no EC legislation laying down emission limits from industrial installations, but a proposed directive on integrated pollution prevention control will, if it comes into effect, provide for the control of emissions, including noise, by means of a permit, taking into account local circumstances.

The World Health Organisation has defined health as 'A state of complete physical, mental and social well-being, and not merely the absence of disease or infirmity'. It has published a number of target values for community noise exposure, consistent with this definition including the following:

- to prevent the majority of people being moderately annoyed, L_{Aeq} should be less than 50 dB(A) outdoors;
- to prevent the majority of people being seriously annoyed, L_{Aeq} should be less than 55 dB(A) outdoors;
- at night L_{Aeq} should be less than 45 dB(A) outdoors so that people may sleep with bedroom windows open.

In the UK the numbers of complaints about noise which are made to local authority environmental health departments is published annually by the Chartered Institute of Environmental Health. The total number each year increases, and at an ever increasing rate corresponding to a doubling every ten years. The largest category, which is increasing at an even faster rate, is of noise from neighbours. The numbers for 1999 are: industrial 17737, commercial/leisure 29779, domestic 148006, vehicles

4738, equipment in the street 3835, construction/demolition sites 8232, traffic 1502, aircraft 2654, railway 554, other 6050. When comparing numbers in the different categories it must be remembered that members of the public are probably aware that the only situations where the local authority traditionally has powers to act are in connection with industrial/commercial noise, domestic noise and noise from construction sites, and it is unable to do anything about traffic, aircraft or railway noise.

The annual *Health of the Nation* report, issued jointly by the Departments of Health and the Environment contained the following objective in its November 1996 publication: 'to minimize noise pollution from all sources in order to improve local environmental quality and minimize the health risks posed by noise'.

The cost of noise in the community

Attempts to quantify the cost of noise in the community have been based on a number of factors including:

- willingness to pay (for less noise exposure);
- change of market value of properties;
- cost of abatement measures;
- cost of avoidance or prevention;
- cost of medical care and production losses.

The cost of community noise in Europe has been estimated as between 0.2% and 2% of GDP, with estimates based on 'avoidance costs', in the poorer countries, falling towards the lower end of this range, and those based on 'willingness to pay', in the richer countries, lying closer to the upper end of the range. The total cost for Europe as a whole is estimated as over ECU12 billion per year.

Summary

1 Sound is transmitted by the outer and middle ear to the inner ear or cochlea, where it is converted to biological signals transmitted to the brain and interpreted as sound.

2 It is permanent and irreparable damage to the hair cells in the cochlea caused by excessive exposure to noise which is responsible for noise-induced hearing loss.

3 Hearing sensitivity is described in terms of the hearing level, which is the threshold of hearing of the test subject, measured using an audiometer, and compared with a standardized hearing level. Audiograms show the subject's hearing level for each ear at different frequencies plotted as a graph.

4 Continuous exposure to high levels of noise at work causes temporary threshold shift, noise-induced permanent threshold shift, loudness recruitment and can also cause tinnitus.

5 Risk of noise-induced permanent threshold shift is related to the duration and level of exposure to noise, measured as continuous equivalent level, L_{Aeq}, over an 8 hour period.

6 Noise-induced permanent threshold shift, combined with the effects of aging (presbycusis) can cause difficulty in understanding speech, resulting in severe social handicap for the sufferer.

7 Noise-induced hearing loss at work is one of the major industrial health problems in Europe and the UK, with millions of employees exposed above 85 dB(A) and with large numbers of people receiving industrial injury benefit and being awarded compensation claims.

8 The cost to employers of complying with the Noise at Work Regulations has been estimated at £37 million per annum, or £35.60 for each noise-exposed worker. The major components

of this cost are from carrying out assessments, implementing noise reduction measures (including purchase of new, quieter machinery), issuing hearing protection and training. The benefits to the employer are difficult to quantify, but have been estimated at 25% of the costs. There are further benefits to the individual employee and to society.

9 The attitude of senior management is the critical factor which influences the success of hearing conservation programmes in a company. Noise exposure assessments that give an action plan for managers to implement are a key stage in the programme. Although hearing protection is widely issued throughout industry it is often not being used effectively by employees because of poor training and management supervision. In general there is a wide gap between knowledge and awareness of the Noise at Work Regulations and effective action.

10 Other effects of noise on people include interference with speech communication, disturbance of sleep, annoyance, effects on task performance, and effects relating to stress caused by noise.

11 Guideline limits have been proposed by the World Health Organisation relating to some of these effects.

12 Noise from road traffic is by far the biggest single source of noise in the community, followed by other transportation-related sources (railways and aircraft) and then by industrial noise.

13 Large sections of the community are exposed to levels of noise which are unacceptable, and a number of government and other public bodies have declared objectives and programmes aimed at reducing noise exposure.

14 The cost of community noise in Europe has been estimated to be between 0.2% and 2% of the GDP.

3

Sound generation, radiation and propagation

Introduction

This chapter explains how sound is generated, and how it travels from source to receiver. The aims are to understand the factors which can be used to minimize the radiation and transmission of noise, and to be able to predict noise levels, which is important if potential noise problems are to be solved at the planning stage.

In the previous chapter it was explained that a sound wave consists of vibrations of the air particles. It is useful to consider what can cause the air to vibrate in this way. One important mechanism is the radiation of sound from a vibrating solid surface, such as a loudspeaker or the surface of a machine such as an engine or motor. The vibration of the surface causes the adjacent layer of air to vibrate, and this is transmitted to the next layer of air, and so on. In this chapter the pattern of radiation from noise sources is considered, and in particular the generation of plane and spherical waves because these are important models used for the prediction of noise from sources.

The chapter starts with a general discussion of the behaviour of sound waves and how they may be reflected, diffracted, refracted and absorbed. An appreciation of this behaviour is important in understanding how sound travels from source to receiver. This is followed by a description of sound transmission, both outdoors and inside buildings.

The mechanisms of sound generation are discussed in more detail in Chapter 4, with emphasis on methods for reducing noise at source and on the application of the principles discussed in this chapter to the reduction of noise during its transmission.

The behaviour of sound waves

We may all remember from school that light travels in straight lines and that objects in its path cast sharp shadows, and that light is reflected by mirrors and absorbed by black surfaces. Cameras, spectacles and binoculars use glass lenses which cause the direction of rays of light to change when the rays pass from air into the glass, a phenomenon called refraction. If we use a microscope to look in detail at how a light ray passes through a narrow aperture in the form of a slit we see a complex distribution of light intensity, called diffraction patterns, that shows that the 'straight-line' behaviour is an oversimplification, and that light waves can sometimes interfere with each other to produce intricate patterns of light and dark.

Sound waves exhibit all these phenomena but there is an important difference, and that is, for the light waves all objects and obstacles are large compared with the wavelength of visible light. Even a pinhead is several hundred light wavelengths across, whereas for audible sound waves the wavelengths are very much of the same order of magnitude as the size of everyday objects. They may be of similar size, or larger or smaller depending on the size of the object and the frequency of the sound. It is helpful to understand, at least in qualitative terms, the properties which determine how sound waves travel, even if we decide to leave the detailed prediction calculations to noise consultants.

Diffraction

The simplest example is that we all know from experience that sound does not travel in straight lines but bends around corners. A consequence of this is that walls erected as noise barriers are not one hundred per cent effective because some of the sound bends around the edges of the barrier to the reception point, even if the line of sight to the noise source has been cut off by the barrier. The phenomenon that describes this process is called diffraction, and the sound reduction achieved by the barrier may be calculated using diffraction theory, but suffice it for the moment to note that it is the size of the barrier compared with the wavelength which is important. This has the practical consequence that it is much easier to erect a barrier to shield a high frequency noise source such as an electric drill that has a small wavelength of a few centimetres than it is to shield a low frequency noise, for example, from a pump or a compressor where the wavelength may be several feet.

Reflection

Light is reflected by a plane surface according to the laws of reflection, i.e. that angle of incidence equals angle of reflection (see Figure 3.1). A snooker player uses knowledge of the same law to calculate how the ball will bounce off the side of the table. A concave mirror can bring reflected light to a focus and a convex mirror can produce distorted images. The architect and acoustic designer must also be aware of sound-focusing problems caused by concave surfaces, for example, domed ceilings and curved rear walls in theatres and concert halls. Convex surfaces diffuse or spread out the sound more evenly.

Similar effects occur with sound waves but we should realize that a surface must be large compared with the wavelength in order to reflect sound in this way, and that smaller surfaces and obstacles will scatter (or diffract) the sound in a more complex manner. A nearby wall or floor can reflect sound and increase sound levels by up to 3dB compared with positions at similar distances from the source but well away from reflecting surfaces. For this reason 'facade corrections' are often made when comparing noise levels in the open with those close to buildings. When we are holding a sound level meter, reflections from our body can affect the sound level at the microphone and so we should always hold the meter

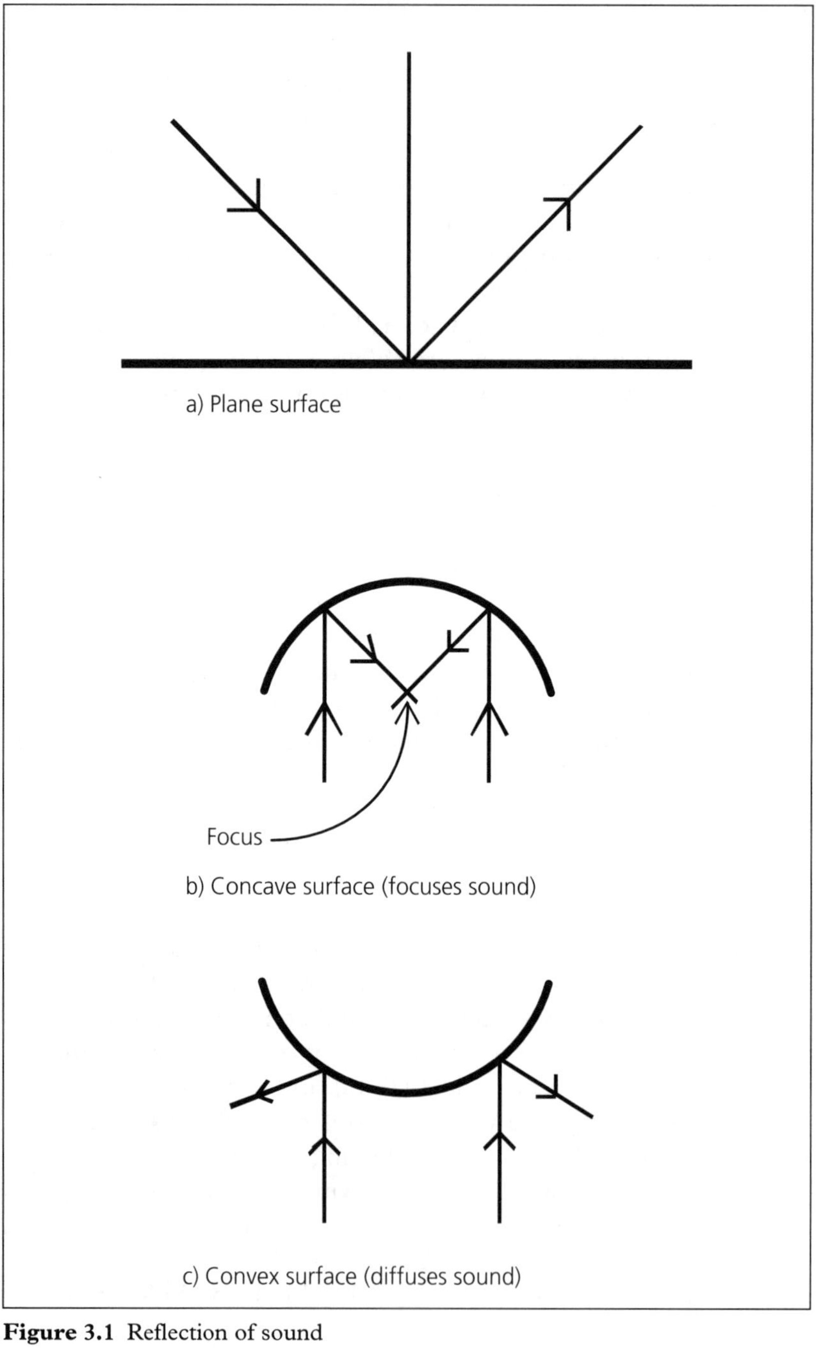

Figure 3.1 Reflection of sound

at arm's length away from the body or use a tripod in order to minimize these effects.

As a general rule, surfaces that are hard, such as brick, concrete or plaster, are good sound reflectors. The amount of sound reflection may be reduced by lining these surfaces with soft fibrous and foam materials such as carpets, curtains and upholstery, which are poor reflectors and tend to absorb rather than reflect the sound. When a noise source is indoors, multiple reflections from the walls, floor and ceiling will occur, leading to a jumble of reflected sound commonly called reverberation. The amount of reverberation will affect the level of sound in the room and may be controlled using sound-absorbing materials either to line the floors and walls or freely hanging as space absorbers. This is discussed in more detail in the section on noise indoors later in the chapter.

Interference

The phenomenon of interference describes what happens when two or more sound waves meet. In the vast majority of situations the waves will not have similar waveforms, or, in the terminology of the subject, they are said to be incoherent. The most likely circumstance in which the waves would be coherent is if they are both pure tones derived from the same source so that they have the same sinusoidal waveform and the same frequency. If they also have the same or similar amplitudes it is possible that at a particular moment at a particular position the two waves could either cancel each other out (called destructive interference) or reinforce each other with doubled amplitude (constructive interference) (Figure 3.2). This could happen, for example, at a point in between two loudspeakers facing each other, with both being supplied by exactly the same pure tone signal. Under these circumstances, however, the net effect would simply be a 3 dB increase in level because as the waves from each source travel onwards the pattern of interference at a particular point would be continually changing from constructive to destructive and back again.

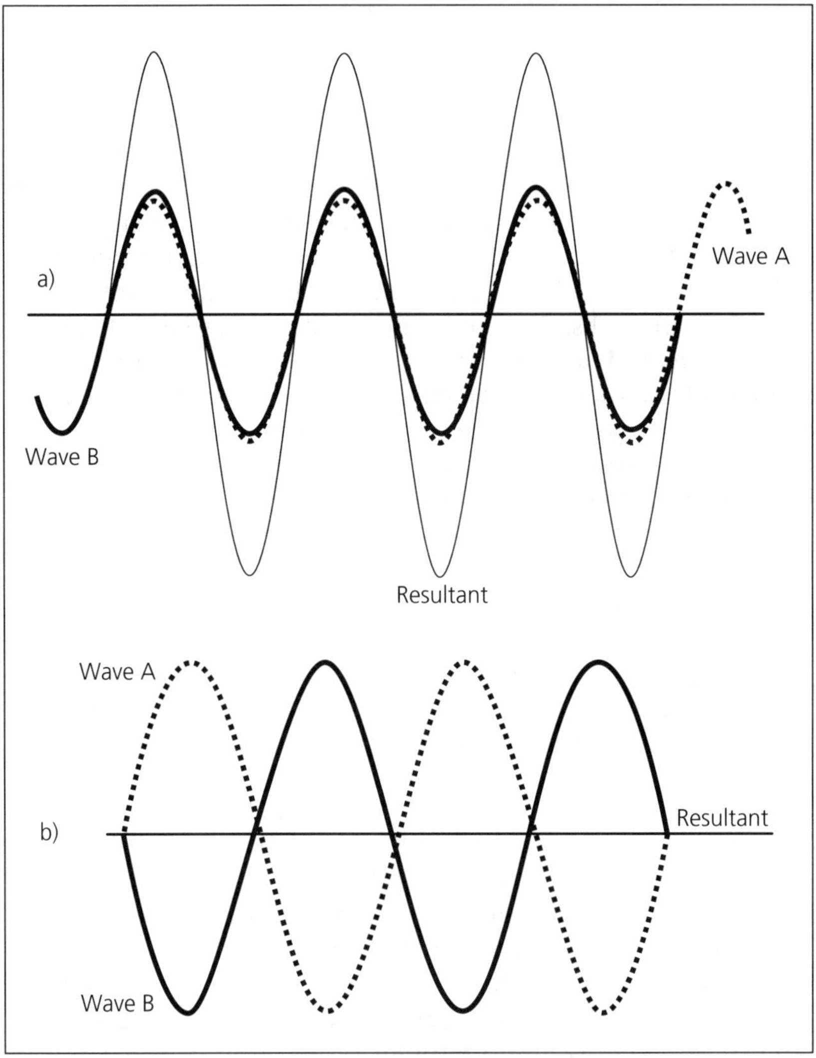

Figure 3.2 Constructive (a) and destructive (b) interference

Reflection of sound produces waves which are coherent and which can interfere constructively or destructively with the original incident wave. Under certain circumstances stationary or standing waves are produced. These are steady patterns of interference characterized by large variations in sound level with position, so that there will be alternate positions where the sound pressure level is a minimum, called nodes, as a result of destructive interference, and positions of maximum sound level (called antinodes) resulting from a constructive interference.

Standing waves in pipes, strings and rods are important in the operation of musical instruments but they may also occur in spaces such as rooms, corridors, stair wells and chimneys. An example would be a fan producing a pure tone relating to the blade-passing frequency that is connected to a length of duct or chimney. For certain lengths of ducting, standing waves would be set up as a result of interference between the waves passing along the duct in both directions. This results in a large increase in the sound pressure level radiated from the duct. The remedy is either to alter the length of the duct or the speed of the fan or to line the duct with sound-absorbing material.

Partial interference can also occur outdoors between sound reaching a receiver directly from the source and that which arrives after the reflection from the ground. This results in a reduction in sound level at the receiver called ground attenuation. More details of this are given later in this chapter in the section on sound outdoors.

Refraction

The speed of sound changes slightly with air temperature from about $330\,ms^{-1}$ at 0°C to $340\,ms^{-1}$ at 20°C. It also changes with wind speed depending upon whether it is travelling with or against the wind, which typically may vary its speed from $0\,ms^{-1}$ to $10\,ms^{-1}$. Both temperature and the wind speed vary with height above the ground, therefore so does the speed of sound. This results in refraction effects similar in principle to those that occur when light enters a glass lens, except that in this case the changes in the speed of sound are far smaller and more gradual. These effects become significant for the transmission of sound over long distances and are discussed in more detail later in this chapter in the section on outdoor sound.

Sound absorption

Sound absorption is a process whereby sound energy is lost from a sound wave and converted to heat. Since the energy content of sound waves is usually very small the actual temperature rises which result from sound absorption processes are usually negligible. Sound absorption can usually be thought of in terms of some frictional process that occurs between vibrating molecules which are transmitting the sound. Frictional processes also occur in vibrating bodies (for example, vibrating panels) but in these cases the energy loss is usually referred to as damping. The two terms damping and absorption have much in common.

Absorption processes can occur within the sound-transmitting medium, or at the interface with another medium, during reflection and scattering. All of the sound absorption mechanisms are frequency dependent, the amount of absorption increasing with the frequency of the sound. Sound absorption in the air is discussed in more detail later, in the section on outdoor sound, and sound absorption by surfaces in the section on sound indoors.

The radiation of sound from noise sources

The most important factors that determine the level of noise at a point are the sound power of the source and the distance of the reception point from the source. This section considers the relationship between sound level and distance from the source, starting with idealized models of the source, and then showing how the theory may be extended to real noise sources such as machines. It is assumed that the noise source is operating in so-called free-field conditions, i.e. that there is no reflecting surface close to either source or receiver. The effects of reflections are then considerd in later sections.

Point sources and plane waves

We can learn much about the behaviour of sound by observing ripples on the surface of a pond or even in the bath. The reflection of the ripples by large surfaces can be contrasted with the way the ripples bend around edges or through small gaps. If a small stone is dropped into the water then circular ripples are generated, whereas a long straight plank would generate straight ripples, except at the ends. The equivalent models for sound are spherical waves (i.e. spherical ripples) and plane waves. The ideal source of spherical waves is a small, ideally point-sized, pulsating sphere, but in practice any source which is small compared with the wavelength will radiate spherical wave. In theory an infinitely long source would be needed to produce perfect plane waves, but in practice a source that is large relative to the wavelength will have the same effect. Even spherical waves produced by a point source will, in effect, become plane as the circular ripples flatten out at long distances from the source.

The directionality of sound radiation

A good example of how the directional pattern of the radiation from the source depends on frequency is given by the behaviour of a typical loudspeaker hi-fi cabinet used in the home. Within the cabinet there are usually two loudspeakers: a large one called a woofer and a small one called a tweeter. At low frequencies the sound radiated by the large loudspeaker will be radiated more-or-less in all directions into the room because even for the large loudspeaker, maybe 20 cm in diameter, the wavelength of the sound at low frequencies will be very large compared with this loudspeaker size. However, for medium and high frequencies the wavelengths become smaller and at the very high frequencies the large loudspeaker would tend to beam sound along a narrow cone in front of the loudspeaker, which is not ideal for the good listening conditions that are required anywhere in the room. Therefore, the cabinet contains an electronic device called a crossover network so that the high frequency sounds in the signal are fed to the tweeter, which can then again spread these sounds fairly evenly throughout the room.

The practical relevance of all this to noise control is to realize that high-frequency sources may be highly directional and therefore there is the possibility of directing the sound from them away from the receiver. An example would be exhaust noise from a steam or air release jet that could be pointed towards the sky and perhaps away from nearby houses.

Effect of distance on sound levels

It is a matter of common experience that the level of sound from a noise source outdoors reduces with the distance from the source. Using the idea of a simple source radiating spherical waves we can easily understand why this is so, and calculate the effect of distance.

First we must assume so-called free-field conditions, that is that there is no reflecting surface nearby. Let us assume that the source is radiating sound power at a constant rate of watts. This sound power is first of all concentrated over a small area close to the source but as the sound waves radiate outwards from the source then the radius of the spherical wavefront increases and, more importantly, the area of that wavefront increases. If we consider two points, one of which is twice as far from the noise surface as the other, then, the area of the spherical waves at these points will be in the ratio of 4 to 1, in other words when the distance from the source doubles, the area over which the sound power is spread increases by a factor of 4.

It is here that the concept of sound intensity, i.e. sound power per unit area, is useful because it is the sound intensity that is related to the magnitude of the sound that we hear. If the distance from the source is doubled, the intensty, i.e. the sound power per unit area, reduces by a factor of 4 according to the inverse square law. Expressing this in decibels, a factor of four times in power or intensity corresponds to a change of 6 dB. Therefore every time the distance from the source is doubled the sound level drops by 6 dB.

As an example, supposing the noise level at 1 metre from a simple point source were 90dB(A), then according to the '6dB per doubling of distance' rule the level at 2 metres will be 84dB(A), at 4 metres 78dB(A), at 8 metres 72dB(A), 66dB(A) at 16 metres, and so on until eventually the noise level from the machine merges with the background noise level.

This approach is fine until we need to work out the level at some intermediate distance that we cannot find simply by doubling. In this case the following formula may be used to calculate the sound pressure level at any distance from the machine:

$$L_1 - L_2 = 20\log\left(\frac{r_2}{r_1}\right)$$

where L_1 is the sound pressure level at distance r_1 and L_2 the sound pressure level at distance r_2.

As an example, suppose that the level at 10 metres from a source is 70dB(A). What would the level be at 120 metres? Substituting these values into the formula:

$$\begin{aligned} L_1 - L_2 &= 20 \log\left(\frac{120}{10}\right) \\ &= 21.6 \text{ dB(A)} \end{aligned}$$

The expression $L_1 - L_2$ on the left of the equation is sometimes called the 'distance attenuation', and in this case is 21.6dB(A) or 22dB(A) to the nearest decibel. Therefore the level at 10 metres, 70dB(A), has been reduced by 22dB(A), to 48dB(A) at 120 metres.

An alternative approach is to plot a graph of level in dB(A) against the log of distance in metres using a slope of 6dB for every doubling of distance. This is shown in Figure 3.3. From this graph we may read off the level at any distance we require. The use of this formula or graph based on the 6dB per doubling of distance rule is the fundamental basis of noise level predictions outdoors and is widely used. Sometimes in practice the rate of reduction of level with distance may not be exactly 6 but it is usually found that plotting level versus distance on the log-graph will produce a straight line. As an example, if the transmission from source to receiver is close to the ground, over soft ground such as grassland which yields a high ground attenuation, then in addition to so-called distance attenuation there will be an extra reduction due to ground attenuation and the level with distance will drop off at a rate in excess of 6 dB per doubling. In contrast, the level with distance plotted along a street or down a corridor where the sound does not disperse as in the free field but is directed back because of reflections will show a slope of less than 6 dB per doubling of distance. However, once the attenuation rate with distance has been determined, perhaps by measurement for a given situation, such a graph can be used in future predictions.

This approach to predicting level at distance is fine if we have data about the sound pressure level at a particular distance from a noise source. However, sometimes we do not have these data, but we may have the sound power level, L_W, of the source. In this case we may use another equation to predict the sound pressure level, L_p, at any distance r from the source using the following formula:

$$L_p = L_W - 20\log r - 11$$

This formula, which is not derived here, comes from the simple equation that the sound intensity, I, is equal to the sound power, W, divided by $4\pi r^2$. As an example, suppose that the sound power level from a machine is known to be 120 decibels, then what is the sound pressure level at 20 metres?

$$\begin{aligned} L_p &= 120 - 20\log 20 - 11 \\ &= 120 - 26 - 11 \\ &= 83\,\text{dB(A)} \end{aligned}$$

Effect of ground reflections

So far we have considered a point source under free-field conditions. In practice, even if it is located outdoors well away from

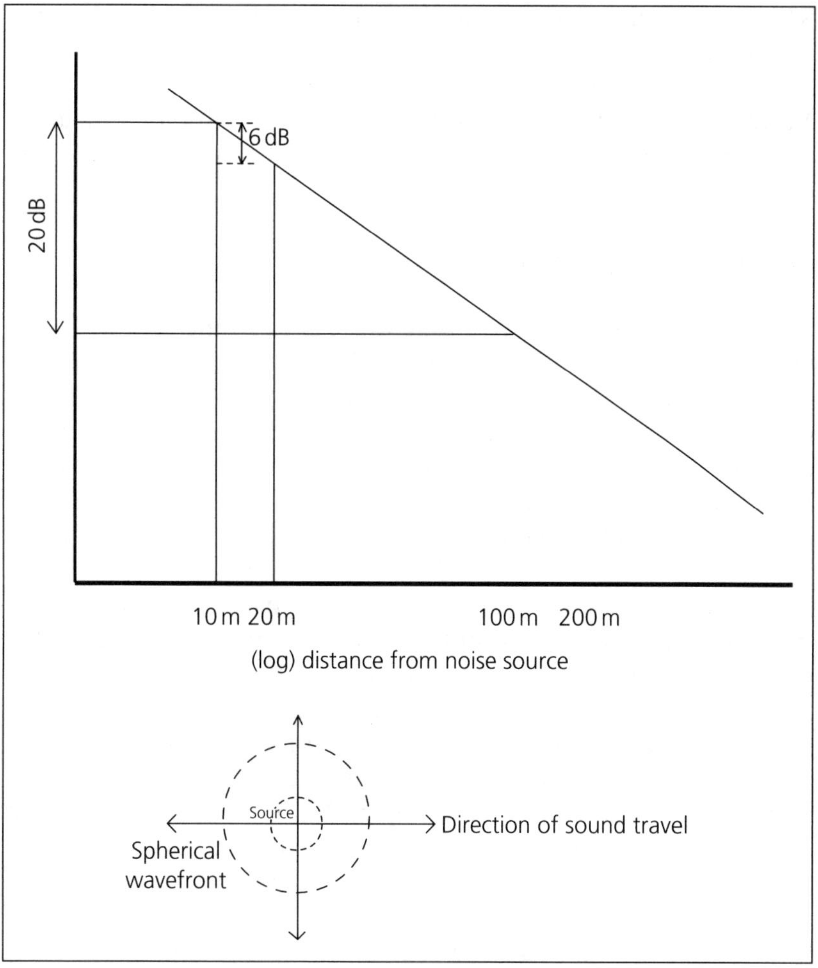

Figure 3.3 Graph of sound level against distance (log) for a point source, illustrating the 6 dB per doubling of distance rule

other reflecting surfaces the source often stands on hard, sound-reflecting ground such as concrete or tarmac. In these cases the half of the sound energy which is radiated downwards is reflected upwards by the ground. This means that at all points above the ground the sound intensity is doubled, and the sound pressure level increased by 3 dB as compared to the free-field situation. Hence the factor of −11 in the above equation becomes −8 for hard ground. When the sound is soft and acoustically absorbing, which is the case for grassland or cultivated ground, the factor −11 is retained.

More complex effects of ground reflections, which can lead to additional 'ground attenuation', are discussed later in the section on sound outdoors.

Line and plane sources

So far we have considered point sources of sound. An infinitely long acoustic line source radiates cylindrically shaped wavefronts (Figure 3.4). In this case the sound pressure level decreases with distance from the line source at a rate of 3 dB per doubling of distance. The noise from a motorway approximates to a line source. So too may the noise radiated from long lengths of pipes or ducts. A long train may behave as a line source for an observer fairly close to the track, but for an observer several train lengths away it behaves more like a point source. The transition point between the line source and the point source behaviour occurs at a distance from the track of $1/\pi$ times the length of the train. An infinitely large plane surface would radiate perfectly plane waves, but the pattern of radiation from a finite plane source, such as a machine panel, a window or from the facade of a building, will vary with distance as shown in Figure 3.5. Close to the source, at distances small compared with the source dimensions, the sound pressure level will be independent of distance, as for a plane wave. At very large distances, much greater than either of the source dimensions, the radiating surface behaves as a point source. At intermediate distances the source may behave as a line source, particularly if one of the dimensions is much greater than the other, as with a long, low building.

Real noise sources — near and far fields, directivity

The point source theory of the previous section can be applied to real noise sources such as machines, with two provisos:

- that the distance from the source is great enough;

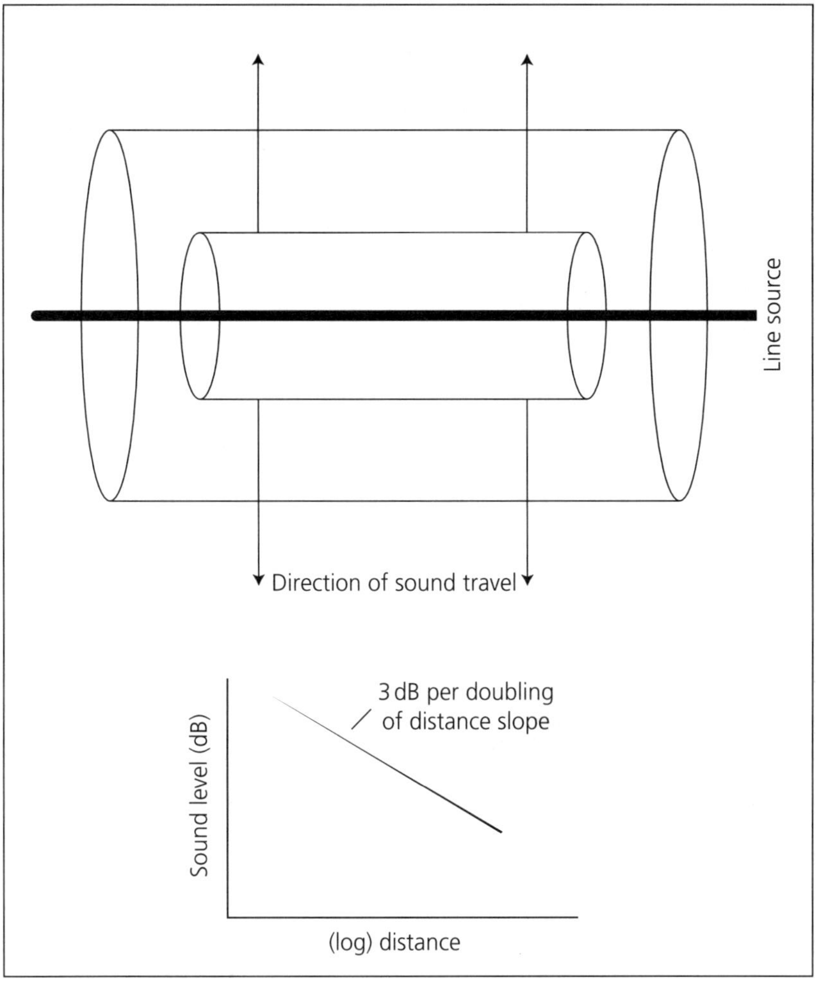

Figure 3.4 Cylindrically shaped waves from a line source

- that account is taken of the fact that the machine may not radiate sound equally in all directions.

Near and far fields

Real noise sources such as machines with vibrating surfaces have a definite size, i.e. they are not point sources. Each part of the machine surface radiates sound. Near to the machine the contributions of the various parts combine in a complex way, and it is

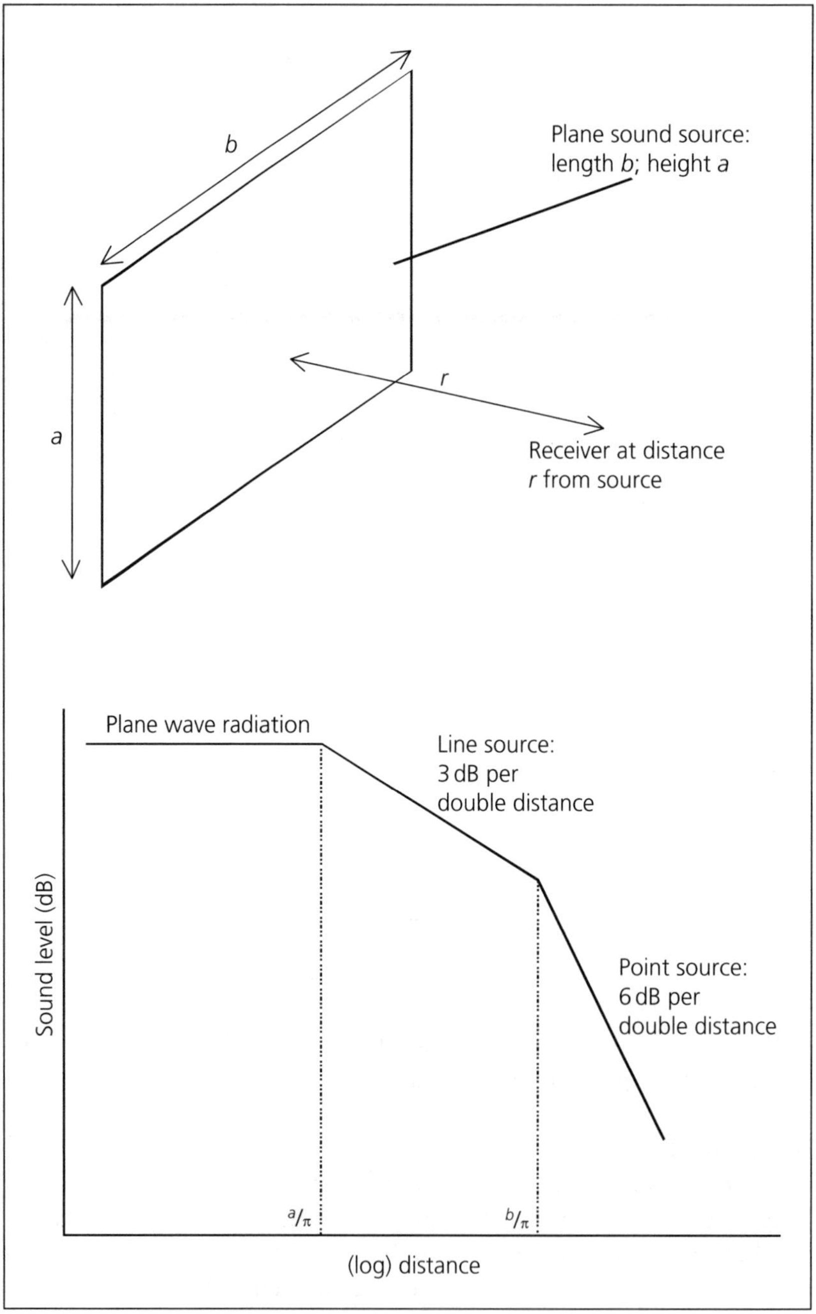

Figure 3.5 Showing the variation of sound level with distance from a plane sound source

difficult to predict the local variations in sound pressure level. This region close to the machine is called the near field of the noise source (see Figure 3.6 where the near-field region is shown hatched).

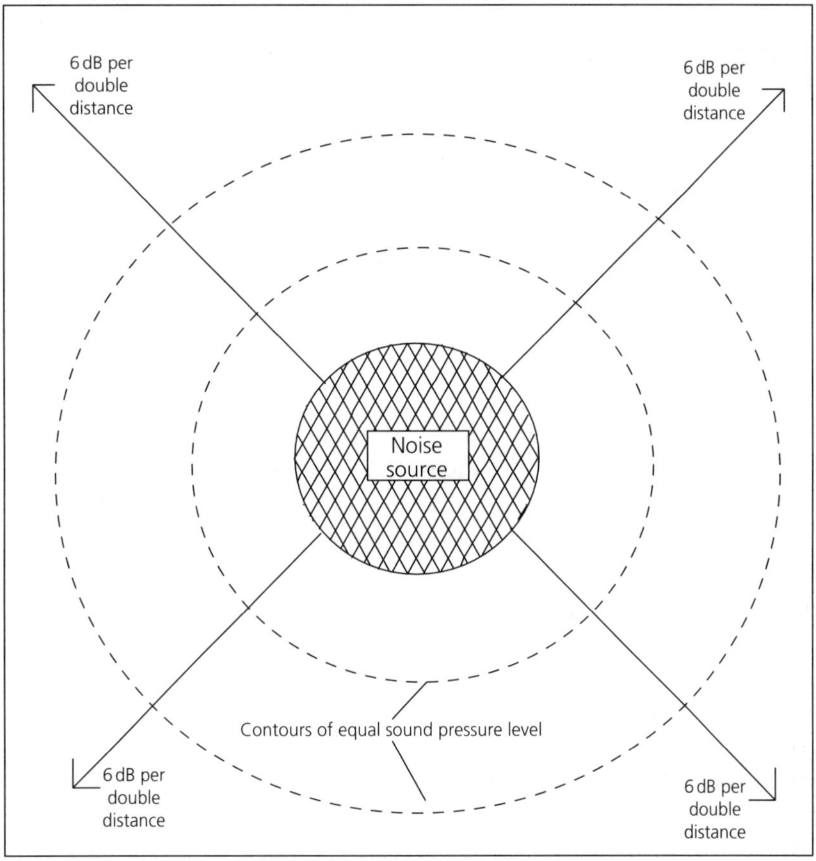

Figure 3.6 Illustrating near and far fields for a real noise source

Further away from the machine the individual contributions from different parts of the source merge and the machine is radiating as a whole. Provided that the distance from the machine is large enough the inverse square law will be obeyed, and the sound pressure level will decrease with distance at a rate of 6 dB per doubling of distance in any particular direction. The region in which this occurs is called the far field of the source (see Figure 3.6).

The extent of the near-field region depends on the size of the machine and on the wavelength of the sound being radiated. There is no sharp division between the two regions, but in order to ensure far-field conditions measurements of machinery noise should be taken at distances from the machine which are several times the typical dimensions of the machine and also several times the sound wavelength. Several usually means at least two or three. For small machines radiating high frequencies, like many electrically powered hand tools, grinders and drills, far field might begin at about 1 metre away, but for a much larger machine, like a compressor, that radiates predominantly low frequencies with large wavelengths, then even distances of 3 or 4 metres may still be in the near field.

Far-field measurements may be used as the basis for predicting noise levels at greater distances from the source, as in the above example, whereas near-field measurements may give unreliable predictions when used for this purpose.

It may, however, be difficult to take far-field measurements indoors, especially for large machines, or for low frequency sources in small rooms, or where there is a high background noise from other machines. Measurements of noise in the workplace are often of necessity taken at near-field positions close to machines, at operators' ear positions.

Directionality or directivity

The directionality of a noise source may be described either in terms of its directivity factor, Q, or its directivity index, D. The directivity factor in a given direction is simply the ratio of the sound intensity radiated in that direction to the average intensity, i.e. averaged over all directions, at the same distance. The corresponding directivity index, in decibels, is the difference between the sound pressure level in the given direction and the average level, i.e. averaged over all directions, at the same distance. The two measures are simply related:

$$D = 10\log Q$$

The formula developed earlier may now easily be extended to predict the sound pressure level in a given direction from a real sound source:

$$L_p = L_W - 20\log r - 11 + D$$

For the simple source, which is nondirectional, situated above hard, sound-reflecting ground, D is in effect +3 dB, leading to the −8 in the formula discussed earlier. Such a source situated indoors will also have an effective directionality, depending upon its position in the room, arising from its proximity to reflecting surfaces. If it is located between two reflecting surfaces, for example, at the junction of a wall and floor, then the directivity factor, Q, is 4 and the directivity index, D, is +6 dB. For a position in the corner of the room, i.e. at the junction of three reflecting surfaces, $Q = 8$ and $D = +9$ dB.

Outdoor sound propagation

In addition to the distance attenuation calculated so far, i.e. the effect of the inverse square law, sound outdoors may be further attenuated by:

- air absorption;
- ground attenuation;
- sound velocity gradients;
- barriers.

The physical processes involved in these mechanisms have already been described. Much research goes on into the prediction of the attenuation of sound outdoors. A number of prediction methods are available in the acoustics literature for each type of attenuation. These are often simplified approximations to much more complicated analyses, and sometimes different schemes are not always in total agreement. An international standard, ISO9613 *Acoustics: Attenuation of sound during propagation outdoors. Part 2: A general method of calculation* has been published, which gives details of prediction methods, and the information which follows is taken from this source.

Air absorption

Absorption of sound in air is caused mainly by molecular absorption involving the oxygen molecules and water vapour molecules. Hence the absorption of sound in air is strongly dependent on the relative humidity of the air. It also depends on the temperature of the air.

An approximate expression for the excess attenuation due to air absorption is given in ISO9613. At a temperature of 20°C and 50% relative humidity the predicted attenuation is:

0.5 dB/km at 500 Hz

1.5 dB/km at 1 kHz

6 dB/km at 2 kHz

24 dB/km at 4 kHz.

These figures illustrate that air absorption increases rapidly with increasing sound frequency, and that it will only be important over very long distances or for very high frequencies.

Ground attenuation

Excess attenuation occurs when sound travels within a few metres of soft ground such as grassland or cultivated ground. The attenuation arises from destructive interference between the sound reaching the receiver directly from the source and that which arrives after reflection from the ground. This produces little effect when the ground is hard, but with soft ground the reflected sound undergoes a change of phase on reflection and at a certain frequency, depending on the distance, cancellation between the direct and reflected waves occurs at the receiver. The attenuation is greatest in the frequency range 200–600 Hz and it depends on the heights of the source and receiver and the distance between them and the acoustical properties of the ground. Excess attenuations can be as high as 25 dB for distances of 1000 m and source and receiver heights of about 1.5 m.

ISO 9613 gives formulae for predicting the soft-ground attenuation in any octave frequency band, and also a simpler method for predicting the overall ground attenuation in dB(A) for a broadband noise with a fairly flat frequency spectrum. For a source to receiver distance of 150 m and an average source and receiver height of 1.5 m. the predicted soft-ground attenuation is:

14 dB at 250 Hz

10 dB at 500 Hz

4 dB(A) overall attenuation

These figures show that the effect of ground attenuation can be significant even at quite short distances.

The ISO standard also offers a method of dealing with situations where the nature of the ground surrounding a noise source is a mixture of both hard and soft ground. Different corrections are given for ground near to the source, ground which is close to the receiver and for ground which is in the middle area.

Sound velocity gradients

Sound velocity gradients can give rise to large fluctuations in sound levels. The principles were explained earlier in this chapter.

Both temperature and the wind speed vary with height above the ground, therefore so does the speed of sound. This results in refraction effects similar in principle to those that occur when light enters a glass lens, except that in this case the changes in the sound speed are far smaller and more gradual. Refraction results in sound rays being bent either towards the sky or towards the ground (see Figure 3.7). These effects only become noticeable over considerable distances, more than a kilometre, but are responsible for our observations that noise from a distant motorway or factory carries better on some days than others, depending on wind direction and weather conditions. For our purposes it is sufficient to know that these effects exist, that they make prediction of sound levels over very long distances notoriously difficult and they can cause day-to-day variation in sound level at these distances of many decibels (10–20 dB).

Sound levels are reduced in the so-called shadow zones which can occur downwind of the noise source because the sound rays from the source are refracted upwards, away from the receiver. Similar effects occur during normal daytime weather conditions, when temperature decreases with height.

At night, temperature inversions often occur, and the sound is bent the other way, towards the ground, causing the transmission of sound over long distances to be improved. The effects of inversion are all the more noticeable because background levels at night are much lower than during the day, particularly on still, calm nights when there is no wind generated. Refraction effects similar to those caused by inversions occur upwind of the noise source.

It is difficult to predict attenuations (which may be either positive or negative) due to velocity gradients, but they can quite easily

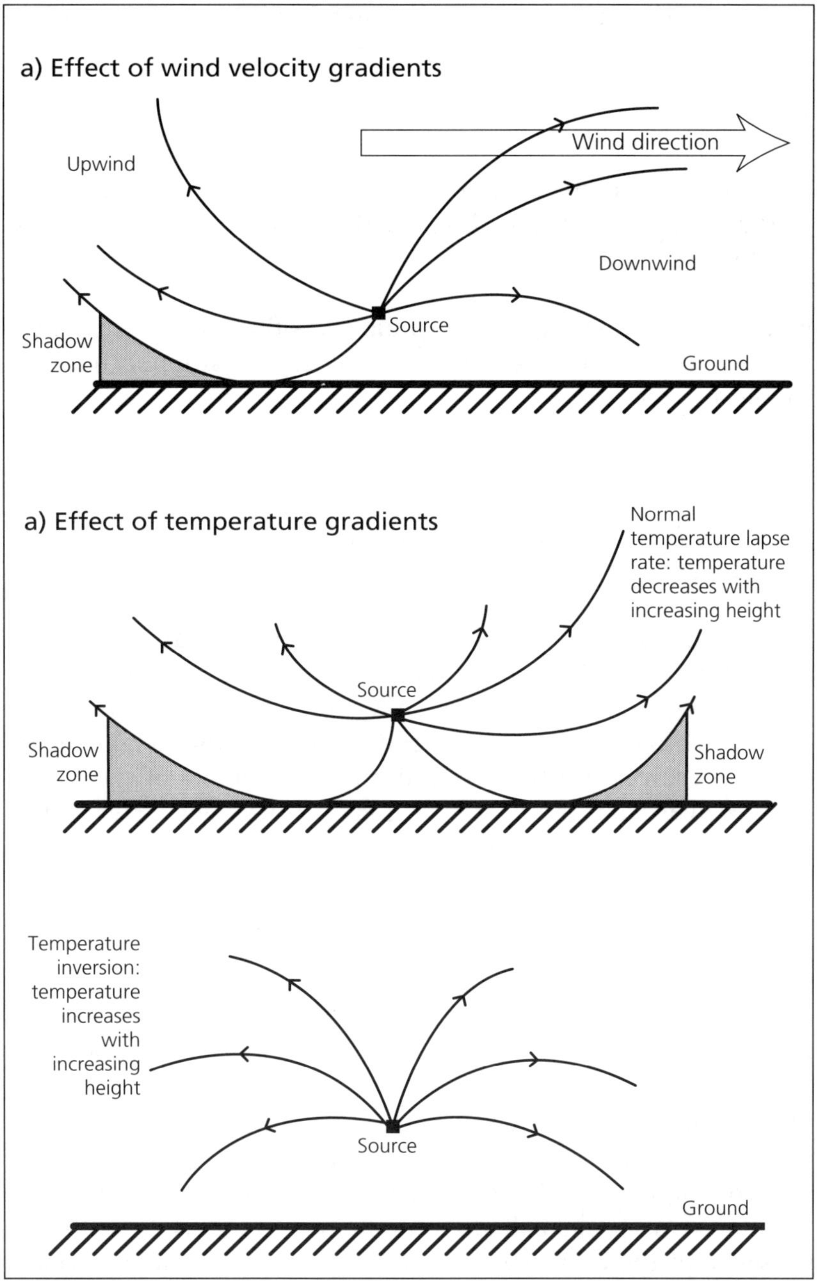

Figure 3.7 The refraction of sound in the atmosphere due to sound velocity gradients

produce variations of between 10 and 20 dB over distances of a few hundred metres.

Barriers

The most commonly used method for predicting the attenuation produced by a barrier is the path difference method originally developed by Maekawa.

The following approximate formula gives the predicted attenuation, E_b, produced by a thin, rigid barrier positioned between source and receiver.

$$E_b = 10\log(3 \pm 20N)\,\text{dB}$$

where N is defined by $N = 2\,\delta/\lambda$, and $\delta = (a + b - c)$ where λ is the wavelength of the sound (see Figure 3.8).

The quantity δ is the difference between the path lengths of sound travelling from source to receiver over the top of the barrier $(a + b)$ and sound travelling directly, in the absence of the barrier (c). The path difference, δ, depends on the relative heights of the source, receiver and barrier, and on the distances of the source and receiver from the barrier. It may be obtained either from a scale drawing of the situation or by calculation using trigonometry, and Pythagoras' theorem in particular, as shown in the example below.

The options of using either the plus or the minus sign in the above formula relate to the two possibilities that the reception point may either be in the shadow zone of the barrier, i.e. when there is no direct line of sight between source and receiver, or in the 'illuminated' zone, when there is line of sight. The plus sign should be used for situations when the receiver is in the shadow zone of the barrier. Because of the nature of wave diffraction there may still be a small amount of attenuation produced by the presence of the barrier even in the illuminated zone, where the barrier does not cut off direct line of sight, and the minus sign should be used in the formula in this case.

Example

A compressor is to be used 30 m away from a bungalow, and a temporary barrier is to be erected to reduce the noise. The ground between the compressor and the bungalow is hard, flat and level. The barrier is 2 m high and is erected 5 m from the compressor. The centre of the compressor is 0.5 m above the ground. Calculate the noise reduction produced by the barrier at a height of 1.5 m above the ground at the bungalow. The barrier is long enough for the effects of diffraction around its sides to be negligible. Take the velocity of sound in air as $330 ms^{-1}$.

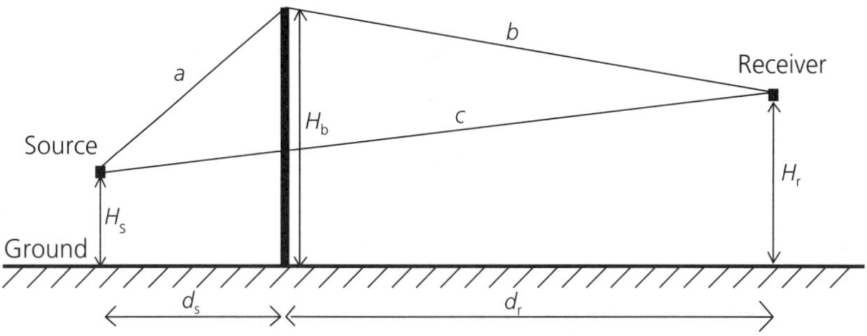

H_s = height of source

H_b = height of barrier

H_r = height of receiver

d_s = distance of source to barrier

d_r = distance of receiver to barrier

path difference $\delta = a + b + c$

$a = \sqrt{(H_b - H_s)^2 + d_s^2}$

$b = \sqrt{(H_b - H_r)^2 + d_r^2}$

$c = \sqrt{(H_r - H_s)^2 + (d_s + d_r)^2}$

Figure 3.8 The method of calculating sound attenuation due to noise barrier

A diagram of the situation is shown in Figure 3.8, which also shows the method for calculating the path difference, which in this case is 0.21 m. In the 500 Hz octave band:

$$\text{wavelength } \lambda = \frac{330}{500}$$
$$= 0.66\,\text{m}$$
$$N = 2\frac{\delta}{\lambda}$$
$$= 2 \times \frac{0.21}{0.66}$$
$$= 0.64$$
$$\text{barrier attenuation } E_b = 10\log(3 + 20N)$$
$$= 10\log(3 + 20 \times 0.64)$$
$$= 12\,\text{dB}$$

The attenuations in the other octave bands are calculated in the same way. The results are given in Table 3.1.)

Table 3.1 Octave band barrier attenuations

Octave band (Hz)	125	250	500	1000	2000	4000
Barrier attenuation (dB)	8	10	12	15	17	20

It can be seen from Table 3.1 that attenuation increases with frequency. It has been shown that, in practice, there is an upper limit of about 25 dB for the attenuation produced by barriers. This is due to the scattering of sound by turbulent air into the shadow zone of the barrier. The above calculation, based on diffraction theory, has assumed that the transmission of sound through the barrier is negligible. In practice this means that the sound insulation produced by the barrier material is sufficient to ensure that the level of transmitted sound is at least 10 dB below that of the sound diffracted around the barrier. The sound insulation depends mainly on the mass of the structure as explained more fully in Chapter 4. A surface density of 20 kg m^{-2} is usually adequate for barriers. It is important that there are no gaps or holes in or underneath the barrier.

Other factors

Thick vegetation such as shrubs and trees often provides a visual screen from the source of noise. The extra sound attenuation provided is, however, usually very small, unless the growth is extremely dense and several metres thick. As an example, a figure of about 6dB per 100m at 400Hz has been quoted for the attenuation of sound in thick forests. There are other benefits: the noise of the wind in bushes and trees can mask more disturbing noises, and the vegetation can also provide a visual barrier which hides the source from the receiver, and this can sometimes make the source of noise seem less unacceptable.

Other factors such as fog, mist and rain have been shown to have very little direct effect on sound transmission through the air.

The attenuations predicted from the various mechanisms are added together to produce a total excess attenuation *E*, which is deducted from the predicted noise level:

$$L_p = L_W - 20\log r - 11 + D - E$$

It must be emphasized that the accurate prediction of the total attenuation is extremely difficult. The various mechanisms may combine in a complex way, as when wind and temperature gradients and atmospheric turbulence affect the attenuation produced by a barrier. Another example is the effect that a barrier may have on reducing ground attenuation, since the sound reaching the receiver has travelled over the top of the barrier and has not been reflected by the ground. For this reason ground attenuation should not be included when there is a barrier.

Propagation of sound indoors

This section is concerned with the distribution of sound within indoor spaces and the transmission of sound through partitions between these spaces. First it is necessary to consider how sound may be reflected, transmitted or absorbed by these surfaces.

Acoustic properties of panels and partitions

Airborne sound striking a panel or partition, such as a wall or window, will be partially reflected as described earlier. However, some sound energy will be transmitted through the panel and radiated into the air on the other side. Some of the sound energy will be converted into heat as a result of frictional processes in the material of the panel. This fraction of the sound energy is said to be absorbed. The surface of the panel is sometimes covered with material (such as foam or fibre) to reduce reflection and increase the absorption of sound.

It is worth clarifying what happens during sound transmission. The incident sound wave striking the panel causes vibration of the particles of material in the panel, i.e. causes sound to be transmitted into the panel. Because panels are usually thin in comparison with their height and width the transmitted energy is usually in the form of a flexural wave, i.e. causing the panel to flex or bend, rather than a compression wave. The vibrating panel then acts as a radiator of sound into the air on the other side — and so sound is transmitted 'through' the panel.

The amount of energy reflected and transmitted by a panel will depend on its density, thickness, stiffness and the way in which it is supported at the edges, and also on the frequency of the sound.

The fractions of sound energy striking the panel which are transmitted and reflected are useful properties of the panel and are called the transmission (t) and reflection (r) coefficients respectively:

$$t = \frac{\text{Sound energy transmitted by the panel}}{\text{Sound energy incident upon panel}}$$

and

$$r = \frac{\text{Sound energy reflected by the panel}}{\text{Sound energy incident upon panel}}$$

The transmission coefficient is an important property of a partition, determining its effectiveness as a sound-insulating material. This is more commonly expressed in decibels as the sound reduction index or transmission loss of the partition. This is discussed in Chapter 4.

The absorption coefficient, α, is much more widely used than the reflection coefficient. It is simply the fraction of sound energy not reflected by a surface:

$$\text{Absorption coefficient } \alpha = \frac{\text{Sound energy absorbed/transmitted by a panel}}{\text{Sound energy incident upon the panel}}$$

The absorption coefficient (for a perfect absorber), which does not reflect any sound, $\alpha = 1$, and that of a perfect reflector which does not absorb any sound is $\alpha = 0$. An α of 0.6 simply means that a surface absorbs six-tenths, or 60%, of the energy striking it, and reflects the remaining 40%. In practice, values for surfaces range from about $\alpha = 0.01$ for hard reflecting surfaces such as smooth brickwork, plaster or concrete, to values of more than 0.9 for very good sound absorbers.

The absorption coefficient is used to calculate the amount of sound reflected back into a room by its walls and other surfaces. On this basis a hole in the wall which lets the sound out would be a good absorber. Usually, however, the absorption coefficient does express the fraction of the incident sound energy that is actually absorbed, i.e. turned into heat by frictional processes.

All of these coefficients, α, r and t, will depend upon the frequency of the sound and the angle of incident of the sound waves upon the surface. Values are often quoted for normal incidence (i.e. angle of incidence of 0°), or for random or field incidence. Field incidence conditions represent a range and distribution of incidence angles which are representative of practical situations.

Under normal circumstances the absorption of sound by air is not considered important when compared with other factors involved in sound propagation such as the spreading of the sound wavefront, scattering and diffraction. Air absorption only becomes significant when considering propagation outdoors over long distances (more than a few hundred metres), and particularly when high frequency sound is involved. Air absorption is much more important at ultrasonic frequencies and is the reason why many technical devices (burglar alarms and so on) employing ultrasonic beams have a limited range in air.

Sound absorption by surfaces

Air absorption of sound energy only becomes significant in sound propagation indoors at the very highest frequencies and for the very largest spaces such as theatres and concert halls. Usually it is negligible compared with the absorption which occurs when the sound strikes a surface such as a wall or floor.

All surfaces will produce some sound absorption, but in the case of hard smooth surfaces this will be very small. Good sound absorbers fall into two categories: porous and tuned (resonant) absorbers.

Porous absorbers

The first category consists of porous materials such as certain types of foam, mineral fibre, felt, carpet. Sound enters the large number of small interlocking air passages in the material and sound energy is lost as a result of friction between the air and the walls of these pores. A typical graph of absorption coefficient versus frequency for a porous material is shown in Figure 3.9. This type of absorber works over a broad band of frequencies, but porous absorbers are much more effective at high frequencies than at low frequencies. Porous absorbers are often used as a lining to a hard surface such as a wall, floor or ceiling, or to line a duct in order to reduce fan noise, but they can be mounted independently, for example, hung from the ceiling in factories, in which case they are called space absorbers. The effectiveness of porous absorbers at low frequencies depends on the thickness of the porous layer. The low frequency absorption coefficient increases with the thickness of the porous layer, and is also increased by an air-space between the porous layer and the backing wall.

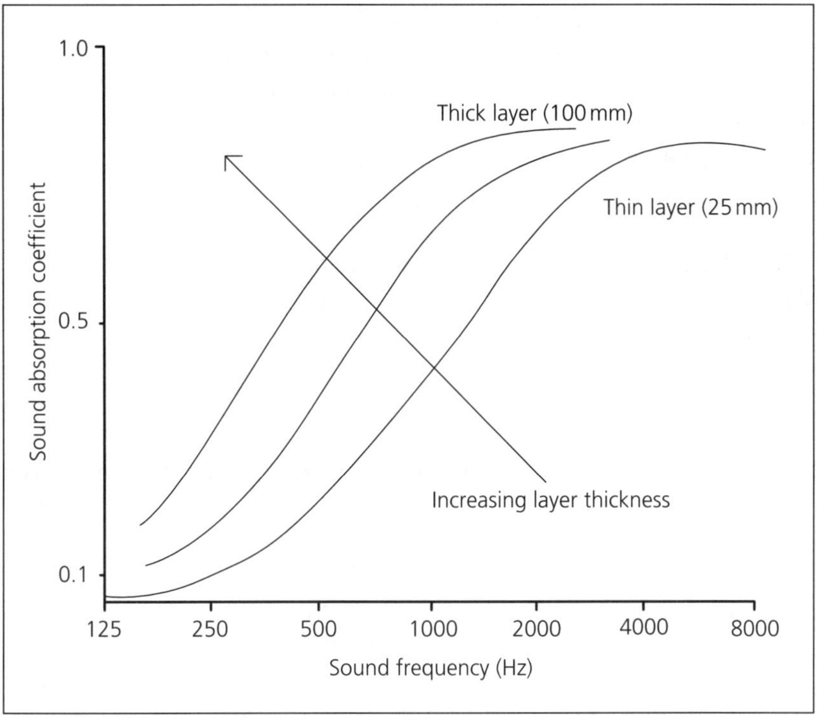

Figure 3.9 Typical variation of sound absorption coefficient with frequency for porous material

There are two requirements for a material to be a good absorber. First, the sound must be able to penetrate into the material and not be reflected at its surface. This means that the material must have an acoustic impedance similar to that of air. Foam and fibrous materials naturally tend to meet this requirement because they consist mainly of air-spaces, but it is important to ensure that the surface of the material facing the sound waves is not treated or lined in any way with a hard sound-reflecting layer. The second requirement is that the material should have an appropriate structure of small interconnecting passages that promotes friction in the vibrating air particles and thereby the maximum amount of sound absorption. Open cell foams, with interconnecting air passages, are much better sound absorbers than the closed cell type.

The amount of sound absorption is measured in terms of the equivalent area of a perfect sound absorbing surface. The American physicist W Sabine, who pioneered much of the work in this area earlier this century, coined the term 'open window units', an open window being taken as a perfect absorber. In his honour the sabine is used as a unit of absorption.

The amount of sound absorption produced by a surface will depend upon both the area of the surface, and its absorption coefficient:

$$A = \alpha . S$$

where A is the absorption in square metres absorption units (or sabines), S is the surface area in square metres, and α is the absorption coefficient.

A simple example illustrates this formula. A carpet of area $10 m^2$ is introduced into a room. The absorption coefficient of the carpet is 0.6. This means that the absorption of the carpet is $6 m^2$, i.e. the carpet is equivalent to $6 m^2$ of perfect absorber.

Tables of values of absorption coefficients are available for a wide variety of surfaces for a range of frequencies. A few typical values are given in Table 3.2. In some cases, for people and for items of furniture, equipment or machinery for example, it is more useful to specify the total absorption of the whole object.

Tuned or resonant absorbers

In contrast to porous absorbers, a tuned or resonant absorber is effective only over a narrow range of frequencies. It consists of a vibrating mechanical system with its own natural frequency of vibration, very much like a mass oscillating to and fro on the end

Table 3.2 Typical values of sound absorption coefficient for some common materials

	Octave band					
	125 Hz	250 Hz	500 Hz	1 kHz	2 kHz	4 kHz
Brick	0.05	0.04	0.02	0.04	0.05	0.05
Concrete	0.01	0.01	0.02	0.02	0.02	0.02
Plaster (on brick or block)	0.04	0.05	0.06	0.08	0.04	0.06
Plasterboard	0.30	0.20	0.15	0.05	0.05	0.05
Steel	0.05	0.05	0.05	0.05	0.05	0.05
Glass	0.25	0.25	0.18	0.12	0.07	0.05
Timber	0.15	0.11	0.10	0.07	0.09	0.03
Carpet (thick pile)	0.15	0.25	0.50	0.60	0.70	0.70
Carpet (standard)	0.02	0.06	0.154	0.40	0.60	0.70
Curtains (heavy)	0.07	0.30	0.50	0.75	0.70	0.60
Mineral fibre (25 mm)	0.07	0.25	0.50	0.80	0.90	0.80
Mineral fibre (50 mm)	0.39	0.91	0.99	0.97	0.94	0.89
Unoccupied seat (wood or padded)	0.03	0.05	0.05	0.10	0.15	0.10
Occupied seat (wood or padded)	0.15	0.25	0.40	0.40	0.45	0.40

of a spring. The energy in the sound waves striking the surface of the absorber is converted first of all into vibrational energy and ultimately, because of frictional processes taking place with the vibrator, into heat.

Cavity resonators (also called Helmholtz resonators) consist of a volume of enclosed air (the cavity) which communicates with the outside air via a narrow neck. This arrangement acts as a mass–spring system, with the plug of air in the neck vibrating to and fro and in so doing alternately increasing and decreasing the pressure of the air in the cavity, which acts as the spring. The natural frequency of this mass–spring system is determined by the volume of the cavity and the length and cross-sectional area of the neck. The note produced by blowing across the mouth of a milk bottle is an example of cavity resonance.

Panel resonators consist of a panel of flexible but massive material mounted away from a wall to leave a cavity of trapped air. As with the cavity resonators the trapped air acts as the spring, but this time it is the panel which acts as the mass.

Graphs of typical absorption against frequency curves for panel and cavity resonators are shown in Figure 3.10. In both cases the introduction of sound-absorbing material into the cavity will lead to a reduction of the maximum absorption but an improved absorption over a wider range of frequencies.

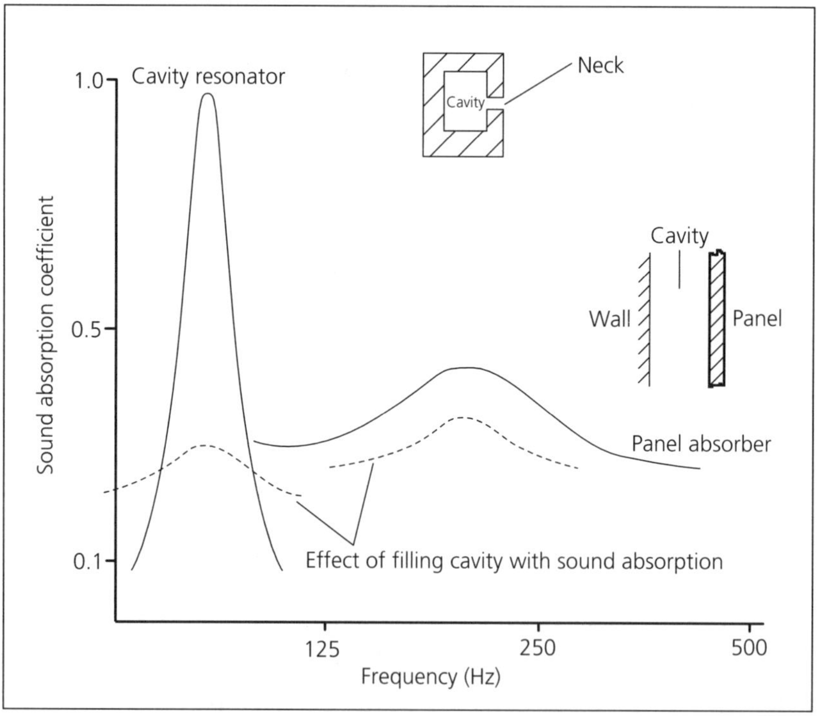

Figure 3.10 Typical variation of sound absorption coefficient with frequency for a cavity and panel resonators

Panel and cavity resonators are most often used in specialist rooms such as theatres and concert halls to provide absorption at low frequencies, where porous absorbers are ineffective, but they can also be used in industrial noise control. Sometimes natural room fittings such as cupboards and cabinets, trunking and false ceilings can act as panel absorbers.

Reverberation time

The reverberation time of a room is the time taken for the sound level in the room to reduce by 60 dB, measured from the time that the sound source in the room is switched off. It depends on the volume of the room, V (in m^3), and the amount of absorption, A (in m^2) in the room. The reverberation time, T, in seconds, is related to V and A by Sabine's formula:

$$T = 0.16 \times \frac{V}{A}$$

The reverberation time is one of the parameters determining the acoustic quality of theatres, concert halls and lecture rooms, and this formula is used in the design of the room to ensure that the surface finishes have the correct amount of sound absorption required to achieve the optimum reverberation time for the particular space. Its relevance to noise control is that since the reverberation time can be measured it gives a method for determining the amount of sound absorption, A, in a room, factory or workshop. This information can then be used to decide whether it is worth introducing additional sound-absorbing material into the room in order to reduce the level of reverberant sound.

Sound distribution in rooms—direct and reverberant sound

Consider a receiver in a room containing a noise source that is emitting sound continously. Sound reaches the receiver in two ways. First, there is the direct sound, i.e. that which arrives at the receiver having travelled directly from the source without being reflected from any of the room surfaces. This is followed by the first few reflections from the walls, floor and ceiling, and from other surfaces in the room, and then by myriad further reflections. The sum total of all these reflections is called the reverberant sound.

The direct sound pressure level (SPL) depends on the distance from the source and on the sound power level and directivity of the noise source. It is the free-field SPL considered earlier in the chapter, and it does not depend in any way upon the room, i.e.:

$$\text{direct SPL } L_p = L_W - 20\log r - 11 + D$$

The reverberant sound builds up to a level where the rate at which sound is being supplied to the room by the source is equal to the rate at which it is being absorbed by the room surfaces during the multiple reflections. A simple theory of reverberant sound assumes that the reverberant SPL is constant throughout the room, and that there is no net flow of sound energy in any direction, i.e. that the sound is diffuse. The reverberant SPL depends on the sound power level of the source and on the amount of acoustic absorption in the room, expressed as a room constant *Rc*. It does not depend on the distance from the source.

$$\text{reverberant SPL } L_p = L_W + 10\log\left(\frac{4}{Rc}\right)$$

where

$$Rc = S\frac{\alpha}{(1-\alpha)}$$

where S is the total surface area of the room and α is the average value of the absorption coefficients of these surfaces. For values α of which are small, $Rc \cong$ A, the total amount of absorption in the room. If $\alpha = 0.2$ then the approximation $Rc = A$ makes an error of about 1 dB in the calculation of the reverberant SPL.

The total SPL at any point in a room is the combination of the direct and reverberant SPLs, i.e. it is obtained by combining the two levels using the usual rules of decibel addition. Alternatively the following equation may be used. It is a combination of the two previous equations:

$$\text{Total SPL } L_p = L_W + 10\log\left[\frac{Q}{4\pi r^2} + \frac{4}{Rc}\right]$$

where Q is the directivity factor of the noise source in the direction of the receiver. The first term in the brackets relates to the direct sound and the second term to the reverberant sound.

Example

A fan is located in one of the top corners of an office of dimensions 6×4×3m (w×d×h). The average absorption coefficient of the room surfaces is 0.2 in the 500Hz octave band, where the fan noise is greatest. The sound power level of the fan in this band is 50dB re.10^{-12} W. Calculate the SPL from the fan in this band at a position which is 3m from the fan.

$$\text{Surface area of room } S = 2 \times (6 \times 4 + 6 \times 3 + 4 \times 3) = 108\ \text{m}^2$$

$$\text{Room constant} \quad Rc = S\frac{\alpha}{(1-\alpha)}$$

$$= 108 \times \frac{0.2}{(1-0.2)}$$

$$= 27\,\text{m}^2$$

$$\frac{4}{Rc} = 0.148$$

For the corner position in the room $Q = 8$:

$$\frac{Q}{(4\pi r^2)} = 0.071$$

$$\text{total SPL } L_p = L_W + 10\log\left[\frac{Q}{4\pi r^2} + \frac{4}{(Rc)}\right]$$

$$= 50 + 10\log(0.071 + 0.148)$$

$$\text{Total SPL 3m from fan} = 43.4\,\text{dB}$$

By calculating the components separately it can be shown that the direct SPL is 38.5dB and that the reveberant SPL is 42dB, which when combined give 43dB.

Figure 3.11 shows how the SPL in a typical room varies with the distance from the noise source in the room. Close to the source, where the SPL falls with increasing distance, the direct sound is predominant. At greater distances the graph levels off, as the reverberant sound becomes the major component of the total SPL. In this region the SPL depends on the room constant, so that the same noise source can give rise to different SPLs, measured at the same distance but in different rooms.

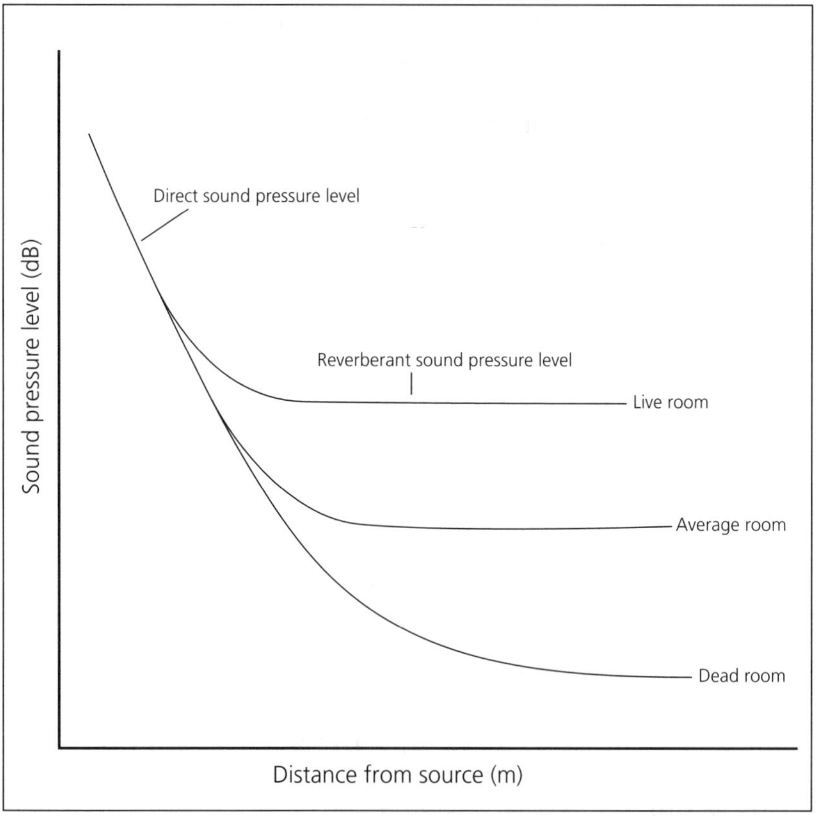

Figure 3.11 Typical variation of sound pressure level with distance from a noise source in a room

Nonstandard rooms

The simple theory of a constant reverberant level throughout the room seems to be fairly accurate for rooms in which the length, breadth and height are all of similar dimensions. In large open-plan offices, however, the length and breadth may be very large compared with the height. Under these circumstances reflections from the ceiling and floor become more important than from the walls. The simple theory then no longer holds true and the SPL continues to fall with distance from the source, and does not 'level out' as in Figure 3.11. This may also happen in factories, where there are also the added complications of unusual ceiling or roof constructions, and arrays of machines which emit, scatter and absorb sound.

Special acoustic test rooms — anechoic and reverberant rooms

An anechoic room is one in which the walls, floor and ceiling have been lined with sound-absorbing material so that there is no reflection of sound and measurements on sound sources may be carried out under free-field conditions. Anechoic rooms may be used to measure the sound power levels and directivities of machines and other sound sources. A semi-anechoic room is one with anechoic walls and ceiling but with a hard, sound-reflecting floor.

A reverberant room is one with hard, sound-reflecting surfaces, designed to produce as diffuse a distribution of sound as possible within the room. Reverberant rooms are used to measure the absorption coefficients of materials and the sound power levels of sound sources, but not their directivity.

A suite of two adjacent reverberant rooms is used for laboratory testing of the sound insulation of panels and partitions which are built into an aperture in the common wall between the two rooms.

All of these test rooms are designed to have a high degree of sound insulation to eliminate interference from noise from external sources, such as traffic. Their performance is governed by British and international standards.

The specification of machinery noise — sound power and sound pressure levels

An important part of any company noise control policy is a requirement to take the noise output into consideration when selecting and purchasing new and replacement equipment. European Commission regulations require manufacturers and suppliers to provide information about noise output of certain items of plant and equipment. The UK Noise at Work Regulations have a similar requirement. The philosophy behind the EC regulations is that the availability of information will help users to make an informed choice about noise output when selecting equipment, and that this will encourage manufacturers to develop quieter products in future.

It is therefore important to have clear, unambiguous and standard methods for specifying the noise output from equipment. One method is to specify the sound power level. An alternative is to quote a sound pressure level measured at a certain distance from the device. There are advantages and drawbacks to each approach.

The main advantage to using sound power level is simplicity of approach. The noise output is specified by a single figure (either in dB(A) or in octave bands) which relates only to the item of equipment and does not require any other information about the test environment. In principle the sound pressure level at any distance from the equipment may be predicted, using the methods described above. One of the disadvantages of sound power level is that it is difficult to measure, by comparison with sound pressure level, and specialist test rooms, either anechoic or reverberant, and measurement equipment are needed. Another disadvantage is that a sound power level figure does not have any meaning to most individuals: it does not immediately and obviously relate to any level of noise, but is just a number from which noise levels may be calculated. A third disadvantage is that, as we have seen, it is sometimes difficult to make accurate predictions of sound pressure levels — near-field situations being a good example.

The disadvantage of using sound pressure levels is that the measurement distance must also be specified. In addition, information about the test conditions must be given, for example, about the room if tested indoors, or about weather, ground conditions etc. if outdoors. However, sound pressure levels are fairly easily measured using a sound level meter, and can be easily understood and related to everyday experience.

Transmission of sound in buildings

In this section we consider how sound is transmitted from a source of noise and vibration in one room to other rooms in the building.

Let us first consider what happens to sound radiated from one source into a room (Figure 3.12). The source could be, for example, a human voice, the loudspeaker of a radio or hi-fi system or some item of machinery. Reverberant sound is set up in room A and the sound pressure on the room surfaces (walls, floor and ceiling) causes these surfaces to vibrate. The radiation of sound from these vibrating surfaces causes sound energy to be transmitted into adjacent rooms.

In the mechanism just described, airborne sound in room A enters room B by the direct transmission of airborne sound. The effectiveness of this transmission depends on the airborne sound insulation of the partition wall between A and B. There are, however, several other paths for the transmission of sound energy from room A to room B involving the transmission of vibration between the surfaces that flank the partition. A number of possible flanking paths are shown in Figure 3.12.

In many cases the flanking paths are not significant compared with the direct transmission path, but this is not always the case, and particularly when the partition wall is designed to give a high degree of sound insulation flanking paths can be important. Flanking paths become relatively more important in the transmission of sound between nonadjacent rooms.

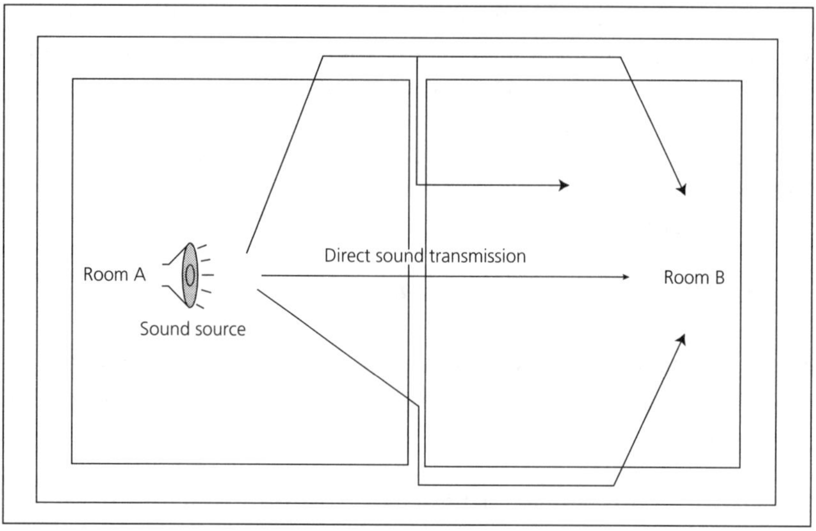

Figure 3.12 Sound transmission between rooms

In standard tests for airborne sound insulation a loudspeaker generates sound in a source room (say in room A) and sound pressure levels are measured in this room and in an adjacent room (say B), and the level difference is found.

In addition to radiating airborne sound into room A the source may also transmit vibrational energy directly into the building structure. This often happens when heavy vibrating machinery such as fans and motors are mounted on the floor of the room without effective isolation between machine and floor. Another important source arises from impacts from footsteps and furniture movement. This vibration is then transmitted through the building structure and results in radiation of structure-borne sound into adjacent rooms, and even into rooms remote from the source, since vibrational energy often travels efficiently through building structures with very little loss of energy.

The important case of the transmission of impact-generated vibration, for example, from footsteps, from a floor to the room below may be measured and assessed using the standard impact sound insulation test of BS2750/ISO2740. A standard impact source is set into operation on the floor and average one-third octave band sound pressure levels are measured in the room below.

Calculation of airborne sound transmission between rooms
The direct transmission of sound between two rooms is determined by the sound reduction index, R, of the partition (also called the transmission loss), measured in decibels. This is closely related to the transmission coefficient, t, of the partition that gives the fraction of incident sound energy transmitted by the partition.

$$\text{Sound reduction index } R = 10\log(1/t) \text{ dB}$$

As examples: if $t = 0.001$ then $R = 30$ dB, and if $R = 0.00001$ $= 10^{-5}$ then $R = 50$ dB.

The level difference between two adjacent rooms depends not only on R, but also on the surface area of the partition, S, and on the amount of absorption, A, in the receiving room. It can be shown that:

$$L_s - L_r = R - 10\log S + 10\log A$$

where L_s is the level of reverberant sound in the source room, and L_r is that in the receiving room. This formula applies only to direct sound transmission and does not take into account transmission via flanking paths.

Example
A foreman's office of dimensions $4 \times 3 \times 2.5$ m high is to be built as an acoustic refuge in a paper mill, where the reverberant sound level is 85 dB in the 1000 Hz octave band. The office is to be situated in the corner of the workshop so that only two sides and the flat roof have to be built on to the existing walls. The office is to be made of chipboard with an area of glazing and a door. The average sound reduction index of the construction is estimated as 27 dB and the amount of sound absorption in the office as 6.3 m^2 in the 1000 Hz band. Calculate the sound

pressure level inside the office in this octave band resulting from the workshop noise outside.

The area of the partition in this case is the area of two walls and of the ceiling of the office:

$$
\begin{aligned}
S &= 4\times2.5 + 3\times2.5 + 4\times3 \\
&= 29.5\,\text{m}^2 \\
L_s - L_r &= R - 10\log S + 10\log A \\
&= 27 - 10\log 29.5 + 10\log 6.3 \\
&= 27 - 14.7 + 8 \\
&= 20.3\,\text{dB} \\
L_r &= 85 - 20.3 \\
&= 65\,\text{dB (to the nearest dB)}
\end{aligned}
$$

The predicted noise level in the office is 65 dB.

Similar calculations for the other octave bands will allow the A-weighted sound pressure level, or the NR (noise rating) or NC (noise criteria) value to be estimated. It should be noted that an average sound reduction index must be used in this prediction that takes into account the differing individual values for the materials of the wall, window and door, and also their relative areas. The method of calculating this average may be found in standard textbooks on the subject.

Unfortunately it is not easy to predict the level of sound transmitted by flanking paths or by structure-borne sound, although the rapidly developing technique of statistical energy analysis may make these predictions more feasible in the future.

The prediction of noise levels — conclusion

The purpose of this chapter has been to explain how sound travels from source to receiver, both indoors and outdoors. The explanations have deliberately been explanatory and qualitative as far as possible, rather than theoretical and mathematical, and where equations and formulae have been introduced they have not been derived or proved, and the number of worked examples and calculations has been kept to a mimimum. There are many textbooks that can provide further detailed information if required. A list is given at the end of this book.

An understanding of sound generation and propagation is essential for formulating principles for reducing noise, and so the material of this chapter forms the basis for the noise control methods described in the next two chapters.

However, the best method of noise control is always to plan in advance to eliminate or minimize noise problems before they happen. In this way potential noise problems can be dealt with far more effectively and economically than by hastily adopted 'retrofit' noise control measures implemented when the problem has become urgent. This advance planning can only be done if it is possible to predict noise levels in advance of the source being installed and coming into operation. Therefore a second important objective of this chapter has been to show how, in principle, noise levels may be predicted, both inside and outside of buildings.

Fairly simple calculations may be performed by hand using an electronic calculator. An example would be the prediction of sound pressure levels to be expected at a works' boundary or at nearby residences from the proposed installation of a new compressor or extractor fan to be located externally.

Most noise level predictions are based on simple models of real situations — idealized 'point source' radiation patterns or reverberant sound fields, for example — and it is always important to understand the assumptions on which a prediction is based and to be aware that its accuracy will be limited by the extent to which the model represents the real situation. Nevertheless, it is always better to attempt a prediction, albeit of limited accuracy, than to operate in complete ignorance.

The uncertainties of prediction are particularly acute for outdoor sound propagation over considerable distances (of greater than a few hundred metres). There are many methods, of differing accuracy and complexity, for predicting the effects of ground attenuation and atmospheric effects. An international standard (ISO 90631) has been published on the prediction of sound outdoors. The advantage of using such a standard is that predicted noise levels used in decision making, for example, about planning developments at public inquiries, are at least based on standardized prediction procedures, even though these will contain a considerable degree of uncertainty.

Although there are in the UK standard procedures, with legal significance, for predicting noise from road traffic and trains, there are no such standard methods, apart from the above ISO standard, for predicting industrial noise. However, methods described in BS 5228 for noise from construction and demolition sites are useful and generally applicable to many other industries.

Even though predictions may be based on simple models the calculations soon become complicated, and tedious if not impossible to do by hand if there are many noise sources or many different reception points. Many of the calculations may be adapted to computer spreadsheets, and there are many commercially available software packages for noise prediction. In addition to removing the drudgery from repetitive calculation these usually have impressive graphics which allow noise maps and contours to be produced, and enable the effects of different layouts and arrangements, including noise control (for example, the use of a barrier) to be investigated. However, it must be remembered that the accuracy of predictions produced by such packages can only be as good as the acoustic principles and models on which they are based. It is always necessary to enquire about these when considering using or purchasing a noise prediction software package, and to require a demonstration of the prediction capability for a situation of reasonable complexity for which the noise levels to be predicted are already known.

One major limitation of any prediction method is the quality of the input data, and in particular of data relating to sound output of noise sources. Ideally the sound power levels of all plant and equipment, or alternatively, sound pressure levels at specified distances, should be available from manufacturers or suppliers, in octave bands, as a result of measurements carried out under specified standard test conditions. Unfortunately this may not always be so, in which case a 'second best' alternative is to use empirically based formulae for sound power levels, and 'typical' figures from data books. Other data that will affect the accuracy of predictions include the performance of building materials such as absorption coefficient and sound reduction index values.

Summary

1 In order to fully understand how sound propagates, both in and out of doors, it is necessary to understand the wave properties of reflection, diffraction, interference, refraction and absorption.

2 The sound intensity produced by a point source under free-field conditions varies inversely as the square of the distance from the source. Under these conditions relationships may be developed between either the acoustic intensity or the acoustic pressure and the sound power of the source, and the distance from the source.

3 These relationships may also be simply expressed in decibel form, allowing sound pressure levels to be predicted at any distance from a point source (under free-field conditions), given either the level at some other distance or the sound power level of the source.

4 A simple correction may be used to take into account the effect of sound-reflecting ground.

5 Similar relationships for predicting the change of sound level with distance from the source may be developed for line and plane sources.

6 These relationships for a point source may be extended to real sources for distances that are in the far field of the source. The sound pressure level in the near field of a noise source varies with position in a complex way. The directionality of a real noise source may be described either in terms of a directivity index or a directivity factor. The two terms are simply related.

7 For sound propagation outdoors extra attenuation in addition to that caused by distance may arise from: air absorption, ground attenuation, sound velocity gradients and from barriers.

8 Sound energy striking partitions may be absorbed, reflected or transmitted, and reflection, transmission and absorption coefficients may be defined. These will depend upon the frequency of the sound and its angle of incidence, and upon the nature of the partition.

9 The reverberation time of a room may be calculated using Sabine's formula. The formula may be used to design rooms for optimum reverberation time. It also allows room absorption to be calculated from the measured reverberation times.

10 The sound pressure level at any point in a room may be obtained by combining the direct sound pressure level, which depends on the distance from the noise source in the room, with the reverberant sound pressure level, which depends on the room constant. Anechoic and reverberant rooms are extreme cases of rooms where only direct or only reverberant sound is present. These special rooms are used for the measurement of sound power level of sound sources.

11 Noise may travel from source to receiver in a building as a result of both airborne and structure-borne sound transmission. Sound pressure levels arising from the direct transmission of airborne sound through partitions may be calculated. In addition, transmission also occurs by a number of flanking paths.

4
Principles of noise generation and control

Introduction

The aim of this chapter is to review and explain the range of methods which are available for reducing noise, starting with commonsense 'good housekeeping' methods. The use of engineering methods to reduce noise involves understanding how noise is produced, and so the noise-generating mechanisms involved in some common sources of noise in industry are explained, and the principles of noise reduction described. The reduction of noise during its transmission path between source and receiver, using the techniques of sound insulation, sound absorption and vibration isolation, are discussed, as well as methods for the control of machinery noise at source. Methods for diagnosing which are the most important noise sources and paths, and for the specification of noise from machinery, are described. The chapter concludes with a discussion of hearing protection policies and the use of personal ear protectors.

Good planning, management and housekeeping

Although there are many technical solutions to noise problems the best approach is to avoid or minimize problems wherever possible so that such solutions are not necessary.

- Avoid using noisy machines and processes where quieter alternatives are available.

- Avoid making unnecessary noise, for example leaving machines running when not necessary.

- Locate noisy machines and processes away from noise-sensitive areas.

- Avoid making excessive noise at sensitive times, for example late at night or at weekends.

- Consider noise issues when planning changes to operations in the future so that steps can be taken well in advance to minimize disturbance.

- Maintain machinery and equipment in good repair so that unnecessary increases in noise levels are avoided. This also applies to the fabric of buildings so that doors and windows, for example, are always a good fit and do not transmit noise through holes and gaps.

The mechanisms of noise generation

It is useful to identify three main mechanisms: the radiation of sound from a vibrating solid surface to the adjacent fluid, the direct disturbance of the fluid flow, and noise generated by impacts. The first category includes noise from machine panels and the external casings of motors, gearboxes and fans. Many machines have a stiff inner framework designed to withstand the working forces generated by the machine, such as cutting, drilling, pressing, but the outer covers are often of thin sheet steel panels which vibrate and radiate noise. The second category includes all so-called aerodynamic and hydrodynamic noise, in which sound is generated by a disturbance to the fluid that causes turbulence. This includes noise from fans, pumps, whistles and jets. The third category includes not only machinery based on impacting processes such as riveting, punching and pressing but also mechanical handling processes where items fall into trays, hoppers and bins.

In each case it is possible to identify the main factors which affect noise radiation, and which therefore provide some basic principles for noise control. The sound power radiated from a vibrating panel will depend on the vibration amplitude of the panel, its area and on a factor called its radiation efficiency. A reduction in any of these will reduce the sound energy radiated. The possibilities for reducing the vibration amplitude are to reduce the vibratory forces reaching the panel from the machine frame, and then to design the panel so that these forces produce the minimum vibration amplitude. The first aim may be achieved either by reducing the forces themselves, at source, or by preventing their transmission to the panel. The mass, stiffness or amount of damping in the panel will affect its vibration response. If the noise-radiating panel is a machinery guard, it may be possible to use a cover in the form of a grille rather than a solid sheet, in order to reduce the noise-radiating area. The radiation efficiency of a panel depends upon its size compared with the wavelength of the sound, and upon the panel stiffness.

Noise generated by fluid flow increases rapidly with flow velocity and so an important principle is to keep the flow speed *as low as possible*. Turbulent flow conditions produce much more noise than streamlined, or laminar, flow, and so any factor which causes turbulence, such as sudden changes in flow conditions, changes in flow speed or direction or obstacles in the fluid which spoil the smooth flow, will cause extra noise. Therefore another important principle is to ensure that flow conditions are always *as smooth as possible*.

When a hard metal object falls onto a sheet of mild steel there are two components to the noise which is generated: the impact itself, and the ringing of the impacting components which continues after the impact has ceased. The amount of sound energy generated by the impact depends on the momentum of the impacting parts, i.e. upon their mass and their relative velocity at impact. Thus the possibilities for noise reduction are to reduce the mass of the colliding components or to slow down the collision speed by cushioning the impact with a resilient layer, or to reduce the drop height. In addition, the impact causes the sheet to ring 'like a bell'. The ringing noise may be reduced by increasing the damping of the panel.

Noise control during sound transmission

The simplest model of sound transmission shows the noise travelling from the source via a transmission path to a receiver (Figure 4.1a). Even with this simple model we can see that there are three ways to reduce the noise level: by reducing the noise (1) at source, (2) by the transmission path, or (3) at the receiver. An example would be a situation where an individual sitting in his garden is affected by sound from a radio in a neighbour's garden, where the path is direct transmission through the air. Control at source would involve the neighbour reducing the volume. Control via transmission might be achieved either by moving away, i.e. increasing the distance between source and receiver, or by erecting some sort of barrier. Control at the receiver might involve the receiver wearing ear plugs or moving indoors.

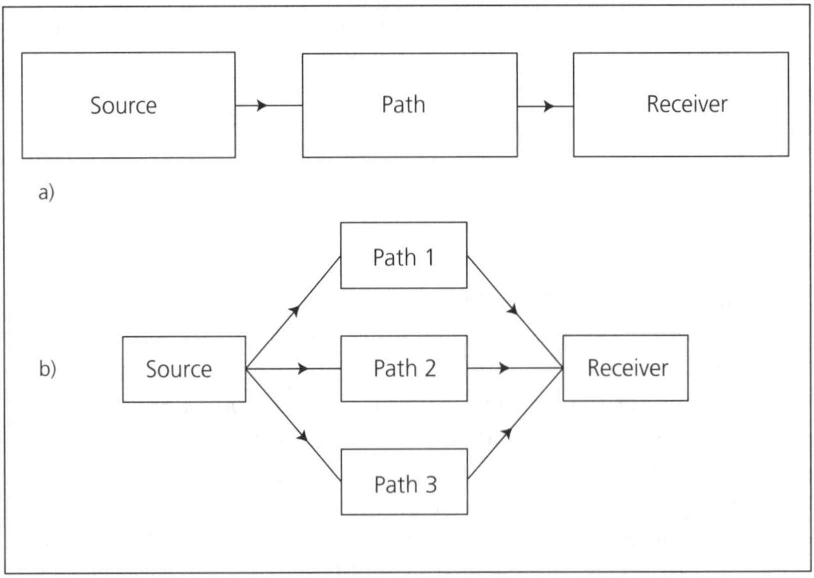

Figure 4.1 Simple source-path-receiver models of sound transmission

It is often stated that noise control at source is the preferred option, and the reason for this is best understood by considering an extension to the simple model, in which sound is transmitted to a single receiver by a number of different paths (Figure 4.1b). Control during the transmission stage would now require three different control remedies, one for each path, whereas a single noise control at source measure would reduce the transmission via each of the paths.

A very simple example is illustrated in Figure 4.2 in which the noise source is a machine in a room. Sound from the source reaches the receiver, in the same room, by three different paths. The first of these is direct airborne sound. The second is also airborne sound but reaches the receiver after multiple reflections by surfaces in the room. This is often called the reverberant component of the airborne sound. The third transmission path, called structure-borne sound, arises from transmission of vibration energy from the source into the building structure (via the floor in this case) and subsequent radiation from the structure as airborne sound.

The methods for controlling the sound transmission via the three different paths use the standard techniques of sound insulation, sound absorption and vibration isolation (Figure 4.2). Transmission via the first path may be reduced by interposing a sound-insulating screen between source and receiver. Although this would reduce the transmission of the direct airborne sound it would not be completely effective on its own because sound would be able to 'bypass' the screen and reach the receiver via reflections at room surfaces. This path may be reduced by lining the room surfaces with sound-absorbing materials, which would reduce the amount of reverberant sound in the room. However, structure-borne sound may still reach the receiver, unless this third path is controlled by the use of vibration-isolating material placed between the source and the structure.

The source-path-receiver model will obviously become more complicated still if there are multiple sources as well as different paths, and the complexity will be increased further if different

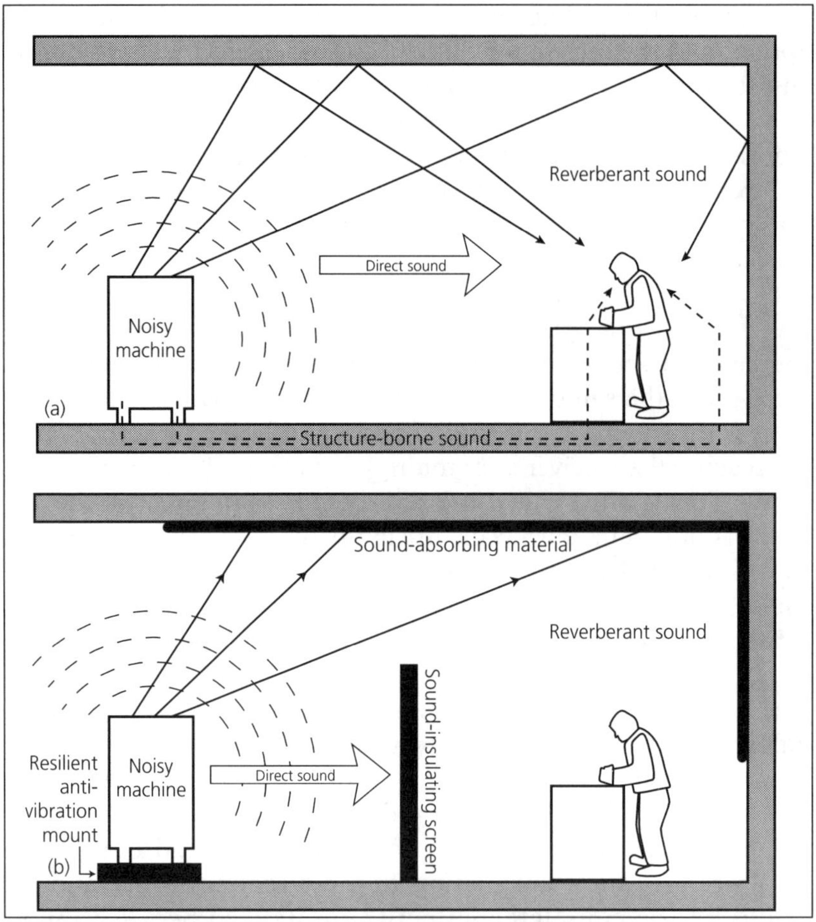

Figure 4.2 (a) Transmission of noise by different paths
(b) Methods of noise control

receivers are also considered. Therefore correct diagnosis of sources and paths becomes an important aspect of noise control.

Sound insulation

Sound-insulating materials are used as barriers, partitions and as complete enclosures around machines. In each case a requirement is that the sound-insulating material shall have a sufficiently large sound reduction index in each frequency band. It is also important that the insulation is complete with the minimum amount of holes and gaps around the edges. Good seals are important if high sound insulation is to be achieved. The sound reduction index of a single-leaf partition will depend upon the mass, stiffness and damping of the material, but in many cases the mass is the most important factor. The mass law of sound insulation is an approximate law that assumes that the sound reduction index of a partition may be predicted entirely from a knowledge of the surface density of a partition expressed in kilograms per square metre. This is illustrated in Figure 4.3. According to the mass law, the sound reduction index will increase with frequency by 6 dB for every octave and also will increase by 6 dB for every doubling of mass. Although the mass law may be approximately obeyed by many materials the neglect of the influence of damping and stiffness leads to discrepancies at high and low frequencies, as shown in Figure 4.4. At low frequencies there are panel resonances and at high frequencies above the mass law region, flexural waves in the panel also cause resonances, a phenomenon called the coincidence effect which occurs above a critical frequency. Typical values of sound reduction index for some single-leaf partitions are shown in Table 4.1.

Although the sound reduction index of a partition may be increased by increasing its thickness and thereby its mass, only 5 dB increase is achieved even for a doubling of mass and thickness, and so trying to increase insulation by this means rapidly leads to a law of diminishing returns. One way of getting around this difficulty is to use double-leaf constructions in which two-sound insulating leaves are separated by a cavity. There are, however, some important design principles if double-leaf constructions are to be effective.

- The cavity should be filled as far as possible with a sound-absorbing material in order to reduce the build-up of reverberant sound within the cavity.

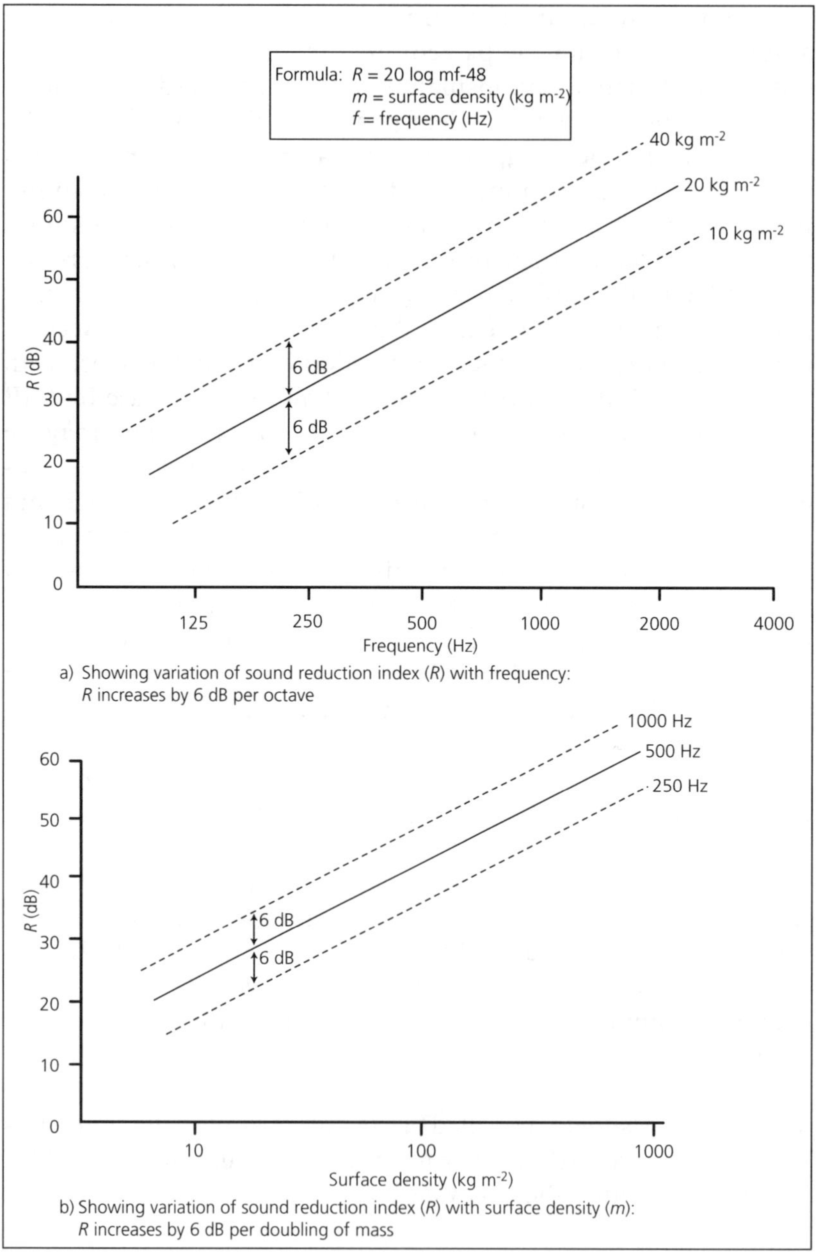

a) Showing variation of sound reduction index (R) with frequency: R increases by 6 dB per octave

b) Showing variation of sound reduction index (R) with surface density (m): R increases by 6 dB per doubling of mass

Figure 4.3 The mass law for predicting the sound reduction (R) of a single-leaf partition

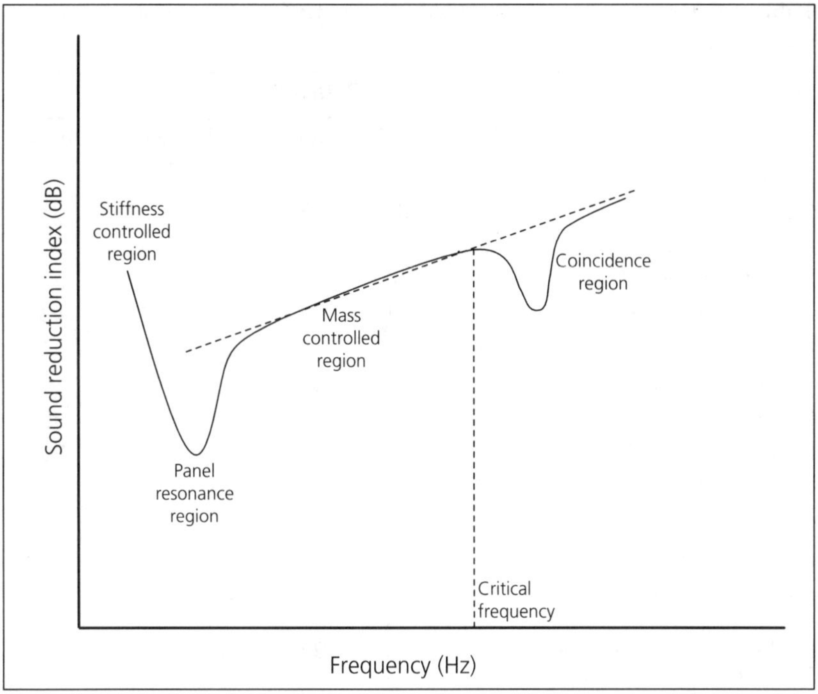

Figure 4.4 Typical variation of sound reduction index with frequency for a single-leaf panel

- It is also important to prevent flanking of the double-leaf structure as a result of structure-borne transmission via the framework between the two leaves. This can be achieved by isolating each leaf from the framework and from the other leaf.

These principles are illustrated in Figure 4.5.

Sound absorption

The principles of sound absorption were described in Chapter 3. Sound-absorbing materials reduce noise by reducing the reflection of sound at surfaces and turning sound energy into heat via frictional processes within the material. Sound-absorbing materials may be used in rooms and other spaces to reduce reverberant sound, to line ducts and, as indicated above, to absorb sound between the leaves of double-skinned structures.

Table 4.1 Typical values of sound reduction index in dB for some common building elements

	Octave band (Hz)					
	125	**250**	**500**	**1kHz**	**2kHz**	**4kHz**
Single-leaf panels:						
1.5mm lead sheet	28	32	33	32	32	33
3.0mm lead sheet	30	31	27	38	44	33
1mm sheet steel	8	14	20	26	32	38
1.6mm sheet steel	14	21	27	32	37	43
Plastered brick	36	36	40	46	54	57
Thermalite blocks	27	31	39	45	53	38
Plasterboard	15	20	24	29	32	35
Plywood	9	13	16	21	27	29
Chipboard	17	18	25	30	26	32
6mm glass	24	26	31	34	30	37
Double-leaf partitions:						
Cavity brick wall (50mm cavity)	37	41	48	60	61	61
Double glazing (6mm glass, 12mm cavity, 6mm glass)	26	23	32	38	37	52
Plasterboard stud partition (two 12.5mm plasterboard sheets with 50mm cavity filled with glass fibre quilt)	21	35	45	47	47	43
Machine enclosure panels (16 gauge steel, 100mm mineral fibre, 22 gauge perforated steel sheet)	21	27	38	48	58	67

Additional sound absorption introduced into a room or space will reduce the level of reverberant noise. The additional sound-absorbing materials may be used to line walls, floor and ceiling of the space or, if this is not possible, may be hung as space absorbers from the ceiling. The amount of sound reduction will depend on the degree to which the amount of sound absorption in the room is increased so that this treatment will be most effective for rooms and spaces that have initially very little absorption in them, i.e. rooms with hard surfaces, such as plaster or concrete. This is the case with many factory spaces. The level of reverberant sound reduces by 3dB each time the amount of absorption is doubled,

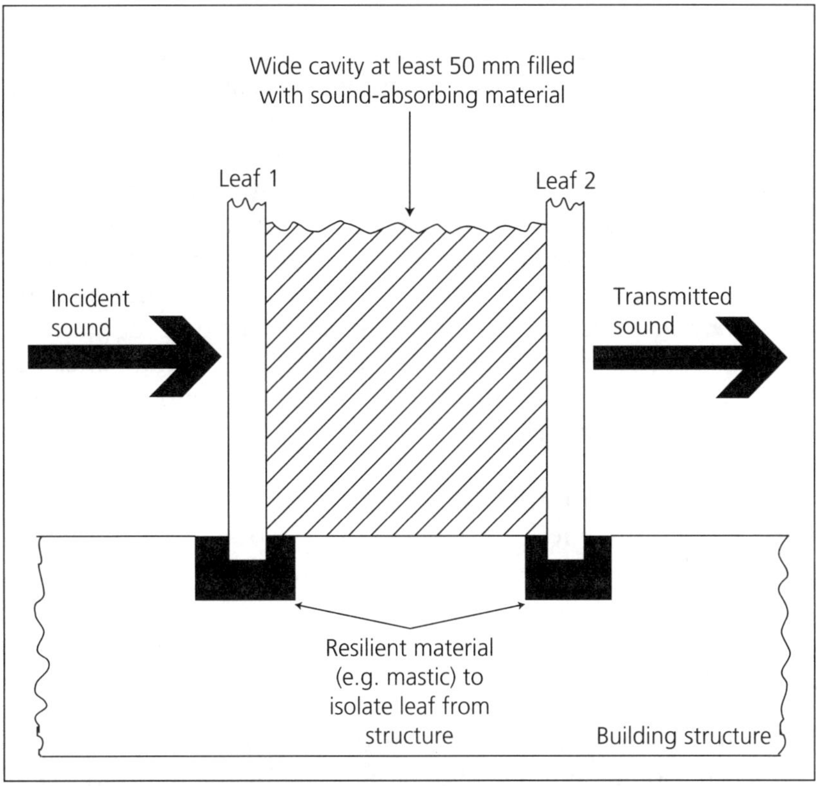

Figure 4.5 Design features of a double-leaf construction necessary to achieve good sound insulation

or it will reduce by 10 dB if the amount of absorption is increased tenfold. The following equation allows the amount of sound reduction to be calculated:

$$L_1 - L_2 = 10\log\left(\frac{A_2}{A_1}\right)$$

where L_1 and L_2 are the levels of sound with the old and new levels of absorption, A_1 and A_2 respectively. Since even hard surfaces such as brickwork, plaster and concrete do provide some absorption, the amount by which reverberant sound may be reduced by introducing extra absorption is limited. For example, a typical absorption coefficient value for these materials would be 0.01 at low and medium frequencies, so a tenfold increase would increase the average absorption coefficient from 0.01 to 0.1 and this would produce a 10 dB reduction. Even theoretically there is only the possibility of another tenfold increase to increase the average absorption coefficient from 0.1 to 1. Therefore it can be seen that this method of reducing noise can never produce more than 20 dB reduction and in practice the limit is usually no more than 10 dB and often only around 5 dB at most. Nevertheless, the subjective response to such a reduction is often favourable because the reduction is entirely of reverberant sound and the effect may be to produce a less diffuse sound field in the space so that the direction from which the sound is coming and hence the source of the noise is more apparent. The noise control treatment is also very apparent, visually.

This type of sound-absorbing treatment will not provide any noise reduction benefit for a person who works close to a noisy machine and receives the major part of his/her noise dose directly from that source.

Vibration isolation

Isolation is the reduction of the transmission of vibration or structure-borne sound in a machine or building by the use of resilient material placed between the source and the structure of the machine or building. The simplest example to consider is a machine such as a pump or motor which is placed on springs or antivibration mounts in order to reduce the vibration from the machine to the floor beneath, as shown in Figure 4.6.

The important property of such a system is called the transmissibility and this is the ratio of the vibration amplitude at the base of the machine to that on the floor beneath, i.e. the ratio of the vibration amplitude across the isolator or spring. Figure 4.7 shows how this transmissibility varies with the forcing frequency that in the case of a rotating machine such as a pump or motor is related to the rotational speed in revolutions per minute or RPM. The machine and isolator system are modelled as a mass and spring system in which the machine acts as the mass on top of the isola-

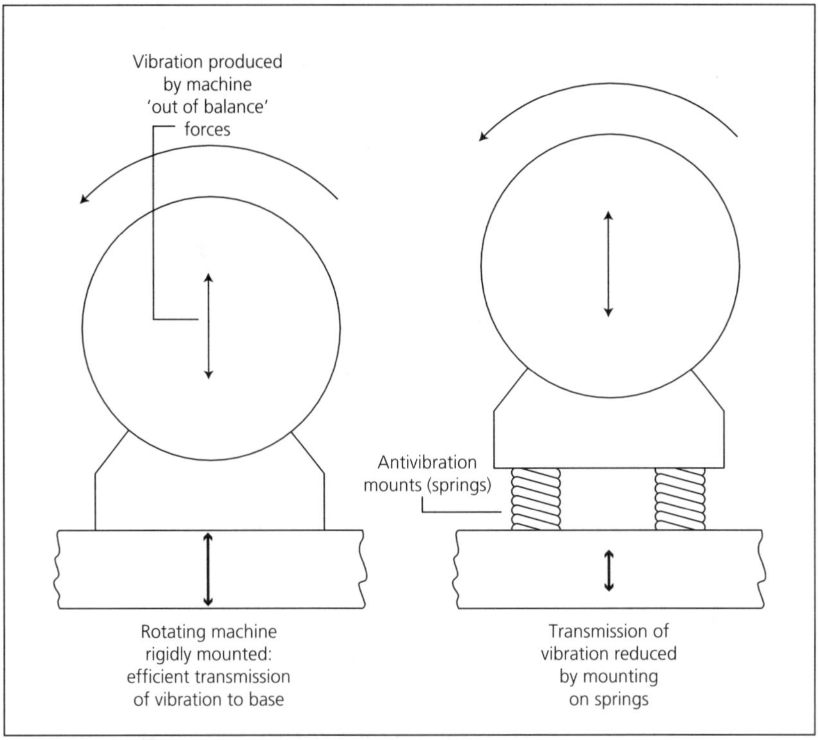

Figure 4.6 The isolation of vibration from a machine using anti-vibration mounts

tors, which is the spring. Such a mass–spring system has its own natural frequency depending upon these two parameters, mass and stiffness.

The graph of Figure 4.7 shows that at low speeds corresponding to forcing frequencies below the natural frequency of the mass–spring system the transmissibility is close to unity, in other words the springs are in effect rigid and all of the vibration from the motor is transmitted to the floor below. As the forcing frequency, i.e. the speed of the machine, is increased the transmissibility increases to a sharp peak at the speed corresponding to the natural frequency of the mass–spring system. This is the phenomenon of resonance, and in this situation the isolators are actually making matters worse and the vibration transmitted to the floor

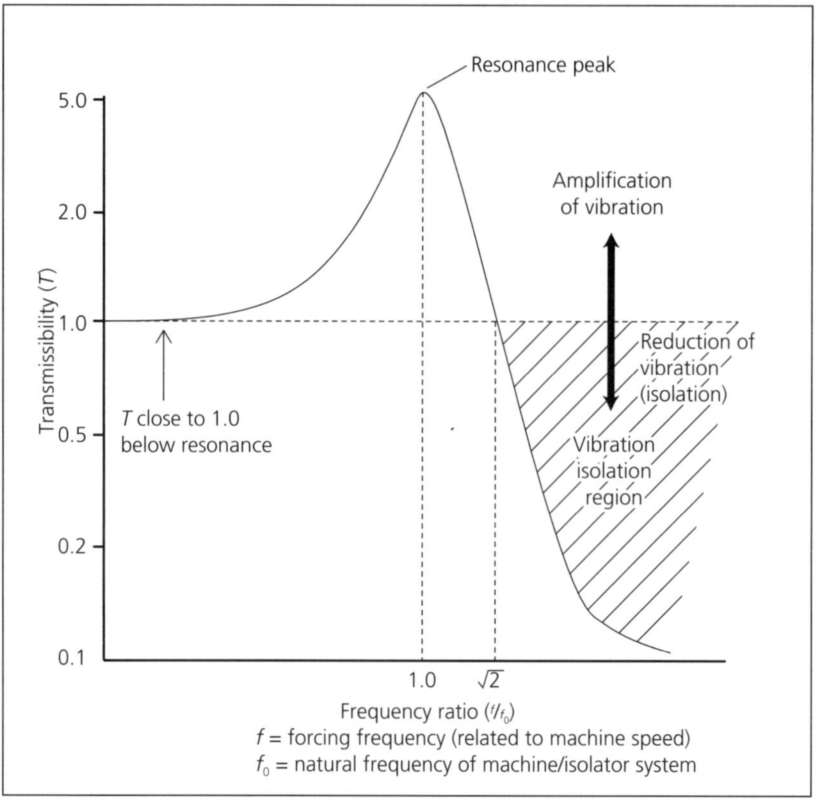

Figure 4.7 Typical variation of transmissibility with frequency for a machine mounted on vibration rollers

will be amplified rather than reduced. As the frequency increases above resonance the transmissibility decreases until at a frequency of $\sqrt{2}$ × natural frequency it falls to one, and for higher frequencies the transmissibility falls below one. In this region and for all higher frequencies where the transmissibility is less than unity, isolation is occurring and the vibration on the floor is less than on the motor, and the isolators are having the desired effect.

Antivibration mounts will normally be selected for the lowest usual operating speed of the machine. The stiffness of the spring is chosen in order to produce a natural frequency when used in conjunction with the mass of the motor which is well below the frequency corresponding to the normal running speed. This means that under normal running conditions the mass–spring system will be forced or driven at a frequency well above its natural frequency and so the transmissibility will be much less than unity and isolation will be achieved.

A variety of materials may be used for isolation depending upon the frequency range and machine speed of interest. The natural frequency of the machine/isolator system is also related to the static deflection of the isolators — the 'softer' the isolators (i.e. the lower their spring stiffness) the lower the frequency for which they will be effective, and the higher the static deflection. Above frequencies of about 25 Hz, corresponding to static deflections of less than 1 mm, sufficient resilience may be achieved using pads of cork or foam plastic or mineral fibre. At lower frequencies from about 15 Hz upwards, corresponding to static deflections of up to 10 mm, vibration isolators made of rubber are common, but for the lower frequencies below about 10 or 15 Hz, where static deflections exceed 10 mm, metal springs are usually used. Exactly the same principles that are used to isolate a complete machine from the structure of a building may be used to isolate parts of a machine, or to isolate whole floors (i.e. floating floors) or ceilings (i.e. suspended ceilings). In all cases it is important that the isolation is complete and that there is no bridging of the isolation or flanking paths. Therefore if a pump or motor has been isolated from the floor by antivibration mounts, any connection to this machine such as ducts, pipes, cables or conduits must be made flexibly, otherwise there is the possibility that vibration from the machine can travel down these alternative paths to the floor, short-circuiting or bridging the isolation provided by the antivibration mounts.

Acoustic enclosures

An acoustic enclosure is a complete box, i.e. four sides and a roof, built around a machine in order to contain or confine noise from the machine within the enclosure, and so to reduce the noise transmitted to the surrounding area. A well designed acoustic enclosure employs all three principles of insulation, absorption and isolation.

The principles of design are first of all that the walls of the enclosure should have sufficient sound reduction index to achieve the desired noise reduction. Secondly, it is advisable to line the inside of the enclosure with sound-absorbing material. This will reduce the noise level inside the enclosure and thus supplement the effect of the sound insulation by further reducing the level of sound transmitted through the enclosure walls to the outside. If the enclosure is to be large enough for people to work inside it then this sound-absorbing lining is essential, because without it the level inside the enclosure will be higher than before the enclosure was built because of a build-up of reverberant sound. The third design principle is that the machine inside the enclosure should be isolated from the floor in order to reduce structure-borne sound transmission. Any service pipes or ducts fitted to the machine must be connected flexibly at the machine and pass through the walls of the enclosure with a flexible seal so that structure-borne sound is not transmitted via the enclosure walls. In most cases it will be necessary for there to be holes and gaps in the enclosure in order to feed services and materials into and out of the machine. The effectiveness of the enclosure will depend upon the extent to which the effect of these apertures can be reduced, so that the potential noise reduction obtainable from the material of the enclosure is as nearly as possible achieved.

The use of acoustic enclosures as a noise control device has a number of possible advantages and disadvantages. The main advantage is that the concept of an acoustic enclosure is extremely simple and as a solution can be adapted to almost any machine or noise source. Provided that material of sufficient density and thickness is used, acoustic enclosures may be designed to achieve almost any reasonable amount of noise reduction, up to 30–40 dB(A). At one extreme, enclosures may be made of brick and designed to reduce high levels of low-frequency noise from large diesel generator, set close to noise-sensitive areas. At the other extreme, they may be made of thin plastic sheet and designed to reduce high-frequency noise from an office printer. Figure 4.8 illustrates the main features of a successful acoustic enclosure.

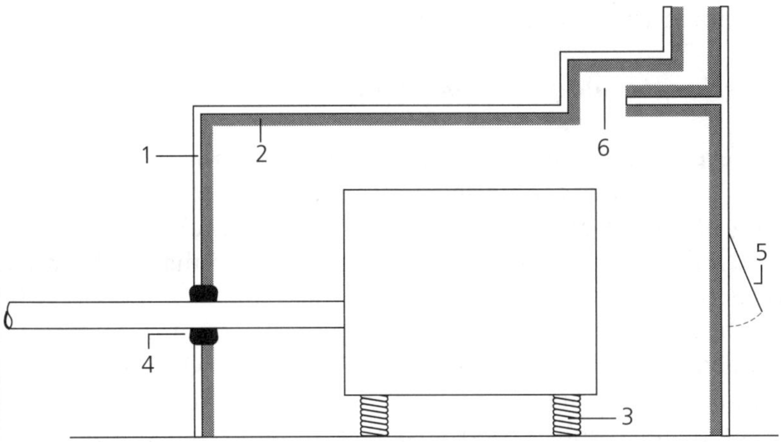

1 Sound-insulating enclosure wall (typically of 16 or 18 gauge steel).
2 Sound-absorbing lining (typically 2–4 inches of mineral fibre, faced on the inside with 22 gauge perforated sheet steel) to reduce the build-up of reflected sound inside the enclosure.
3 Antivibration mounts (springs) to isolate machine from floor.
4 Pipes and ducts carrying materials and services into the machine should be well sealed, using resilient material to prevent bridging of the isolation.
5 Inspection hatches, doors and windows must be constructed to the same standard of sound insulation as the rest of the enclosure, and must be well sealed.
6 Ventilation should be via ducts lined with sound-absorbing materials to minimize the escape of noise.

Figure 4.8 Typical features of a noise enclosure

One of the disadvantages of acoustic enclosures is that they can interfere with the normal operation of machines; for example if operators have to feed or remove material, or change settings on the machine. Another disadvantage is that many machines will become unduly heated when enclosed unless provision is made for air to circulate inside the enclosure, and if forced ventilation is necessary this will require a fan which will produce noise and will require acoustic treatment. Acoustic enclosures may be relatively expensive and will take up valuable floorspace.

Partial acoustic enclosures can give up to 10 dB(A) noise reduction if lined with sound-absorbing material.

Acoustic attenuators or silencers

Whenever sound travels with a ducted air or gas supply then it is possible to reduce the noise transmitted via the duct by using a lining of sound-absorbing material. The principle is that the sound will travel to and fro across the duct and that each time it strikes the wall of the duct some of the acoustic energy will be absorbed by the lining. The principle of a lined duct may be extended to an acoustic attenuator or silencer in which in addition to lining the sides of the duct, sections of sound-absorbing materials, often called splitters because they separate the airway in the duct into sections, are inserted into the duct in order to increase the surface area of the sound-absorbing material and thus the amount of noise reduction achieved. Figure 4.9 illustrates the structure and typical performance of an acoustic attenuator. The sound-absorbing slabs of material are usually protected against abrasion by thin perforated metal sheets, and sometimes also by thin plastic films to prevent fibre shedding or to protect against moisture or for reasons connected with hygiene.

The amount of attenuation provided by the silencer will depend upon several factors:

- the absorption coefficient of the sound-absorbing material;
- the thickness of the sound-absorbing linings;
- the number and thickness of the splitters;

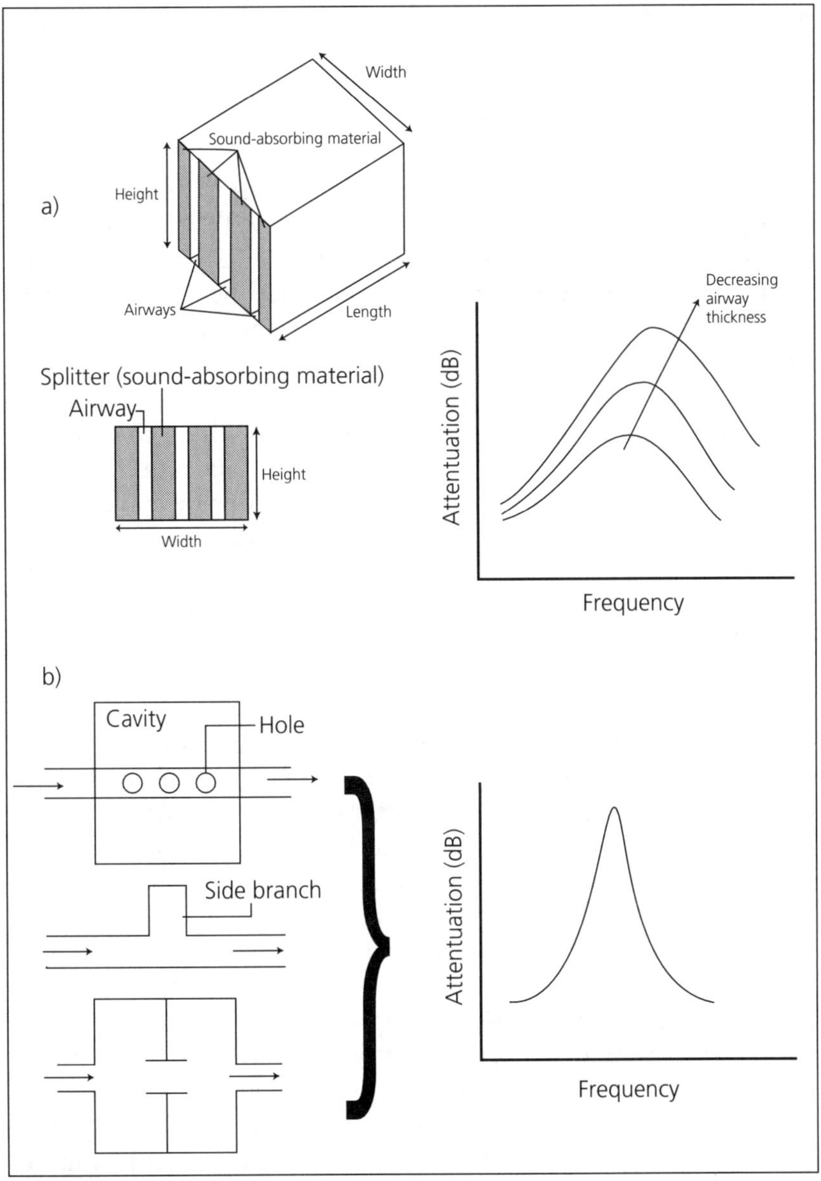

Figure 4.9 Typical construction and sound attenuation performance of
(a) absorptive or dissipative silencers
(b) reactive silencers

- the width of the airway passages between the sound-absorbing slabs (splitters);
- the length of the silencer.

The absorption coefficient of the splitters, and thus the attenuation produced by the silencer, increases with increasing frequency, and at low frequencies in particular depends upon the thickness of the splitters. At high frequencies the attenuation falls off because the sound becomes more directional and tends to travel down the airways and be less affected by the sound-absorbing material linings. The attenuation is therefore improved by reducing the width of the airways, but this will have the effect of increasing the flow resistance of the silencer, thus requiring more energy (and more noise) from the fan in order to maintain the flow. Restricted airway thickness can also lead to the creation of noise generated by airflow through the silencer. The design of the silencer is therefore a compromise between attenuation, pressure drop, flow-generated noise, size (length and cross-sectional area) and material cost.

The type of silencer described above is called an absorptive or dissipative silencer because it relies on the properties of sound-absorbing materials. It produces attenuation over a wide range of frequencies, but is least effective at low frequencies, when very large and expensive units are required to obtain significant noise reductions. Tuned, or resonant, sound absorbers, described in Chapter 3, form the basis of reactive silencers which may be used to obtain large attenuation over a narrow range of frequencies. They utilize the principles of resonance and of interference between waves reflected at different points in the system. A simple example is the expansion chamber, for which the attenuation is maximum when the length of the chamber corresponds to one-quarter of the wavelength of the sound. The useful range of frequencies can be extended by combining chambers of different length, and also by introducing pipes between the different sections so that additional resonances and anti-resonances are introduced, relating to reflections in the pipes. The Helmholtz resonator is perhaps the best known example of a reactive attenuator. It consists of a volume or cavity connected to a short open neck. The device acts as a simple mass–spring system with a sharply defined natural frequency. Blowing across the top of a partly full milk bottle illustrates the principle. The sound wave causes the air in the neck (the mass) to vibrate and cause pressure fluctuations in the cavity (the spring). At the natural frequency the cavity absorbs large amounts of energy from the sound wave. A similar effect is produced when a series of holes in a pipe allow the air or gas flowing through the pipe to communicate with a chamber surrounding the pipe, or by a closed side-branch pipe or duct, that produces a maximum attenuation when the length of the side-branch is one-quarter of a wavelength. These various devices are illustrated in Figure 4.9. In many cases they adopt a combination of absorptive and reactive principles. Reactive attenuators are used for low frequency sounds where solely absorptive types are relatively ineffective, and they are particularly useful for reducing the level of low frequency pure tones, caused by machinery operating at low and fixed speeds, because the dimensions of the device can be designed to produce maximum attenuation at the frequency of a particular tone. They are widely used for silencing vehicle exhausts, compressors, pumps, and fans that produce pure tones.

Damping

Damping is a mechanism or process whereby vibrational energy in a material is converted into heat by some form of frictional mechanism. Certain materials such a mild steel, for example, have very little inherent damping and will ring like a bell if struck. Other material such as timber and some forms of plastic have much more damping. Increasing the amount of damping in a sheet or panel of a machine will be effective in reducing noise and vibration in two circumstances. First of all, if the sheet or panel is subjected to a series of impacts and is relatively undamped, each impact will produce a ringing noise and this may be reduced by using a material with more damping, or by applying damping material to the panel. Examples where this application would be suitable would for panels used as bins or hoppers or chutes in the handling and transport of material. The second application is where the panel is subject to resonant forced vibration. This could be the case, for example, if a mild sheet steel gearbox cover or fan casing is resonating because the driving speed produces a frequency of forcing vibration which coincides with the natural frequency of the panel. In this case increased damping will reduce the amplitude of the resonant vibration and hence the noise.

The amount of damping of a sheet steel panel may be increased by applying a layer of highly damped material, for example some sort of viscoelastic polymer, as illustrated in Figure 4.10. This is called unconstrained layer damping. The vibration of the sheet steel panel is transmitted to the polymer layer and the damping mechanisms within this layer extract sound and vibrational energy. A more effective treatment is to apply a second constraining sheet on top of the damping layer, thus making a sandwich. This is called constrained layer damping. A number of proprietary products are available for use as damping materials. They can be painted on as a mastic or applied as a stick-on sheet. Sheets of sandwich materials employing constrained layer damping are also available.

Close shielding or acoustic lagging

Sometimes, rather than attempting a complete enclosure around a machine, it is better to shield only those surfaces which are known to radiate most of the noise, for example thin sheet steel panels. An arrangement that is suitable is shown in Figure 4.11. The shield should consist of two layers: a resilient layer next to the noise radiating surface and a heavy, massive layer. The resilient layer may be of mineral fibre or foam. The thickness of the resilient layer should be 25–50 mm depending on the noise reduction required and the frequency of the sound to be shielded. The mass layer could be of sheet steel, lead sheet, plasterboard, mortar, or of timber such as fibreboard or chipboard. The noise reduction process is a complex one but the major mechanism is probably the effect of isolation. The resilient layer and the mass layer form a mass–spring system that effectively isolates the mass layer from

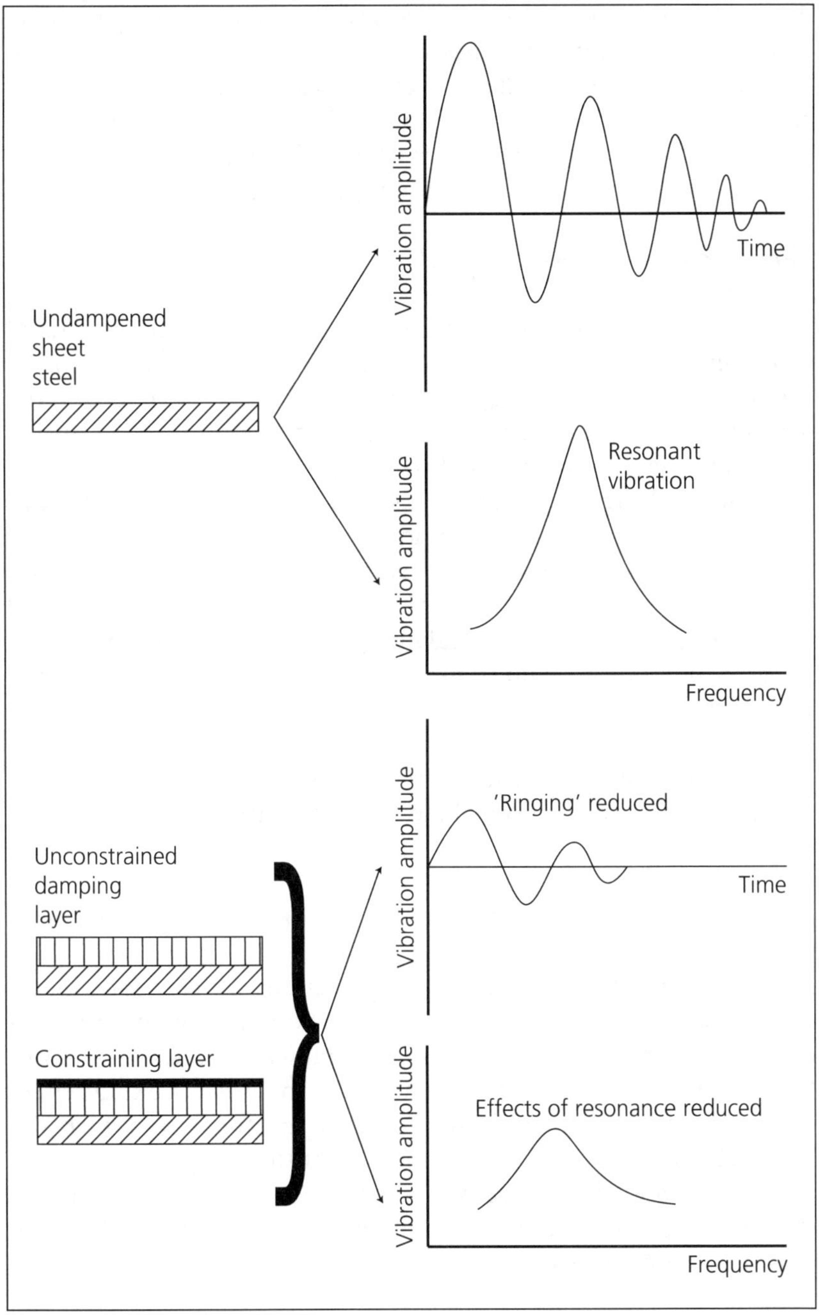

Figure 4.10 Damping of vibrating panels

the noise-radiating surface. However, there may also be an effect of sound absorption, of damping, and of sound insulation as well. The treatment is most effective at high frequencies and it is difficult to obtain high noise reductions at low frequencies. As well as being used for reducing noise from panels, this treatment is also suitable for the acoustic lagging of pipes and ducts.

Terminology of noise control

It is important to distinguish between the three mechanisms of sound insulation, sound absorption and vibration isolation and to use the correct terminology. Incorrect use of terms can lead to the wrong type of material being used: for example a sound-absorbing material being used when insulation is required. Since sound-absorbing materials are usually light they are often poor sound insulators and since sound-insulating materials often have hard, smooth surfaces they are usually poor absorbers of sound. Confusion also arises because mineral fibre quilts are good sound absorbers but poor sound insulators, but also good thermal insulators. Mineral fibre quilt is also used for its resilient properties as a vibration-isolating material.

The term 'sound attenuation' may be used to describe the amount of noise reduction whatever mechanism is used to reduce the noise level.

Specification of the performance of noise control materials

There are British and international standards which define methods for testing the sound reduction index and absorption coefficient of materials, and comprehensive tables of data are available for commonly used materials. There can, however, be differences between laboratory performance and that obtained with the materials in use, particularly if the size of the sample and the fixing method are very different in the two situations. There is also a standard method available for testing the sound attenuation produced by absorptive silencers.

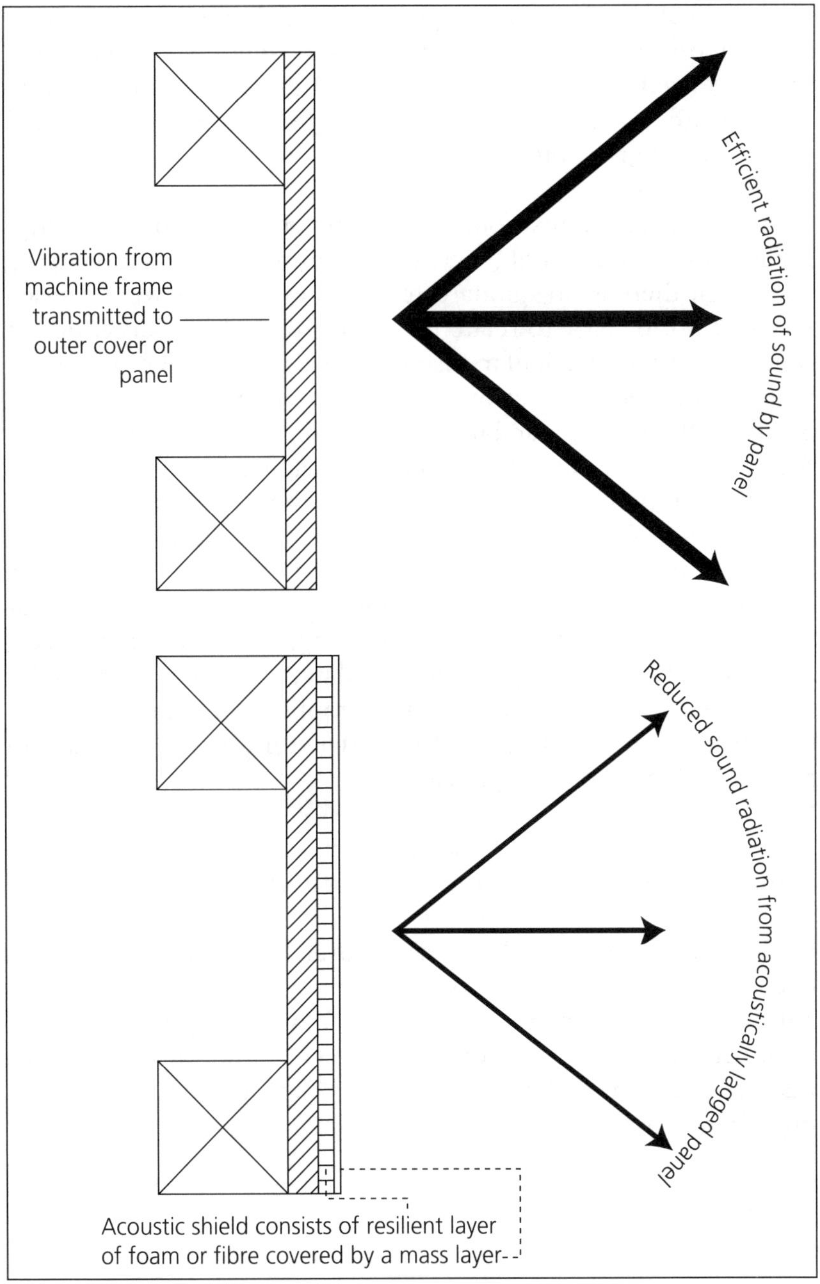

Figure 4.11 Close shielding or acoustic cladding (or lagging) of noise-radiating panels

A great deal of selection and performance data is available from manufacturers and suppliers of vibration isolators (antivibration mounts) used for isolating machinery. Less information is available for other applications of isolation, for example the isolation of structure-borne sound.

Although there are textbook definitions of the amount of damping in a sheet of material (such as the damping ratio and damping constant), there is no standard test, and even if one were devised it would not be easy to relate the results to the decibel reduction obtained in any particular case by substituting a damped panel for an undamped one, or by adding damping material to a panel. Similarly there is no standard way of testing or specifying the performance of close shielding or acoustic lagging materials. There is a large variety of acoustic material products available commercially, some of which are clearly designed for damping applications and others as acoustic lagging, but many of which offer a combination of properties combining the effects of sound insulation, absorption, isolation and damping. Manufacturers' datasheets usually offer test performance data, perhaps showing noise reductions achieved for a particular application. This should be carefully scrutinized to see to what extent the test situation resembles the proposed application.

All of these data should be available in octave bands. The user should beware of overall dB(A) reduction claims, because although they may be given in good faith, they can only at best be for 'typical' cases, and the overall dB(A) reduction obtained in each case will depend on the frequency spectrum (in octave bands) which is to be reduced. If the frequency spectrum of the application is different from the 'typical' one then a different dB(A) reduction will result — usually performance is better at high than at low frequencies.

Noise control at source

Machinery noise — generation and control

The source–path receiver model may also be applied to the analysis of noise radiated from machines. The source in this case is the noise-producing mechanism, which is often a dynamic force, producing vibration that is transmitted via the structure of the machine to the external surfaces, which radiate the noise. An example is the combustion forces occurring within the cylinder of an internal combustion engine which are transmitted through the engine structure to noise-radiating surfaces such as crankcase panels and thin sheet metal covers, such as the sump and rocker cover. Often the main structural framework of the machine may be strong and stiff, designed to withstand the working forces generated within the machine, but most of the noise is generated by much more flexible sheet steel covers attached to the external parts of the frame. A good example would be a punch press.

A full understanding of the noise-generating forces and mechanisms and the way in which they are transmitted to the noise-radiating surfaces is essential if the noise is to be reduced at source by modification to the design of the machine.

Apart from devising an entirely different process, the opportunities for reduction are in reducing or changing the vibration-producing forces, changing the transmission paths by which these forces reach the radiating surfaces, or by changes to these surfaces.

The forces are often the same as the working forces that perform the machine function. They include:

- cutting, pressing and shaping forces;

- gear and bearing forces;

- electric and magnetic forces (in motors and generators);

- combustion forces;
- out of balance forces (in rotating machines);
- frictional forces, for example, in brakes;
- pneumatic and hydraulic forces, for example, in pumps;
- stick-slip forces which can result in squeal of brakes and cutting tools.

Research has been carried out to modify these forces without reducing the working efficiency of the machines. Thus it is now possible to obtain machines with quieter gears and bearings, or to replace gears by belt drives, better balanced rotating machines and quieter motors. In many cases the modifications involve better quality engineering and hence more expense. It is possible to design quieter cutting tools for presses and other material-forming tools.

It is the rate of change of force that is important, as well as its magnitude. Smooth forces that change slowly are quieter than those that vary rapidly. A good example is the sharp rate of increase in combustion pressure which occurs in diesel engines, which gives rise to the characteristic 'diesel knock' which is absent from the noise from petrol engines. There are ways of modifying the combustion forces that reduce noise but they also have effects on gaseous emissions (hydrocarbons, oxides of nitrogen and so on) and on fuel efficiency. Another example is the cutting of sheet metal using a guillotine, which because the cutting force is applied smoothly and steadily is a very quiet process, although the impact of the offcut onto the floor is often noisy, unless measures are taken to cushion the blow.

Once the vibration has reached the vibrating surface there are a number of measures that can reduce the noise. These are:

- to reduce the surface area of the noise-radiating surface;

- to reduce the forces by isolating the panel from the frame of the machine;
- stiffening or damping the panel;
- close shielding or applying acoustic lagging to the panel.

If the surface is relatively stiff, a cast panel for example, then damping which relies on large vibration amplitudes will be ineffective, and isolating the panel may be the best option. If the surface is a flexible thin sheet steel panel, damping will be an appropriate treatment. A possible alternative would be to stiffen the panel either by increasing its thickness or by attaching stiffening ribs, and if necessary isolating the stiffened panel from the frame. The effect of increasing stiffness may be complex and difficult to predict. Changing the stiffness changes the natural frequencies of the panel and also its radiation efficiency.

In many material-forming processes the workpiece being formed may also radiate a significant amount of noise. When a blacksmith's hammer strikes a metal bar on an anvil then the noise generated by the impact will be radiated by the hammer, the workpiece, the anvil and the bench to which the anvil is attached. Similarly, timber planks passing through woodworking machinery will also radiate noise, as will sheets of metals being drilled, punched or riveted, or metal castings being dressed by chisels, grinders or chipping hammers, or machined by lathes or milling machines. Noise radiated from workpieces can be reduced by clamping or supporting the workpiece to provide temporary increased damping and reduce vibration. Hollow castings may be filled with sand to provide damping and reduce ringing noise during machining, and clamping and damping of sheet metal will have a similar effect. Sometimes, enclosures around woodworking machines are fitted with long entrance and exit tunnels, lined with sound-absorbing material in order to enclose the wooden planks whilst they are being machined and to attenuate noise escaping through the work access holes.

The noise levels from most rotating machines increase sharply with increasing speed. Therefore any changes which reduce machine speed will provide a useful reduction in noise. Large, slow-speed fans, for example, are usually much quieter than smaller, high-speed versions which move similar volumes of air.

The level of noise from pneumatic jets and nozzles widely used for cleaning purposes in industry increases rapidly with air pressure, and any reduction in pressure will lead to significant noise reductions.

Good maintenance will reduce noise caused by the movement of worn or loose parts and correct lubrication will reduce noise from bearings and gears. Keeping the cutting edge of tools sharp will also reduce noise as well as maintain the efficiency of the process.

Fans and blowers

Fans of one sort or another are responsible for about 30% of complaints about noise nuisance from industry and commerce. They are used for moving air in ventilation systems, removing fumes and waste gases and for transporting particulate material, either in the form of process material (powders, granules) or waste particulate material. The axial and centrifugal types widely used for moving air and waste gases produce a broadband noise but tonal components can be produced by interaction with obstacles such as guide vanes placed too close to the fan blades. For other types such as propeller fans, and high pressure industrial blowers for transporting particulate material, the tonal component may be much more prominent.

The control of noise from fans starts with the selection of the fan. The main criterion for selection is the volume flow rate of air that has to be moved and the pressure drop against which it has to work. Within these parameters a fan with the lowest noise output when working at its optimum efficiency should be selected. This may need to take into account the shape of the noise spectrum, because it may be better to accept a fan that has the lowest sound power level at lower frequencies (that are difficult to reduce) even though it may produce higher levels at the more easily controlled high frequencies.

The size of the fan is also an important factor because, in general, larger fans operating at lower speeds move the same amount of air with less noise than smaller, higher-speed fans. The noise output increases rapidly with speed so that variable speed fans can be used to reduce noise by reducing the speed when the load requirement is low.

Once the fan has been selected it should be installed so as to make the minimum noise possible and this requires a smooth flow of air into the fan since input turbulence can increase the noise level by several decibels. There should be no obstructions to flow, no bends or changes of cross-section within at least one duct diameter, either up- or down-stream of the fan. Noise from the inlet and supply side of the fan may be reduced by using in-line silencers, and airborne noise radiated from the casing of the fan itself may be reduced by an enclosure around the fan. The transmission of structure-borne sound should be reduced by fitting antivibration mounts between the fan and the building structure, usually the floor, and using flexible connectors between fan and ductwork. The sound power produced by the fan may be augmented by noise generated by the flow of air through the duct system, and this should be minimized by designing the system to keep the airflow as smooth and as slow as possible. If the airflow carries particulate material then there is additional noise generated by impact of the particles with the duct walls. Noise generated within and emanating from the duct system may be reduced using a secondary silencer, and noise breaking out from the duct through the duct walls may be reduced by application of acoustic lagging treatment to the duct.

In summary, noise problems from fans may be minimized by:

- careful location of the fan, and of inlet and outlets to avoid noise-sensitive areas;

- planning and prediction of noise levels before installation, if possible, so that noise control can be incorporated at the design stage rather than retrospectively;
- careful selection of the most appropriate type and size of fan, operating at lowest possible speed;
- reduction of fan speed, if possible, at periods of reduced load and at sensitive times, e.g. at night;
- correct installation to ensure that fan is operating at maximum efficiency;
- design of duct system to ensure smooth airflow into fan and smooth airflow at lowest possible speed through ductwork to minimize additional noise generation;
- use of silencers, fan enclosure and acoustic lagging of ductwork, if necessary, to provide additional attenuation.

Jets and exhausts

A jet is a flow of fast-moving gas or air moving from the end of a tube or pipe into free air. The structure of a jet is shown in Figure 4.12. The noise-producing mechanism is the turbulence created by the viscous forces which operate between adjacent layers of air in the boundary layer between the jet and the surrounding air, where there is a very high velocity gradient. The sound power level produced depends on the cross-sectional area of the jet and the efflux velocity. The level increases sharply with increasing velocity, so that any velocity reduction which can be achieved will produce significant noise reductions — more than 20 dB reduction if the velocity is halved. The noise has a broadband spectrum with a peak at a frequency which depends on the jet velocity, v (in ms^{-1}), and diameter, d (in mm), according to the formula:

$$f = 200 \times \frac{v}{d}$$

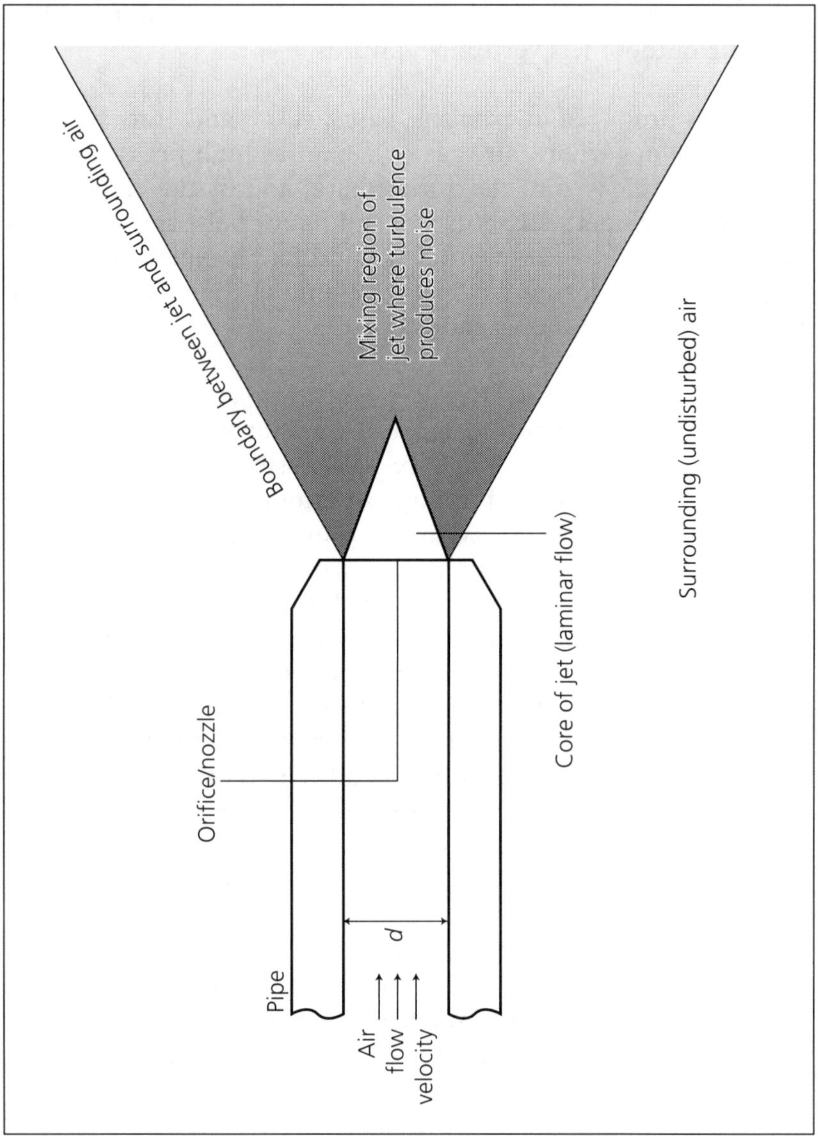

Figure 4.12 The structure and important features of a jet

Thus small diameter, high velocity jets will have a high frequency spectrum, whereas the much larger diameter and lower velocities in exhausts produce a much lower frequency spectrum. The radiation is directional and so some benefit can be obtained by directing outdoor jets vertically upwards.

Jet noise is produced in exhausts, vents, valves and other pressure release devices where air, gas or steam at high pressures and velocities is released to the atmosphere, and by the exhausts of pneumatically operated actuators and hand tools, and by 'working' air-jets used to eject workpieces and for cleaning and cooling purposes. Compressed air hoses are among the most universal high-level noise sources in industry.

The principles of diffusion and absorption are used to reduce noise from exhaust jets. Figure 4.13 shows examples of an exhaust silencer suitable for process exhausts, in which the initial high flow velocity is forced through a perforated diffuser. This has the effect of reducing flow velocity, promoting frictional effects, and also converting one single jet, which for a large diameter process exhaust system may be predominantly low frequency noise, to many smaller high frequency jets which are more easily attenuated by the sound-absorbing material lining the silencer. Exhaust silencers working on the diffuser principle, which can easily be screwed onto pneumatic exhausts, are relatively cheap and readily available, and can produce reductions of up to 25 dB(A). The diffusing medium may be sintered plastic, compacted wire wool or layers of woven wire cloth. In addition to the noise reduction to be achieved, the selection of the most appropriate type will need to take into account the effects of any back pressure caused by the silencer, and arrangements for cleaning, maintenance or replacement in order to avoid blockage of the diffuser by debris in the airflow. An alternative to fitting a diffusing silencer is to lead the exhaust away through a length of flexible tubing to exhaust in a less noise-sensitive area.

Where the air-jet is required to do some useful work a variety of 'low noise' nozzles are available. Most of these work on the 'air entrainment' or 'induced flow' principle, in which a flow of air of intermediate velocity is introduced into the boundary layer between the fast-moving jetstream and the stationary surrounding

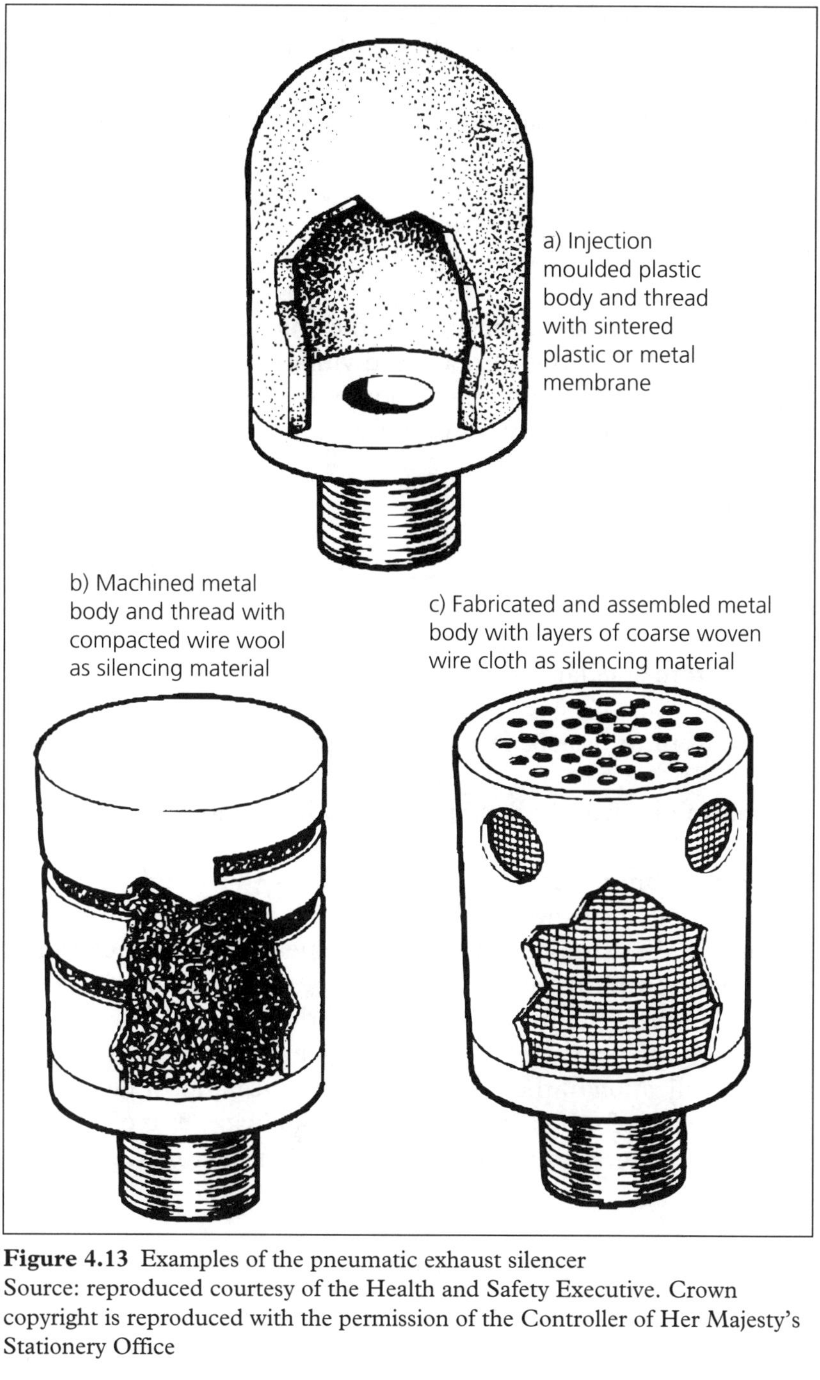

Figure 4.13 Examples of the pneumatic exhaust silencer
Source: reproduced courtesy of the Health and Safety Executive. Crown copyright is reproduced with the permission of the Controller of Her Majesty's Stationery Office

air, in order to reduce the velocity gradient, and so to reduce turbulence and noise generation (Figure 4.14).

More detailed information on reducing noise from a pneumatic air-jet is given in HSE Guidance Note PM56 *Noise from pneumatic systems*.

Punch presses

Punch presses are used throughout the engineering industry and can produce high levels of noise and vibration. In addition to the impact noise produced by the action of the die on the workpiece there are many other sources of noise, including:

- compressed air-jet noise;
- transmission of vibration to external noise-radiating surfaces of the press, and to other surfaces;
- noise from ancillary equipment, fans, motors, gears and so on;
- noise from workpiece feed mechanisms;
- impact noise from collection of workpieces and offcuts.

Some possible noise control treatments that might be used include: total enclosure, partial enclosure, close shielding/acoustic lagging of existing panels, or replacement by 'acoustic' panels with good sound-insulating properties, exhaust silencers, vibration isolation of the press from the building, and of parts of the press from the press frame, damping of panels and of collection bins, modification of the punch tools to reduce impact noise. Figure 4.15, taken from HSE Noise Guide 4, illustrates typical noise sources on a press, and some noise reduction treatments.

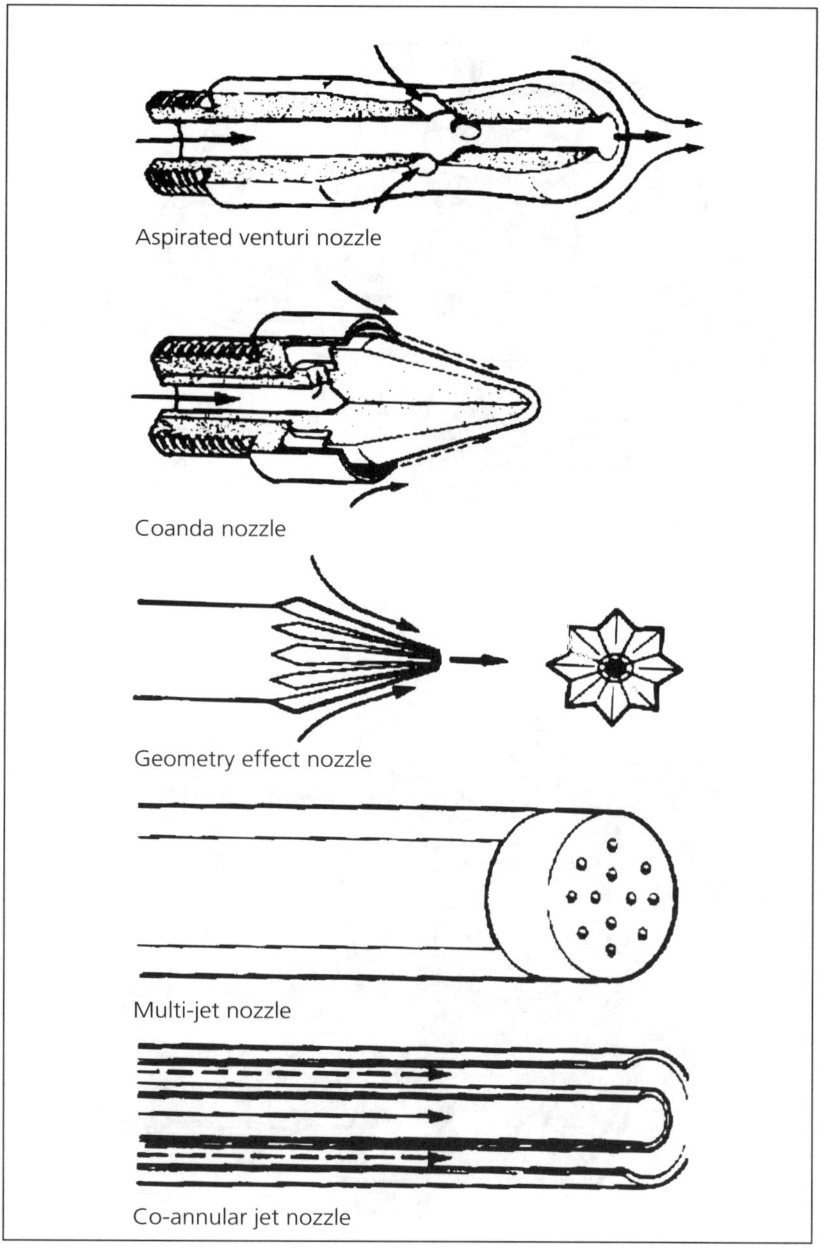

Figure 4.14 Examples of the 'induced flow' jet nozzle
Source: reproduced courtesy of the Health and Safety Executive. Crown copyright is reproduced with the permission of the Controller of Her Majesty's Stationery Office

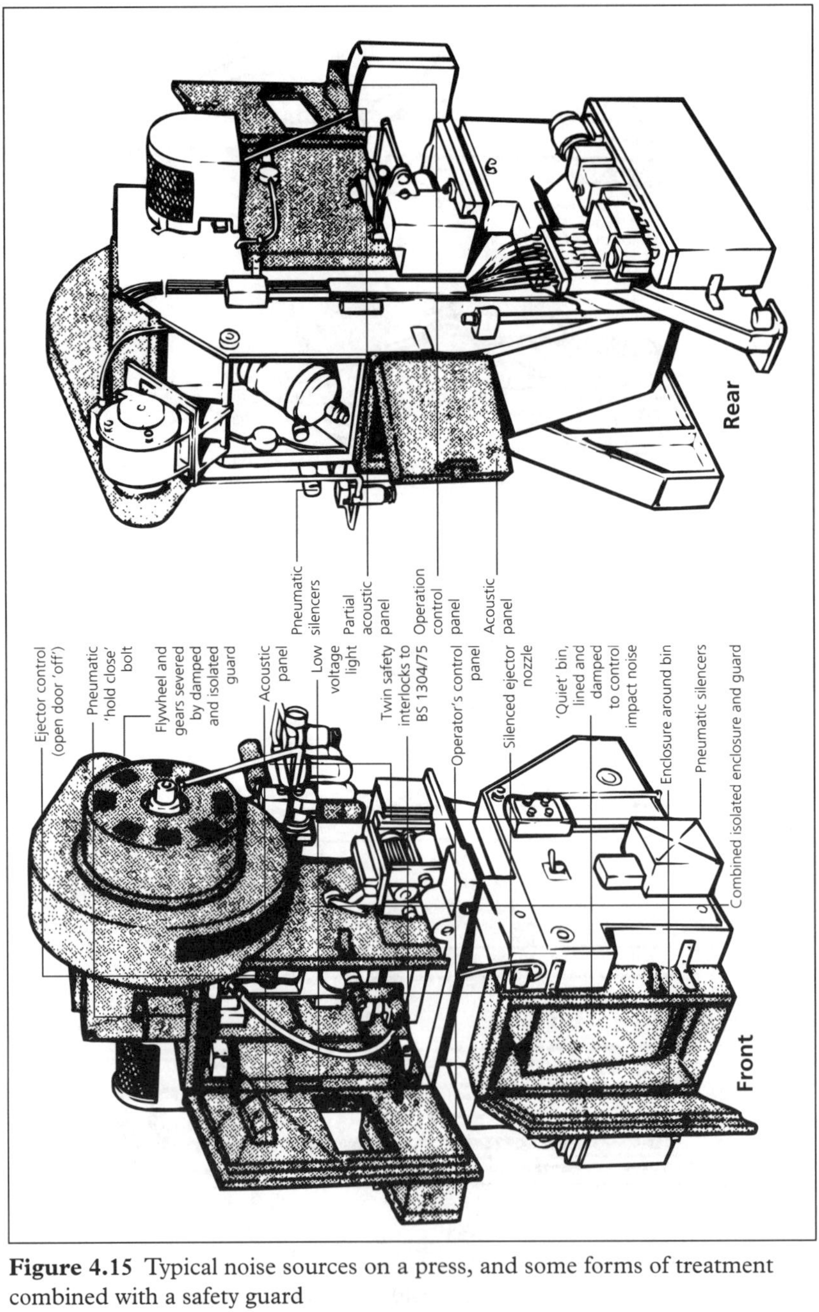

Figure 4.15 Typical noise sources on a press, and some forms of treatment combined with a safety guard

Source: reproduced courtesy of the Health and Safety Executive. Crown copyright is reproduced with the permission of the Controller of Her Majesty's Stationery Office

Mechanical handling of materials

In most industries, materials have to be moved about and collected using conveyor belts, or airflow in ducts used to transport material in particle and pellet form. These processes generate impact noise from materials dropping into chutes and hoppers, and from the pellets striking the walls of ducts, cyclones and collectors. Suitable methods of noise control are:

- line surfaces of conveyors, hoppers and chutes with resilient material to reduce impact noise;
- use damped material, or apply damping treatments instead of undamped sheet metals for trays, bins, hoppers etc. to reduce ringing noise;
- reduce impact velocity by reducing height from which objects drop into hoppers. This can sometimes be achieved by breaking the fall into several smaller stages, with cushioning at each stage;
- cover ducts, cyclones and other surfaces conveying pellets with acoustic lagging.

Printing presses

Much of the information in this section is taken from the booklet *Noise Reduction at Web-fed Presses*, published by the Health and Safety Executive, and from information supplied by the Noise Control Centre.

In common with much other large and complex plant, a printing press will have a large number of different noise sources including motors, gears, fans, pumps, conveyors, compressors and waste extract, and many noise-radiating panels. Noise-producing mechanisms which are specific to printing are those associated with the transport, inking, folding and cutting of the paper. There are many panels, covers and guards attached to the frame of the press which are caused to vibrate and radiate noise by the various forces resulting from press operations, including: impacts from paper folding and from gear teeth, cams and eccentrics associated with paper transport; out of balance forces from uneven loading on rotating rollers; hydraulic forces associated with ink flow, and stick-slip friction that can occur at reel stand brakes, resulting in brake squeal. The major noise sources are the folder, printing unit, drive mechanisms, dryer and auxiliary equipment. The folder is usually the most important noise source but the other sources will also require treatment if overall noise is to be reduced to satisfactory levels. Typical levels for noise from regional newspapers and commercial printers (given in the HSE booklet and measured in 1984/85) are:

reel stand	87–98 dB(A)
print units	86–102 dB(A)
control console	87–100 dB(A)
folder take-off	87–104 dB(A)

Noise levels vary with make and type of press, running speed, webbing configuration, and type of paper. A typical noise spectrum in a print hall is shown in Figure 4.16 and at a folder in Figure 4.17, indicating how both levels and spectrum change with speed.

The scope for reduction of noise at the design stage of the press includes:

- reduction of noise-generating mechanisms such as the various impacts described above and through improved engineering such as selection of quieter gears and bearings;
- improved balance and alignment;

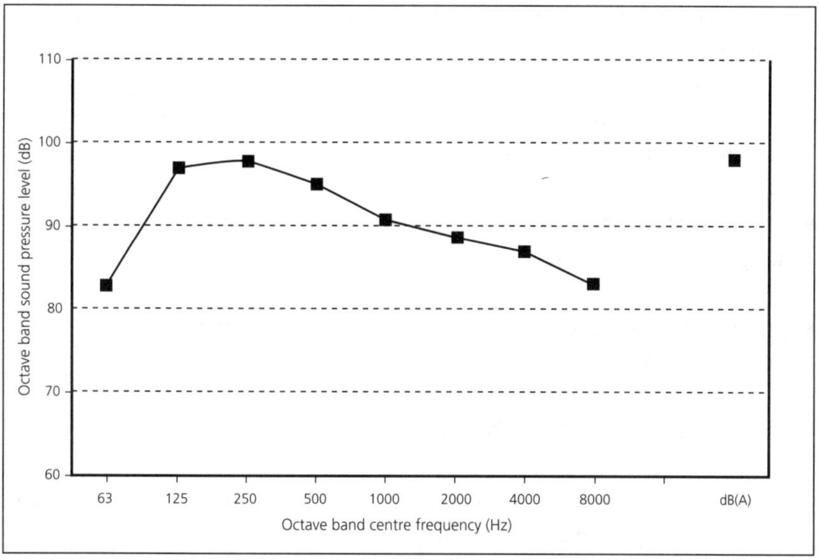

Figure 4.16 Press hall: typical sound levels running 32 pages at 32000 cph
Source: reproduced courtesy of the Noise Control Centre

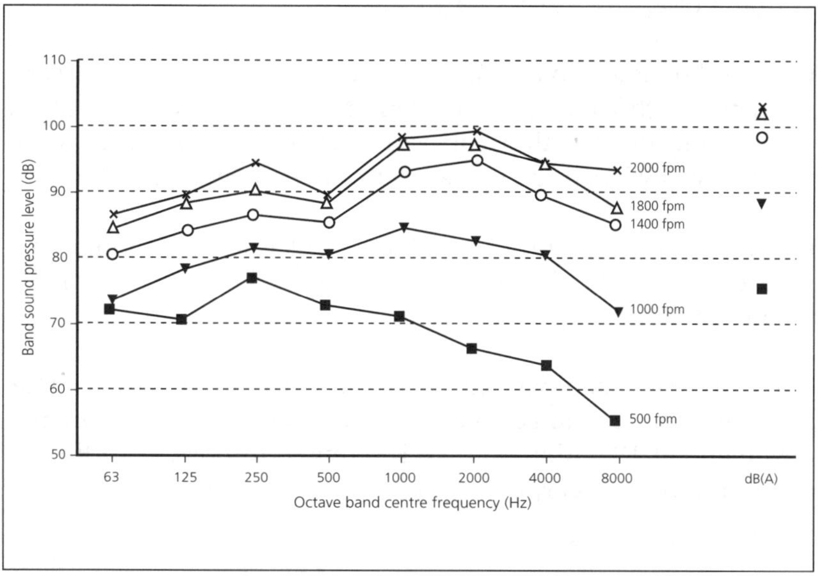

Figure 4.17 Folder noise spectra showing change relative to speed
Source: reproduced courtesy of the Noise Control Centre

- isolation of noise-producing forces from the noise-radiating panels;
- use of sound-absorbing materials to reduce build-up of airborne sound within the press;
- treatment of noise-radiating panels by damping and acoustic lagging treatments;
- operating procedures which minimize noise, for example reduced operating speeds;
- layout of plant within the building;
- automation and remote control of plant to allow more personnel to be separated from noisy areas;
- use of enclosures, screens and havens to separate personnel from noise;
- control of noise from auxiliary equipment such as compressors, pumps, extractor and air conditioning systems, either by including them within enclosures around the press, or separately, or by locating them away from operatives;
- design of the building in which the press is located to minimize reverberation within and breakout of sound to the environment outside.

Some of these techniques can be applied retrospectively, after the press has been installed, but at greater cost and inconvenience (see Figure 4.18). Maintenance is required to prevent additional noise created by wear, poor lubrication, looseness and misalignments.

In multilevel presses where the reel rooms are directly below the press hall the main cause of noise in the reel room is usually breakthrough from the press hall of noise from the folder and the

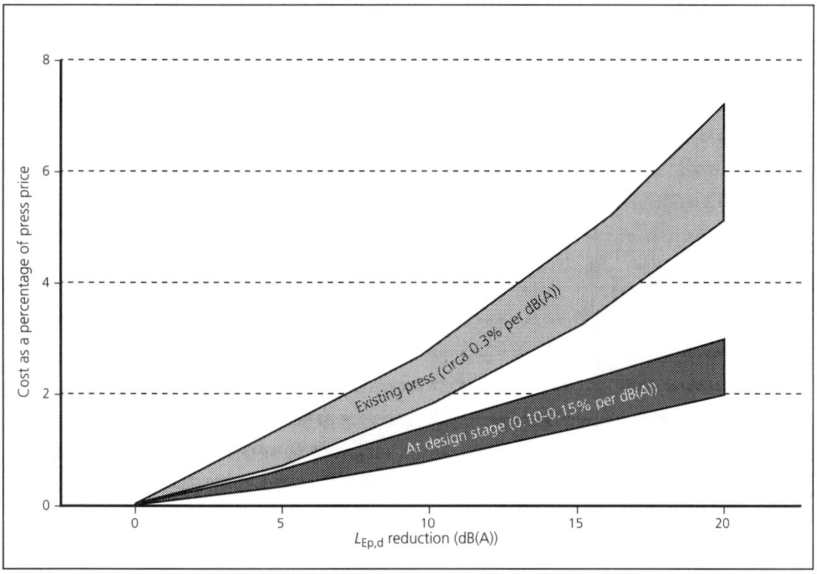

Figure 4.18 Estimated costs of noise control assuming treatment to existing press
Source: reproduced courtesy of the Noise Control Centre

print units, either by structure-borne sound or airborne transmission through web feed slots. Noise levels may be minimized by isolation of the press from the pressroom floor, to reduce structure-borne sound transmission, and by using sound-absorbing material in attenuators, in the form of lined tunnels, at the web slots, and in the reel room generally, in order to reduce reverberant sound levels.

Figures 4.19 and 4.20 show typical variations of noise levels with position in a press hall and reel room, and also indicate typical noise reductions that can be achieved using sound-absorbing treatments. Figures 4.21 and 4.22 give some indication of the effect of different types of acoustic treatment on the noise exposure of operatives.

Some of the case studies in Chapter 5 relate to noise from printing presses.

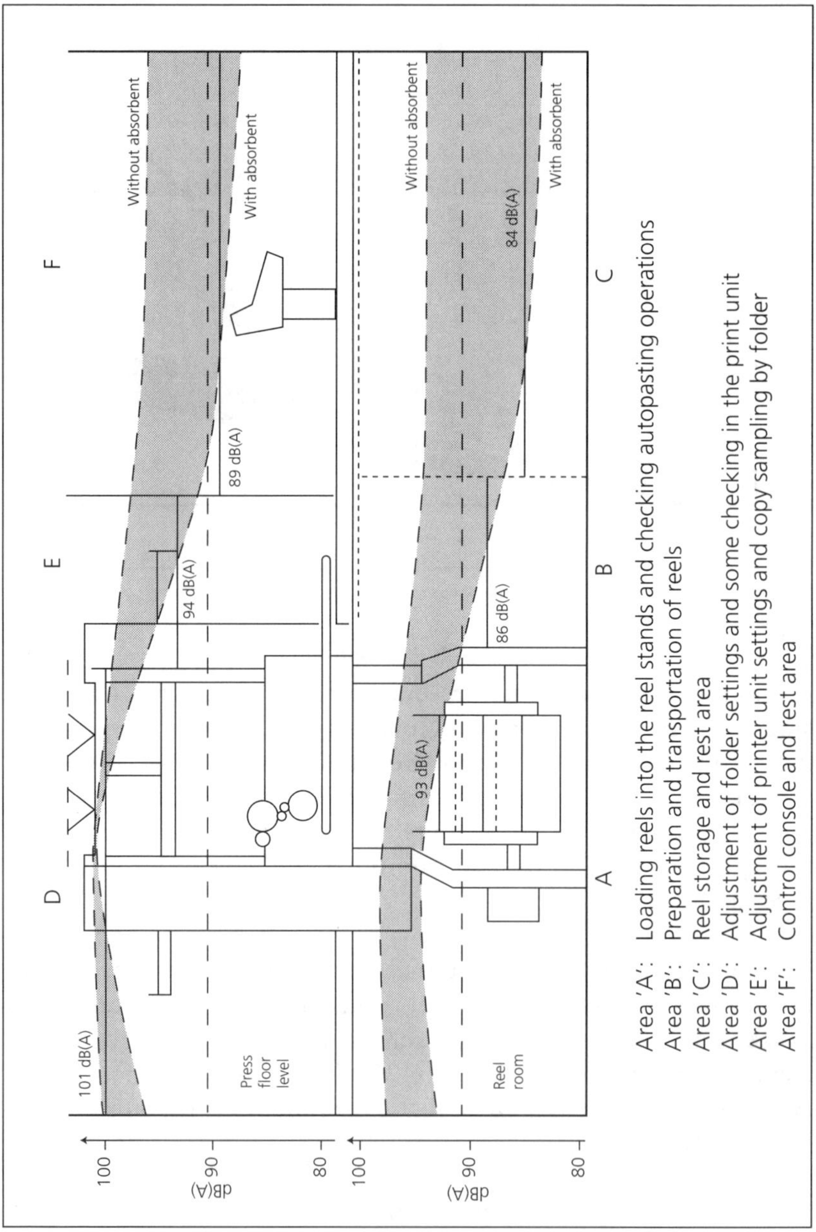

Figure 4.19 Typical variation of noise level with position in press hall and reel room
Source: reproduced courtesy of the Noise Control Centre

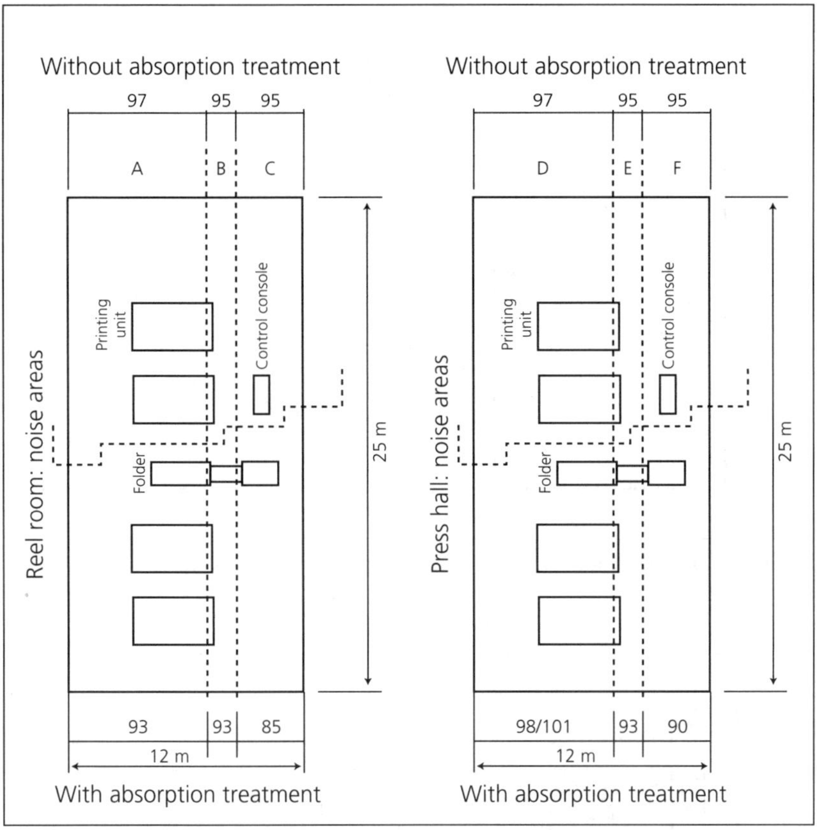

Figure 4.20 Sound level variation across press hall and reel stand room
Source: reproduced courtesy of the Noise Control Centre

Paper making

The range of noise sources, typical noise levels and noise control treatments that occur in the papermaking industry is described in an HSE booklet *Protection of Hearing in the Paper and Board Industry.* The range of noise levels measured at fixed locations around various items of plant in a survey carried out by the HSE is shown in Figure 4.23. The survey included mills that manufactured a range of paper and board products on a variety of machines under different operating conditions and speeds. The highest noise levels occurred in woodchipper and refiner areas. The levels

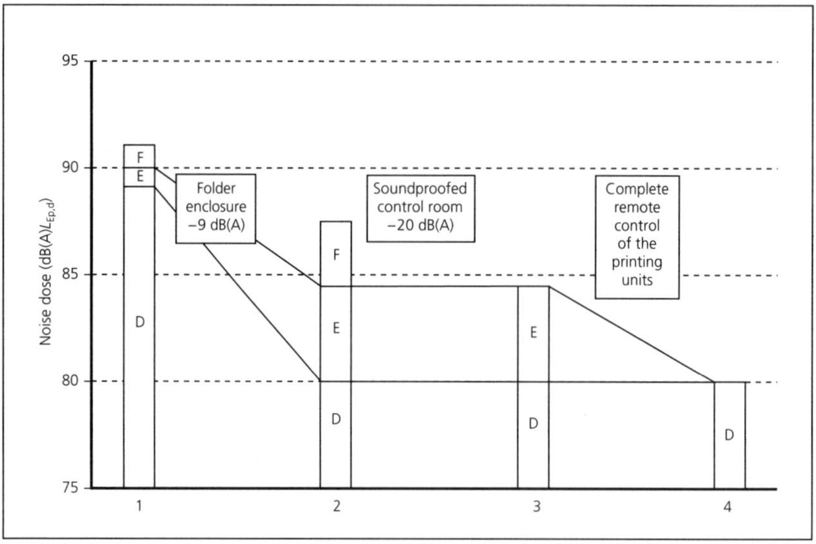

Figure 4.21 Press room noise dose reductions for different noise control measures
Source: reproduced courtesy of the Noise Control Centre

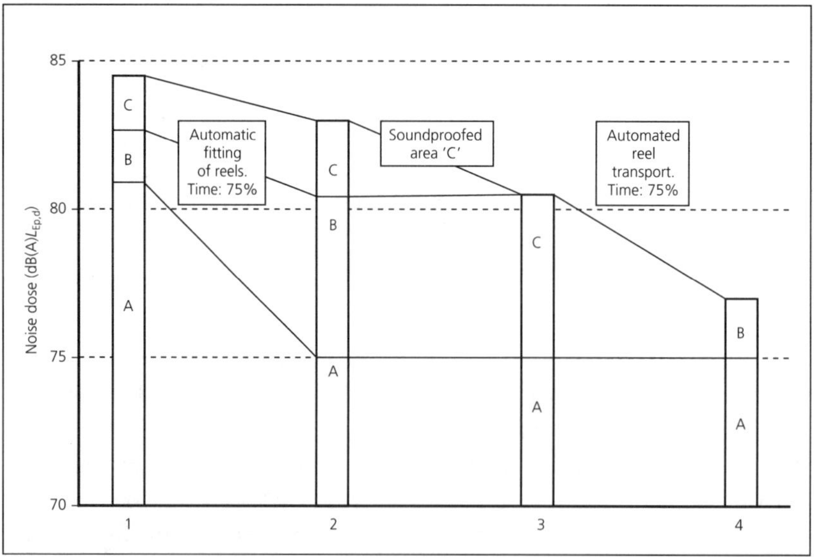

Figure 4.22 Reel room noise dose reductions from automation and soundproofing
Source: reproduced courtesy of the Noise Control Centre

varied at different points along papermaking machines, but were generally highest close to the couch suction rolls. Important noise sources are: gears, electric motor drives, air and steam leaks, vacuum pumps, couch and other vacuum rolls, press and other rolls. High noise levels are also produced by refiners and reelers/slitters (winders). The booklet gives suggestions for and examples of possible noise control techniques for: steam plant, boilerhouse, chipper, debarking drums, pulpers, refiners and for the various stages in the papermaking process: headbox, wire part, press section, dryer section, reel up, calender stacks, rewinder and finishing machinery.

The booklet also emphasizes the need for good maintenance and the importance of drawing up noise specifications for the purchase of new machinery. Some of the case studies in Chapter 5 refer to noise in the papermaking industry.

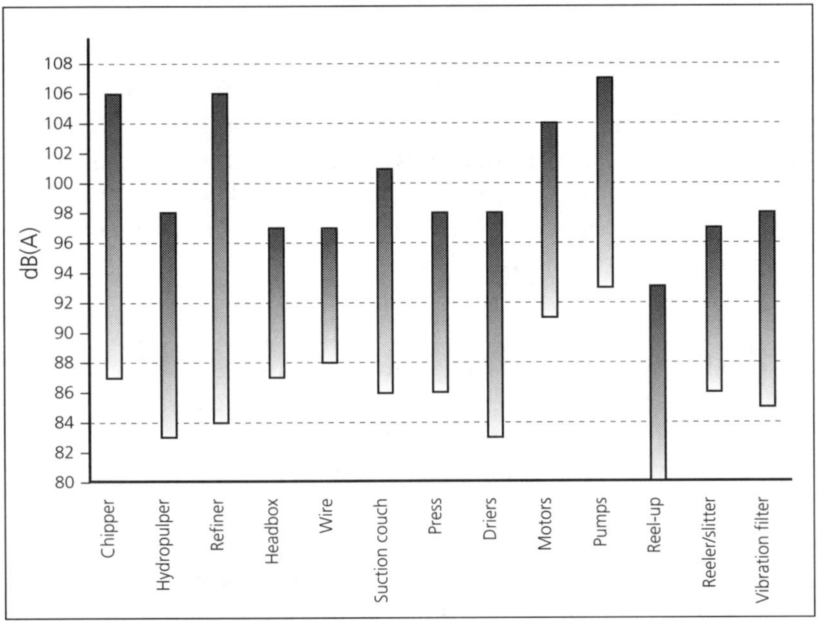

Figure 4.23 The range of noise levels at operator positions at web-fed presses
Source: reproduced courtesy of the Health and Safety Executive. Crown copyright is reproduced with the permission of the Controller of Her Majesty's Stationery Office

Active noise control

In active noise control systems the principle of destructive interference is applied to cancel the noise using an 'anti-noise' signal from a loudspeaker. The main features of an active noise control system installed in a duct are shown in Figure 4.24. A microphone picks up the noise signal from the fan, and the signal processor produces a signal of equal amplitude, but opposite phase, which is fed to a loudspeaker downstream of the microphone. Although the idea is simple in principle it is difficult to carry out in practice. In order to achieve a reduction of 20 dB, for example, the intensity of the noise must be reduced by a factor of 100, which gives an indication of how exact the cancellation must be. The situation is complicated by the need for the processor to take into account the phase shift introduced by the time it takes for the sound to travel between the microphone and the loudspeaker. This depends on the speed of sound, which varies with temperature and with airflow speed. Other problems are that the loudspeaker will also feed sound back to the microphone, as well as cancelling the fan noise, and that the noise from the fan may change with time. These difficulties are overcome by using a second microphone positioned downstream of the loudspeaker in order to detect any imperfections in the cancellation process and to send an error signal back to the processor that adapts the cancelling signal to the loudspeaker.

Active noise control has been successfully applied to a wide variety of noise sources including industrial fans, ventilating systems in buildings, generators, compressors and exhaust stack noise. It is best suited to reducing noise levels in small, enclosed spaces such as the interior of sports cars and aircraft cabins, to ducts and pipes and to industrial noise havens. Communication headsets and ear muffs fitted with active noise control are available. The method is also best suited to the cancellation of low frequencies, for which the wavelengths are long, and so the sound level and phase change gradually with variation in position. Since the alternative 'passive' control methods, such as absorptive silencers, are least effective at low frequencies, hybrid noise control systems

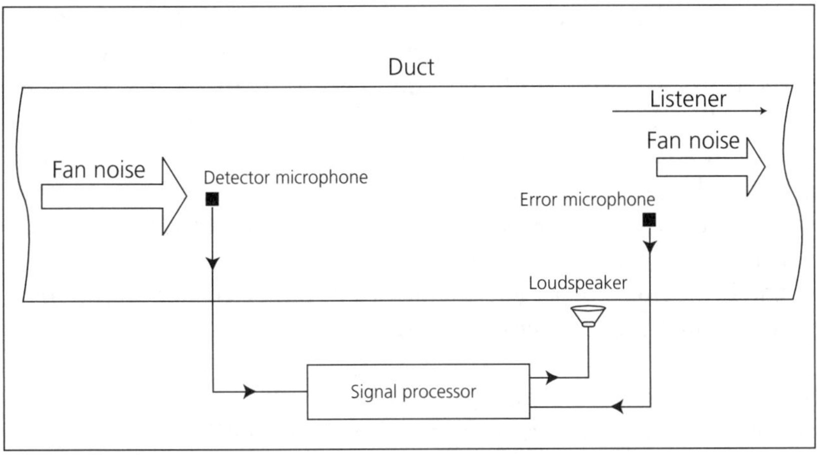

Figure 4.24 Active noise control applied to fan noise in a duct

which use active methods at low frequencies and passive methods at high frequencies are sometimes used. There are still some concerns about the ruggedness of active noise control devices such as microphones and loudspeakers when exposed to hostile industrial environments for long periods, but continuing development is likely to lead to improvements in both software and hardware, and to new applications.

Case study 2 in Chapter 5 illustrates the application of active noise control.

Specification of machinery noise

An important part of any company noise control policy is a requirement to take noise into consideration when selecting and purchasing new and replacement equipment. It is therefore important to have clear, unambiguous and standard methods for specifying the noise output from plant and machinery. The relative advantages of using either sound power level or sound pressure level at a specified distance were discussed in Chapter 3. European Commission directives on noise emissions from machinery are discussed in Chapter 6. Under these regulations a series of noise test codes are being developed for each type of machine, indicating how the machine is to be tested, its operating and mounting conditions during the test, the measurement standard to be used, and how the measurement results are to be declared and verified. The use of both sound power levels and emission sound pressure levels is recommended in these codes and standards, which are designed to help manufacturers, suppliers, purchasers and users of machinery. The methods of measuring machinery noise are discussed in Chapter 7, including details of the draft noise test code for printing, paper converting, papermaking machines and equipment.

The importance of drawing up noise specifications for the purchase of new machinery is emphasized in an HSE booklet *Protection of Hearing in the Paper and Board Industry.* The advice is applicable to all industries. The booklet also emphasizes the need for good liaison between purchaser and supplier of the machinery. The noise specification should include:

- noise limits for the installation;
- responsibility of purchaser and supplier, particularly with regard to the accuracy of information supplied by each;
- methods and materials to be used for noise control, including any possible restraints on these, because of working practice, environmental, safety or other considerations.

The discussions between purchaser and supplier should include consideration of installation and operating conditions and work patterns for the new plant, noise from any associated new auxiliary plant and from existing plant, and servicing maintenance arrangements and programmes.

Diagnosis of noise sources, paths and mechanisms

Diagnosis is an important first step in any noise reduction programme. It attempts to answer the following questions:

- Which are the most important noise sources?
- What are the most important sound transmission paths?
- What are the noise-producing mechanisms?
- Which are the main noise-radiating surfaces?

Good diagnosis enables noise control to be conducted in a systematic manner and the appropriate noise control treatments to be specified and prioritized. Incorrect diagnosis can result in the application of the wrong noise control measures, leading to a waste of time, effort and money, and bringing the noise control programme into disrepute.

If there are several different noisy machines the best way to find out which ones are the noisiest is to switch them all off and then to measure the noise level with each one being switched on in turn. The alternative method, of measuring the noise whilst switching one off at a time can often be ineffective, as shown by the following example.

Ten identical machines each produce a level of 80 dB(A) at the receiver. Using the rules of combining decibels introduced in Chapter 1 it is possible to calculate how the noise level at the receiver increases as each one is turned on: 80, 83, 85, 86, 87, 88, 88.5, 89, 89.5, 90. This tells us that switching just one source off, leaving the other nine still running, will reduce the total noise by less than 0.5 dB. Even switching four of the sources off will only achieve a reduction of 2 dB. In this case the only way to find the contribution from each source will be the first method, i.e. switching all off and then switching on individual sources singly and in turn. The example also illustrates that the only effective strategy for noise control in this case will be to attempt to reduce the noise levels of all ten sources equally, i.e. it would be more effective to reduce the level of all ten sources by 2 dB than to concentrate attention on only two sources and reduce their level by 10 dB each.

Now let us imagine the situation to change so that one of the ten sources produces a noise level which is 10 dB above the other nine, which remain equal at 80 dB. The first nine sources switched on together will produce a combined level of almost 90 dB, which will increase to 93 dB when the tenth is also switched on. In this case the technique of switching off in turn would be successful in diagnosing the one dominant source, but even switching this one off would only produce a reduction of 3 dB, and switching off the others would not produce any detectable difference. This situation would also require an entirely different strategy for noise control. The first step in this case must be to reduce the noise from the one dominant source, by 10 dB before paying any attention to the other nine. Once the dominant noise source has been treated the diagnosis exercise must be repeated to establish the new order of priorities for noise control treatment.

Two simple extreme cases have been described to illustrate different strategies that may be required. In many cases involving multiple noise sources the choices will not be so clear, but it will still be necessary to draw up a list showing the contributions from each source to the total noise level in order to prioritize noise control treatments. The process will need to be ongoing and to be continually reviewed as the noise control programme proceeds. In the last example the priority will be to treat only the dominant source, but once this has been made 10 dB quieter then, in order to achieve further noise reductions, the strategy must be switched to treating all ten sources equally.

Sometimes it may be possible to turn off equipment, for diagnostic purposes, but only for a very short period of time, perhaps a few seconds. In such cases it is extremely useful to have made tape recordings of the noise for future replay and analysis. If switching off machines is not possible then some idea of the relative importance of noise from different machines may be obtained by measuring sound pressure levels close to each machine, where the noise reading will be largely unaffected by that from other nearby machines.

Some machines contain many different sources of noise. A motor vehicle is a good example. Noise is produced by the engine, exhaust, air inlet, gearbox and transmission, fan, alternator, tyres and aerodynamically as a result of airflow over the vehicle body. The noise from the engine can in turn be analysed into combustion noise and mechanical noise from valves, pistons, bearings and timing equipment. In addition, vibration from smaller machines such as fuel pumps and alternators may be radiated from the engine surfaces to which they are attached, as well as directly.

Although there are specialist acoustic techniques for diagnosing sources, the most effective method is for an engineer with a detailed knowledge of how the machine works to conduct a thorough investigation. By walking around the machine, looking and listening carefully, and observing the effect on the noise as the machine operating conditions, such as speed and load, are changed, and with various parts of the machine not in operation it is possible to obtain a good idea of all the important sources and mechanisms. The experience of the operator who uses the machine every day may also be useful. This is rather like detecting the source of a new noise in a car — some indication of the cause may be obtained by listening to the effect of driving at different speeds, in different gears (including neutral) and engine revs, and of accelerating, braking and cornering.

Sometimes it is necessary to find out which surfaces of the machine are radiating most noise. One effective approach is to cover all possible surfaces with carefully designed and close-fitting acoustic shields or lagging. Then, rather like the method for individual machines, the lagging is removed from each surface in turn, i.e. with all other surfaces covered, and the noise levels are measured in order to detect which surface makes the biggest contribution to the total. This is the classic technique used by the late Professor Priede to detect and rank the important noise-radiating areas of a diesel engine, and has been used by the author to identify a noisy motor as an important contributor to the noise from a large printing plant.

If it is not possible to take valid measurements of machine noise because of the disturbing effect of noise from nearby machines then it may be possible to measure the levels of vibration on the machine surfaces and estimate the noise level from these. Specialist knowledge is needed, however, to interpret the results. Another specialist technique is the use of a sound intensity meter which, unlike an ordinary sound level meter is able to detect the direction and flow of acoustic energy, and may be used to diagnose which are important sources and radiating areas in a machine, or to measure sound power levels of machines in the presence of noise from other nearby sources. Narrowband frequency analysis can be used to identify the exact frequency of a tonal component in machinery noise and causally link it with a particular repetitive process occurring within the machine, such as a particular fan-blade-passing or gear-meshing frequency. Sophisticated signal processing techniques may also be used for diagnosis, such as correlation, in which two signals are compared to determine the degree of similarity between them. The two signals could be, for example, from the noise radiated from a machine and the vibration of a certain part of the machine and it is possible to determine the extent to which the noise is produced by the vibration.

Hearing conservation policies

A hearing conservation policy is a co-ordinated collection of measures operated by a company aimed at protecting its employees from hearing loss damage caused by exposure to noise at work. The ingredients of such a policy are:

- Support and commitment to the aims of the policy throughout the company, particularly at senior management level.

- Regular periodic assessments of the noise exposure of employees. In the first instance this is a statement of the magnitude of the company's hearing conservation problem, and the basis for the design of the other parts of the programme and for setting priorities. Subsequently it becomes a check on the progress in implementing other aspects of the programme and the success of its operation. The assessment is more than a survey of noise levels throughout the workplace, although this is an essential part, because the process should focus attention on the exposure, and so should include an assessment of the times for which employees are exposed to various levels of noise.

- A programme of measures aimed at reducing the exposure to noise of those employees whose exposure is above some criteria, based upon risk of hearing damage. The criteria used will probably be the Action Levels of the Noise at Work Regulations, although some companies will have their own, more stringent, exposure limits. The noise exposure of employees may be reduced by one of the following methods:

  - reducing the noise levels in the workplace;
  - replacing noisy machines and processes by quieter ones;
  - implementing remedial noise reduction measures to existing machinery and processes;
  - separating the employees from the source of noise, using automation and employee refuges;
  - reducing the exposure times, e.g. by job rotation;
  - using personal ear protectors, i.e. ear muffs or ear plugs.

- A programme of information and training for all employees in support of all aspects of the policy and aimed at ensuring that everyone is aware of the goals of the policy and of the part they have in ensuring its success.

- Continuing management of all aspects of the policy, including a continuing programme of noise exposure assessment and reduction.

- A programme of monitoring audiometry. This is the ultimate check that the other parts of the programme are effective, and usually consists of a pre-employment audiometric check for all new employees and regular follow-up tests, perhaps once or twice each year. Further information about regulations and guidance concerning industrial audiometric monitoring is given in Chapter 6, and a brief introduction to the measurement methods is given in Chapter 7.

Government guidance about the setting up and implementation of hearing conservation programmes was first available to employees in the Department of Employment Code of Practice *Reducing the Exposure of Employed Persons to Noise*, issued in 1972, which has now in effect been replaced by the Noise Guides 1–8, issued in relation to the Noise at Work Regulations.

Personal ear protectors

Ear protection should be seen by managers in industry as a last resort method of protecting people's hearing, as a result of failure to reduce noise levels by other means, and as an interim method until a more acceptable method of controlling employees' exposure to noise is in place. Nevertheless, the effective use of ear protectors is likely to be the only practicable means available for protecting the hearing of large numbers of employees for several years to come, and it is therefore important that a well managed programme is in place to ensure that the protectors are always being used effectively. This programme needs to cover aspects such as availability, selection, training and monitoring. Although the cost of each muff or plug is small, the cost of their continued provision for large numbers of employees over several years, together with the cost of managing their use, including time spent on training and monitoring, can be substantial and comparable with the costs of investing in noise control measures.

Types of ear protectors

Ear muffs are fitted over the ears in order to block the path of air-borne sound to the ear canal. They consist of four main parts:

- moulded rigid plastic cups which fit over the ears and which provide the basic sound insulation;

- sound-absorbing foam plastic lining fitted inside each cup to reduce reverberation;

- flexible plastic cushions designed to enable the cups to fit closely over the ears and establish a close seal to the wearer's head in order to minimize leakage of sound around the cups to the ear. The cushions are made out of thin, flexible plastic film, and most types are filled with foam plastic, but there are some which are filled with oil;

- an adjustable elastic, flexible headband which holds the cups in place and help the cushions to make a good seal to the head.

Although all ear muffs conform to this same basic pattern there is a variety of different cup sizes and weights. Muffs are available which fit onto hard hats.

Ear plugs are fitted into the ear canal. There are many different types, made from soft rubber, foam plastic or a special type of mineral fibre (called glass down) — note that ordinary cotton wool is not effective. In each case they are designed to completely fill the ear canal and therefore minimize the sound transmitted to the ear drum. It is therefore important that the types selected are a good fit and are inserted properly, according to manufacturer's instructions.

Canal caps consist of a pair of plastic or rubber plugs connected by a light, flexible plastic headband. They are designed to be quick and easy to fit and remove for personnel who move in and out of noisy areas frequently, such as managers and supervisors.

Specialist types

Specially developed amplitude-sensitive ear muffs are available which allow low amplitude sound, for example from normal conversation, but prevent transmission of high intensities. These are useful in situations where there are sudden, unpredictable bursts of high levels of noise.

Other types of plug are available which are individually moulded and fitted with an acoustic filter designed to ensure that the device produces more-or-less the same attenuation at all frequencies. This type of plug is used by musicians, for example, when it is necessary that the frequency spectrum of the sound being listened to, and hence its character, is preserved.

Ear muffs fitted with communication headsets are also available, so that employees can enjoy protection from high levels of machine noise and also listen to 'piped music' and receive messages from the workplace communications system.

Ear muffs fitted with active sound attenuation are available, i.e. the muffs contain a miniature microphone and loudspeaker which detect the sound waveform and provide a cancelling 'antiphase' signal.

Performance of ear protectors

The first requirement is that the ear protectors should provide sufficient noise attenuation to reduce the noise at the wearer's ear to a level that will prevent risk of noise-induced hearing loss. This obviously depends on the levels and frequency spectrum of the noise.

The performance of ear protectors is specified as a mean attenuation, measured in each of seven octave bands (from 125 Hz to 8 kHz), according to a test method specified in BSEN24869-1 (formerly BS5108), according to which the hearing thresholds of test subjects are measured with and without ear protectors, the attenuation being the difference between the two measurements. The attenuation obtained from individual test subjects will be different, because of differences in quality of fit, and the test specifies that the standard deviation from the mean shall also be specified. If the mean value of the attenuation were to be used in calculations of noise exposure then half the population of wearers would receive a lower value of protection than predicted. Therefore the HSE, in Noise Guide No. 5 suggests that an assumed protection value of attenuation of the mean value minus the standard deviation be used in such calculations of noise exposure. Assuming that the spread of attenuation values follows Gaussian statistics, 68% of the wearing population will receive the assumed level of protection. If a value of mean minus two standard deviations is used then 95% of the wearing population will receive the calculated level of protection.

In order to calculate the amount of protection afforded in any particular application it will be necessary to measure the level of noise at the wearer's ear, in octave bands. The assumed protection provided by the protector in each band is then subtracted to obtain the band level at the 'protected' ear. These levels are then A-weighted, and combined, to give the level at the protected ear, in dB(A). Ideally this should be well below 85 dB(A) and preferably below 80 or even 75 dB(A). However, it must be remembered that it is the exposure level, which depends upon duration as well as sound level, which is important, and so higher levels may be acceptable for shorter periods. The Noise at Work Regulations require that the protectors should provide sufficient attenuation to reduce exposure levels to below the Second Action Level (90 dB(A) $L_{Ep,d}$), although the First Action Level would be a better, i.e. safer, objective. The method is illustrated in the following example.

Example

The sound pressure level close to the folding machine in a printing works is 104dB(A) and the octave band spectrum of the noise is given below. Calculate the assumed protected level at the ear of an employee working near to the folder who is wearing ear protectors having the performance given in Table 4.2.

Table 4.2 Calculation of hearing protection

(1)	(2)	(3)	(4)	(5)	(6)	(7)	(8)
Octave band frequency	Octave band noise level	Mean attenuation of the ear protectors	Standard deviation of the ear protectors	Assumed protection of the ear protectors	Octave band noise level at the ear	A-weighting	A-weighted protected level
(Hz)				(dB)			
63	87	20	4	16	71	−26	45
125	90	19	3	16	74	−16	58
250	95	18	5	13	82	−9	73
500	90	18	6	12	78	−3	75
1000	99	21	4	17	82	0	82
2000	100	31	4	27	73	+1	74
4000	95	37	4	33	63	+1	63
8000	94	38	6	32	62	−1	61

The assumed protection of column 5 is given by subtracting the standard deviation of column 4 from the mean attenuation of column 3. The A-weighted protected band level of column 8 is obtained by subtracting the assumed protection value of column 5 from the band level of column 1, to give column 6, and then adding the A-weighting value of column 7. The overall protected level is obtained by combining the levels in column 8, using the rules of decibel arithmetic (see Chapter 1), to give an assumed protected level of 84dB(A). Thus for this particular application the overall protection provided in reducing the level at the ear from 104dB(A) to 84dB(A), is 20dB(A). If an assumed protection of the mean minus two standard deviations is used then the predicted level at the ear is 88dB(A), i.e. 95% of wearers will be exposed to 88dB(A) or below.

There are many different charts, graphs, nomograms, calculators and computer programs available to automate and simplify the above calculation, including those that incorporate a database of attenuation values for the different types of ear protectors which are commercially available.

Many attempts have been made to simplify the above procedure, both in terms of the need to measure the noise level and specify the performance of protectors in octave bands, and in terms of the complexity of the calculation. These have mainly centred around attempts to find one single-figure value to specify protector performance, but it is difficult to do this because both the level of the sound and the attenuation of the protectors vary so much with frequency. One such method, the HML method, has, however, been adopted in the ISO4869-2. HML stands for high, medium and low frequency, and the manufacturers provide three different performance figures to be used depending on the frequency spectrum of the noise. The noise level is measured using both the A and C frequency weighting scales, and the difference between the two readings is indicative of the type of spectrum. The H, M and L values are the predicted noise level reduction (PNR) of the hearing protector for noises with values of $L_C - L_A$ equal to –2, 2 and 10dB respectively. Where the difference $L_C - L_A$ is different from one of these three values the value of PNR is obtained by interpolation, for example by drawing a graph of PNR against $L_C - L_A$ and reading off the appropriate value of PNR from the graph.

For the noise from the folding machine in the above example the measured value of L_C is the same as the dB(A) value, i.e. 104dB, and the manufacturer's values for the ear protectors are: H 25dB, M 17dB and for L, 15dB. The interpolation is very simple in this case, and a graph is not needed, because the measured value of $L_C - L_A$, i.e. 0dB, is exactly halfway between –2 and 2dB, and so the appropriate value of PNR is exactly half way between the H and M values of 25 and 17, i.e. (25 + 17)/2 = 21 dB. This gives a predicted level at the wearer's ear of 104 – 21 = 83 dB, which in this case is 1 dB different from the prediction using the calculation method based on octave bands. Note that this method does not require octave band analysis, but it does require a sound level meter which can measure dB(C) as well as dB(A). The full method has the advantage that it is easier to select protectors for the particular application. In the above example it can easily be seen from column 6 that it is improved performance in the 1000 Hz band which is the most important if it is required to further reduce the dB(A) level at the ear.

The noise level of 104 dB(A) in the example is very high, so that without ear protectors the exposure level equivalent to the First Action Level would be reached within a few minutes (see example in Chapter 3). In such a case it is certainly necessary to perform the above calculation in order to check that the protectors being used provide sufficient protection. At lower levels, say 92 or 93 dB(A), any reputable plug or muff should provide ample protection if in good condition and fitted properly, and emphasis should be placed on providing a selection of types for the wearer to choose from in order to reduce discomfort and inconvenience to a minimum, and therefore to maximise the chances that the protectors will be worn for the entirety of the time for which they should be worn.

Sometimes it is necessary for employees to be exposed to very high noise levels, say above 110 dB(A), and the above calculations may show that neither plugs nor muffs will reduce the noise level at the ear to a low enough level. If both muffs and plugs are worn together then this may provide an increased amount of protection, but only by a few extra decibels, and it is not easy to predict the combined performance. Under these circumstances it is strongly recommended that alternative working procedures are found, and that exposure times at these levels are reduced to an absolute minimum and are strictly monitored, even with ear protectors being worn.

Other aspects of ear muff performance such as size, weight and durability are specified in BS 6344.

Selection of ear protectors

Apart from performance, other factors influencing selection are considerations of comfort, convenience and hygiene. Ear muffs are easier to fit than ear plugs, and they can be worn by almost everyone, whereas some people may have a medical condition which prevents them from wearing plugs. Ear muffs generally, but not invariably, provide higher levels of attenuation than plugs (depending upon the particular types) and this attenuation is less variable because less skill is required in fitting them properly. Ear muffs can be inconvenient, uncomfortable, hot and heavy, particularly when they have to be worn for several hours in warm and restricted spaces, and plugs will be lighter and more comfortable in such circumstances. Good hygiene is essential when ear plugs are used, and hands should always be washed before inserting or removing the plugs into the ear canal. Ear muffs are therefore preferable in dirty areas where adequate washing facilities are not available, or where they have to be frequently taken on and off because the wearer is moving into and out of ear protection zones. People who wear glasses or earrings, or who have long hair may receive a reduced amount of protection from ear muffs if the quality of fit of the seals of the muffs to the head is reduced, and there can be problems if other safety equipment has to be worn such as goggles, face masks or other respiratory equipment, although special types of muffs are available to deal with some of these situations, for example muffs attached to hard hats.

Difficulties and limitations of ear protectors

The difficulties are that ear protectors may not be worn, and even if they are worn they may not be giving the estimated degree of protection, either because they have not been fitted correctly or because they are defective in some way.

Many employees understandably do not like having to use ear protectors, particularly if they have to be worn for several hours each day. Apart from the discomfort and inconvenience several other reasons for concern are often given, including that they impair the wearer's ability to detect changes in the noise emitted by the machines they are operating, or to hear alarm signals and communications from fellow workers and the public address system. In fact the protectors reduce both the level of the background noise as well as of the wanted signal, and it has been shown that for wearers with good hearing the detection of these signals is undiminished, or even increased, but there are problems for wearers who have hearing impairment. Sometimes those already suffering from noise-induced hearing loss put forward objections to wearing ear protectors, either on the basis that they are not needed because they have 'got used to the noise', or alternatively that 'it is too late' since they already have hearing impairment. The guiding principle in such cases should be to safeguard all the more carefully the hearing that remains. It is important to counter and overcome all such concerns with a programme of training that explains the need to wear ear protectors and the consequences of not doing so.

The importance of the need to wear ear protection for the whole of the time the worker is exposed to high levels of noise cannot be overestimated. No matter how good the assumed protection provided, and this can be in the region of 20–30 dB, it will be reduced to only 3 dB if they are only worn for 50% of the time, and even if they are worn for 90% of the time the degree of protection can only be 10 dB. This is particularly important when the noise levels are very high because the exposure level increases rapidly even in a short time. At a level of 102 dB(A), for example, the Second Action Level of the Noise at Work Regulations is reached after 30 minutes, and this falls to 15 minutes at 105 dB(A) and 7.5 minutes at 108 dB(A). In these circumstances it is obvious that failure to wear protectors even for a few minutes will be harmful. It is important to explain and emphasize this degree of urgency in training sessions.

The attenuation figures provided by manufacturers are obtained from tests under standardized measurement conditions. They represent the maximum attenuation likely to be met under laboratory conditions, when protectors are new and always fitted properly. Much lower levels of protection are obtained if the protectors are not fitted properly. It is particularly important with plugs, which must always be inserted exactly according to manufacturers' instructions. Training is needed to demonstrate the proper procedure and to ensure that each employee is able to fit the plugs properly, and even then they may work loose in time. Even with ear muffs, which are much easier to fit properly, it is necessary to sweep back the hair, ensure that the cups are completely surrounding the ears, and adjust headband tension to ensure a good seal with the side of the head. It has been shown that a few minutes spent demonstrating and explaining these points leads to higher levels of attenuation.

After prolonged use plastic plugs may become inflexible, the seals of muffs may become worn or hard, or the headbands may lose their elasticity or the cups may become damaged. In all cases the degree of protection will be drastically reduced until the protectors are replaced. Training must therefore cover inspection of protectors to alert wearers to these defects.

Therefore it can be seen that if a company's hearing protection policy relies heavily on the use of ear protectors, particularly if there are high levels of noise, then for all of the reasons described above there will be some risk that employees may not be receiving the amount of protection predicted on the basis of assumed protection calculations. It is for this reason that regular audiometric monitoring is used as a check on the effectiveness of the hearing protection policy, and is the reasoning behind government regulations relating to health surveillance in noisy industries, described in Chapter 6.

Information instruction and training

Training is needed to cover the aspects indicated below.

- Why protectors should be worn, i.e. training should include an explanation of noise-induced hearing loss and its consequences, first of all in terms of risk of hearing loss and its possible effects on the individual, and also any legal and disciplinary consequences. The persuasive arguments relating to personal and social consequences of loss of hearing should be presented, and not just the more coercive approach emphasizing duties relating to the law and/or company policy.

- Where and when hearing protectors should be worn, i.e. in which areas of the workplace and when certain machines or processes are in operation. This information should also be clearly marked by signs at the entrances to all ear protection zones. Information about noise levels and noise exposure levels should be provided or made available.

- How to obtain protectors, i.e. from where and from whom in the organization.

- Introduction to a range of different types, with the opportunity to exercise personal preference regarding convenience and comfort.

- Careful instruction into correct fitting procedures for both muffs and plugs.

- Instruction about care of protectors, e.g. washing, and how to inspect to ensure they are still effective, and when to replace.

- Importance of wearing for 100% of the time in ear protection zones.

- Duties of employees under the Noise at Work Regulations, and any specific conditions of employment relating to wearing of ear protectors.

- Where to obtain further information and where to go and whom to see about any future queries and concerns.

- Training should be given to managers as well as shopfloor employees. It is particularly important, for motivational reasons, that senior managers in the company are seen to be actively involved in the hearing conservation policy, and that they always wear ear protectors in ear protection zones, even if present for only a short period of time. Provision for the training of new employees should be made, and monitoring and supervision should be used to identify when further updating and reinforcement training is needed either on a collective or on an individual basis.

- The provision of information, instruction and training is not only an important duty of employers under the Noise at Work Regulations, but also an important defence against future civil law claims from employees and former employees for compensation for loss of hearing caused by noise exposure at work, and it is therefore essential that complete records are kept of all training activities.

Hearing protectors — conclusion

The use of ear muffs and ear plugs may be a necessary last resort in order to protect employees' hearing, but their use as an interim measure must not detract from efforts to reduce noise exposure by other more acceptable and reliable means. The widespread use of ear protection by employees needs to be managed properly, is not necessarily a cheap and simple option, and has limitations and difficulties. It is essential that employees are fully informed, trained and supervised. There are legal requirements under the Noise at Work Regulations relating to the provision of ear protectors.

Summary

1 Much can be done to minimize or avoid noise problems without resorting to technical methods of noise control, by good planning and management and by good housekeeping.

2 It is useful to understand that all noise is generated either by vibrating surfaces, by impacts or by aerodynamic or hydrodynamic forces, since in each of these three cases it is possible to state some simple general principles which can be used to minimize noise production.

3 Noise travels from source to receiver by a number of paths involving either airborne or structure-borne sound transmission.

4 The four principal methods of reducing noise transmission between source and receiver are using sound insulation and sound absorption (for airborne sound) and vibration isolation and damping (for structure-borne sound).

5 Standard noise control solutions for reducing sound transmission using these four methods are: screens, enclosures, havens, attenuators and close shielding or acoustic lagging.

6 It is important to select and use the most appropriate materials for controlling noise, and this involves understanding and using both the correct terminology and the performance specification of noise control materials.

7 The control of machinery noise at source involves understanding how the noise-producing forces are being generated by the machine, and how these forces are transmitted to surfaces such as panels, covers and guards which radiate the noise. This understanding can then lead to methods of reducing the forces or of preventing their transmission to the noise-radiating surfaces.

8 Noise generation and control methods are considered for some industrial noise sources: fans and blowers, jets and exhausts, punch presses, mechanical handling of materials, printing and papermaking.

9 Active noise control involves the use of loudspeakers to produce out-of-phase acoustic signals which 'cancel' noise according to

the principle of destructive interference. The technique works best for low frequencies and has been used to reduce the noise from fans, pumps, and communication headsets.

10 Managers should specify the noise output of any new machinery. Codes and standards on emission of noise from machinery are available to inform the drafting of such specifications. It is important that purchasers and suppliers of machinery should liaise to ensure that new machinery, when installed, does not lead to unforeseen noise problems.

11 When there are several different sources of noise it is important to be able to establish priorities for noise control. This requires the diagnosis of which are the most important noise sources and transmission paths. Some methods for diagnosis are reviewed.

12 Hearing conservation policies involve carrying out surveys of noise levels and assessments of exposure of employees, implementing a programme of measures to reduce noise, the issuing of ear protectors to employees supported by a programme of information, instruction, training and supervision to ensure that the protectors are used properly, specification of noise limits for new machinery introduced into the workplace, the use of audiometric monitoring, and the effective management and review of all aspects of the policy. The commitment of senior management is an important factor in the success of such policies.

13 The use of ear muffs and ear plugs may be a necessary last resort in order to protect employees' hearing, but their use as an interim measure must not detract from efforts to reduce noise exposure by other more acceptable and reliable means. The widespread use of ear protection by employees needs to be managed properly, is not necessarily a cheap and simple option, and has limitations and difficulties. It is essential that employees are fully informed, trained and supervised. There are legal requirements under the Noise at Work Regulations relating to the provision of ear protectors.

5
Case studies

Introduction

The purpose of this chapter is to illustrate the various techniques and principles described in previous chapters. The case studies cover a wide range of topics and most of them relate to the printing and papermaking industries. The first case study describes how the problem of noise in the papermaking industry has been tackled over a number of years by one manufacturer. Case Study 3 illustrates the use of active noise control, and several others give examples of the use of standard noise control techniques, such as the use of silencers, havens and enclosures. Case Study 4 features examples of noise control at source, and numbers 7 and 8 illustrate the techniques for the assessment of workplace noise exposure levels in the printing industry. Case Study 10 describes the stages in the resolution of an environmental noise complaint about a printworks, written from the point of view of actions taken by the local authority environmental health officer dealing with the case. The last section of the chapter is not really a case study at all, but provides more detailed information on audiometric monitoring from an expert in this important subject.

In addition to the case studies described in this chapter the Health and Safety Executive has produced two volumes of noise control case studies, and many of these will be relevant to numerous different industries, including printing, papermaking and packaging. The first volume, entitled *100 Practical Applications of Noise Reduction Methods*, was published in 1983 and contained several case studies that were related to printing, papermaking and packaging. A possible criticism was that rather too many of the cases featured enclosures of one sort of another, rather than innovative examples of noise control at source. A second volume entitled *Sound Solutions*, published in 1995, contains a further sixty cases, including eight examples of enclosures. There is one example about a noise haven from the packaging industry, and one describing the partial enclosure of a small printing press. Very many others are equally relevant to printing, papermaking and packaging, including control of noise from fans, jets, air dryers, compressed air lines, compressors, pneumatic hand tools and pipes conveying pellets and granules. One example describing acoustic lagging for conveying pipes in a flour mill is equally applicable to pipes conveying plastic pellets or wastepaper or cardboard trim.

CASE STUDY 1

The control of noise in a paper mill

This case study is based on an interview with the health and safety manager of a paper mill. It is an account of how one company has tackled the problem of noise, and covers all aspects of a noise control policy. It is typical of the experience of many medium-sized manufacturing and engineering companies.

The paper industry certainly did have, and to a degree still has, a great many noise problems because of the nature of the plant that is operated. This particular company does not have the very high wet-end machine problems of dandy roll and suction boxes, but it does have, in common with virtually every other paper mill, vacuum pumps, the exhausts from which are extremely noisy. It also has slitting and cutting machines that have the trim chopped and led away by suction to some distant venting point, and the travel of the trim through the ducts can often cause high levels of noise, both from the airflow and from the impact of the small bits of paper and card on the sides of the duct walls. There are also a number of very large electric motors driving pumps and gearboxes. Careful noise measurement, including frequency analysis, made it clear that most of the noise was coming from the cooling fans at the back of these motors, and the noise problem can be alleviated either by using a different type of cooling fan, or by partially enclosing the cooling end of the motor with a cowl-type arrangement that allows free flow of air but is a barrier to the noise that is emitted. The cowl must be lined with two or three inches of sound-absorbing material.

The company also has to be concerned about noise to the external environment as well as noise affecting workers in the factory because it is sited within a rural environment. Using a noise consultant, an independent survey of the noise levels around the factory was carried out at houses, street corners and other positions at the factory boundary. These measurements are now updated on a routine basis to ensure that any modifications or any new plans introduced by the plant are not causing noise emissions to be any higher than they were, and also to see if changes have actually made reductions in noise levels.

On one occasion a newly installed vacuum pump produced noise complaints from the general public and the noise was measured and found to be nearly 20 dB(A) above the ambient noise level. Most of the noise seemed to be coming from a one inch pipe carrying exhaust away from the pump. The noise was reduced by fitting a home-made silencer based on a car exhaust. This removed the high frequency noise but this then revealed a lower frequency noise from the exhaust itself which was dealt with by designing an attenuator fitted to the exhaust line which did not produce any restrictions in flow. The home-made silencer simply consisted of substituting a section of pipe by another section that was perforated by holes drilled at about one inch intervals throughout its diameter and length and then surrounded by a glass fibre blanket to absorb sound and then enclosed by another sheet steel layer. This had the effect of acting as a combination of a reactive and absorptive silencer. This was so effective that it was impossible to detect the noise at the external measuring point.

The company initially used an acoustic consultant to carry out a comprehensive noise survey and to give advice about noise control solutions, but engineers within the company then learnt and managed to solve on their own a number of noise problems as they arose with continuing advice from the consultant as and when necessary. A local engineering firm was used to produce the noise control hardware such as attenuators and enclosures.

The company's concern with noise in the workplace started in the late 1970s but was given impetus in the mid 1980s when the Noise at Work Regulations were at the draft and consultation stages. By the time the regulations came into place the company was well on the way with its hearing conservation programme. The first stage was to educate all the personnel about noise and how it affected them, how it damaged their hearing and how that would affect their lives and their future. This policy of raising awareness and understanding of the effects of noise would inevitably provoke civil compensation claims, which in fact did happen, but these would have come anyway, and probably at a later date when the damage was more acute. These were from employees who had been working for the factory for many years and in this respect this company was no different from the majority of other large engineering factories at the time. In industry generally there were peaks in employers' liability claims for noise-induced hearing loss in the late 1980s and early 1990s very much as a result of efforts of the unions. This has now very much reduced; for example this particular company had about forty claims in the first year but it has not had a claim for the past three or four years. Maybe the large increase in claims was an inevitable consequence of the awareness campaign and possibly was an indication that this message had been successfully transmitted.

However, in addition the company took steps to determine in which parts of the factory noise levels exceeded 90 dB(A). These were made mandatory hearing protection areas where hearing protectors must be worn, and the company undertook to provide enclosures and sound havens for people and also to engineer noise out as far as possible. Also, a policy of taking noise into account when new plant and equipment was purchased was initiated so that the noise has become one of the criteria when buying new machinery. A maximum level of 85 dBA at one metre from the equipment is used as the criterion, and this ensures that further noise problems are not introduced into the factory.

When the company first started its hearing conservation programme something like 50% of the work area was in the 90 dB(A) region. Now it is less than 20%, and this has been achieved within the past 5–10 years. The noise in the plant is, on the whole, of a reasonably steady nature. There are variations, for example if a new wire is placed on a machine: then, for a day or so there will be a high frequency noise emission, but in most of the cases the noise is constant and exceptions or changes are dealt with as they arise.

The company's policy to noise, then, has three components:

- Educating everybody about the effects of noise so that they will co-operate with noise reduction measures.
- Making sure that any new plant brought into the factory is not going to increase the noise levels.
- Continuing to reduce and design out the existing noise.

Initially there were the usual problems of persuading people to use ear protection and the full gamut of excuses as to why employees could not wear the ear defenders they were given ranging from 'it's hot and sticky' to 'it makes me sterile'. These were overcome by arranging for a wide variety of protectors to be available, both muffs and plugs, so that individuals could choose which ones they wished to wear. At the start of the hearing conservation programme a campaign of twenty or so talks about the effects of noise and about wearing hearing protection was held. At that time the company employed about 430 people and over 400 attended those presentations. This effort is now much reduced and is not quite as necessary as it was.

Although persuasion has been effective in getting employees to wear hearing protection, there will inevitably be individuals who will not comply, and on occasion disciplinary procedures have been used. Nevertheless, the persuasion policy is the preferred option because it is impossible to be monitoring people all of the time. The health and safety manager will take note as he moves about the factory and if he sees someone not wearing protection he will certainly take them aside and explain and re-emphasize the need to wear hearing protection and make sure that they do. Equally, members of the workforce who have been persuaded about the importance of wearing personal hearing protection will feel quite free to challenge senior managers who enter hearing protection zones without wearing hearing protection. Having said that, he would expect his senior colleagues to set an example, which in the main they do.

The policy relating to buying-in equipment with only low noise levels extends to all plant and machinery. Where it is not possible to buy a quiet piece of equipment then noise control measures are bought with it at the same time, but suppliers of equipment are becoming more aware of noise and now use reduced noise levels of their equipment as a selling point.

Regular noise exposure assessments are carried out throughout the factories using both dosemeters and type 2 sound level meters. The health and safety manager underwent training and carries out these assessments himself. Noise surveys are carried out on areas of the factory and of individual machines. Records are kept of noise exposure assessments and of noise levels from various machines and of various areas of the plant. The company has three sound level meters, one for the safety manager, one for the production management team, and one for the trade union safety representatives so that they can also monitor noise levels for themselves as this approach gives a better involvement from employees.

An important factor in obtaining employee co-operation in reducing noise and wearing ear protection is that employees can see that measures are being taken to reduce noise as well as simply issuing ear protectors. At each machine in the mill there are noise havens and there are lots of examples where noise reductions have been carried out. An example was a new paper machine which was bought at a cost of £11 million, and many innovations in the design of this machine were introduced to reduce noise such as replacing alternate drive wheels of cylinders with plastic so that metal-to-metal contact was avoided. Another measure was to gather all the vacuum pumps and refiners that produced a high noise level into one area and separate them off by locating them inside an acoustic enclosure. This actually meant knocking down offices to extend the machine house. A series of panels on overhead runways were designed to partition off the noisy machines from the rest of the building, using thick, heavy plastic curtains. This area is not normally manned and the only time that employees will need to enter is for maintenance purposes; on those occasions ear protection must be worn. However, apart from the occasional emergency, maintenance is carried out at weekends when machines are closed down and therefore the need for employees to go into this very noisy area is minimized.

The success of the noise control policy relies heavily on shopfloor participation, including the contributions of the trade union safety representatives. This means that faults and defects in noise control equipment, such as worn seals, would usually be reported and maintained regularly.

The control of environmental noise and noise inside the factory is closely interrelated. Measures taken to reduce noise in the workplace are inevitably going to reduce emissions to the environment. Since the company started a major programme to reduce noise levels in the workplace the external noise levels have also been reduced, not by as much, but by approximately 2–3 dB(A) at the external measuring points. The motivation behind the attempt to reduce the noise is partly that organizations are being driven by the obvious good business sense of a good safety system and a good safety environment. A few years ago civil claims were a comparative rarity, but nowadays they are very much a fact of life and such civil legislation, of course, affects the company's insurance premiums which also will reduce their profits. Some insurance companies employ their own noise experts and have given advice on noise matters to companies. However, the more important motivation for reducing noise is a caring attitude within the company towards the people that it employs and to the surrounding environment. The company has been in the area for 150 years and looks forward to being in the same position for another 150, and the only way that it is going to attract and retain the right sort of people is by making sure that they are looked after, and that is why there is a relatively low employee turnover of about 2–3%.

One environmental noise complaint that did occur had in fact nothing to do with the papermaking process. It arose when the company was remaking a machine and using external building contractors who were using jack hammers at night to dig it out. The problem was solved by instructing the contractors that noisy equipment could not be used except in the day between 7am and 7pm. The company visited the complainants to apologize and to explain what was going to happen to solve the problem in future.

Environmental noise affecting nearby houses arises mainly from exhaust ventilation. Also, in the summer when factory doors are open this will increase noise. Mechanical handling from lorries is not really a problem because deliveries to and from the mill are usually in working hours. There are one or two wagons leaving the factory at 1 or 2 in the morning. Forklift trucks are used but most of the work is done externally in daylight hours when pulp products and other materials are moved for the dayshift and also during the day to anticipate the demand during the night. Therefore only in exceptional circumstances will a forklift truck be used at night.

The health and safety manager of the company becomes involved in the planning stage when any changes are to be made either in the layout of the plant or in the purchase of new equipment which might affect anything to do with health and safety and environmental emissions. An example currently under consideration is the purchase of a new cutter and, as with all other equipment, health and safety features are an integral part of the decision and noise levels are important features of this aspect.

The company policy so far has been not to use monitoring audiometry of workers. However, this policy is being reviewed and the health and safety manager is investigating the possibility of using pre-employment audiometric monitoring. The purpose of this would be to protect the company from deafness claims from employees who had received their noise dose before joining the company. Although the company does not currently employ an occupational health nurse there is possibly enough work to occupy one employed on a part-time basis. The alternative of purchasing audiometric equipment and carrying out the screening in-house is being evaluated against buying-in audiometric screening for the forty or so applicants for employment each year.

It would be difficult to quantify the benefits of the noise policy in a company like this in monetary terms, but to some extent the costs could be quantified. At the start of the company's drive to reduce noise in the mid to late 1980s about £50000 a year for three years was spent on noise reduction. This includes hearing protection, noise monitoring, and noise reduction equipment. After the initial three-year noise reduction programme the amount spent on noise control has been very much reduced, especially since the policy of buying only quiet machinery was introduced. During the initial three-year period, probably 30% of the safety manager's time was spent on noise; now this is down to about 5%. The cost of noise to the company could also be evaluated by the cost of claim settlements for which there were about forty in the first year. The amount the claimant received depended on the degree of hearing loss according to an approved scale agreed between the trade union and the company's insurer. This approach to settling claims has advantages for all concerned: the employees, the trade unions, the insurers and the company. One advantage for the trade unions and employers is that claims for individuals would not be contested on the basis of employees' previous history of noise exposure. One of the claimants, for example was a blacksmith, who also played the drums in a band.

The company was motivated to reduce noise levels by the threat of impending legislation, i.e. the Noise at Work Regulations. Also at this time the company's insurers were pressing for action against noise because anticipated hearing loss claims would have been reflected in the premiums. However, perhaps because the company introduced measures to reduce noise ahead of the regulations the HSE has never actually had a factory inspector who has imposed an improvement notice on the company and apart from the one occasion there has not been a nuisance claim. Neither has there been any occasion when planning permission has been refused because of a noise issue.

The company's attitude towards using a noise consultant is that it was extremely useful at the start of the noise reduction programme to employ such a person, first of all to take independent noise readings around the factory to satisfy neighbours that the noise readings really were independent, and secondly to give the health and safety manager guidance, information and setting him along the correct route towards noise control. In addition to the health and safety manager several of the project engineers in the company have some knowledge of noise reduction techniques. A consultant might be called in again to give advice for any major redesign and implementation. If the consultant is called in at the start of such an event his main purpose would be to bring to light problems which can best be dealt with at the design stage of the project rather than subsequently. However, over the ten years that the noise policy has been in existence a considerable body of expertise has been built up within the company so that many routine noise problems could now be solved without the use of a noise consultant. In the period preceding the introduction of the Noise at Work Regulations there were a number of industry-based regulations, but since the legislation has been introduced these initiatives seem to have stopped. Nevertheless, it is still essential to work at noise reduction; there is no one-stop solution, rather a permanent work ethic to reduce noise. Noise reduction must always feature in the considerations of the company, otherwise it would be easy to slip back.

CASE STUDY 2

The acoustic design of a new paper board machine KM8 at Stora Billerud mill in Skoghall, Sweden

— L Landstrom, Ingemanson Technology AB

The paper industry in Sweden is very much concerned with environmental issues, including noise. It produces ecological products which today are to a large extent recycled. This concern extends to the production process and work environment. Low noise and vibration levels in the workplace are important factors in establishing this favourable environmental image, and for influencing the recruitment and retention of highly qualified personnel.

This case study concerns the design of a machine for producing board for the waste liquid packaging used in the food industry. The company policy for the machine hall is 'Bright, Clean and Silent'. The project managers have set the following noise targets in terms of equivalent continuous sound pressure level L_{Aeq}:

For the board machine, on the operator's side	$L_{Aeq} = 75\,dB(A)$
For other production areas	$L_{Aeq} = 80\,dB(A)$
For noisy equipment (in limited areas)	$L_{Aeq} = 85\,dB(A)$

For the external environment, the total allowable sound power level externally from the plant is to be limited to $L_{WA} = 83\,dB(A)$.

For the external environment the target value must be guaranteed. However, for the internal environment the values are target values which suppliers are requested to meet as far as is possible. It would not be possible to demand guarantees from suppliers because they would not have complete control over how their products were going to be used. This is because there are so many other suppliers involved in the project and also because the customer may influence the way in which the supplier's product is to be used.

Therefore, a policy of purchase negotiation has been adopted into the contract, instead of guaranteed sound level values. During the months prior to signing the contract, negotiation takes place between all the suppliers and the customer's noise consultants DNV Ingemansson. During this time modifications and noise control measures are specified. Some of the noise control measures which have been adopted are given below.

In the wire section of the plant the vacuum system used to remove water from the paper web is normally a dominating noise source. Silencers have been installed on the control valves, and steam leakage points where noise is generated have been removed. Hole patterns in the suction rolls that are perforated and under vacuum have been optimized so that audible tones have been extinguished. The design of air bleeding arrangements has resulted not only in lower noise levels but also in a better solid content in the paper. Modifications to the suction box have also been made.

In the press section of the plant, machine noise is created by a shoe press driven by built-in gears. Noise reductions of 4 dB(A) have been achieved by specifying extra-high precision for the manufacture of the gears and modifications to the design of the shape of the gear teeth. The steel frame of a machine has been damped by viscoelastic damping cassettes welded to sections of the frame.

Modifications to the dryer hood have also produced noise reductions.

Board coating is accomplished using blow boxes of the single type, i.e. paper drying is attained with air blown from one side only. Modifications to this system, developed by the noise consultants and the supplier working together, have achieved a 5–8 dB reduction in noise generated in separate one-third octave bands, and in addition the blow capacity has been increased by approximately 5%. This has been achieved by installing a flow resistance in the assembly box preceding the nozzles so that the turbulent flow has been made more laminar, and in addition the nozzle length has been extended.

The noise outputs from all sources in the plant are entered into a computer program that predicts noise levels throughout the various areas of the plant.

The plant is not yet in operation, but six months before the start-up date noise targets have been met in 75% of the areas. Only when the plant is fully commissioned will it be known whether all of the targets have been met, but even so, on the basis of what has already been achieved it is quite clear that the KM8 machine will be one of the quietest paper board machines ever built.

Acknowledgement
This case study has been provided by L Landstrom of Ingemansson Technology AB, Goteborg, Sweden. It is based on a paper presented at the Internoise 96 Conference, Liverpool, 1996: L Landstrom, Acoustic design of a new paper board machine KM8 at Stora Billerud Skoghallsverken, *Proc. Internoise* 96, 449–452.

CASE STUDY 3

Active control of noise from vacuum pumps

— *Digisonix, Inc.*

Vacuum pumps are widely used in the pulp and papermaking industries. The pumps are used to draw water via felt filters from paper slurry. Often, many vacuum pumps are exhausted to a common exhaust manifold. High levels of noise are caused both inside the mill and outside as a result of noise radiating from exhaust stacks. The use of passive, i.e. absorptive-type silencers, in this situation can be difficult primarily because the noise is dominated by low frequencies. Often, too, the noise is tonal and frequencies are determined by the number of pump blades and the rotation rate of the motor. In addition there are harmonics at multiple higher frequencies. Added to that, the exhaust gas is generally corrosive, saturated with water vapour and often contains solid debris that may coagulate on the surface of any silencers and lead to blockage. Passive silencers may also require additional energy because of pressure loss in the system caused by the introduction of the silencers. Therefore, this is an ideal application of active noise control.

In the first example two sets of pumps on either side of the plant facing a residential neighbourhood are connected to a manifold and exhaust stack. The noise emitted by these stacks is dominated by pure tones, one at 120 Hz and the other at 240 Hz. These were causing objections in neighbouring homes at considerable distance — up to 1.5 miles or more — especially at nighttime. Figure 5.1 shows active noise control components on an 18 inch discharge pipe between the vacuum pumps and an exhaust stack. Figure 5.2 shows the noise reduction achieved. A reduction of 37 dB in a 120 Hz primary tone was achieved.

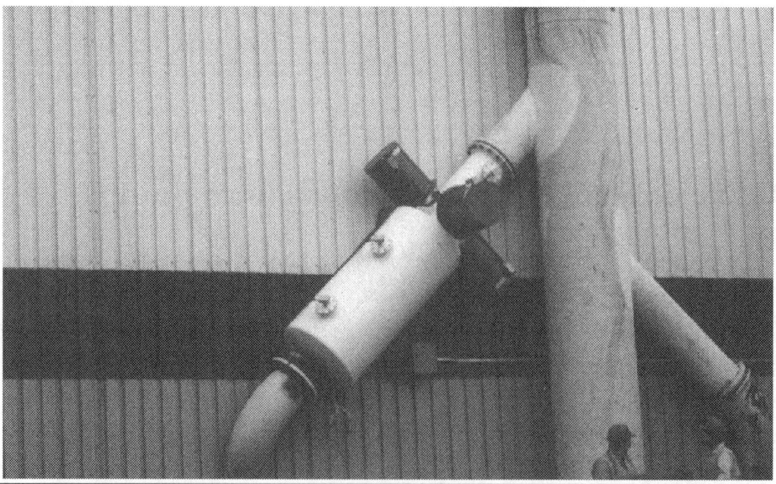

Figure 5.1 Active noise control components are shown on an 18″ discharge pipe between vacuum pumps and an exhaust stack
Source: reproduced courtesy of Digisonix, Inc.

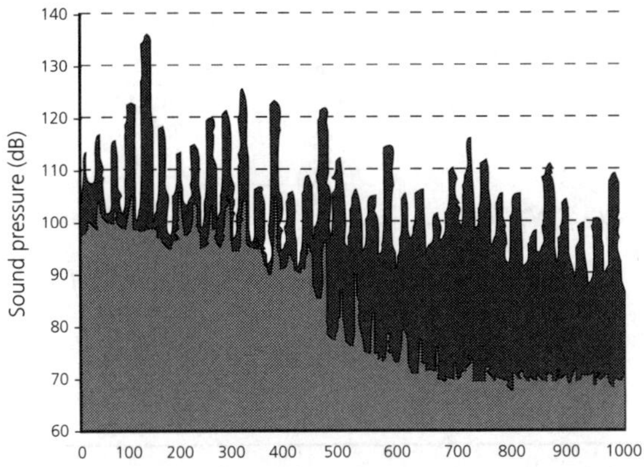

Figure 5.2 Narrowband plot of vacuum pump noise reduction measured at the exhaust stack
Source: reproduced courtesy of Digisonix, Inc.

In the second application eight vacuum pumps were connected to a common manifold and produced complaints of an annoying low frequency rumble. Figure 5.3 shows a narrowband spectrum of the noise measured close to the stack discharge. There were two dominant pure tones at 89 Hz and 93 Hz and the level of these tones varied by up to 10 dB as a result of interference between the noise from the different pumps. Nearby residents found the result beat frequency particularly annoying. An active noise control system shown in Figure 5.4 reduced the noise of the pure tones by 20 dB which was sufficient to render the noise from the stacks acceptable to the local residents. The active noise control unit was mounted outside the airstream and therefore did not produce any back pressure and its components were protected from a hostile stack environment. Microphones mounted on the stack send primary and residual noise signals to the controller that then drives a number of loudspeakers to produce the noise cancelling energy. Since this signal processing system is adaptive it is able to respond to changes to the frequency and amplitude of the noise caused by changes in pump speed, temperature, moisture and rate of flow, and also to changes in characteristics of the loudspeakers or the microphones. A controller is self-calibrating and will remain on-line during pump shutdowns.

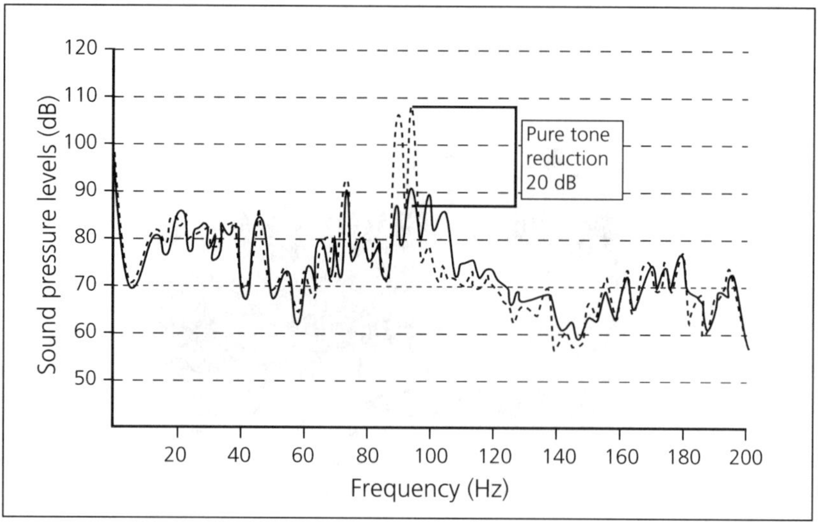

Figure 5.3 A narrowband spectrum of the noise measured close to the stack discharge
Source: reproduced courtesy of Digisonix, Industries Inc.

Figure 5.4 A 52″ diameter exhaust stack
Source: reproduced courtesy of Digisonix, Industries Inc.

Acknowledgement
This case study has been provided by Digisonix, Nelson Industries, Inc, 8401 Murphy Drive, WI 53562, USA. Tel 608 836 3999.

CASE STUDY 4

Examples of noise control at source

— *The Industrial Noise and Vibration Centre*

Case A: Printing press

Problem
A Roland RDK printing press was generating noise levels of up to 95 dB(A) at typical operator positions, requiring the mandatory use of hearing protection. Enclosure was ruled out as a potential treatment for reasons of both cost and access.

Diagnosis
The various noise sources on the press were diagnosed and then ranked. The dominant source was found to be air noise from the second print-head air-drum. Additional sources included product-radiated noise, suction system and drying-head noise. Frequency analysis showed most of the noise energy to be at high frequencies (1000 Hz and above), i.e. directional. This indicated that acoustic close shielding would be effective.

Solution
A number of close shields were designed for the machine in conjunction with the operators, including modifications to existing guarding and machine cladding. Once implemented, the modifications reduced the noise level at the noisiest occasional operator position from 95 dB(A)L_{eq} down to 83.5 dB(A)L_{eq}, a reduction of 11.5 dB(A) as shown in Figure 5.5.

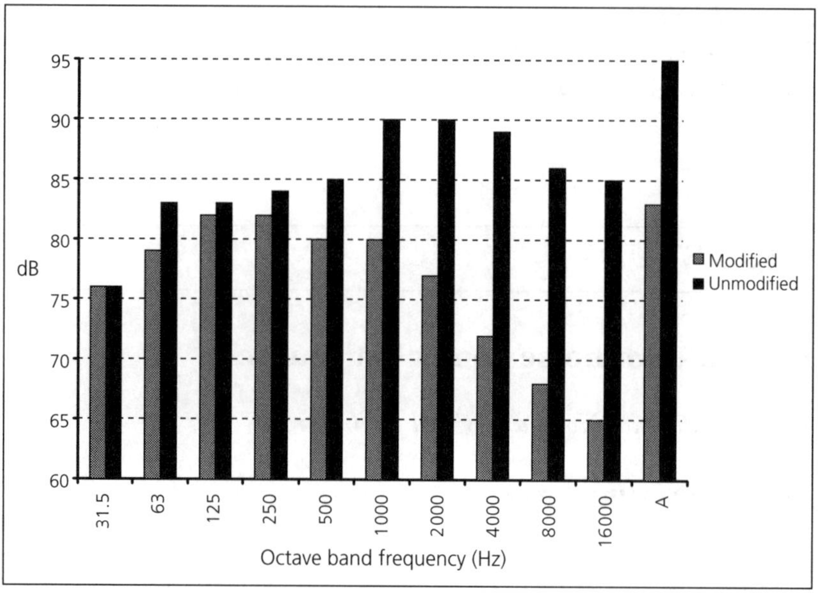

Figure 5.5 RDK printing press noise reduction
Source: reproduced courtesy of the Industrial Noise and Vibration Centre

The highest machine noise level at 1 metre was 83.5dB(A) rising to a maximum of 85.5dB(A) at one location close-in. Operators considered that the modifications had little effect on normal access. The nature of the modifications and the fact that they were implemented in-house made for a very cost-effective treatment.

Other applications

This solution demonstrates the large and highly cost-effective noise reductions that can sometimes be achieved by modifying existing machine guards and components. Accurate initial diagnosis and an understanding of the sources and noise paths involved coupled with operator involvement in the design can lead to simple, low-cost solutions to a wide range of noise problems.

Case B: Cyclone separators

Problem

The company manufactures PVC granules. These are transported along each production line by air from a fan, terminating in a cyclone separator. The arrangement is typical of the transport systems commonly found in industry. Within each cyclone, the air exhausts through a perforated steel tube. This acts as a sieve, avoiding the small plastic wastage that would otherwise occur.

The cyclones were producing a very shrill, penetrating whistle (at 4975 Hz). This dominated the entire production area. As well as being extremely annoying, the whistle produced 110 dB(A), posing a very high risk of hearing loss.

Diagnosis

Based on previous extensive experience it was diagnosed that the whistle was generated by a flow-induced acoustic resonance. This was confirmed by inserting a 10 inch square piece of cardboard into the cyclone. The cardboard broke up the aerodynamic resonance and totally eliminated the whistle — a reduction of 50 dB (see Figure 5.6). The overall noise fell by 25 dB(A) to 85 dB(A).

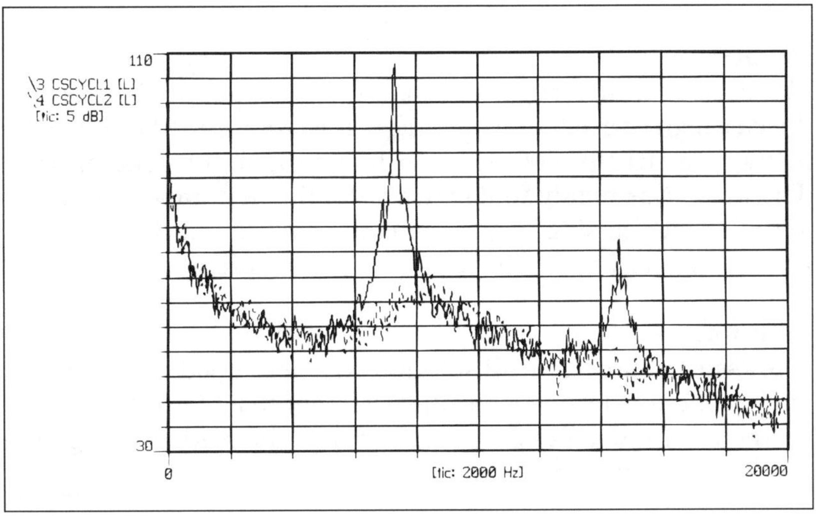

Figure 5.6 Graph showing the effect of a technique to reduce whistle generated by flow-induced acoustic resonance
Source: reproduced courtesy of the Industrial Noise and Vibration Centre

Solution

The production version of the solution comprised a steel plate fixed inside each cyclone. The geometry of each plate was carefully 'tuned' to provide maximum performance, matching that of the prototype. Since each steel plate costs less than 50 pence, for a 50 dB noise reduction this represents an extremely cost-effective noise reduction solution. Even a very expensive, high performance enclosure built around the cyclones cannot normally provide such a high noise reduction.

Other applications

Noise associated with the transport of materials is a common problem in industry, and the fans are often an important contributor. Over the years, a number of elegant and inexpensive engineering solutions both for fans and for complete transport systems have been developed.

Case C: Boiler air supply fans

Problem

The centrifugal fans supplying combustion air to three boilers produced a high level of noise that was readily transmitted through the lightweight structure of the boiler house to the surrounding area. The noise was highly tonal with a dominant component at the 490 Hz blade-passing frequency; complaints about the noise had been received from the residents of adjoining properties.

Solution

A low-cost source control solution was developed. The existing fan was modified using a retrofit treatment that alters the internal geometry of the fan casing. This reduced the blade-passing tone by 22 dB as shown in Figure 5.7.

This approach provided a highly effective solution at substantially lower cost than conventional silencing without requiring major changes to the installation or reducing space for maintenance access in the boiler house.

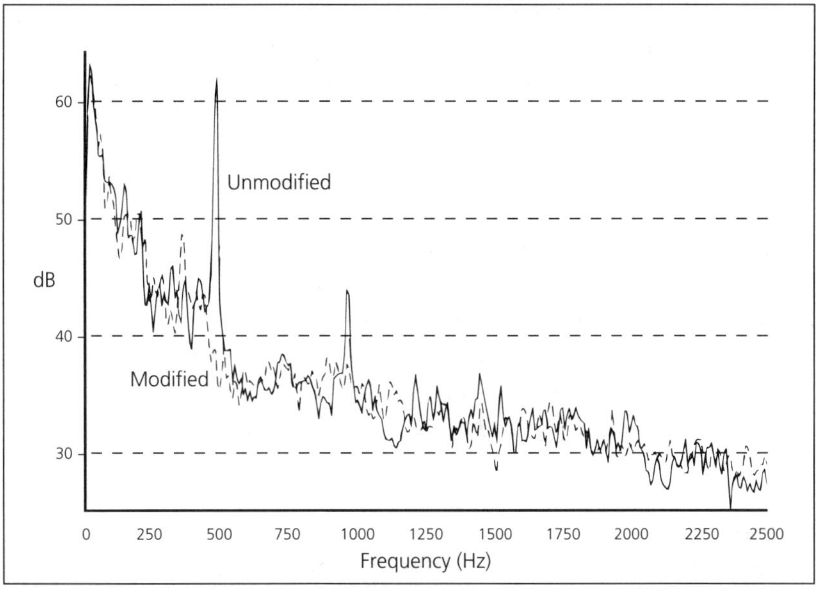

Figure 5.7 Graph showing the effect of a technique to reduce noise emitted by centrifugal fans with dominant component of 490 Hz
Source: reproduced courtesy of the Industrial Noise and Vibration Centre

Other applications

Low frequency fan tones (at blade pass and harmonics) are a common source of industrial and environmental noise, for example in material transport systems. Conventional silencers are inefficient at low frequencies and reduce both tonal and broadband noise equally, so that the tone may still remain audible above the general fan noise. Internal fan modifications that are tone specific are simple and low cost (as little as £100 to manufacture and fit). They are also useful for applications where conventional sound-absorbing materials might cause hygiene problems or where expensive structural modifications (for example to roofs) would be required to fit conventional silencers.

Case D: Dryer oven

Problem

Typical noise levels generated by the dryer ovens used in malting (grain) were 92 dB(A). This increased to 95 dB(A) close to each of the individual burners that were the dominant noise sources. Moreover, the burners also generated high amplitude tones at low frequencies which were highly irritating. A further complication was the fact that hygiene considerations ruled out the use of acoustic absorbent.

Diagnosis

Analysis of the noise showed that the low frequency boom that dominated the burner noise was a tone at 82 Hz. As it occurred only at low firing this was diagnosed as a flame instability that developed into an oscillation at the half-wavelength standing wave frequency of the combustion tube. The precise cause of this flame instability was determined to be an excessively weak mixture at low firing.

Solution

A motor-controlled valve usually used for controlling weld fume extraction was adapted and fitted to the combustion fan intake. Triggered by a microswitch, this was used to reduce the air-flow at low loads to improve the combustion characteristics. This reduced the low frequency tone by 21 dB and the overall noise level by 8 dB(A) to well below 90 dB(A), as shown in Figure 5.8. The bought-in units were hygenic, had no effect on normal operation, cost £98 per burner (at 1992 prices) and could be retro fitted during normal plant use.

Other applications

Poor combustion conditions are a common cause of high noise levels from burners, particularly at low frequencies. In this case the problem was occupational noise. However, environmental noise is often an issue owing to the low frequency tonal nature of the sound. Accurate diagnosis and engineering experience can result in low-cost and elegant solutions to noise problems that would be difficult to treat using traditional techniques.

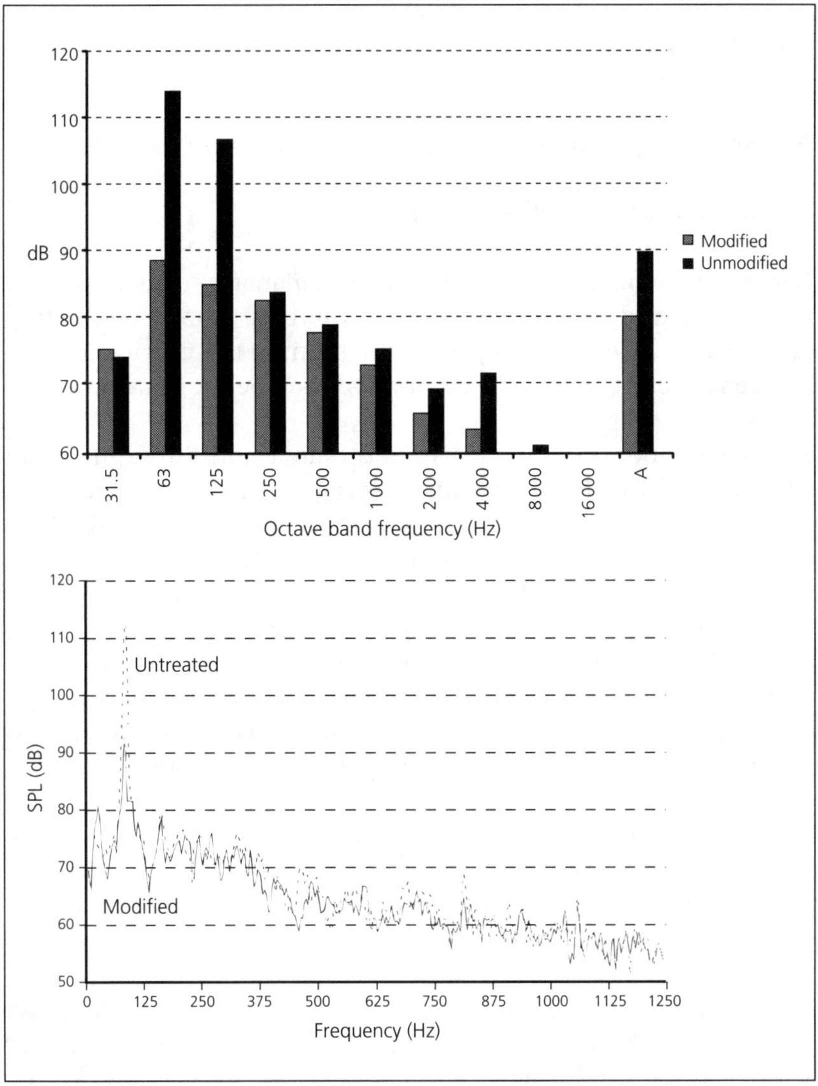

Figure 5.8 Drier oven burner noise reduction
Source: reproduced courtesy of the Industrial Noise and Vibration Centre

Acknowledgement
These case studies have been provided by the Industrial Noise and Vibration Centre, Burnham House, 267 Farnham Road, Slough, Berkshire SL2 1HA. Tel 01753 570044/530414.

CASE STUDY 5

Noise control in the corrugated board industry

— *Mr R Hobbs, Noise Reduction Ltd*

Noise in the corrugated board industry emanates mainly from the machinery and its interaction with the board once converting takes place. The main culprit in the plant is the corrugator and this generates high noise levels at all of the operator positions.

At the wet end of the plant where the liner and fluting medium are prepared for the roll stands/splicers, the area noise levels are dominated by the single facer. This machine corrugates the fluting medium and combines the liner to create single face. There are numerous types of facer and these can be simple with a fixed roll system, integrated dual roll systems or cartridge dual facers. Most of the facers produce noise levels of between 100 and 120 dB(A), although for some modern types with a new design and integrated noise control package it is between 90 and 100 dB(A), depending on speed, paper and installation.

The noise from the glue machine and double backer is in the range 90–100 dB(A) with the older heated beds very similar. Some more recent types, and the new low-crush systems, produce noise levels nearer to 90 dB(A).

The order change knife and the main chop unit are between 90 and 100 dB(A). The later generation slitter scorers are producing 100 dB(A) level at the higher speeds. These are located towards the dry end of the process where the new machines have fully automated computer-controlled stackers running at high speed, whereas the older, slower machines have hand take-off and stacking.

Modern installations have a computer control room at the dry end of the process which runs the machine, including order input, on line, diagnostic fault-finding/rectification and a quality control laboratory making this the nerve centre of the plant. Some box plants stop here and supply the cut sheets to the converters; others convey the stacks of board to the converting sections where the boards are cut, scored, printed, folded, glued and banded for despatch. The machinery ranges from a simple creaser or slitter to folder gluers, rotary die cutter or complete printer/slitter, folder gluers, depending on the type of box. The product can be a single plain box, one-colour flexo, to high colour photographic quality, with a varnished finish for point-of-sale display packaging.

The noise levels in the converting areas are generally between 90 and 95 dB(A) depending on machine type, density and building construction. One noise source that is common to the community and the corrugator is the waste system. The noise is usually from fan drone and from the chopper conveyor system piped from the machines to the cyclone/bailer. Traditionally, overhead tube systems have been popular; however, modern underfloor belt and pneumatic systems have been recently introduced.

The new plants are high volume, high quality, fully automated pull–pull systems driven by the 'customer's order'. Generally, over the past 20 years noise levels have increased as the speed and sophistication of the plants have increased; however, manning levels have decreased. In the past 2–3 years new machinery has had noise control integrated at its conception; however, it is difficult to manufacture machines of this power and size that will be below 85 dB(A) in the vicinity of the operator, and noise levels below this are unlikely. Zoning will help the control of noise, dust and fumes in the future.

Community noise from a cyclone and ancillary equipment

The project followed the traditional procedure with qualified and experienced noise control engineers initially conducting a community noise study around the sites after 11 pm to establish the extent of the nuisance and the major noise sources. Specific plant operating conditions were simulated with the offending items running in isolation, thus allowing the extent of each necessary acoustic treatment to be determined. The background level was established without the plant running.

From these data a report for the management was compiled exploring the feasibility of various engineering and operating procedures, with their associated costs. The selected solutions were detailed and submitted to the relevant local authorities and a suitable noise level was agreed that would satisfy the local authority nighttime noise criteria.

The solution for the plant was a combination of new equipment, with a positional change for the waste system and palliative measures for the single facers, dry-end equipment, corrugator bay roof, access doors and the plant ventilation systems.

The new cyclone body was fitted with additional damping during its manufacture and the transfer fans were fitted into acoustic enclosures. Six metre long in-line silencing for the waste/transfer fans was incorporated in the new duct runs to reduce aerodynamic noise, with additional damping and/or acoustic lagging being added to the appropriate bends to further reduce the trim impact noise.

Noise refuges

Noise refuges are used when it is easier to treat the operators than the machinery. At the take-off end of the corrugator the noise levels are between 90 and 100dB(A). The refuge can reduce these levels by up to 30dB(A).

Refuges are built as a control centre for the whole corrugator. A modern refuge is designed as a fully air-conditioned enclosure, consisting of double-skin acoustic panels that incorporate acoustic glazing to give good all round visibility into the production areas. Internally the refuge is finished to office standards, i.e. with antistatic tiled floors and acoustically absorbent ceiling and walls.

Fans

Fans exist in just about all industries. There are basically two fan types: the axial fan is normally used for air movement and the centrifugal fan is used for both air and product movement. In the corrugated board and folding carton industry, fans are used as conveying systems for cardboard scrap. Here the fans perform three functions: (1) to suck in the scrap, (2) to chop up the scrap, and (3) to convey it to the installation via ductwork where the waste is collected in a cyclone. Although easily treated they give rise to both on-plant noise and community noise problems, whether vented direct to atmosphere or via a cyclone.

The main problem of the centrifugal fan design is that it produces a pure tone at blade-passing frequency which is usually in the 125–250 Hz band. This type of noise spectrum is usually more difficult to attenuate, and may become important when considering community noise problems, where background noise levels could be approximately 30–40 dB(A).

There are three noisy areas: (1) the fan inlet, (2) noise from the fan casing, due to impact with the chopped-up scrap, and (3) airborne noise at the fan outlet. In order to deal with these a silencer is fitted on the inlet, a close-fitting enclosure is fitted around the fan body, and the distribution ductwork is usually fitted with acoustic lagging for 3–4 metres downstream of the fan. If the fan is vented direct to atmosphere a silencer fitted to the outlet will be needed, or damping/acoustic lagging treatment to the cyclone, if fitted, as discussed earlier.

Enclosures for the control of noise from single facers

Ear muffs and plugs can give good protection, and when fitted with a communication system can offer a reasonable compromise. However, the necessary back-up services of maintenance, hearing tests, supervision and replacement, sometimes four times daily, make the potential costs worthy of careful investigation.

A properly designed and proven acoustic enclosure, although initially more expensive than the issue of ear protectors, gives rise to other benefits and offers the possibility of a good working environment in which board of high quality can be repeatedly produced.

Acoustic enclosures have been sucessfully used on single facers for more than twenty years and during the past few years the new type of fingerless facers has demanded greater achievements from the environmental engineers. Acoustic enclosures were introduced primarily to provide hearing protection for the operators and noise reduction for the staff in adjoining areas and sometimes for local residents. Many board plants have working environmental noise levels of less than 85 dB(A).

Additional benefits of acoustic enclosures

The second function of the acoustic enclosure is to control the temperature, fumes and dust. Prior to the introduction of these enclosures it was difficult to see down a corrugator bay because of the fog.

Efficient extract ventilation systems have been fitted for these enclosures to control the plant fog and to reduce the cleaning requirements. This has saved the replacement of many roofs due to corrosion, which is much reduced. The systems allow for the temperature to be controlled, and to a lesser degree the humidity, for both winter and summer conditions, and this provides a microenvironment in which the quality of the board may be controlled. It also provides an improved working environment around the single facers in which the crews can communicate with each other without difficulty, and work efficiently.

Acknowledgement

This case study has been provided by Mr R Hobbs, Noise Reduction Ltd, Phoenix Park, Chickenhall Lane, Eastleigh, Hampshire SO50 6RP. Tel. 01703 611611.

CASE STUDY 6

Noise control in the production of sheet plastic film

— *Mr D Bull, dB Acoustics*

The purpose of this case study is to demonstrate what can be achieved on an in-house basis by an engineer who has been properly trained in noise control, applying more-or-less standard principles and techniques in a systematic and persistent manner.

The process starts with plastic granules which are heated, injection moulded and extruded to produce sheets of plastic film. Reject material is recycled through a granulator.

The main noise sources are many different fans, the granulators, jet noise from discharges of cooling air, and noise radiated from large-diameter pipes conveying granules.

The case study concerns a factory where the average overall factory noise was reduced from 100dB(A) to below 85dB(A). Apart from in a small number of areas nobody on the factory floor now has to wear ear protectors. Figure 5.9 shows the layout of one part of the factory and lists ten measures that were introduced to achieve the noise reduction.

The reduction was achieved by one of the company's own engineers who had attended a training course in the measurement and control of noise. The starting point is careful measurement of existing noise levels in all parts of the factory. A noise map, giving dB(A) contours, resulting from such measurements for another part of the factory is shown in Figure 5.10. This was used to establish priorities for noise control action, on a step-by-step basis, which in this case included enclosures around noisy machines, a noise haven, replacement of old, noisy equipment by quieter plant, in-line silencers to air blowers, and the fitting of better quality gears to some machines.

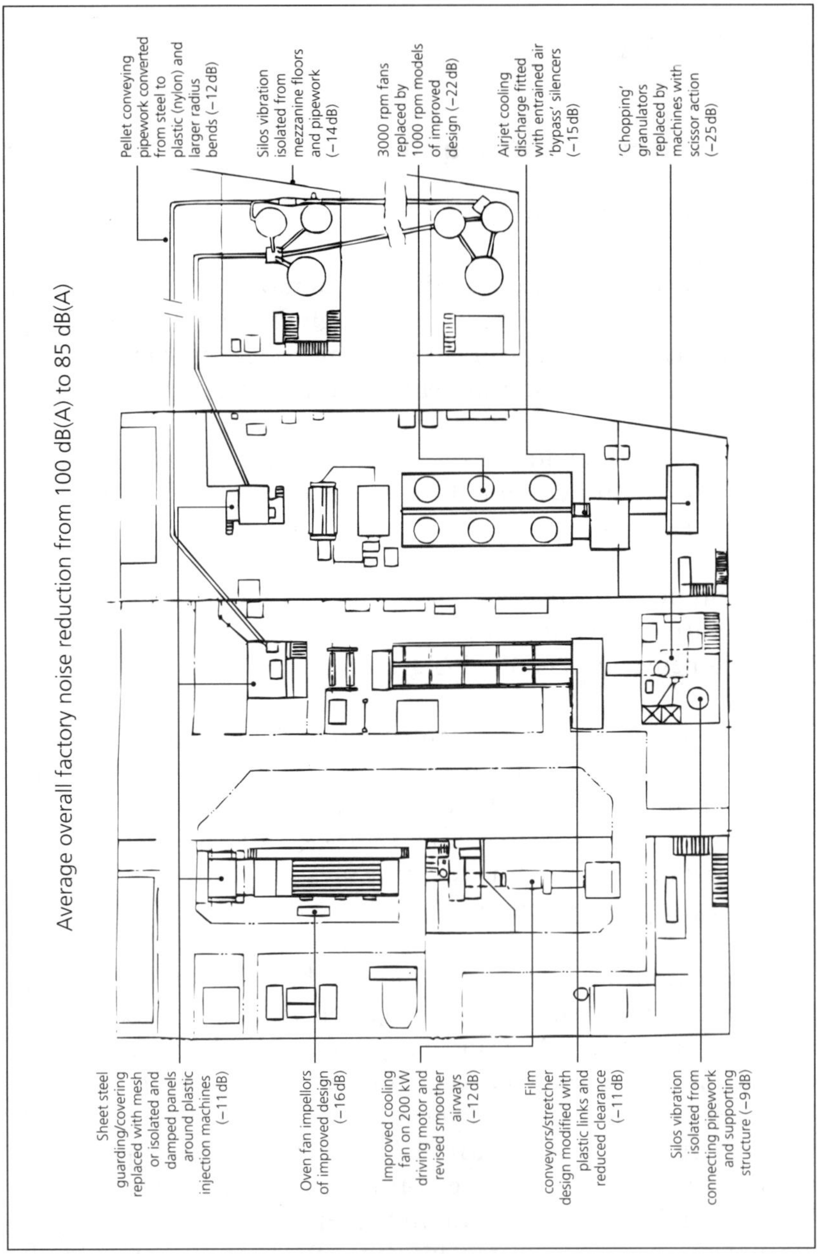

Figure 5.9 Factory layout showing different noise reduction measures
Source: reproduced courtesy of dB Acoustics

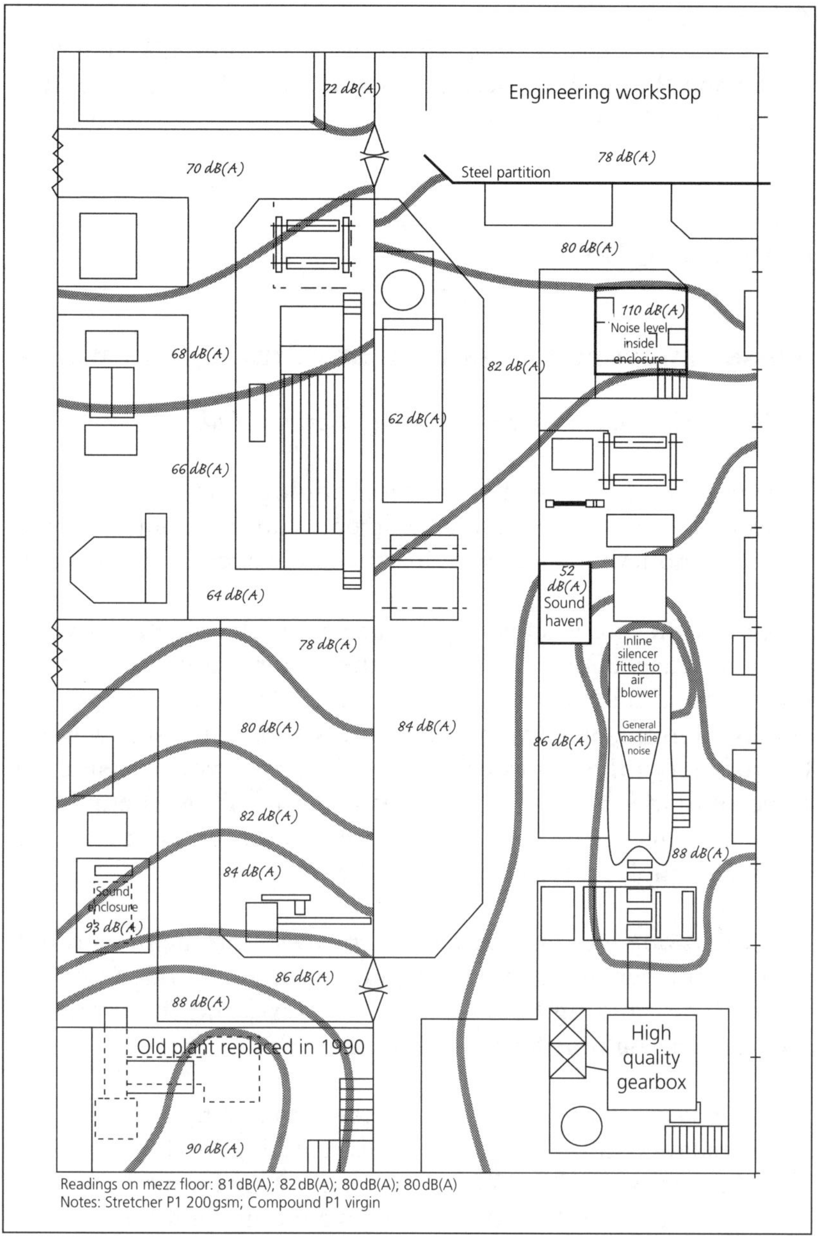

Figure 5.10 Noise map showing dB(A) contours resulting from measurements for another part of the factory
Source: reproduced courtesy of dB Acoustics

Acknowledgement
This case study has been provided by Mr D Bull, dB Acoustics, 25 Albany Road, West Bergholt, Colchester, Essex, CO6 3LB. Tel. 01206 241684.

CASE STUDY 7

Noise exposure assessment at a small print works

— *Mr A Watson, Acoustic Consultancy Services Ltd*

This case study illustrates the methodology for carrying out a fairly simple noise exposure assessment, and the complementary use of sound level meters and dosemeters in such an assessment.

A plan of the site is shown in Figure 5.11. A initial brief visual and aural inspection revealed that the major source of noise was the printing machine in the press room. There are ten persons employed in the press room: six printers and four casual workers. Up to thirty other workers are employed to work outside but adjacent to the press room, on a casual basis. All other employees work in offices remote from the press room or in other quiet areas. All employees have access to the press room.

The works operates on four days each week, and the press is only running for part of each day, depending upon workload, which varies. The working hours for the printers, and the estimated average running time for the press are:

Mondays 08.00–14.00	press not running
Tuesdays 09.00–19.00	press running for 3.5 hours
Wednesdays 11.00–23.00	press running for 6.5 hours
Thursdays 09.00–18.00	press running for 4 hours

Working hours for casual employees vary with print runs but is usually less than for the printers.

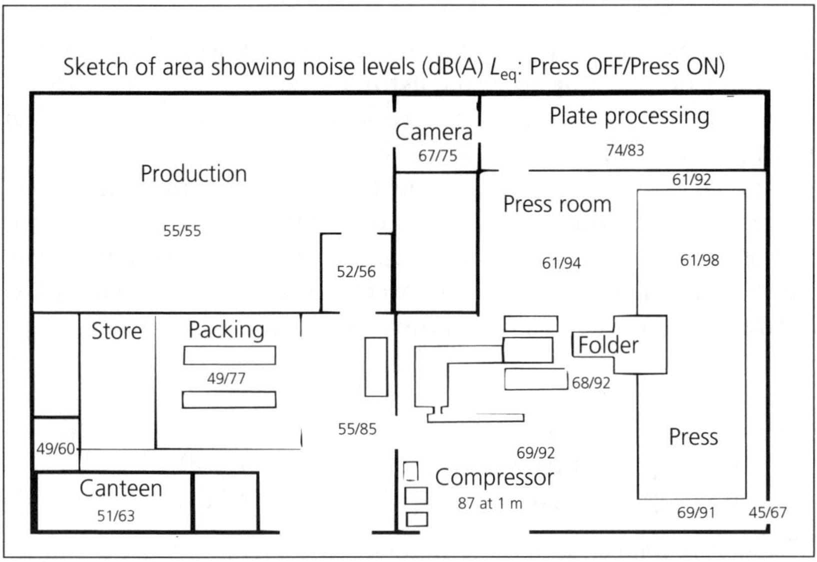

Figure 5.11 Site plan showing noise levels in print works
Source: reproduced courtesy of Acoustic Consultancy Services Ltd.

A survey of noise levels in all areas of the works was carried out using a type 1 integrating sound level meter which also had the capability to measure peak noise levels and in octave bands. The meter, which carried current calibration certificates from an accredited laboratory, was calibrated satisfactorily before and after the measurements and was used in accordance with manufacturer's instructions. Short period L_{Aeq} measurements, sufficient to give a representative sample of the noise level (of about three minutes) were taken both when the press was operating and when it was silent. The results are given in Figure 5.11, and they confirm that it is only in the press room that sound pressure levels exceed 90 dB(A) when the press is running, ranging from 87 dB(A) to 98 dB(A). The highest levels are close to the press where access is required by the printers during normal print runs. The casual employees work near to the folder and sometimes outside the press room in the adjacent packing area.

The personal daily noise exposure level, $L_{Ep,d}$ of employees depends upon whereabouts in the press room they are working, and for how long. It is obvious, however, that the printers and possibly also the casual workers could be exposed above the First, if not the Second Action Level of the Noise at Work Regulations. It would be possible to make estimates of the $L_{Ep,d}$ for various combinations of sound pressure level and exposure duration using either the formula or the nomogram described in Chapter 1. In fact this was not necessary because the sound level meter readings were supplemented by fitting dosemeters to two of the printers and to two of the casual employees working in the press room. The measurements were carried out on a Thursday, between 09.00 and 17.00 and the results were as follows:

Printer no. 1 L_{Aeq}	= 94.7 dB(A)
Printer no. 2 L_{Aeq}	= 94.3 dB(A)
Casual operator no.1 (at folder) L_{Aeq}	= 88.2 dB(A)
Casual operator No.2 L_{Aeq}	= 88.6 dB(A)

These were data logging dosemeters, so as well as giving the single-figure overall L_{Aeq} for the measurement period they stored the values of each individual one minute L_{Aeq} occurring throughout the measurement period. These values are plotted in Figure 5.12 for casual operator no. 2. The times when the press was running, for which the dosemeter reading was 94 dB(A) approximately, can be clearly seen from the graph: 11.05 to 11.40, 13.20 to 13.40, 14.50 to 15.55, and 16.03 to 17.00. This is a total duration of approximately 4 hours, at which the noise level from the graph was approximately 94 dB(A), thus giving good confirmation of the sound level meter readings, and of the estimated press running time.

It should be noted that the L_{Aeq} values measured using the dosemeters (95 dB(A) for the printers and 89 dB(A) for the casual workers) result from four hours with the press operating and four hours at much lower levels of exposure when the press is silent. It is thus possible to conclude that the L_{Aeq} values whilst the press is in operation will be 3 dB higher, i.e. 98 and 91 dB(A) respectively. From these data it is possible to estimate $L_{Ep,d}$ values for each day, assuming press operating times given earlier:

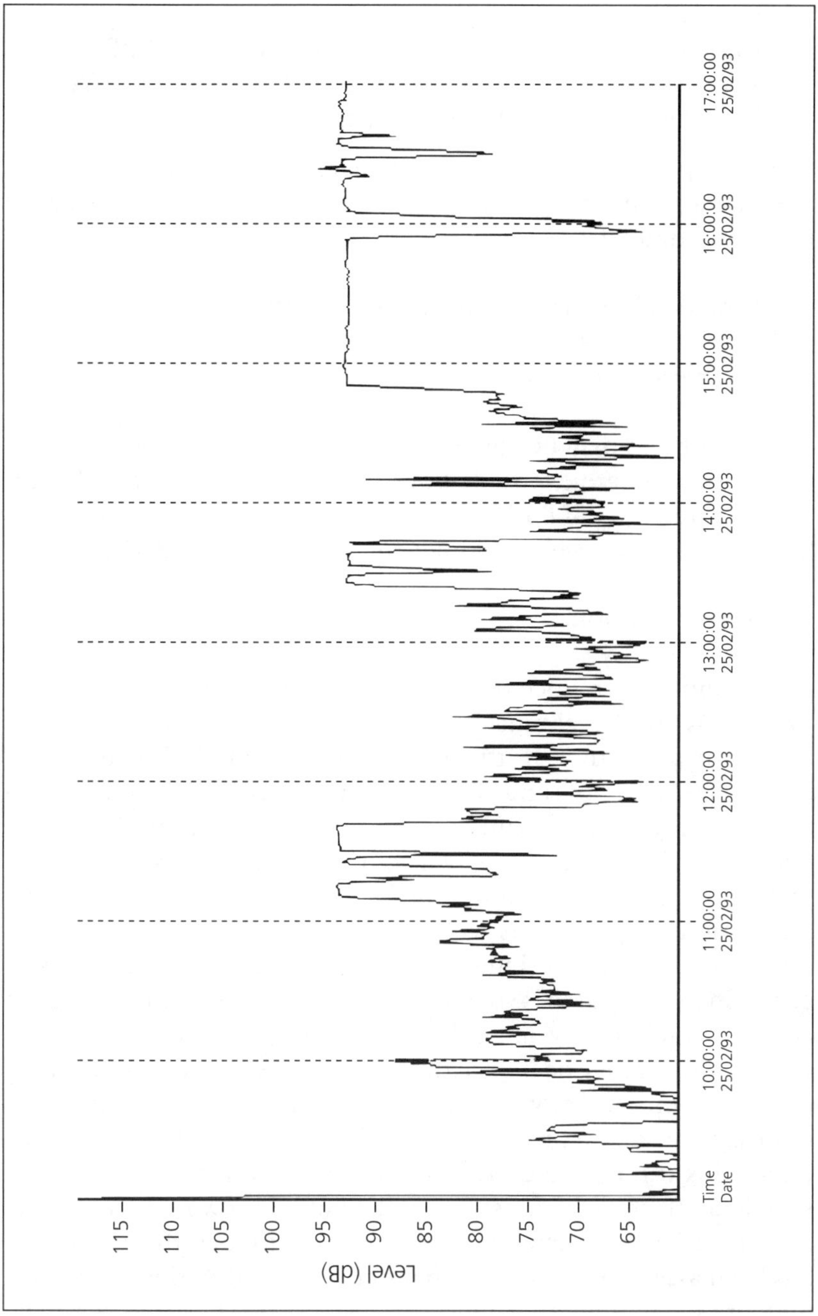

Figure 5.12 Noise levels for casual operator No. 2 taken from data logging dosemeters
Source: reproduced courtesy of Acoustic Consultancy Services Ltd.

Monday	below 75 dB(A)
Tuesday	printers 95 dB(A), casual workers 89 dB(A)
Wednesday	printers 97 dB(A), casual workers 91 dB(A)
Thursday	printers 95 dB(A), casual workers 89 dB(A)

It is also possible to estimate the level averaged over a normal five-day working week of 40 hours, assuming that the press runs for a total time of 14 hours:

printers 93 dB(A), casual workers 88 dB(A)

Assessment of noise exposure

Although there may be some day-to-day variations it is clear that the six printers are exposed above the Second Action Level, with an estimated $L_{Ep,d}$ of 93 dB(A), and the four casual workers above the First Action Level, with an estimated $L_{Ep,d}$ of 88 dB(A).

Recommendations

A programme to reduce the exposure of the six printers below the Second Action Level must be produced, by means other than the use of ear protectors. If it is not reasonably practicable to do this immediately, suitable and effective ear protection must be issued to these employees and training given to inform them of the risk of damage to their hearing, to instruct them in the use of ear protectors, and of their duties under the Noise at Work Regulations. The Regulations require areas with employees exposed to the Second Action Level to be designated ear protection zones and marked accordingly. If an area is so marked then all employees entering the zone are required to wear ear protection irrespective of the duration of their visit. It may be impracticable to create a zone within part of the press room, and more sensible to insist that the entire press room be designated an ear protection zone, but only when the press is running. This can be achieved using illuminated notices that can be switched off when the press is switched off. This would require the casual workers to wear ear protection even though their exposure has been assessed as less than that of the Second Action level. This measure seems advisable, however, because it is possible that they, or indeed any other employee could, under unusual circumstances, spend sufficient time in the area close to the press to be exposed above the Second Action Level. Therefore the programme of training should be extended to the casual workers and to all employees who are likely to enter the press room whilst the press is running.

Although it may not be practicable to reduce noise levels or noise exposure levels by operational methods or by engineering noise control at the moment, it is important that the effects of noise exposure of employees is taken into account when planning and before implementing any changes to working arrangements, or before introducing any new plant into the workplace.

Acknowledgement
This case study has been provided by Mr A Watson, Acoustic Consultancy Services Ltd, 2 Belhaven Terrace Lane, Glasgow G12 9LZ. Tel. 0141 339 7536.

CASE STUDY 8

Noise exposure assessment in a large printing press

— *Mr D Bull, dB Acoustics*

This case study illustrates that even with noise control measures in place, in this case an acoustic enclosure, it is still necessary to carefully monitor the exposure of employees.

There are three printing presses. Each is a large two-storey structure approximately 75 metres long, surrounded by a noise enclosure, and used for the colour printing of magazines at a rate of about 40000 copies per hour. Figure 5.13 is a plan view showing typical operator and noise monitoring positions.

Measurements of equivalent noise level, L_{Aeq}, were carried out at the operator positions over periods of time (usually a few minutes)

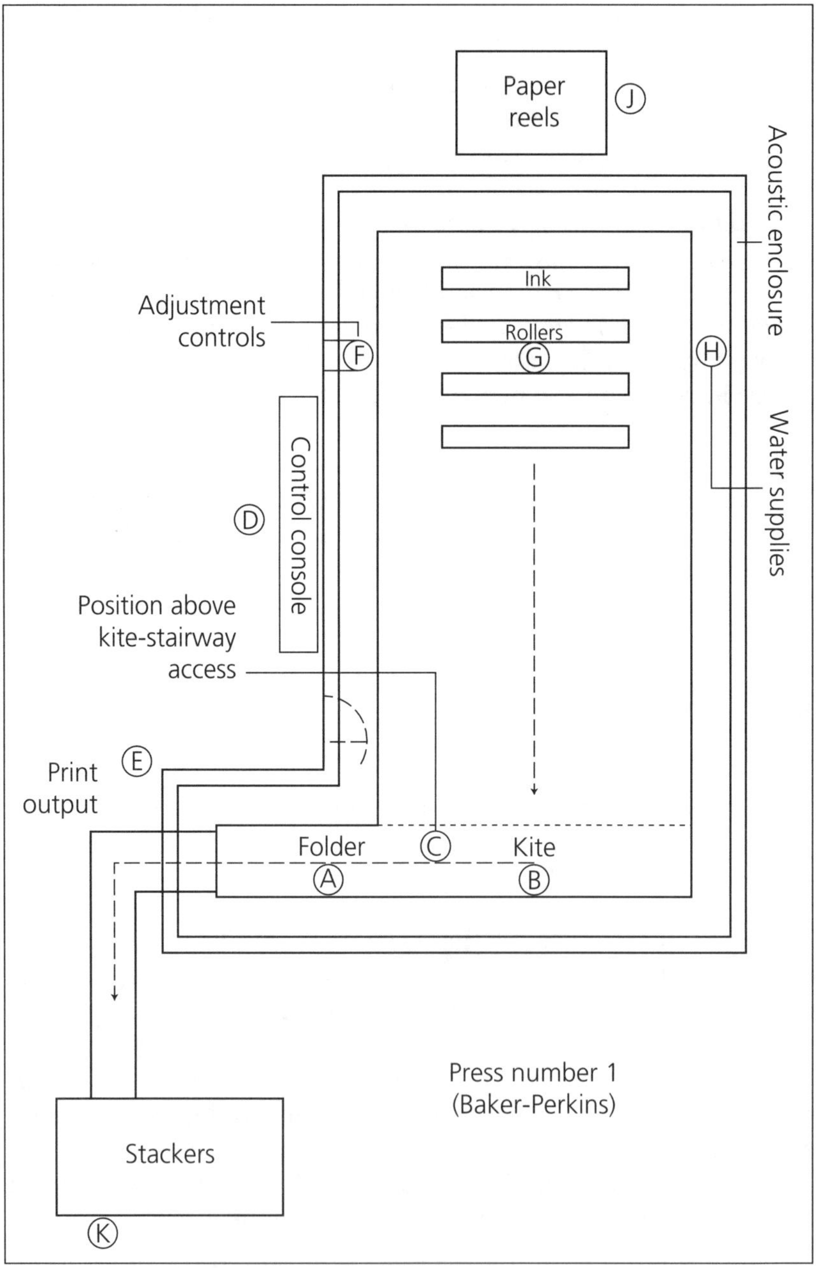

Figure 5.13 A plan view showing typical operator and noise monitoring positons on a large printing press
Source: reproduced courtesy of dB Acoustics

necessary to establish a representative sample of the noise at that position, using a type 2 integrating sound level meter that also had the capability of measuring peak noise levels and noise levels in octave bands. The meter, which carried current calibration certificates from an accredited laboratory, was calibrated satisfactorily before and after the measurements and was used in accordance with manufacturer's instructions. In accordance with guidance given by HSE the measurements were taken either at representative ear positions with the operator temporarily moved aside, or, where this was not possible, at a short distance of 5–20 cm from the operator's ear.

Noise exposure times were obtained by talking to both managers and workers, and by direct observation over several visits to the plant.

Some examples of noise exposure patterns, i.e. noise levels and exposure times, are given below, with the calculated $L_{Ep,d}$ value in each case. Each employee worked a 12-hour shift.

Employee exposure pattern no. 1

Inside the press enclosure, making folder adjustments:

Position A .... 93 dB(A) for 30 minutes
Position B .... 98 dB(A) for 15 minutes
Position C .... 93 dB(A) for 15 minutes

Outside the press enclosure:

At control console D .... 78 dB(A) for 5.5 hours
At print output E .... 83 dB(A) for 5.5 hours

The calculated $L_{Ep,d}$ value for this exposure pattern is 88 dB(A), which is above the First Action Level of the Noise at Work Regulations.

Employee exposure pattern no. 2

Inside the press enclosure, making ink adjustments:

Position F .... 94 dB(A) for 20 minutes
Position G .... 99 dB(A) for 20 minutes
Position H .... 92 dB(A) for 20 minutes

Outside the press enclosure:

At control console D .... 78 dB(A) for 5.5 hours
At print output E .... 83 dB(A) for 5.5 hours

The calculated $L_{Ep,d}$ value for this exposure pattern is 88 dB(A), which is above the First Action Level of the Noise at Work Regulations.

Employee exposure pattern no. 3 — reel stand operator

Close to Paper Reel, position J.... 86 dB(A) for 12 hours

The calculated $L_{Ep,d}$ value for this exposure pattern is 88 dB(A), which is above the First Action Level of the Noise at Work Regulations.

Employee exposure pattern no. 4 — stacker operator

Close to stacker, position K... 84 dB(A) for 12 hours

The calculated $L_{Ep,d}$ value for this exposure pattern is 86 dB(A), which is above the First Action Level of the Noise at Work Regulations.

Similar noise exposure patterns were recorded for the other two presses.

Note that in the case of patterns 1 and 2 even short duration exposure to high noise levels inside the enclosure has increased the exposure level to above the First Action Level, and that in case 4 the 12-hour duration of the exposure has had a similar effect.

The report contained a number of observations which indicated that improved maintenance would lead to a reduction in noise exposure: occasional very loud, high-pitched squealing noises emitted from the reel stand brake unit; occasional banging noises from the stacking machine (possibly indicating a worn bearing); excessive levels of air discharge noise, small gaps between panels and badly worn and poorly fitting seals in the enclosure; and doors were often left open. There was no evidence of the use of ear protectors by employees either inside or outside the enclosure except by the reel stand operator when severe squealing occurred.

Although none of the estimated exposure levels was above the Second Action Level, it is possible that under unusual circumstances in which employees are required to spend additional time working inside the enclosure their exposure could increase to that of the Second Action Level. It was therefore recommended that the area inside the enclosure be designated an ear protection zone when the press is running, with notices displayed to that effect at entry points to the zone. Improved supervision and maintenance, a programme of information and training for employees, and a planned programme of noise reduction measures was also recommended.

A similar approach was adopted to assess noise exposure of employees working in the bindery, at positions such as copy feeders, stitcher control panel, loading, stacking, inserting and guillotine. A notable difference from the press areas was that at several of these workstations there was no source of noise and employees were exposed mainly to reflected sound from other sources. It was recommended that sound-absorbing materials be used to reduce the levels of reverberant sound.

Acknowledgement
This case study has been provided by Mr D Bull, dB Acoustics, 25 Albany Road, West Bergholt, Colchester, Essex, CO6 3LB. Tel. 01206 241684.

CASE STUDY 9

Control of noise from newspaper presses using acoustic enclosures, havens and partitions

— *Mr J Charman, The Noise Control Centre*

Modern newspaper presses which can print, cut and fold more than 100000 copies an hour contain thousands of moving parts and hundreds of noise sources. Although the press manufacturers may attempt to build noise reduction features into each new generation of plant, this will be offset, partially at least, by the demand for ever larger and faster operating equipment. Noise levels can be in excess of 100 dB(A) at certain points close to the presses. Except in a few cases, retrofit noise control cannot be applied to so many different noise sources, and therefore the usual solution, when planning the installation of the press, has to be to use sound-insulating panels within the press hall to separate, the operatives from the entire press as far as possible.

There are in principle three approaches:

- an acoustic enclosure around the press;
- a noise haven, i.e. an enclosure built around the operatives. This could be entirely free-standing, i.e. separated from the press, or could be built close to the press in order to facilitate access to controls from within the haven;
- the use of acoustic screens or barriers around the press. To be fully effective these must extend from floor to ceiling.

Each individual situation will be different, depending upon the size and number of presses, the layout and arrangement of plant, and the size and geometry of the press hall. Often a combination of the above methods will be used. Sound-absorbing materials may also be used to complement the effects of sound insulation and sometimes the press may be built on concrete rafts and isolated from the rest of the building to reduce the transmission of structure-borne sound.

In addition to the acoustic requirements, which are that there shall be sufficient sound insulation between the press and the operatives, there are many other requirements including:

- easy access to all areas of the press to ensure that the noise control system does not interfere in any way with the uninterrupted operation of the press, and for maintenance;
- glazing to enable good visual contact to be maintained;
- other aspects of employee comfort, e.g. lighting, ventilation and control of air quality both for the machinery and for the operatives;
- architectural and aesthetic considerations — the appearance of sound-insulating treatments must be compatible with that of the rest of the press hall;
- cost;
- other safety considerations;
- remote control of press from quiet areas as far as possible;
- penetrations to the sound insulation for services and conveyor outlets.

It is often these other requirements which determine the design of the noise control treatment. Figure 5.14 an example of noise control treatment.

Large newspaper presses are often constructed on three levels, with the reel room beneath the two-storey press. Web slots in the floor of the press room transmit noise from the press room to the

Figure 5.14 Examples of noise control treatments
Source: reproduced courtesy of Industrial Acoustics Co.

reel room below, and require treatment to reduce noise levels in the reel room. The press drive shaft also often runs just beneath the press room floor and may need to be enclosed. The series of sketches in Figure 5.15 show various possible sound insulation arrangements for both the press hall and the reel room, together with their various advantages and disadvantages.

Acknowledgement
This case study has been based on information provided by J Charman, The Noise Control Centre, Crown Business Park, Leicester LE14 3NQ. Tel. (01664) 821811 and also by B Jaffrey, Industrial acoustics Co.

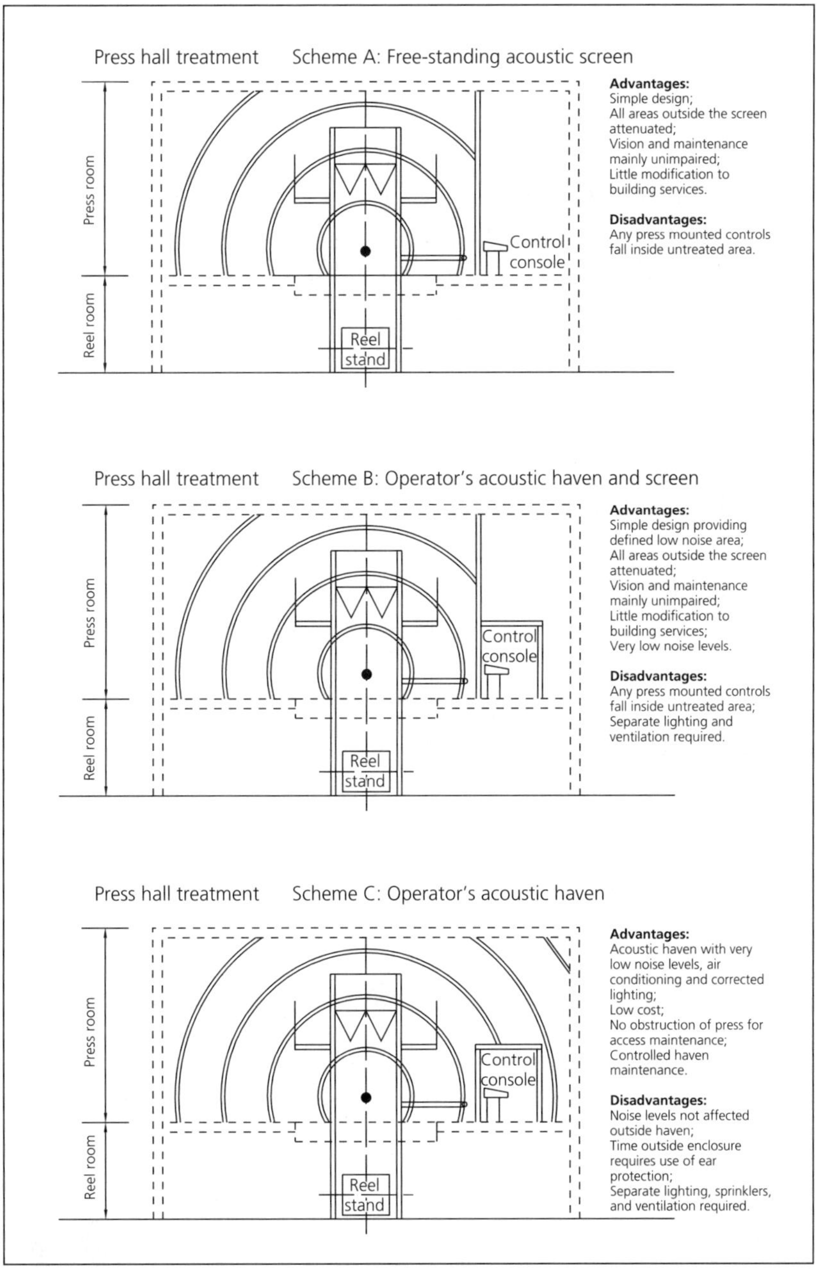

Figure 5.15 Various sound insulation arrangements for both the press hall and the reel room
Source: reproduced courtesy of the Noise Control Centre

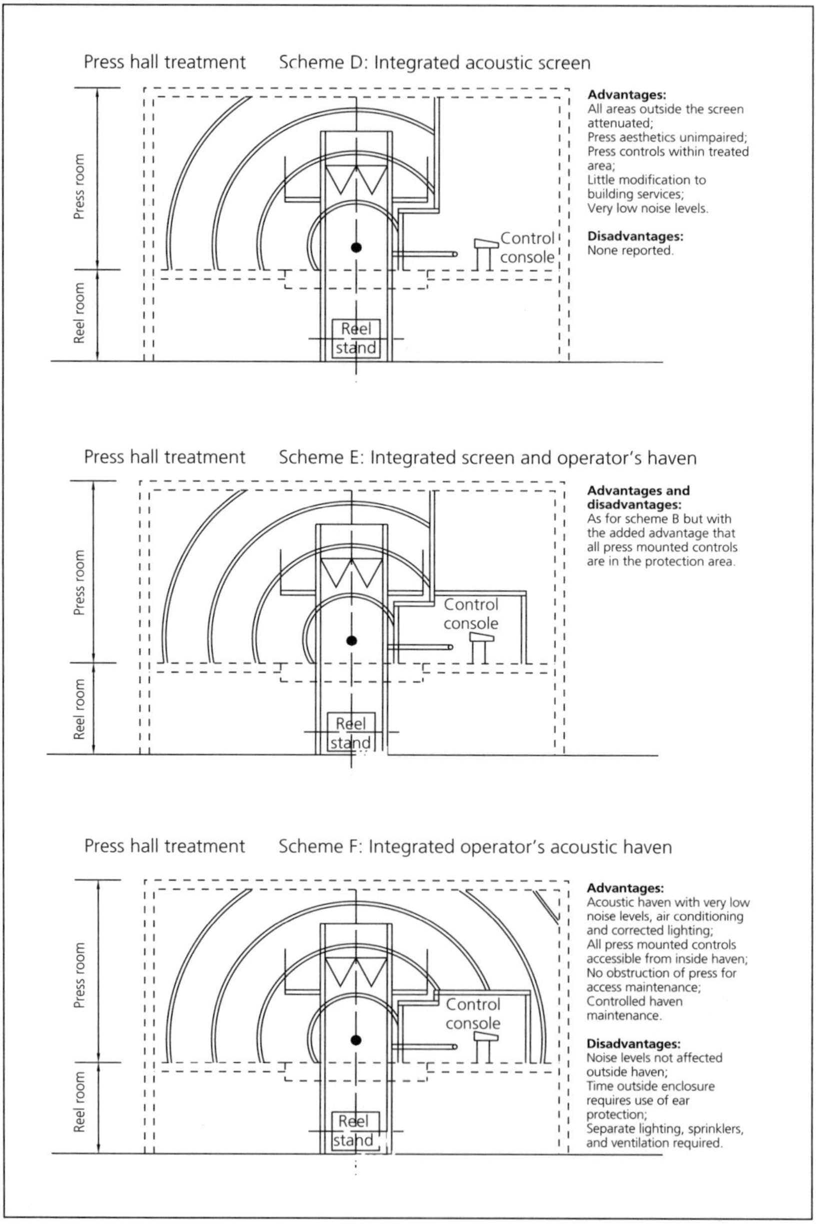

Figure 5.15 (cont'd) Various sound insulation arrangements for both the press hall and the reel room
Source: reproduced courtesy of the Noise Control Centre

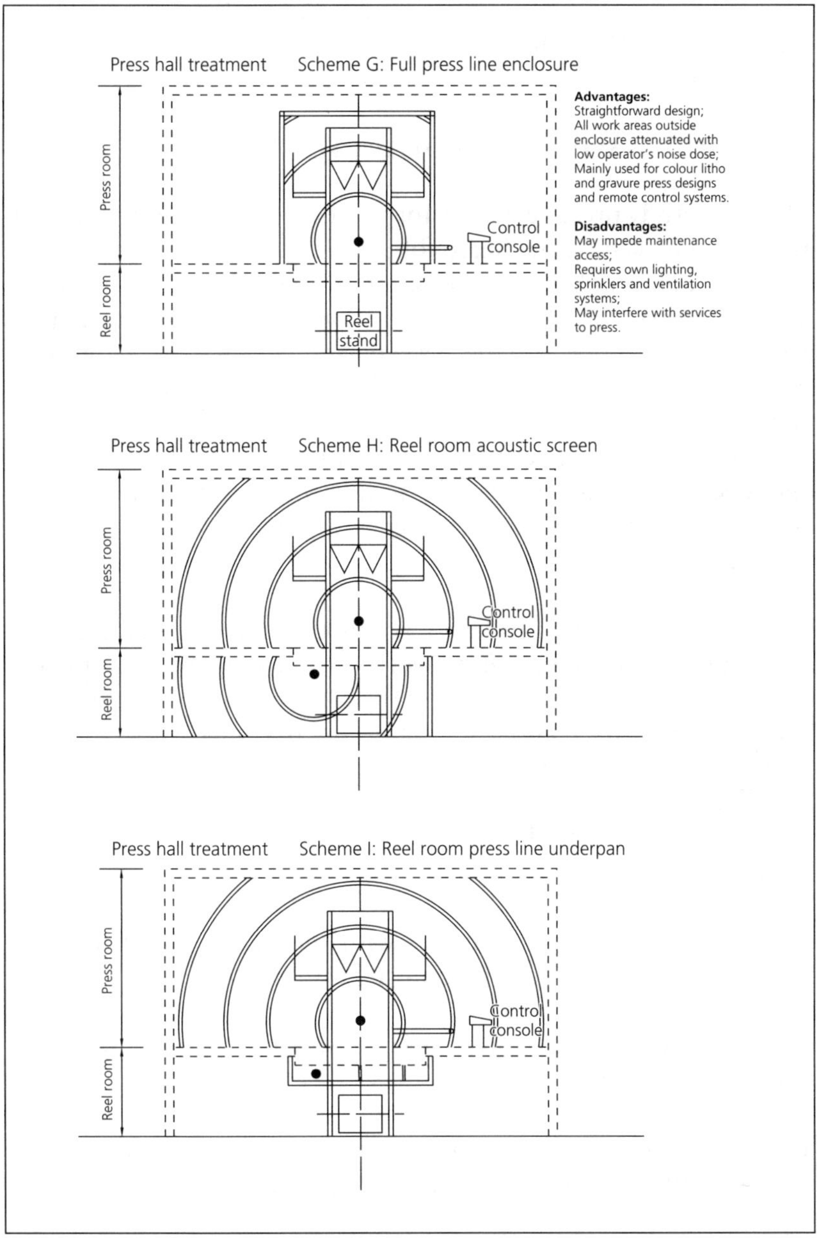

Figure 5.15 (cont'd) Various sound insulation arrangements for both the press hall and the reel room
Source: reproduced courtesy of the Noise Control Centre

CASE STUDY 10

Noise nuisance from a printing works

This case study presents the history of a case as seen from the local authority environmental health officer's viewpoint. The resolution of the problem took about twelve months and the case study illustrates that persistence, patience and co-operation among all parties is necessary in order to achieve a satisfactory outcome. Although a statutory noise nuisance was issued by the local authority the company was, from the outset, very willing to try to reduce the noise in order to maintain good relations with nearby residents, and co-operated with the local authority to this end. Nevertheless, several attempts at noise control were necessary before all sources were satisfactorily reduced.

The case concerns complaints about the noise in the evenings and nighttime from a printing works on the edge of an industrial estate near to residential property. The premises had formerly been a warehouse, and the change of use was subject to the following planning conditions:

The design and installation of any plant or equipment shall be such that:

- any associated noise complies with the NR25 criterion when measured within any neighbouring dwelling house;
- no structure-borne vibration is perceptible within any neighbouring dwelling house.

The case is presented chronologically in the form of the environmental health officer's (abbreviated) log of events.

Week 1	About six weeks after the granting of planning permission. First complaints received, from residents in two different nearby houses. The printing works not yet fully operational. Works production manager contacted and visited. It is assumed that most of the noise is coming from an exhaust stack, although there are a number of other fan/flue outlets at roof level. The production manager proposes lagging the stack with mineral fibre and fitting a windshield cowl to the top of the stack. He is advised that this is very unlikely to be effective, and that it is likely that an in-line silencer will be needed. He is also advised to seek the help of a professional noise consultant.
Week 2	Noise measurements attempted in the day are abandoned because daytime background noise levels are too high. Arrangements are made with the resident to make noise level measurements in the bedroom late one evening, and with the Works to switch sources on and off as required. All future noise measurements are made in the late evening.
Week 3	Octave band noise measurements carried out in bedroom — 46dB(A), NR25 exceeded by up to 16dB, in 250–2000Hz octave bands. Production manager arranges for works (lagging and cowl) to be carried out.
Week 5	Continuing complaints. A statutory nuisance notice is issued to the Works and they are also informed of the exceedance of the planning consent condition. Production manager contacts acoustic consultant.
Week 8	Further measurements taken after works have been completed. There is a slight improvement (44dB(A)) but still a substantial problem — NR25 still exceeded by up to 14dB. Letter sent to factory confirming noise measurements and also advising about the possibility of noise breakout of high internal noise levels through lightweight roof.

Week 9	Letter received from factory enclosing noise consultant's report which advises in-line silencer to reduce extract fan noise. Silencer to be specified, manufactured and installed.
Week 12	Works complete, i.e. in-line silencer installed. Arrangements made with resident and with factory for more nighttime noise measurements to be made in bedroom. Resident acknowledges big improvement in noise levels.
Week 14	Further measurements show a substantial improvement (of up to 15dB in some octave bands), but the internal noise level still exceeds NR25, by up to 6dB at 250Hz. The Works are again advised to investigate breakout. Production manager to re-call acoustic consultant for further investigation.
Week 17	Further noise measurements carried out with both the environmental health officer and the noise consultant present.
Week 19	Vibration survey carried out inside the Works by consultant, revealed no problems. Vibration survey carried out in resident's house by environmental health officer to check compliance with planning condition. Vibration was not detectable.
Weeks 22–23	Further complaints from resident. Works are ordering further silencers following consultant's report. Residents informed of further improvements in progress.
Week 28	Production manager reports that further work almost complete. Silencers have been fitted to all boiler flues at just below roof level. However, the fan has not yet been enclosed. It is suggested to the production manager that the paper compactor which is located externally at the rear of the factory may also be a significant contributor to the noise, together with open doors at the rear, and that both should be investigated as part of the next measurement survey. Suggested that heavy duty plastic curtain across the opening may help with the problem of the door being left open.

Week 32	All work now completed, including an acoustic hood type of enclosure fitted over the large fan above the printing plant.
Week 33	Further measurements were carried out. The noise in the bedroom still exceeds NR25.
Week 39	Discussions take place between the noise consultant and the environmental health officer about further work to be carried out.
Week 50	Further work complete. Further measurements arranged.
Week 54	Further measurements carried out. Noise level now below NR25. The nuisance has been abated and the planning condition satisfied. Although further complaints continued from one resident the environmental health officer was satisfied that a statutory nuisance no longer existed, and no further action was taken. The position was explained to the resident, including his right to take individual nuisance action against the factory.
Week 70	(Three months later). Further measurements were carried out in response to a further complaint and because new equipment had been installed in the Works. The results showed an increase in the noise levels (of 2–3 dB(A)) since the nuisance had been abated. The levels were still, however, just below the planning limit of NR25, and so no further action was taken, apart from alerting the Works of the increase in noise levels, and advising them to consider further noise control treatment in order to build a 'safety margin' between existing levels and the planning condition, and in particular to deal with noise escaping through open doors at the rear of the factory.

CASE STUDY 11

Protecting the hearing using industrial audiometry

— Dr SJ Karmy, SJK Scientifics Ltd

Industrial audiometry represents a cost to industry — this case study shows why this is money well spent from the point of view of both the employer and the employee.

The legal reasons

The 1992 Management of the Health and Safety at Work Regulations require audiometric surveillance if industrial noise is causing a risk to hearing.

This has been interpreted in the 1995 HSE guidance document *Health Surveillance in Noisy Industries — Advice for Employers* as meaning that at $L_{EP,d}$ levels of 90 dB(A), external to any hearing protection worn, hearing checks are good practice. When this $L_{Ep,d}$ level rises to 95 dB(A) the HSE states that employers should normally provide audiometry.

In view of the above it would be safest if employers commence audiometry at the 90 dB(A) $L_{Ep,d}$ level. Employers not offering audiometry at these exposure levels could be left, at some later date, defending against the claim that they had not followed good practice as defined by the HSE.

Financial and medical reasons

The large variation in susceptibility to noise-induced hearing loss existing between individuals creates difficulty in assigning causation correctly to a measured deafness.

This leaves the employer vulnerable to spurious claims for noise-induced hearing loss. These may have been launched maliciously, or in the honest but mistaken belief that the employer's noise had caused the problem. Data given in ISO 1999 and tables produced by the National Physical Laboratory relate a given noise exposure to the size of likely noise-induced hearing loss, but both are intended for use with populations, not individuals. Calculations made using these tables show the percentile of the population to which an individual must belong if the measured loss was to have resulted from the given noise exposure. This does, however, leave a sufficiently determined individual able to argue that his level of loss occurred from that noise exposure because he belonged to an extremely susceptible segment of the population.

Furthermore, diagnostic audiometry is less precise than many imagine in determining the cause of a hearing loss, particularly if the loss is sensorineural in nature. This is the class of loss to which noise-induced hearing loss belongs. For example, the configuration of deafness resulting from exposure to leisure noise and that resulting from exposure to industrial noise cannot be differentiated if both have been sufficiently intense. Similarly, diagnostic testing cannot separate deafness caused by the current employer from losses caused by previous employers.

In view of the above factors, therefore, a prudent employer should ensure that a pre-employment audiogram is obtained, or at least one should be measured as soon as possible during the individual's career with the company.

The benefits of a pre-employment audiogram to the employer and employee are as outlined below:

- It establishes a baseline.

This can:

  - prevent deafness caused by an earlier employer or agency from being blamed on the current employer;

  - prevent the employee from later claiming that although his hearing is within normal limits, it was actually better than normal when he joined the company;

  - help in preventing an employee from wrongly considering noise as being the cause of a hearing loss which had been subjectively unnoticeable at the pre-employment stage, but which had recently worsened;

Later deviation from this baseline can:

  - trigger immediate remedial action within the company to prevent significant loss if exposure to industrial noise is considered to be the cause;

  - establish the period during which the loss occurred;

- It promotes well-being by detecting remediable conditions of the ear.

- It allows assessment of whether a prospective employee would be a risk to himself or his colleagues as a consequence of a hearing loss, or under undue stress as he attempted to complete his work.

- It indicates those prospective employees apparently susceptible to noise-induced hearing loss. Possible evidence for this would be:

  - a notch in the audiogram at 4kHz;

  - a strong history of exposure to noise.

The fact that a prospective employee is thought to fall into this category should not immediately cause him to be rejected for employment in an intractably noisy area for the following reasons:

- this is forbidden under the Disability Discrimination Act 1995 without ascertaining the feasibility of adapting the workplace to ameliorate any problems which are perceived to exist as a consequence of his disability;

- personal hearing protection plus regular monitoring audiometry is capable of safeguarding his remaining hearing;

- unless the situation is very clearly thought out, such a policy can lead to later complications.

However, irrespective of the final decision made, pre-employment audiometry will have succeeded in alerting the company to problems that could emerge in the future if this individual is employed. Without this warning, a company can build a reservoir of problems for itself that may be difficult or expensive to resolve at a later date. For example, if an employee is found to have a hearing loss, then the company has an 'increased duty of care' towards this employee to ensure that the loss is not worsened by industrial noise (*Parish* v. *Stepney Borough Council* (1952)). There are different ways of discharging this duty of extra care, but all naturally mean extra effort and thus extra expenditure.

- It assists in obtaining a TTS-free initial audiogram.

TTS (temporary threshold shift) is a temporary worsening of the hearing which can be caused by unprotected exposure to high levels of noise immediately prior to the test. A baseline audiogram obtained at the pre-employment stage is more likely to be free of this effect than one measured after the individual has commenced work with the company. A more accurate baseline improves the chances of detecting small changes in auditory threshold on subsequent tests, and thus protecting the employee's hearing from further damage by swiftly instigating remedial action to reduce noise exposure, if this is thought to be the cause.

The benefits of regular monitoring audiometry to the employee are that it acts as the quality control procedure for the hearing conservation programme. Owing to the logarithmic nature of the decibel, apparently small failures in the hearing conservation programme can quickly result in a hazardous noise dose being received. Regular monitoring audiometry throughout the career of the employee provides a final check on the effectiveness of the hearing conservation programme by checking, for example, that employees are:

- continuing to utilize correctly the noise control procedures or barriers provided by the company;
- making full and proper use of any hearing protection issued;
- receiving the anticipated level of protection from the hearing defenders issued.

Monitoring audiometry is particularly cost effective because it offers the additional benefits of:

- reaffirming the interest of management in the hearing conservation programme;
- providing a forum at which the hearing protection message can be reinforced, and ear defenders checked;
- ensuring the availability of a series of audiograms on an individual. In the case of a sudden acoustic accident suffered by an individual these will allow an assessment of whether a consequential increase in hearing loss has occurred. The series of audiograms also permits an assessment to be made of the validity of any audiogram measured for use as the basis of an out of court settlement.

An audiogram should, ideally, be obtained from an employee immediately prior to him leaving. Should the employee sustain a noise-induced hearing loss whilst working for a new employer, the existence of this audiogram will permit the first employer to disclaim responsibility for the subsequent hearing loss. It will also allow the current employer to resist the retrospective backward apportionment of damages paid to an ex-employee by a subsequent employer's insurers.

The cost of failure

- The primary cost of failure is loss of hearing by the employee. There is no cure for a noise-induced hearing loss — a hearing aid can only offer an amelioration of the problem, not a replacement of the lost sense. Noise-induced hearing loss is not simply an inability to pick up quiet sounds, many other auditory problems also occur.

- Approximately one-third to a half of all employees with a noise-induced hearing loss will also have an associated tinnitus. This is a subjective noise that only the sufferer can hear, and in the worst cases can lead to severe depression, inability to concentrate and loss of quality of life.

- The civil courts are compensating deafened employees substantially for the presence of tinnitus. Damages awarded in the civil courts are a function of many factors, including age, effect on future work prospects, and pain and suffering. Currently, a 35 year old with a 30 dB hearing loss averaged over 1, 2 and 3 kHz, a level of loss once recognized as the onset of definite auditory disability, can expect an award in the region of £7000 in the courts. Add a moderate tinnitus and the award could rise to £13 500. A severe tinnitus could cause the damages to reach approximately £21 000. The same combinations of loss and tinnitus in a 60 year old might be worth between £5400 and £16 100.

- One of the largest awards in the civil courts for a combination of deafness and tinnitus was made in 1990 to Mr Douglas Kentish who had worked for the CEGB. Aged 51 years at the time of the award, Mr Kentish received £129 000 for a hearing loss and a severe tinnitus. A large proportion of this award was for the loss of earnings. Through depression brought on by deafness and particularly the tinnitus, Mr Kentish had lost a promising career as a technical author with an American publishing company.

- Perhaps of even greater concern to a company not providing at least pre-employment audiometry, is the case of *Hunter, McPoland and Williams* v. *Robinson Wiley Ltd* (1992). Three employees exposed to moderate levels of industrial noise were awarded £3000 each plus costs in respect of noise-induced hearing losses which they were deemed to have sustained. The points of interest in this case are twofold. Firstly, none of the hearing thresholds measured would have been thought excessive if they had been noted during the measurement of a pre-employment audiogram. Secondly, the defence used reputable and modern scientific data to argue that the hearing losses forming the bases of the claim were indistinguishable from the average hearing levels expected in individuals of the plaintiffs' ages. Judge Lachs, however, accepted the plaintiffs' contention that their hearing had been better than average and had deteriorated due to noise exposure. It is certain that the existence of a pre-employment audiogram would have given the defence a better chance of success.

- Most settlements are not reached in the civil courts, but by means of out of court payments made between employer and employee. These claims are usually funded through an insurance claim. Employers, however, should try to insist that their insurers investigate some claims thoroughly, and resist the temptation to settle all as quickly as possible. Currently, noise-induced hearing loss claims represent 80% by number of all claims for industrial ill health, and 50% by value. Employers who build up a poor claims record due to noise-induced hearing loss must find their premiums rising in subsequent years. Moving to a new insurer in an attempt to obtain lower premium costs then becomes less of an option because of their claims record.

How to set up an audiometric programme

Two HSE documents published in 1995 describe what is required of an audiometric programme, and how to set this up: *A Guide to Audiometric Testing Programmes* and *Health Surveillance in Noisy Industries — Advice for Employers.*

Equipment

Figure 5.16 shows the type of audiometer most frequently used in industrial audiometric programmes. Giving the required air-conduction audiogram, it offers the Bekesy technique of audiometric measurement. This produces the zigzag output trace that is the most accurate way of measuring a hearing threshold. The machine automatically analyses the audiograms following the HSE five category system. It continuously checks the trace for reliability, and retests dubious sections. The audiometer has an on-board database for 850 audiograms that simplifies comparison of audiograms in later years. It can also send results to a computer or receive audiometric data from the computer.

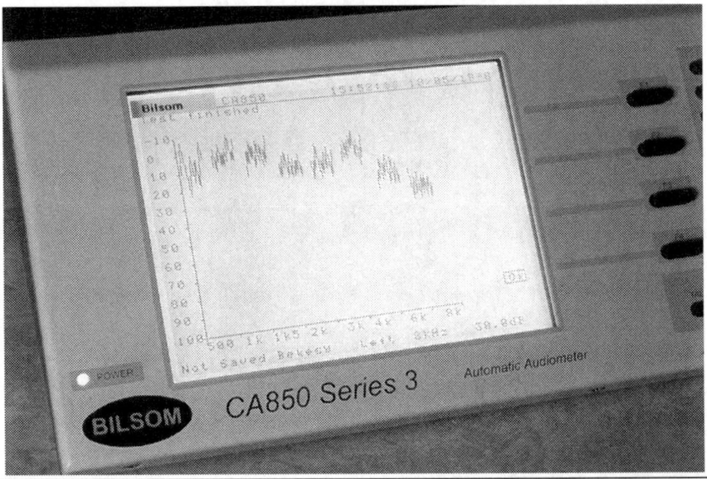

Figure 5.16 Type of audiometer commonly used in industrial audiometric programmes
Source: reproduced courtesy of Bilsom International

Figure 5.17 An audiometric booth
Source: reproduced courtesy of Bilsom International

Figure 5.17 shows an audiometric booth. Background noise levels must be very low if an accurate audiogram is to be produced, and these are specified in BSEN26189: 1991. It is difficult to achieve these very low sound levels without the use of a booth. However, somewhat laborious techniques do exist for attempting to overcome this problem without a booth if the budget cannot be stretched to cover such a purchase.

Training

Naturally, any person using an audiometer should be competent to do this type of work. The HSE does not describe the requirements for competence in exact terms, but does suggest in its guidance document that attendance at one of the courses approved by the British Society for Audiology would be a good route to ensuring the correct level of competence.

Further assistance

Additional information about setting up an audiometric programme can be obtained from the provider of this case study, Dr SJ Karmy, at SJK Scientifics Ltd, Epsilon House, University Research Park, Chilworth, Southampton, SO16 7NS. Tel. (01703) 767954.

Reproduced courtesy of Dr SJ Karmy.

6

Control of industrial noise by application of the law, standards and codes of practice

Introduction

The legislative and administrative control of industrial noise in the UK is based on a variety of Acts, regulations, standards and codes of practice. Some aspects of this provision, such as the control of nuisance, have their origins in the beginning of the century and earlier. In other cases the measures originated in the 1960s and 1970s. Noise first became a serious problem in our society in the late 1950s and early 1960s with the postwar rapid growth of industry, roads and air traffic. Many of the provisions for controlling noise which are in use today have their origins in the final report of a committee appointed by the government to examine the problem of noise (usually called the Wilson Report, after the committee's chairman) issued in 1963. This was a very thorough and far-reaching investigation that reported and made recommendations on every aspect of noise in society ranging from noise in towns from industry to noise sources affecting the countryside.

Many of the control measures introduced in the 1960s and early 1970s, most of which are still in operation today, have their origins in the recommendations of the Wilson Report including:

- Control of Pollution Act 1974;

- British Standard BS4142 on the rating of industrial noise 1967 (the most recent version was published in 1997);

- Noise Insulation Regulations 1975 (for compensation for traffic noise) issued under the Land Compensation Act 1973;

- BS5228 on construction site noise;

- Circular 10/73 Guidance Note on Planning and Noise (now replaced by Planning Policy Guidance Note 24).

In 1990, prior to the enactment of the Environmental Protection Act the government established a Noise Review Working Party to review the framework of measures used to control noise and make recommendations. In comparison with the earlier Wilson Committee this was mainly a 'fine-tuning' process of the measures already in existence.

The purpose of this chapter is to outline the legal and administrative measures in place for the control of noise from industry concentrating mainly on nuisance, planning and hearing protection legislation. The primary sources — the Acts and Standards themselves — should always be consulted before taking any action based on them.

Noise in the environment

Noise nuisance

The word 'nuisance' has a specific legal meaning that is much more restrictive than its everyday use.

There are three types of nuisance in law: private nuisance, public nuisance and statutory nuisance. The first two types are dealt with under common law. A private nuisance action may be taken in the civil courts against a neighbour causing a nuisance. Public nuisance is a nuisance which is so widespread, i.e. affecting a whole street or area that it is considered unreasonable that any one individual should have to take common law action to deal with it, and therefore action may be taken by the Attorney General. Any noise emitted from premises which is a nuisance or prejudicial to health is declared a statutory nuisance, and is dealt with under criminal law by the local authority environmental health department. A statutory nuisance is currently dealt with by the provisions of the Environmental Protection Act 1990, which is discussed later.

Interpreting whether a particular noise is or is not a private nuisance is difficult, and it is certainly not possible to define a single noise level above which a noise may be declared to be a nuisance. The Act does not define the word 'nuisance' so the common law case law must be used. Certain factors have, however, emerged from case law which are considered to be relevant to the existence of nuisance, such as the time of day and week at which the noise occurs and its duration, the type of area or locality in which it occurs, and the degree to which it causes disturbance. Judgements about nuisance should be based upon the likely effects of the noise on the average reasonable person and not on persons who are unusually sensitive to noise, perhaps because of illness, or because they work, and therefore sleep at unusual hours. The noise must not merely cause transitory disturbance but also substantially interfere with comfort or convenience. Private nuisance protects only interest in land, so that the fact that someone is made ill by the noise will not give rise to payment of damages. Only if there is an interference with the use of the land, for example so that someone cannot use a bedroom to sleep in, will damages be awarded. Such interference must be significant unless there is some physical damage to the property, for example cracks.

The following quotation from a case illustrates some of these points:

> Every person is entitled as against his neighbour to the comfortable and healthful enjoyment of the premises occupied by him and in deciding whether, in any particular case his right has been interfered with and a nuisance thereby caused it is necessary to determine whether the act complained of is an inconvenience materially interfering with the ordinary physical comfort of human existence not merely according to elegant or dainty habits of living but according to plain and sober or simple notions obtaining among English people. (*Vanderpant* v. *Mayfair Hotel Company Limited* (1930))

The type of area is also of significance since a noise that may be considered acceptable in one area, for example an industrial city site, may not be acceptable in another area such as a suburban or rural area, as illustrated by the famous and much quoted judgement: 'that which is a nuisance in Belgravia may not be a nuisance in Bermondsey' (*Sturges* v. *Bridgeman* (1879)). However, this does not necessarily give a license to create additional noise simply because an area is already noisy, as illustrated by the judgement in the case of *Rushmer* v. *Polsue and Alfieri Ltd* (1907). In this case the defendant introduced a printing press into his premises in Fleet Street and operated it at night. Although this was at that time a noisy area the noise from the new equipment was far in excess of what was normal for the area, and the court decided that this constituted a nuisance:

> 'It does not follow that because I live, say, in the manufacturing part of Sheffield, I cannot complain if a steam hammer is introduced next door, and so worked as to render sleep impossible, although previous to its introduction my house was a reasonably comfortable abode, having regard to the local standard.'

The time factor is obviously important, since a noise that might be acceptable during normal working hours can become highly disturbing at nighttimes or at weekends, and a noise that occurs occasionally and for brief intervals may be more acceptable than one that is continuous or occurs over long periods.

The level of noise is obviously also a factor, as is the character of the noise, as characterized by its frequency spectrum, whether it is continuous, and, if not, on its pattern of occurrence. Noises that contain features such as pure tones (i.e. whistles, whines, tones) and impulsive characteristics (thumps, clatters, bangs) are usually considered to be more annoying than noises of similar level and spectrum that do not contain these features, and this is recognized in rating methods such as BS4142 and BS7445, discussed later.

There are a number of defences to private nuisance, for example consent or statutory authority. It is, for example, not an acceptable defence that the complainant came to the noise, but it may defeat a claim for an injunction that is only awarded at the discretion of the judge.

Unlike the situation in statutory law, discussed later, the argument that the best practicable means have been used to reduce the noise is not in itself an adequate defence in a common law case, as illustrated by the case of *Walter* v. *Selfe* (1851):

> '...the making or causing of such a noise as materially interferes with the comfort of a neighbour, when judged by the standard to which I have just referred constitutes an actionable nuisance, and it is no answer to say that the best known means have been taken to reduce or prevent the noise complained of or that the cause of the nuisance is the exercise of a business or trade in a proper manner'

and also by the case of *Rushmer* v. *Polsue and Alfieri Ltd* (1907), mentioned earlier:

> '...and it would be no answer to say that the steam hammer is of the most modern approved pattern and is reasonably worked.'

Nevertheless, the efforts which have been made by the defendant to reduce the noise may be taken into account in the judgement.

In England and Wales the most common remedy sought via a court action for nuisance at common law is an injunction (interdict in Scotland) restraining the defendant from continuing his nuisance. If the plaintiff proves his case then he is entitled to damages as of right but the award of an injunction is discretionary. If only an injunction is asked for, and refused, then there is no automatic right to damages, so both remedies must be asked for.

Public nuisance is a strange combination of public and private law and covers many 'nuisance-like' activities, from running a brothel, obstructing a highway to operating a quarry causing noise and dust. In *AG* v. *PYA Quarries* (1957) public nuisance was defined as 'an act or omission that materially affects the reasonable comfort or convenience of life of a class of Her Majesty's subjects.' It covers a wide spectrum of activities and at one end would be dealt with in the crown court as an indictable criminal offence by the police and Crown Prosecution Service. At the other, nearer private nuisance, where, for example a village is affected by quarrying activities, the Attorney General is approached to take on the case in a relator action on behalf of the villagers. (Alternatively, the local authority may do so under s222 of the Local Government Act 1972). If an individual suffers over and above the other villagers, a claim for his own special damages (apart from a general injunction) may be applied for, even for damages to his health. This is different from claims for private nuisance (see above).

The Environmental Protection Act 1990

Part 111 of the Environmental Protection Act, ss79–82, deals with noise nuisance. The powers given to local authorities are both preventative and remedial, i.e. they may be used to remedy an existing nuisance or to prevent a nuisance occurring in the future. Section 79 states that any noise or vibration which is emitted from a premises and which is prejudicial to health or is a nuisance is a statutory nuisance. Nuisance is not defined in the Act, and so the same considerations as apply under common law have to be used in deciding whether or not a nuisance exists. Fixed premises include factories, shops, discos, dwellings and land. This section places a duty upon local authorities to require its area to be inspected from time to time to detect whether a statutory nuisance exists. They must also take such steps as are reasonably practicable to investigate any complaints of noise nuisance.

According to s80 of the Act, where a local authority is satisfied that a statutory nuisance exists or is likely to occur or recur, it shall serve an abatement notice requiring:

- the abatement of the nuisance or prohibiting or restricting its occurrence; and/or

- the carrying out of such works or other action necessary to abate the nuisance.

The abatement notice may specify noise levels, hours of operation and equipment that may or may not be used. The conditions of the notice should be reasonable. The person receiving the notice may appeal.

Section 82 of the Act also allows an individual to take action against an alleged statutory nuisance, if for whatever reason the local authority decides not to do so. Alternatively an individual still has access to remedy via a common law action for private nuisance.

If the noise results from industry or from trade the defence that the best practicable means have been used to reduce the noise may be used and the court shall have regard to cost and to local conditions and circumstances, including technical measures available to deal with the noise.

Informal resolution of noise complaints

Experience has shown that in many cases of complaint against noise from industrial and commercial premises the problems can best be dealt with by informal discussions between the parties rather than resorting to law, whether private or public. If a local resident, for example, complains to a nearby factory owner about new or increased levels of noise it may be possible to resolve the problem before the local environmental health officer becomes involved. Even in cases where the complaint is made directly to the local authority the investigating environmental health officer may prefer to resolve the matter informally rather than by issuing an abatement notice. Even though the officer may not consider the noise sufficient to be a statutory nuisance he/she may still recommend the factory to carry out certain actions to reduce its effect if this is feasible, and the factory will often agree, in the interests of maintaining good relations with neighbours. Only by communicating can disputes be avoided and the effect of inevitable ones minimized. The factory may be unaware of the disturbance being caused to neighbours; the noise may be due to an unauthorized activity, or due to an undetected fault in equipment, or it may be emanating from another nearby industrial premises. Conversely, if the factory takes the trouble to talk to nearby residents, to explain the reasons for the increased noise, which may be temporary or due to some unforeseen difficulty, this may reduce the possibility of complaints. It may be that lower noise reductions and less expensive noise control measures will suffice if neighbours are informed and consulted than would be needed to satisfy complainants once disagreement and conflict have arisen; or it may be that higher levels of noise might have been acceptable if negotiated amicably than those ultimately required by a formal abatement notice issued by the local authority.

Planning and noise

All new developments of any size require planning permission under the Town and Country Planning Act 1990. The planning process provides the ideal opportunity for minimizing the effects of noise and for preventing the need for nuisance actions. The sources of noise and predicted noise levels can be considered carefully and thoroughly, and methods for reducing the impact on the community surrounding the development may be specified. If it is not considered possible to do this then planning permission may be refused unless it can be shown that there is an overriding benefit or need.

Conversely, if the implications of noise issues are not foreseen and considered at the planning stage not only is an opportunity for improvement lost but noise problems may be increased too. If conditions relating to noise impact are not imposed during the planning application process, or are inadequate, this can make it difficult for the local authority to deal with noise nuisance problems that may occur subsequently. This is particularly the case if the development involves a change of use of the site as illustrated by the case of *Gillingham Borough Council* v. *Medway (Chatham) Dock Co. Ltd. and Others* (1992). The planning authority gave approval for change of use from a former naval dockyard to a commercial port, but failed to foresee the extent of noise problems that would arise from the increase of industrial traffic using the site and passing through a nearby residential area, deciding that the costs of the noise were outweighed by other benefits. When the local environmental health department subsequently tried to take action for nuisance it failed to win its case. The approach taken in this judgement has been challenged in more recent cases. Therefore it is important that there is close liaison on noise issues between the local planning authority and the environmental health department.

For many years planning authorities have followed the advice given in Department of the Environment Circular 10/73 *Planning and Noise* (issued in 1973). Following the recommendations of the Noise Review Working Party this has been revised and reissued as Planning Policy Guidance Note (PPG) 24 *Planning and Noise*. The Guidance Note suggests that sites for which planning applications for residential development are being considered be characterized by the use of four noise exposure categories (NEC) — A, B, C and D — depending upon the existing noise levels prevailing at the site. Sites in category A have the lowest noise levels and sites in D the highest. It is recommended that:

- For NEC A Noise need not be considered as a determining factor in granting planning permission, although the noise level at the high end of the category should not be regarded as a desirable level.
- For NEC B Noise should be taken into account when determining planning applications and, where appropriate, conditions imposed to ensure an adequate level of protection against noise.

- For NEC C Planning permission should not normally be granted. Where it is considered that permission should be given, for example because there are no alternative quieter sites available, conditions should be imposed to ensure a commensurate level of protection against noise.
- For NEC D Planning permission should normally be refused.

The PPG gives a recommended range of noise levels, expressed as equivalent L_{Aeq} levels, for each of the NECs for dwellings exposed to noise from road, rail, air and mixed sources. These are shown in Table 6.1. Planning authorities may wish to choose category limits within the recommended bands or take local circumstances into account to define their own bands.

Table 6.1 Noise levels corresponding to the noise exposure categories for new dwellings

Noise source	A	B	C	D
Road traffic				
07: 00–23: 00	<55	55–63	63–72	>72
23: 00–07: 00	<45	45–57	57–66	>66
Rail traffic				
07: 00–23: 00	<55	55–66	66–74	>74
23: 00–07: 00	<45	45–59	59–66	>66
Air traffic				
07: 00–23: 00	<57	57–66	66–72	>72
23: 00–07: 00	<48	48–57	57–66	>66
Mixed sources				
07: 00–23: 00	<55	55–63	63–72	>72
23: 00–07: 00	<45	45–57	57–66	>66

Source: Department of Environment Planning Policy Guidance Note 24

The NEC procedure is applicable to the situation where residential development close to an existing noise source is being considered rather than the reverse situation, where new noise sources are to be introduced into an existing residential area. The procedure is relevant to a mixed noise site where industrial noise is present but not dominant but is not particularly suitable for situations where it is proposed to introduce residential development close to industrial noise sources. This is because the nature of this type of noise and local circumstances may necessitate an individual assessment, and because there is insufficient information on people's response to allow detailed guidance to be given.

The PPG recommends the use of BS4142 for assessing noise from industrial and commercial premises, with the rating level defined in this standard as being an appropriate method of specifying permissible noise limits.

Examples of specimen planning conditions are given in Annex 4 of the Guidance Note. It is suggested that for industrial and commercial sites local authorities may wish to consider two types of planning conditions:

- Noise limits to be met at specified points, for example outside the nearest noise sensitive properties or at points around the site boundary. Different limits may be set for daytime and nighttime periods. Noise limits may be absolute levels in which case L_{Aeq} is recommended as the noise index, over a specified period of time, or they may be relative to the background noise level at the site. In this case the procedures of BS4142 are recommended. Limits on maximum noise levels may also be used, but they may be difficult to monitor and to enforce.

- Restrictions or limitations relating to:

  - the types of activity which may or may not be carried out on different areas of the site, including processes and types of machinery and equipment;

  - the sound insulation of buildings enclosing noisy equipment;

- the layout of buildings, including, for example, access to the site and areas where traffic movement and loading and unloading operations take place;
- the times of day during which operations are allowed.

The first type of condition (noise limits) has the advantage of allowing freedom to the developer to decide how best to meet the noise limit, for example by noise control at source or by limiting transmission of noise to the receiver, but the disadvantage that the condition will involve the time and expense of monitoring noise levels. It will be easier for the local authority to check compliance using the second method (specifying operating conditions) but these may be less effective over the long term as the situation at the site changes. A combination of the two types of condition may also be used. It may be possible, for example, to specify a noise limit and allow the developer to put forward a plan for the operation of the site that will meet the limit. If the planning authority is satisfied with the developer's plan then it can be incorporated into the planning conditions.

Planning conditions must be necessary, relevant, enforceable, precise and reasonable in all other respects. Appeals against decisions of the local planning authority are considered by the Department of the Environment (DOE). If a development proposal is particularly sensitive or of national interest, or if significant objections to it have been received then the DOE may decide to hold a public inquiry, and will appoint an inspector. After considering all the evidence presented at the inquiry the inspector will convey his decision to the DOE and this will subsequently be announced by the Secretary of State. Noise issues are quite often important in public inquiries, with evidence being presented by expert witnesses on behalf of both the planning authority and the developer. The expert witnesses may then be examined on their evidence by the barrister acting for the other side.

BS4142: 1997 Method for Rating Industrial Noise Affecting Mixed Residential and Industrial Areas

BS4142 describes a method for measuring the noise from industrial and commercial premises and for assessing whether the noise is likely to give rise to complaints from persons living nearby. It is based upon the principle that the likelihood that a 'new' source of industrial noise (called the 'specific noise' in the standard) will provoke complaints depends upon the extent to which its level exceeds the existing background noise level. Other factors such as local attitudes to the particular premises may also have an effect, but the standard does not include these in the assessment procedure.

The method of rating described in the standard compares the level of the specific noise, corrected to take into account certain audible characteristics, with the background noise level. The corrected level of the specific noise is called the rating level. If the rating level exceeds the background noise level by about 10 dB or more then, according to this standard, complaints are likely. If the difference is 5 dB the situation with regard to complaints is marginal. At a difference below 5 dB, the lower the value the less the likelihood that complaints will occur; and if the rating level is 10 dB or more below the background noise level then this may be taken as a positive indication that complaints are unlikely.

The rating level is obtained by adding a 5 dB correction factor to the specific noise level if the specific noise contains a distinguishable, discrete, continuous note (whine, hiss, screech, hum), or if there are distinct impulses in the noise (bangs, clicks, clatters or thumps) or if the noise is irregular enough to attract attention. Only a single 5 dB correction should be made even if more than one of the above characteristics are present.

The standard is intended for assessing noise from factories, industrial premises or fixed installations and sources of an industrial nature in commercial premises. It is the recommended method for assessing these types of noise for planning purposes. It has also been widely used in the past in the investigation of nuisance complaints, a situation that is likely to continue even though this usage has provoked much discussion and criticism, and is specifically ruled out in the introduction to the standard. It must be emphasized that the standard is about predicting the likelihood of complaints. It does not predict the level of community annoyance (as might be obtained, for example, from social survey techniques), nor does it predict the existence of nuisance, although there may be some relationship, not necessarily causal, between these three. On the one hand, the use of the standard to assess the validity of a nuisance complaint seems pointless, given that someone has already complained, presumably because they are disturbed by the noise in some way. On the other hand, an objective measure of the situation taken according to standardized procedures can only be helpful provided that it is used to supplement rather than replace the reasoned professional judgement of the environmental health officer or the court about the noise and the evidence of the plaintiffs. It might also be helpful in deciding the extent of any noise reduction that is necessary in order to render the noise level acceptable.

The standard may be used for assessing the predicted noise from new or modified premises, as well as for the measured noise from existing premises. The noise levels are those measured or predicted outside affected buildings — the method is not applicable to the assessment of noise inside buildings. It is also not applicable to situations where the background noise level is very low, i.e. below 30 dB(A).

Although the principle on which the standard is based is very simple, as indicated above, the first-time reader may be perplexed by the complexity of detail that it contains. This is because the standard has been widely used since its introduction in 1967 by both environmental health officers and noise consultants, and disputes have arisen in the past about the interpretation of the methods of measurement and assessment. For this reason the latest revision, the 1997 version, sought to clarify (but not necessarily simplify) procedures through strict definition of terms and specification of measurement details. This latest version also introduced the use of L_{Aeq} and thus brought the standard into step with the wider-ranging international standard ISO 1996 *Description and Measurement of Environmental Noise*, now also adopted as BS 7445.

The use of the standard would be exceedingly simple if both the new noise to be assessed, i.e. the specific noise, and the background noise were constant in level throughout the day and night. However, this is hardly ever the case. The specific noise may, for example, be steady and continuous, steady in bursts, intermittent and cyclic, or random. The background noise may also vary both over the short term, i.e. over seconds and minutes, and over the longer term, for example throughout the 24-hour period. The standard requires that the specific noise is measured as an L_{Aeq} whereas the background noise level is measured as an L_{A90}. The assessment process thus requires an L_{A90} level (the background noise level) to be subtracted from an L_{Aeq} (the rating level). This is an idea which has also caused some problems, since we are often trained only to subtract 'like from like', and particularly when the L_{Aeq} of the background noise, or residual noise as it is called in the standard, may itself be 10 dB or more above its L_{A90} value — does this mean that we have the likelihood of complaints even before we start?

This, however, is to miss the point, which is best explained by a simple example illustrated by Figure 6.1. This shows a graph of the variation of the level of residual noise with time, over a time period of several minutes. It is made up of various transient noise events such as passing cars, aircraft occasionally flying overhead, and even bursts of bird song, superimposed on a more-or-less steady lower level of noise from a distant main road. The level of the specific noise is also shown on Figure 6.1 — in this case it is fairly constant, a few decibels above the lower levels of residual noise but well below the level produced when the aircraft is passing overhead. It causes disturbance to the resident during those times when the residual noise is at its lowest (i.e. most of the time) even though it may be temporarily inaudible when an aircraft flies overhead. The L_{Aeq} level of the residual noise is probably determined by the occasional noisy events, whereas the L_{A90}

value, i.e. the background noise level as defined in this standard, corresponds reasonably closely to the base level, i.e. to the level of noise enjoyed by the resident outside his/her premises when there is no car passing, no aircraft flying overhead, and no bird song.

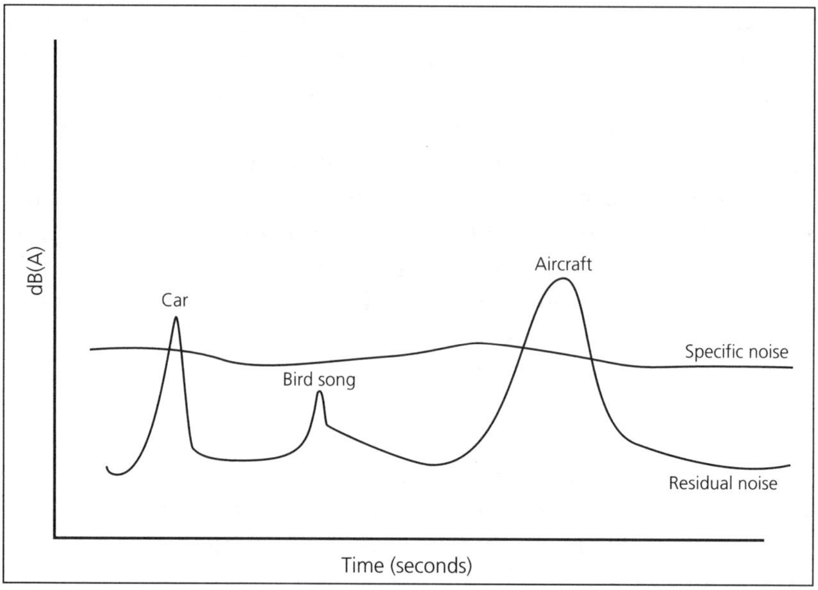

Figure 6.1 Possible variation of residual noise and specific noise with time (re. BS4142)

Therefore it is reasonable that in order to predict the likelihood of complaints it is the L_{A90} of the residual noise which should be compared with the specific noise level.

The L_{Aeq} of the specific noise should always be determined over the same time period, called the reference time interval. This is specified as one hour during the daytime and five minutes at nighttime. The specific noise may, however, be measured over a shorter period. Bearing in mind that the specific noise may show a wide variety of time patterns including continuous, intermittent, cyclic or random, and that the residual noise may also fluctuate, there are a number of measurement problems to be overcome and decisions to be made, including:

- the selection of the most appropriate measurement time interval for the particular type of specific noise, and how to relate the measured level to the specific noise level over the reference time interval;
- the effect of the residual noise on the measurement of the specific noise, in cases where the latter is less than 10 dB above the former;
- the measurement of the background noise level in the presence of the specific noise.

The standard gives detailed advice about these and other measurement issues, and further details are given in Chapter 7.

Although BS4142 is generally considered to be useful and effective it has attracted a number of criticisms. One of these is that it can often lead to a creeping increase in background levels. This could arise, for example, in a situation where an industrial noise source is declared to be statutory nuisance, and is shown to produce a rating level which is, say, 15 dB above the background noise level at the affected noise-sensitive premises. The industrial firm introduces noise control measures which reduce the level by 13 dB (so that it is now only 2 dB above the background noise level). The noise is no longer considered to be a statutory nuisance by the local environmental health department, and the complainant is now satisfied, but the background noise level has been increased, in this case by 4 dB. It should be remembered that even if the 'new' noise level is reduced to the existing background noise level this will still result in a 3 dB increase. The concept of noise abatement zones (discussed later) was introduced to combat the effect of 'creeping' background noise levels.

Another criticism is that the emphasis on numerical comparison of dB(A) levels can often obscure the fact that in some cases the nuisance caused by the noise is related more to specifically annoying features than to its overall level. These features can include the spectral content of the noise, its pattern of occurrence (as, for example in the case of a dripping tap late at night) as well as its tonal or impulsive character, which are already taken into account to some extent. Sometimes, for example, a tone can render a noise particularly annoying even though its effect on the dB(A) level is negligible. The use of dB(A) as the basis of the assessment has also been criticized in the case of low frequency noise, say below 250 Hz octave band. This type of noise can be particularly annoying late in the evening or in the middle of the night when the background noise is very low, and the A-weighted value fails to adequately take this into account. In such cases an octave, or even one-third octave or narrowband analysis is required.

Thus although BS 4142 is of major importance in dealing with industrial noise it is only one of a number of different approaches and rating methods which can be used, including concentration on the investigation of annoying features and the use of noise abatement zones and environmental impact assessment methods (discussed later).

Example 1

A new factory has applied to move into a vacant site on the edge of an industrial estate, near to some residential properties, and will produce continuous noise throughout the daytime. There may be occasions in the future when nighttime operation will become necessary. Background noise measurements made outside residential properties close to the new site give values of L_{A90} of 45 dB(A) during the daytime and 35 dB(A) late at night. Noise levels from the factory are measured at its existing site at positions that are the same distance away as the houses at the new site, under similar prevailing wind conditions. The L_{Aeq} measured over one hour was 47 dB(A). The noise contains a clearly audible hum. The background noise level at the existing site, where there are no houses nearby, was obtained during a period when the plant was switched off for a short while, and was 36 dB(A). Assess the likelihood of complaints if the planned move goes ahead.

The assessment is set out in Table 6.1. Note the significance of the tonal correction in the daytime assessment. Note also that if this investigation had been carried out after the move to the new

Table 6.2 BS4142 assessment for Example 1

	Daytime	Nighttime
Specific noise level	47 dB	47 dB
Character correction (tone)	+5 dB	+5 dB
Rating level	52 dB	52 dB
Background level	45 dB	35 dB
Assessment level	52 – 45 = +7 dB	52 – 35 = + 17 dB
Conclusion	Marginal: some complaints possible	Complaints very likely

site, the measurement of the specific noise would have been affected by the background noise level, and it would have been necessary to make a correction for this, or to measure the specific noise much closer to the factory so that background noise did not affect the measurement, and then apply a 'distance correction' to the measured level.

Example 2

A factory introduces a new noise source which operates for 8 minutes each hour throughout the 24 hour period, into a neighbourhood where the background noise level is 43 dB in the daytime and 33 dB(A) at night. The noise level produced by the new source is measured outside the nearest residence over the 8 minute 'on' period on three occasions and the L_{Aeq}(8 min.) is found to be 56 dB. The noise is reasonably steady during its 'on time' with no noticeable tonal, impulsive or other characteristics. Assess the situation using BS4142.

In this case it will be necessary to correct the measured value of the specific noise over 8 minutes to obtain the L_{Aeq}(1 hour) for the daytime, using the principles described in chapter 2:

$$\begin{aligned} L_{Aeq}(1\text{ hour}) &= L_{Aeq}(8\text{ min}) - 10\log\left(\frac{8}{60}\right) \\ &= L_{Aeq}(8\text{ min}) - 9 \\ &= 56 - 9 \\ &= 47\text{ dB} \end{aligned}$$

This correction is not necessary for the nighttime assessment because the reference period at night is only five minutes. The assessment is therefore as given in Table 6.3.

Table 6.3 BS4142 assessment for Example 2

	Daytime	Nighttime
Measured level of specific noise	56dB	56dB
Specific noise level (over reference period)	47dB	56dB
Character correction	–	–
Rating level	47dB	56dB
Background level	43dB	33dB
Assessment level	47 – 43 = + 4dB	56 – 33 = 23dB
Conclusion	Marginal: some complaints possible	Complaints very likely

This example illustrates the significance of the different reference periods for day and nighttime.

Some more complex examples are given in an appendix to BS4142.

BS 7445/ISO 1996: Description and measurement of environmental noise

This standard aims to provide a method for describing, measuring and rating environmental noise from all different sources (i.e. industry, transport, recreational and so on) which contribute to the total noise at a site, using L_{Aeq} as the basic measure. The standard lays down guidelines for specifying noise limits and describes procedures to be used for checking compliance with such limits, and for gathering environmental noise data which may be useful for making planning decisions about land use. The standard defines a rating level determined over a specified reference time interval, which is obtained by adding adjustments to the measured L_{Aeq} value based on both tonal and impulsive characteristics of the noise. Methods of determining a long-term average rating level and for representing the results in terms of noise zones on a map of the area are described.

BS4142 can be seen as a standard that describes methods and procedures that comply with BS7445, but restricted to commercial and industrial noise.

Environmental assessments

The Town and Country Planning (Assessment of Environmental Effects) Regulations came into force in July 1988, in compliance with Directive 85/337/EEC, and are described in Department of the Environment Circular 15/88. The Regulations require that projects that are likely to have significant effects on the environment by virtue of their nature, size or location shall be subject to an assessment of those effects, in many cases before planning permission is granted. Noise is one of the many possible environmental factors to be considered, together with air, water and land pollution and effects on flora, fauna, soil, buildings, amenity and so on.

The assessment will be required to identify assessment locations close to noise-sensitive premises likely to be affected by noise arising from the development, such as dwellings (including gardens), educational establishments and hospitals. Special consideration should also be given to development that would affect the quiet enjoyment of parks and similar outdoor areas. All significant sources of noise affecting the assessment locations, such as industrial and transportation sources, must be identified. At each of the assessment locations the existing noise levels and those predicted as arising from the development must be determined by measurement and calculation. The environmental assessment study will have to rate the significance of noise impacts in terms of factors such as the number of people affected, magnitude and timescale of impact. Where impacts are considered significant, mitigation measures designed to reduce exposure to noise should be introduced. These could include design and engineering measures aimed at reducing the noise emissions at source, the layout of the development and limiting hours of operation of sources of noise.

In 1995 the Department of the Environment published a Good Practice Guide entitled *Preparation of Environmental Statements for Planning Projects that Require Environmental Assessment*. This publication includes a chapter on noise. A code of practice specifically covering noise aspects of environmental assessments is currently being prepared by a working party organized jointly by the Institute of Acoustics and the Institute of Environmental Assessment.

Noise abatement zones

Under the provisions of the Control of Pollution Act 1974 (s63–67) local authorities may set up noise abatement zones in their area. Once the zone has been established and the noise levels around its perimeter have been measured and recorded in a register, which is available for public inspection, they may not be exceeded except with the consent of the local authority. The main purpose in setting up a zone is to protect the area against upwardly creeping background noise levels. The local authority may require noise levels to be reduced if this is reasonably practicable and would lead to public benefit. These provisions give the local authority an alternative to nuisance legislation for controlling the noise from industrial and commercial premises. The measures for setting up noise abatement zones and carrying out the noise measurements and maintaining the zones are set out in the Control of Noise (Measurement and Registers) Regulations 1976. Unfortunately these procedures are so labour intensive that very few noise abatement zones have been set up and most of these have not been maintained and so have fallen into disuse. The Noise Review Working Party in 1990 recommended that these procedures be simplified in order to encourage the more widespread use of the noise abatement zones.

Noise at work

The Noise at Work Regulations 1989

These regulations were made under the Health and Safety of Work (etc.) Act 1974 in response to EC Directive 86/188 of 1986 on the protection of workers from the risks related to noise exposure at work. The Regulations impose duties upon employers, employees and on manufacturers and suppliers of noisy equipment. The duties depend on the level of noise exposure of employees, as defined by their personal daily noise exposure level, $L_{Ep,d}$. Three Action Levels are defined. The First and Second Action Levels correspond to $L_{Ep,d}$ values of 85 dB(A) and 90 dB(A) respectively. The third, called the Peak Action Level, is an instantaneous peak sound pressure of 200 Pa. This corresponds to a peak unweighted sound pressure level of 140 dB. The same duties are required above the Second and the Peak Action Levels.

The duties required of employers relate to the provision of information, instruction and training of employees, the supply of ear protection, the reduction of noise exposure levels, and the maintenance of equipment relating to noise reduction.

Even when noise exposure levels are below the First Action Level employers have a general duty to reduce noise exposure, as far as is reasonably practicable. Some employees will suffer noise-induced hearing loss even when their exposure is below an $L_{Ep,d}$ of 85 dB(A); and even those who do not will benefit from the improved comfort of a reduction in noise level.

If the noise exposure level of employees is likely to exceed the First Action Level then the employer must arrange for a noise assessment to be carried out by a competent person. This is the first stage in the hearing conservation programme, and is discussed later.

If the exposure level exceeds the First Action Level but is below the Second then employees have the right to ask for and be supplied with suitable and effective ear protection. The employer must also provide a programme of information, instruction and training about the effects of noise, and the risk to the employees' hearing from noise exposure and how this risk may be reduced, about where to obtain ear protectors and how to fit them properly, and how to look after them and inspect them for wear or damage.

If the noise exposure level is above the Second Action Level or if the Peak Action Level is exceeded, then the employer has a duty to reduce the exposure level as far as is practicable by means other than the use of ear protection. This could be either by reducing the noise levels to which the employees are exposed, or by reducing the time for which they are exposed to these levels, for example, by job rotation. This regulation emphasizes that the use of ear protection should always be a last resort in any hearing conservation programme, to be used as an interim measure until noise exposures can be reduced by other more satisfactory methods.

Again, above the Second Action Level the employer must supply ear protectors to employees, together with the programme of information, instruction and training described above, and must ensure that the protection is always properly used by employees. Any area where employees are exposed above the Second Action Level must then be declared a hearing protection zone, and must be indicated as such by appropriate notices. Anyone entering the hearing protection zone must wear ear protectors whilst they are in the zone, even though this may be only for a short period of time. The idea behind this Regulation is that supervisors and managers who may only be passing through the hearing protection zone should set an example, and should be subject to the same rules as those employees who have to suffer the inconvenience and discomfort of wearing ear protection throughout the day.

The employer must ensure that all equipment and devices for reducing noise exposure are maintained and kept in good repair. This includes maintaining the supply of ear plugs and ear muffs, and of seals and other replaceable parts for ear muffs, and the maintenance of acoustic enclosures, silencers and so on.

Employees have a duty to wear ear protectors when in situations where they are exposed above the Second Action Level and whenever they are in an ear protection zone. They must also co-operate with employers in using any devices, equipment or procedures provided in order to reduce their noise exposure and report any defects which may occur in such equipment. An example would be a noise enclosure that has become ineffective because seals on a door or inspection cover have become worn and need replacing.

Manufacturers and suppliers of equipment that is likely to produce noise exposure levels above the First Action Level must supply information about noise levels from their equipment. This will enable employers to compare the noise levels of equipment from different suppliers and to plan control measures that will minimize noise exposure from any new equipment introduced into the workplace.

A summary of these duties is given in Table 6.4. Detailed advice on the implementation of a hearing conservation policy and on satisfying the requirements of the Noise at Work Regulations can be obtained from Noise Guides Nos 1–8 published by the HSE. They should be compulsory reading and on the bookshelf of any manager with responsibility for protecting the hearing of employees.

The Noise at Work Regulations are enforced via the provisions of the Health and Safety at Work (etc.) Act 1974, and the enforcing bodies are either the Health and Safety Executive or the local authority, depending on the size and nature of the workplace. Enforcement is via the issuing of improvement notices or, in extreme cases where there is an immediate risk to the health, safety and welfare of those in the workplace, via a prohibition notice.

Noise exposure assessments

The assessment is the first step in the hearing conservation programme. It should define the magnitude of the problem and be the starting point for an action plan. Each assessment should be kept together with notes of what actions have been taken. It can then be the starting point for the next assessment that should be

Table 6.4 Summary of Noise at Work Regulations.

Action required where $L_{Ep,d}$ is likely to be: (see Note 1 below)	Below 85 db(A)	85 db(A) First AL	90 db(A) Second AL
EMPLOYER'S DUTIES			
General duty to reduce risk			
Risk of hearing damage to be reduced to the lowest level reasonably practicable (Reg 6)	•	•	•
Assessment of noise exposure			
Noise assessments to be made by a competent person (Reg 4)		•	•
Record of assessments to be kept until a new one is made (Reg 5)		•	•
Noise reduction			
Reduce exposure to noise as far as is reasonably practicable by means other than ear protectors			•
Provision of information to workers			
Provide adequate information, instruction and training about risks to hearing, what employees should do to minimize risk, how they can obtain ear protectors if they are exposed between 85 and 90 dB(A), and their obligations under the regulations (Reg 11)		•	•
Mark ear protection zones with notices, so far as reasonably practicable (Reg 9)			•
Ear protectors			
Ensure so far as is practicable that protectors are:			
— provided to employees who ask for them (Reg 8(1))		•	
— provided to all exposed (Reg 8(2))			•
— maintained and repaired (Reg 10(1)(b))		•	•
— used by all exposed (Reg 10(1)(a))			•
Ensure so far as reasonably practicable that all who go into a marked ear protection zone use ear protectors			• (3)
Maintenance and use of equipment			
Ensure so far as practicable that:			
— all equipment provided under the regulation is used, except for the ear protectors provided between 85 and 90 dB(A) (Reg 10(1)(a))		•	•
— ensure all equipment is maintained (Reg 10(1)(b))		•	•
EMPLOYEE'S DUTIES			
Use of equipment			
So far as practicable:			
— use ear protectors (Reg 10(2))			•
— use any other protective equipment (Reg 10(2))		•	•
— report any defects discovered to his/her employeer		•	•
MACHINE MAKER'S AND SUPPLIERS' DUTIES			
Provision of information			
Provide information on the noise likely to be generated (Reg 12)		•	•

Notes
(1) The dB(A) action levels are values of daily personal exposure to noise ($L_{Ep,d}$).
(2) All the actions indicated at 90 db(A) are also required where the sound pressure is at or above 200 Pa (140 dB re. 20 μPa).
(3) This requirement applies to all who enter the zones, even if they do not stay long enough to receive an exposure of 90 dB(A) $L_{Ep,d}$.

Source: reproduced courtesy of the Health and Safety Executive carried out after any significant change affecting noise exposure has occurred.

The purpose of the assessment is to estimate the personal daily noise exposure levels of employees, establish which are exposed over the different Action Levels, and to make recommendations to the employer about what needs to be done in order to meet the requirements of the Regulations in the short, medium and long term. This should include advice about the need for hearing protection, including selection of suitable protectors, about programmes of training and instruction for employees, and about measures to reduce noise exposure levels.

The assessment report will probably be written for a manager with limited understanding of the terminology and technical aspects of noise. Therefore even though the report may well contain much technical information, it must communicate the recommendations and conclusions in good, clear, non-technical English. If it does not do this it is inadequate.

Who should carry out the assessment? The choice is between developing and using in-house expertise or employing an external consultant. The advantage of having the assessment carried out by a company employee, such as the health and safety manager, works manager or an experienced foreman is that he/she will be able to bring detailed knowledge and experience about the workplace to the task. This option will require an investment in suitable training in the principles and practice of noise measurement and control and on how to carry out assessments, and in suitable sound measuring equipment, although this is also available to hire. An external consultant will undoubtedly bring a high level of expertise about noise to the task but will not have the detailed knowledge of the workplace, and it will be important to ensure that he/she is well briefed and given full access to all areas and is able to talk freely to employees who are being assessed if this limitation is to be remedied. The advantage of the in-house option is that the expertise will continue to be available to carry out future assessments and advise on changes that have implications for noise exposure levels.

Methods for carrying out assessments are described in chapter 7.

An assessment which satisfies the requirements of the Noise at Work Regulations will also satisfy the requirements for risk assessment of the Management of Health and Safety at Work Regulations 1992.

Health surveillance in noisy industries — audiometry

Monitoring audiometry, i.e. the measurement of employees' hearing on a regular basis, is the only final direct test that a hearing conservation policy is working. It is the only way to be sure that employees who are being subjected to high levels of noise are not suffering noise-induced hearing loss. Otherwise no matter how thorough the hearing conservation programme, its effectiveness will rely on assumptions about the accuracy of noise exposure assessments, about the effectiveness of noise reduction measures and of hearing protectors, and that employees always behave exactly as they should in matters relating to hearing conservation. If a periodic check shows that an employee's hearing has deteriorated, above that expected from the natural aging process, then the reasons can be investigated. This might show up some defect in hearing protection arrangement, such as not wearing ear protection, ineffective protection (for example inappropriate selection, worn or damaged protectors or protectors being incorrectly fitted), or it might be that the employee is being exposed to high levels of noise outside of working hours. Another possibility is simply that the employee is particularly sensitive to noise-induced hearing loss, and the remedy could be to move him/her to a quieter job. Increasingly, companies are using monitoring audiometry to provide evidence to defend against civil hearing loss damage claims, particularly through the use of pre-employment audiometric tests. It is also sometimes claimed that the audiometric tests encourage employees to be conscientious about wearing hearing protectors.

EC Directive 86/188 contained a requirement for employees to have access to an audiometric test. This was not included in the Noise at Work Regulations because such tests are available under the National Health Service. An earlier draft form of the regulations had a proposed Action Level of 105 dB(A) $L_{\mathrm{Ep,d}}$ above which an employer must arrange for audiometric monitoring of employees so exposed, and this is how any requirements might be introduced if they should become mandatory as a result of any future changes in legislation.

The management of Health and Safety at Work Regulations 1992 includes a requirement (Regulation 5) for health surveillance in relation to the risks to health and safety identified by the risk assessment, which could include monitoring audiometry where appropriate. A leaflet issued by the HSE entitled *Health Surveillance in Noisy Industries* gives advice for employers. It states that

> ...it is good practice for employers to carry out regular checks on all employees whose daily personal noise exposures equal or exceed 90 dB(A). The risk of hearing damage rises significantly at exposures above this level. Therefore even allowing for the use of hearing protection, employers should normally provide hearing checks when noise levels reach or exceed 95 dB(A), except where that exposure is likely to be only temporary, for example for only a few weeks in a year.

The HSE has also issued a Guidance Note (MS 26) entitled *A Guide to Audiometric Testing Programmes.*

The advantages and limitations of industrial audiometry are discussed further in case study 11 of Chapter 5.

Compensation claims for noise-induced hearing loss

Employees suffering from noise-induced hearing loss resulting from their work can take civil action under common law for negligence against their employer. The employee must prove three things: that the employer owed him a legal duty of care at the time of the alleged negligence; that the employer breached this duty (by doing less than the duty required); and must show that not only he is deaf, but that this is a direct result of the negligence. The following are factors to be taken into account in deciding such claims.

- The hearing loss was noise-induced and resulted from working for the employer and not from previous employment or leisure activities.

- The employer should have been aware of the risk to hearing of his employees from high levels of noise. Previous judgements have determined that employers should have been aware of this risk since the publication in 1963 of a booklet entitled *Noise and the Worker*. In 1972 the then Department of Employment published a Code of Practice *Reducing the Exposure of Employed Persons to Noise*. This outlined the main provisions of a hearing conservation programme and included advisory limits for noise exposure of 90 dB(A) over 8 hours, together with an overriding limit of 140 dB, and was in many ways a forerunner of the present regulations.

- The employee has not contributed to the negligence, for example by refusing to wear ear protectors, even though he/she was instructed about how and when they should be used and warned of the risks by the employer. Contributory negligence is only a partial defence, however, and would only reduce damages.

In successful claims damages are awarded on the basis of loss of earnings and loss of amenity, the latter being the more significant factor in most cases. In many cases claims are settled out-of-court on an agreed scale, depending on the amount of hearing loss, negotiated on behalf of employees by trade unions. Much higher damages are awarded in those individual cases where it can be shown that hearing loss has led to loss of earnings.

Since the early 1980s negligence claims for compensation for noise-induced hearing loss have been one of the main sources of payments made by insurance companies for industrial injuries. There have been thousands of claims costing many millions of pounds.

Since 1974, noise-induced hearing loss has been classified as a notifiable industrial disease under the social security legislation. However, compensation paid by the government is restricted to employees in certain industries related mainly to metalworking and wood machining, and to cases where the damage exceeds certain defined levels of hearing loss (a minimum of 50 dB(A)). Nevertheless, noise-induced hearing loss has become one of the main sources of such claims, numbering several thousand each year since 1974.

Insurance companies therefore encourage employers to take all measures necessary to protect the hearing of their employees and to guard against future negligence claims. These measures include not only compliance with the Noise at Work Regulations and the pursuance of an effective hearing conservation policy, but also that these shall be fully documented by a comprehensive system of records of actions taken. The records should include:

- reports of all noise exposure assessments carried out and actions taken as a result;
- records of all other noise surveys, for example of noise levels from particular machines;
- records of all training given to employees;
- records of the issue of ear protection;
- records of surveys carried out to check that ear protection is being worn;
- all measures taken to reduce noise levels in the workplace;
- all measures taken to reduce noise exposure levels of employees, for example by job rotation;
- all changes which may affect noise exposure, for example new machinery, working hours;
- records of audiometric tests and medical examinations carried out.

European Commission regulations

European Community directives are formulated within the Commission and approved by the Council of Ministers, following which they are implemented through legislation introduced within each member state. Directives may be in support of policies of removing barriers to trade, health and safety at work, or protection of the environment. An example is the Noise at Work Directive 86/188, which led to the introduction of the Noise at Work Regulations in the UK.

Noise emissions from machinery

Directives relating to product standards are issued under Articles 100 and 100A of the Treaty of Rome, as part of the policy of removing barriers to trade. Before 1985 a number of such directives relating to noise from machinery were published which required manufacturers to provide information about noise emissions from their products, and in some cases specified upper limits on allowable noise levels.

A new approach to technical harmonization and standards was agreed by Community ministers in 1985 and subsequent directives on machinery include only a statement on essential safety requirements that have to be met before a product can carry the CE mark and be placed on the market anywhere within the Community. The Machinery Directive 89/392/EEC was passed on 1 June 1989, and became part of UK law on 1 January 1993 as The Supply of Machinery (Safety) Regulations.

The Regulations, which relate to all aspects of safety, contain the following extracts which summarize the position relating to noise:

> Machinery must be so designed and constructed that risks resulting from the emission of airborne noise are reduced to the lowest level taking account of technical progress and the availability of means of reducing noise particularly at source.

Where risks remain despite all the measures adopted the manufacturers must provide warnings of such possible risks which may not normally be evident in the normal use of the machine.

Any sales literature describing the machinery must give information regarding airborne noise emissions.

Where necessary, instructions must give the requirements relating to the installation and assembly of the machine in order to reduce noise and vibration.

The following information about the airborne noise emissions must be given:

- L_{Aeq} at workstations where this exceeds 75 dB(A). If it does not exceed 75 dB(A) this must be stated.
- Peak C-weighted sound pressure at workstations where this exceeds 63 Pa (130 dB).
- Sound power level emitted by the machine where the L_{Aeq} at the workstation exceeds 85 dB(A).

In the case of very large machines the L_{Aeq} at specified positions around the machine may be indicated instead of the sound power level.

Where the workstations are undefined, or cannot be defined, sound pressure levels must be measured at a distance of 1 metre from the surfaces of the machinery and at a height of 1.6 metres above the floor or access platform. The position and value of the maximum sound pressure level must be indicated.

The manufacturer must indicate the operating conditions of the machinery during measurements and what methods have been used for the measurements.

In order to assist manufacturers to comply with the Supply of Machinery (Safety) Regulations a hierarchy of three types of harmonized European Standard (EN) is being developed by CEN (Comité Européen de Normalisation):

- Type A standards (fundamental safety standards) giving basic concepts and principles for design and general aspects that can be applied to all machinery.

- Type B standards (group safety standards) dealing with one safety aspect (such as noise) that can be used across a wide range of machinery.

- Type C standards (machine safety standards) giving detailed safety requirements for a particular machine or group of machines.

Standards relating to noise will be of types B and C. The International Standards Organisation (ISO), in collaboration with CEN, is revising existing standards for the measurement of sound pressure, sound power and sound intensity from machinery in order to harmonize them with CEN requirements. These will be type B standards. When eventually adopted, these standards will have the same EN ISO number as the ISO standard on which they were based, and in the UK they will become BS EN ISO standards, also with the same number.

Other standards will also be developed to give guidance on the design of low-noise machinery and low-noise workshops, on the design of noise control devices, and on methods for measuring and specifying their performance. These will be generic standards, i.e. applicable to all machinery, but will form the basis of a large number of type C standards, to be developed for different types of machinery, prepared in consultation with each particular industry, including the printing and papermaking industries. A series of noise test codes will also be produced for each type of machine, indicating how the machine is to be tested, its operating and mounting conditions during the test, the measurement standard (type B) to be used, and how the measurement results are to be declared and verified.

The Machinery Regulations should also assist the manufacturer to satisfy Regulation 12 of the Noise at Work Regulations, which requires suppliers of equipment and machinery to provide information relating to the noise emissions of their products in cases where the operator of the machine is likely to be exposed above the First or Peak Action Levels of the Regulations, provided that the test conditions reflect the way in which the machine is to be used in practice. The Machinery Regulations will also help the user to assess the effects of new machines when brought into a new workplace or when placing the machine in an existing workplace.

Noise exposure at work

The Noise at Work Directive 86/188/EEC was implemented in the UK through the introduction of the Noise at Work Regulations. It was always the intention that these would be only the start of legislation to reduce the exposure of employees to noise, and that they would be reviewed after a period of some years. In 1987 the Single European Act added a new article, 118A, to the Treaty of Rome, to deal specifically with health and safety at work. In 1993 the European Commission published a proposal for a directive on physical agents at work, to be introduced under Article 118A, which would extend and replace Directive 86/188. The proposal sets out three levels to be observed: a ceiling level that must not be exceeded; a threshold level towards which implementation of the directive should be geared; and Action Levels, situated between the threshold and ceiling levels, above which one or more of the specified measures must be undertaken.

The proposed ceiling level is the same as the existing Second Action Level, i.e. a personal daily noise exposure level, $L_{Ep,d}$, of 90 dB(A) and a peak sound pressure of 200 Pa (140 dB). The proposed threshold level is 75 dB(A) $L_{Ep,d}$. Above this exposure level workers must be informed of risks from noise.

Four Action Levels are proposed. Above an $L_{Ep,d}$ of 80 dB(A) and/or a peak sound pressure of 112 Pa (135 dB) workers must be informed of the level of exposure and ear protectors made available to those who request them. Above an $L_{Ep,d}$ of 85 dB(A) and/or a peak sound pressure of 112 Pa (135 dB) a programme of measures to reduce noise exposure by technical or management means must be introduced, and further training and information about noise exposure and its control given to workers. The proposed third Action Level is above an $L_{Ep,d}$ of 90 dB(A) and/or a peak sound pressure of 200 Pa (140 dB). Where these exposure levels are exceeded, areas must be delimited and access restricted, ear protectors must be used, and systematic health surveillance by or under a doctor must be carried out. Activities which exceed the fourth Action Level (above an $L_{Ep,d}$ of 105 dB(A) and/or a peak sound pressure of 600 Pa, or 150 dB) must be declared to the responsible authority, which must take appropriate measures to control the risk. In addition, where rest areas are provided for workers the noise level must be reduced to 60 dB(A) during sleep.

It must be emphasized that these are only proposals, which may never be adopted or may be modified before introduction. If they are ever introduced an indication of the possible timescale may be obtained by comparison with the 86/188 directive, which was first proposed in 1982, published in 1986, and implemented in the UK in 1990. Whether or not these specific proposals are eventually introduced it is likely that, in the longer term, employers will be required to further reduce exposures of employees to noise.

Environmental noise

The EEC first adopted a common environmental policy at the Paris summit of 1972. The Community first announced an 'anti-noise' policy in its Second Action Programme. The latest EC policy towards environmental noise is outlined in the Fifth Action Programme *The Environment — Towards Sustainability*, published in 1993. This acknowledged that noise pollution was 'one of the most pressing problems in urban areas' and determined that the primary objective in relation to noise regulation should be to remedy the problem of noise at nighttime. The following targets have been set for nighttime exposure levels in L_{Aeq}:

- exposure of the population to noise levels in excess of 65 dB(A) should be phased out; at no point in time should a level of 85 dB(A) be exceeded;

- the proportion of the population at present exposed to noise levels between 55 and 65 dB(A) should not suffer any increase in noise exposure;

- the proportion of the population at present exposed to noise levels less than 55 dB(A) should not suffer any increase above that level.

Measures designed to meet these objectives are under consideration. These may include controls on noise immissions (i.e. noise exposure at the reception point) as well as the continuing programme of measures designed to reduce emissions (i.e. noise emitted by the source) via the implementation of noise quality criteria for various environments.

Summary

1 Much of the present framework of legislation for the control of industrial noise in the UK dates from the Wilson Report of 1963, with the exception of nuisance legislation which has a much longer history in common law.

2 There is no legal definition of nuisance and it is not possible to define a single noise level above which a noise may be declared to be a nuisance. Nevertheless, certain factors may be identified from case law that are relevant to determining whether a noise is a nuisance, including the time of day and week at which the noise occurs, its duration, the type of area or locality in which it occurs, and the degree to which it causes disturbance. Private and public nuisance are dealt with under common law.

3 Statutory nuisance is dealt with under criminal law by the local authority environmental health department, under the provisions of the Environmental Protection Act (Part 3, ss79–82).

4 It is advantageous to solve nuisance complaints informally wherever possible.

5 Developments requiring planning permission may be subject to conditions relating to noise exposure levels. Guidance is given in Planning Policy Guidance Note 24, which defines four noise exposure categories.

6 BS4142 gives a method for rating industrial noise affecting mixed residential and industrial areas. It leads to the prediction of the likelihood of complaints arising from the development, and is intended for use in planning, and not for the investigation of nuisance complaints. It is based on the evaluation of the difference between the level of the specific noise under investigation and the background noise level.

7 BS4142 adopts a similar approach, and complies with ISO 1996/BS 7445, which gives a method for describing and measuring environmental noise of all types, not just noise from industrial and commercial premises.

8 Environmental impact assessments are needed for certain types of development, and require noise levels to be predicted, and the impact of the noise to be assessed.

9 Local authorities may set up noise abatement zones to control the level of environmental noise in an area. The provisions have rarely been used because of the expense involved in setting up and monitoring zones.

10 The Noise at Work Regulations impose duties on employers when noise exposure levels of employees exceed certain Action Levels. The duties relate to the assessment and reduction of noise exposure, the provision of hearing protectors, the reduction of noise levels, the provision of information and training, and the maintenance of equipment. There are also duties for employees and for suppliers of equipment.

11 The first step in a hearing conservation programme is to carry out a noise exposure assessment that should lead to a programme of action to reduce noise exposure.

12 Advice given in connection with the Management of the Health and Safety at Work Regulations 1992 suggests that employers should arrange regular audiometric checks of employees when personal daily noise exposure levels exceed 90dB(A).

13 Employees suffering from noise-induced hearing loss resulting from their work can take civil action under common law for negligence against their employer. Since the early 1980s negligence claims for compensation for noise-induced hearing loss have been one of the main sources of payments made by insurance companies for industrial injuries.

14 Since 1974 noise-induced hearing loss has been classified as a notifiable industrial disease under the social security legislation. Even though compensation paid by the government is restricted to employees in certain industries and to cases where the damage exceeds certain defined levels of hearing loss there have been several thousand claims each year since 1974.

15 The Supply of Machinery (Safety) Regulations require manufacturers to supply information about noise levels emitted by machinery, which must be designed and constructed so as to reduce these levels to the minimum possible. A series of standards is to be developed in support of these Regulations, including noise test codes indicating how the noise from the machinery is to be measured and the results declared and verified, and standards which will give guidance on the design of low-noise machinery.

16 A proposed directive on physical agents at work has been published which, if implemented, will eventually replace the Noise at Work Regulations and lead to a requirement for lower noise exposure levels of employees.

17 The EC Fifth Action Programme has set targets for reducing nighttime noise exposure levels in the community.

7
Measurement and instrumentation

Introduction

As far as a manager is concerned, the purpose of noise measurements are to identify and quantify problems, to diagnose their cause and to help solve them, to demonstrate that the solutions are effective and have remained so. It is therefore always important that noise measurement data are valid, reliable and accurate. The aim of this chapter is to provide information about what equipment is needed, how it should be used, and about the recording and reporting of noise measurement information. The need for training in noise measurement will be identified.

Instrumentation and equipment

Sound level meter and calibrator

There is a bewildering range of hand-held sound level meters on the market costing from about £200 to about £5000 at 1999 prices. They may be classified by the range of functions they possess or by their type according to British and international standards which set down their limits of accuracy.

The cheapest and most basic instrument is one which will only be able to measure instantaneous sound pressure level in dB(A). This will certainly be useful for checking levels in the workplace to determine if they ever exceed 85 or 90dB(A). They will only be able, however, to measure noise levels which are constant or steady. If noise of this type occurs in bursts it will be possible to estimate L_{Aeq} values by a combination of measurement and calculation, as shown in Chapter 1. If, however, the noise level fluctuates rapidly or is impulsive then this type of sound level meter cannot be used to give an accurate measurement. If the meter measures dB(C) as well as dB(A) this is useful because the difference between these two levels will give an indication of whether the noise has a predominantly high or low frequency spectrum. A detailed measurement of the frequency spectrum requires a meter with a set of octave or one-third octave filters. Sometimes meters of this basic type can be fitted with octave bands.

For measurements of fluctuating noise an integrating sound level meter is needed, which will allow L_{Aeq} values to be determined.

If it is required to measure impulsive noise and, in particular, if it is necessary to check compliance with the Peak Action Level of the Noise at Work Regulations then it is necessary to have a sound level meter with the facility to measure the true peak value of the impulsive noise. This value should either be unweighted (or linear) or C-weighted, but not A-weighted.

The capability of being able to measure L_{Aeq} over a period of a few minutes (perhaps up to one hour) will probably suffice for sampling workplace activities, but environmental noise monitoring often requires measurements over several hours, whole days, and even several days. Instruments differ over the way the measurement period may be controlled and initiated, from simple manual control of both start and cessation of measurement to completely automated measurements over preset intervals starting at preselected times. Some meters will also have the facility to start measuring when pre-set sound levels are exceeded. Additionally some meters will have the facility to measure L_{An} and single exposure level (SEL). L_{A90} measurements are required for BS4142 assessments and SEL for measuring noise from single events such as bursts of hammering or drilling.

Some sound level meters have output signals suitable for tape recorders, chart recorders and for downloading data to computers for further signal processing.

Calibrator

An essential accessory to every sound level meter is a calibrator which, when fitted over the microphone of the sound level meter, produces a known sound level. The calibrator produces a check that the meter is working properly and the meter should be calibrated before and after every measurement, and sometimes between if a long programme of measurements is being undertaken. Minor fluctuations from the calibration level due to temperature changes can be corrected by adjustment to the meter, but consistent discrepancies could indicate malfunction and the meter should be sent back to the manufacturer for repair.

In addition to day-to-day checks, both sound level meter and calibrator should be periodically checked and calibrated by an accredited laboratory at least once every two years.

Performance of sound level meters

BS5969 (IEC 651) specifies the performance of sound level meters and defines four types: 0, 1, 2 and 3. Type 0 meters that are intended for laboratory use only are the most accurate. Type 1 meters are suitable for laboratory and the most accurate field use, and type 2 for field use only. The standard deals with: the directionality of the sound level meter, i.e. the extent to which it has different sensitivity to sound approaching the microphone from different directions; the accuracy of the A-weighting network within the meter; the time response characteristics; and the sensitivity of the meter to influences such as humidity, temperature, vibration, and electric and magnetic fields.

Although the accuracy obtained with different types of meter will depend on the frequency spectrum of the sound and also its directional characteristics it is possible to give an approximate indication of the accuracy likely to be achieved in typical use. This is ±1 dB for type 1, ±2 dB for type 2 and ±3 dB for type 3.

Selection of sound level meter

It can be seen that the main factors to be considered are: what the meter will do (for example SPL only, L_{Aeq}, peak, octave bands), how accurate it is, and the cost. Other factors are: portability, how easy it is to use, ruggedness, battery life (this is important if the meter is to be used for several hours at a time), service arrangements, and flexibility in terms of possible upgrade at a later date.

Microphones

Microphones used for accurate sound measurement need to be sensitive, stable, have a good frequency response and be able to operate over a very wide range of sound levels. The two types of microphone that satisfy these requirements are the condenser microphone and the electret microphone, sometimes called the prepolarized microphone, which is an adapted form of condenser microphone. Overall, the condenser and electret types are comparable in cost and performance. Piezoelectric microphones are sometimes used on less accurate equipment.

The microphone is the most delicate and easily damaged part of the sound level meter and is expensive to replace, and so needs to be handled with great care. It is the most important part of the instrument, determining overall accuracy of the entire measuring system. In some cases a sound level meter may be upgraded, say from type 2 to type 1 accuracy, by changing the microphone. Condenser microphones need to be supplied with a polarizing voltage (typically 200 volts DC) whereas electric microphones do not, and so different preamplifier stages are needed for the two types. Nevertheless, many sound level meters will accommodate both types provided the correct polarizing voltage is selected. Condenser microphones are sensitive to damage when the sound level meter is operated in wet and humid environments because of the possibility that the polarization voltage across the very small gap (of a few microns) between the metal diaphragm and backing plates of the condenser will cause arcing and sparking if condensation occurs. Electret microphones do not suffer from this problem because a prepolarized polymer film between the plates means that a polarizing voltage is unnecessary.

A good quality microphone will have a flat frequency response and will have the same sensitivity for different frequencies of sound over a range from about 20 Hz to an upper limit in excess of 10 kHz. The high frequency response will depend on the size of the microphone and on the type of sound field for which it is calibrated. Half inch (12.5 mm) diameter microphones have a better high frequency performance than the one inch types which are gradually falling into disuse in modern instruments, despite their increased sensitivity. Quarter inch (6 mm) diameter microphones would allow measurements to even higher, ultrasonic frequencies. Many microphones are calibrated for free-field use and designed to be pointed at the source of sound so that the sound waves strike the diaphragm at 0°, or normal incidence (see Figure 7.1). Pressure response microphones are designed to be used at 90°, or grazing incidence. When the sound field is diffuse, for example in reverberant situations, the ideal microphone is one which has been calibrated for random sound incidence. The manufacturer's handbook will give guidance as to which type has been fitted and how it should be used.

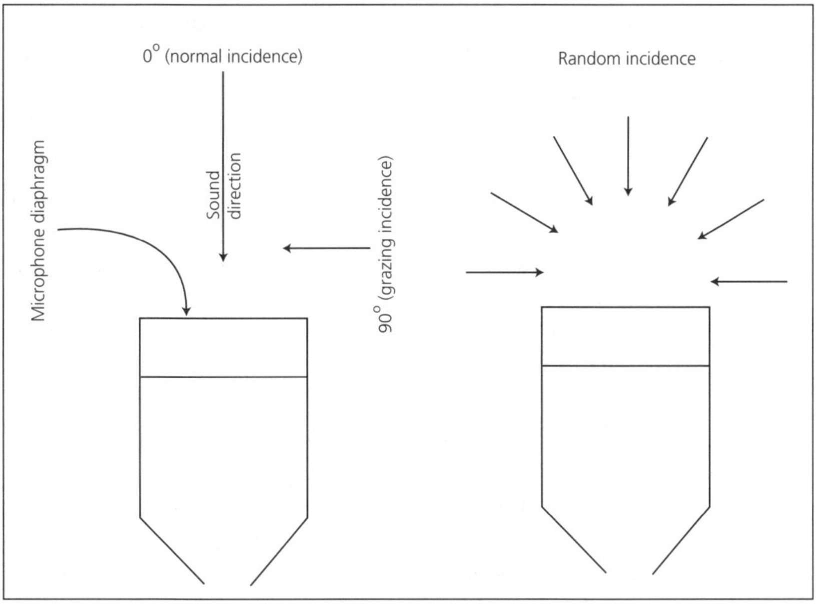

Figure 7.1 Angles of incidence of sound striking a microphone

Windshield
A suitable windshield should always be fitted over the microphone when in use to prevent winds and draughts of air from cooling fans fitted to machinery from producing spurious wind-generated noise in the microphone.

Other equipment

Noise dosemeters or dosimeters

Noise dosemeters are portable devices, also called personal sound exposure meters, that can fit into a breast pocket and be carried about throughout the day by the wearer to measure his/her noise exposure. A microphone connected to the instrument via a short flexible cable can be attached to the wearer's lapel, or to a hard hat if he/she is wearing one. The original types which are still available measure only the accumulated noise exposure dose since the start of the measurement period, either in pascal-squared hours or as a percentage of some dose limit such as the First or Second Action Levels of the Noise at Work Regulations. Sometimes the indicated value is a number which has to be translated into these values via a nomogram or formula. More sophisticated devices, often called data logging dosemeters, can display other parameters such as instantaneous sound pressure level, SEL and statistical L_{An} values. In addition, they may be attached to a computer at the end of the working shift and the data can be downloaded and processed to display a minute-by-minute profile of the noise exposure pattern throughout the shift. The number of times that the Peak Action Level has been exceeded during the measurement period may also be indicated.

The more sophisticated types can also be used as sound level meters satisfying the requirements of type 1, 2 or 3 of BS5969 depending mainly on the quality of microphone used. However, when worn as dosemeters they can only ever achieve type 2 performance because of effects of reflection and scattering of sound from the wearer's head and body.

The performance requirements of dosemeters are described in BS 6402. Their use in carrying out noise exposure assessments is described later in this chapter, including their advantages and limitations.

Tape recorders

Digital audio tape recorders (DATs) are now available with good frequency response and dynamic range that are suitable for recording output from sound level meters or directly from a microphone via a suitable preamplifier. Devices with automatic gain control must not be used. Good quality analogue tape recorders using either the direct record or frequency modulation (FM) signal processing may also be used.

If quantitative measurement data are to be taken from a recording it is essential that a calibration signal, for example a burst of signal from a calibrator fitted over the microphone, is recorded so that a reference level of signal is established on the tape. Many of the more sophisticated sound level meters will have an alternative input to the microphone to enable tape recordings to be analysed. It will then be possible to determine any noise measurement parameter by replaying the tape signal through a suitable instrument.

Tape recorders are useful for the following tasks:

- to capture signals on tape for a more detailed analysis later using more sophisticated equipment. This could be necessary, for example, either because more sophisticated equipment is not available on site or because only limited time was available;

- to enable a subjective impression of the noise to be conveyed to a third party, for example to demonstrate subjectively the effect of a noise control measure;

- to provide evidence of the identity of the source of a particular noise and its time of occurrence, for example in cases of disputes about the onset of bursts of noise late at night;

- to capture rare or unique transient events for later analysis, for example a controlled explosion or a demolition.

Narrowband frequency analysers

If a noise contains tonal components it is often useful to be able to identify the exact frequency, rather than the octave or one-third octave band, as an aid towards identifying the source. In the case of rotating machinery, for example, the frequency may be related to the rotational speed, and to the number of blades on a fan or turbine, or to the number of teeth on a gear, or the number of electrical poles on a motor or an alternator. The most commonly used narrowband analyser is the fast Fourier transform or FFT analyser, which produces a graph of sound pressure level against frequency on a screen. This type of device is used to identify the source of low frequency tonal noise (hums), which can sometimes cause annoyance at nighttime, even at comparatively low sound pressure levels. FFT analysis of vibration signals is also widely used for condition monitoring of machinery. From the variation in the level of the different harmonics of the rotational speed of the machine it is possible to identify the onset of failure and to identify possible causes such as bearing failure, out of balance or looseness of components.

Sound intensity meters

Sound intensity meters are specialist devices that can detect and indicate the direction of flow of acoustic energy as well as measuring the magnitude of sound intensity and sound pressure levels. The usual type has a probe that contains two identical microphones very close together. They can be used to locate sources within machines, identify weak links and flanking paths in sound insulation of partitions and enclosures, and to measure sound power levels of machines in-situ and without the need for a specialist test environment of an anechoic or reverberant room.

Building acoustics analysers

Although sound insulation and reverberation time measurements can be carried out using hand-held sound level meters, the requirement that noise levels have to be the average of measurements taken at several different positions in a room, in two adjacent rooms (in the case of an airborne sound insulation test) and for a range of different frequency bands means that this would be time consuming and would also require a great deal of calculation. Specialist microprocessor-controlled analysers are available which can measure, store and process sound level data gathered from two rooms simultaneously and which provide an enormous saving in measurement time and analysis.

This type of instrument can be used to measure the sound insulation performance of machine enclosures and noise havens, as well as of offices and conference rooms. Reverberation time measurement of industrial spaces can be used to determine the amount of acoustic absorption present in order to assess the potential for reducing reverberant sound by introducing additional sound-absorbing materials. The same equipment can be used for the measurement of sound power levels, which also require the averaging of sound pressure levels, in anechoic or reverberant rooms.

Analogue and digital signal processing in sound level meters

A sound level meter consists of a microphone, various stages of signal processing followed by the output or display of the required measurement parameter (Figure 7.2). The microphone converts a fluctuating sound pressure signal into an electrical signal in which the variations of voltage mimic identically, or are analogous to, the variations in the sound pressure (Figure 7.3).

The signal from the microphone then undergoes several stages of conditioning and processing until it is in an appropriate form to be delivered to the output or display device. These stages include:

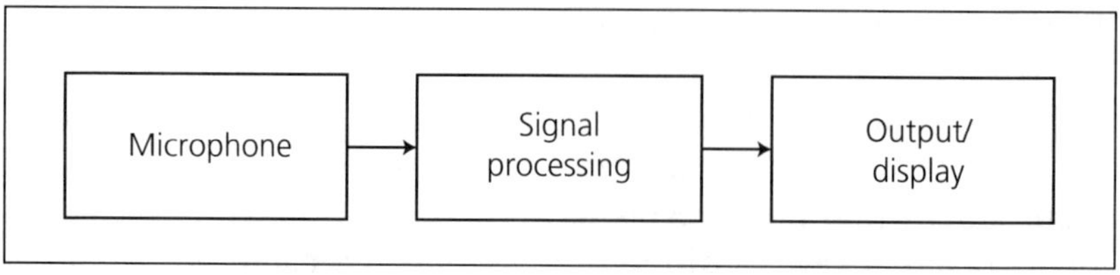

Figure 7.2 Components of a sound level meter

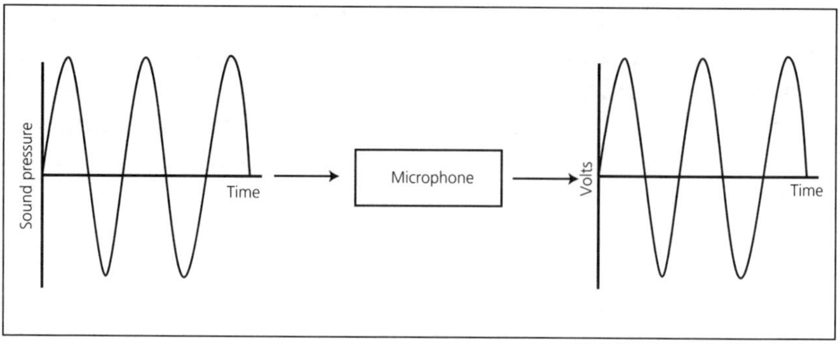

Figure 7.3 The function of the microphone in a sound level meter

- preamplification and amplification, to condition the signal to meet the requirements of the following processing stages;

- frequency weighting, to provide an A or C weighted version of the signal, as described in Chapter 2, or frequency analysis, for example into octave or one-third octave bands;

- further amplification or attenuation in order to bring the magnitude of the signal into the range required by the detector and indicator circuits;

- detector and indicator stages that produce a signal which is proportional to the root mean square (RMS) sound pressure as explained in Chapter 1, and which average this signal over an appropriate time weighting such as fast or slow, and deliver the appropriately weighted and averaged signal to the output or display device. It is at this stage that peak detection and indication of the signal would be included as an alternative to RMS.

In meters of the older type an analogue display device is used, such as a moving needle on a scale. In many modern instruments a digital display is used, sometimes together with a pseudo-analogue display such as a moving column indicating how the measured parameter is varying.

All of the above stages may be carried out by analogue signal processing methods, but during the 1980s and 1990s more and more processing was carried out digitally. An analogue-to-digital converter in the sound level meter samples, digitizes and stores the signal for subsequent digital processing.

The use of digital signal processing enables the technology of the computer to be utilized inside the sound level meter and greatly facilitates processing which involves calculations of L_{Aeq} and L_{An}.

Computers, data loggers and the virtual sound level meter

The use of digital signal processing in sound level meters has led to the increasing interfacing of sound level meters with computers so that signals from the sound level meter can be transferred, or downloaded to a computer, either for storage and continuing display, i.e. data logging, or for further analysis, i.e. post-processing. This has the advantage that noise level data from the sound level meter can be processed by databases, spreadsheets and graphical packages in the computer and easily incorporated into reports in the form of tables and graphs.

A natural extension of this process is to build the signal processing usually contained in the sound level meter directly into the computer, so that a signal from a microphone may be fed into the computer after only the minimum of signal conditioning, consisting of preamplification and some amplification. The processing and display of the microphone signal are then carried out in the computer, with the advantage of great flexibility because different types of analysis that may have required different dedicated instruments, such as for building acoustics or environmental noise, may all be carried out within the same computer simply by changing the software. Thus apart from the microphone and amplifier stages, all of the sound level meter is contained within the software of the computer, hence the term 'virtual sound level meter'. The increasing use and availability, data storage capacity and processing power of lap top computers that can easily be taken to the measurement site means that the trend towards use of computer-based measurement systems will probably increase, but equally the use of dedicated hand-held sound level meters will probably also continue for certain applications.

Measurement and the use of equipment

Correct use of the sound level meter

Correct use of the meter involves:

- preliminary inspection and checks to ensure that the meter is working properly;
- selection of meter functions and settings appropriate to the measurements to be taken, having decided what, when and where to measure;
- precautions to avoid unwanted influence on the meter readings;
- postmeasurement checks and recording of all relevant measurement details.

Before each use the meter and the microphone should be examined for any obvious sign of damage. Most meters have a facility for checking the state of the battery and after this the meter should be switched to measure sound pressure level and a simple test carried out to check that it seems to be responding to ambient noises such as fingers clicking, whistling, talking into the microphone, etc. Sound pressure level mode is best for this rather than L_{Aeq}. The meter should then be calibrated and the windshield fitted. It is then ready for use.

Each type of sound level meter will have different types of controls and the manufacturer's handbook should be consulted, kept safely and its instructions followed carefully. However, in most cases the following selections have to be made:

- appropriate time function: SPL; F, S or I; L_{Aeq}; Peak;
- appropriate frequency weighting function: A, C, linear (unweighted), octave bands;
- appropriate range: some meters are fitted with overload and underload indicators which assist in range selection.

Care has to be taken that the meter is not being affected by wind, unwanted reflections, background noise and extremes of temperature and relative humidity. The use of the windshield will protect against the influence of draughts indoors or mild breezes outdoors but care must be taken to ensure that wind-generated noise, even using a windshield, is at least 10 dB below the measured value. Sometimes this can be checked by taking a measurement with some temporary wind barrier in place or by noting how the indicated sound level fluctuates with gusts of wind. Generally, valid measurements cannot be taken if the wind speed exceeds about $5\,ms^{-1}$, but different measurement standards specify various values.

Sound reflected by nearby objects, including the body of the operator, can be detected by the microphone and influence the measured value of sound pressure level. For this reason the sound level meter should always be held with the arm outstretched away from the body of the operator towards the sound source, or mounted on a tripod. Unless there is a good reason not to do so, the microphone should be positioned well away (at least 1 metre) from hard, reflecting surfaces. If this is not possible then the presence of such a surface should be noted in the measurement report.

Unless there is a good reason for doing so, noise measurements are not usually taken outdoors when it is raining. Apart from the danger of malfunction and damage due to ingress of water into the meter and microphone, the sounds produced by the rainfall will influence the reading, and if noise from a distant noise source is being measured then sound propagation conditions will be very different from those in dry weather conditions.

If noise from a specific source, such as a machine, is being measured then it will be necessary to check that background noise levels are at least 10dB below the measured value. Some meters have a pause button that is useful for cutting out the effects of passing vehicles or aeroplanes on the measurement. The manufacturer's handbook should be consulted with regard to using the sound level meter in extremely hot or cold weather.

When all the measurements have been completed the battery condition and the calibration should be checked again before leaving the measurement site and all the relevant measurement details should be recorded. It is useful to devise a measurement report form (Figure 7.4 for example) which can also act as a prompt and a checklist to ensure that all checks have been made and necessary details recorded.

Measurement aims

The starting point of any noise measurement is to decide on the main purpose of the measurement, since this will influence later decisions. As an example consider the possible reasons that there could be for needing to measure noise levels produced by a compressor. These could include:

- to compare with noise levels from alternative equipment;
- to compare with manufacturer's noise specification;
- to compare with company's own (i.e. customer's) noise specification;
- to assess the need for or effect of machine maintenance;

Noise measurement checklist/report form

Title/location ...*J.T. TIMBER LTD, CRAMPTON*...

Purpose of measurement ...*Noise at work survey*...

Measurement taken by ...*J Smith*... Date ...*12-9-98*...

Type of sound level meter ...*XYZ type 220*... Serial no. ...*1034*...

Wind/weather conditions ...*— (indoors)*...

Noise measurement parameters (SPL, L_{Aeq}, octave bands etc.)

...*Leq over machine cycle (approx. 5 mins)*...

Relevant meter settings (fast/slow etc.) ...*Leq*...

Battery check (tick): Before ...✓... After ...✓...

Calibration check (tick): Before ...✓... After ...✓...

Windshield fitted?: ...*Yes*...

Subjective impressions of noise (tonal/impulsive/steady/intermittent?)

...*Idling — steady, broadband* ... *Cutting — level inceases, tonal*...

Map/plan of location (show microphone positions) *Woodwork shop*

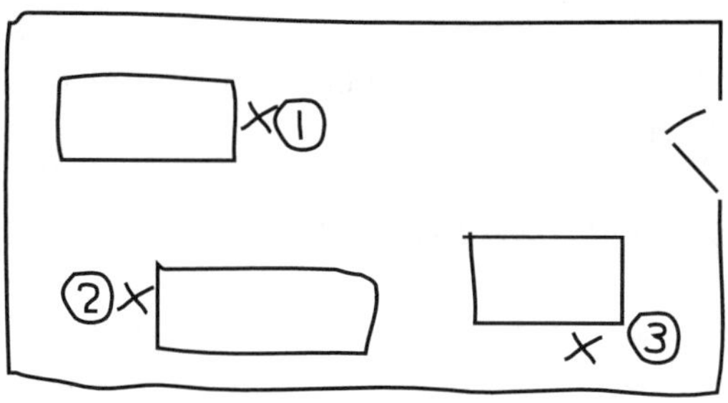

Noise level readings

Thicknesser - position 1 86 dB(A)

Circular saw - position 2 93 dB(A)

Planer - position 3 84 dB(A)

Figure 7.4 Sample measurement checklist/report form

- to assess need for and to quantify noise reduction requirements;
- to diagnose noise sources and mechanisms and specify control methods;
- to assess the effectiveness of noise control measures;
- to measure the sound power level of the machine;
- to assess the noise exposure level of the machine operator;
- to use as a basis for predicting noise levels at other distances;
- to use as part of a noise complaint investigation;
- to use as part of a planning application investigation;
- to use as part of an environmental impact assessment;
- to assess whether a machine is a major contributor to the noise level at the receiver.

Measurement of noise from machinery

Some of these different aims will involve very different measurement procedures — for example in choice of measurement position, type of sound level meter to be used, noise parameter to be measured. Very broadly the type of measurement required to meet the various objectives listed above fall into three categories, discussed in more detail in the sections that follow. The three types are:

- *Noise emission measurements* where the objective is to measure the noise output from a source, such as a machine. Here it is the position of the microphone relative to source that is important, rather than its position relative to the receiver, and the emphasis will usually be on taking measurements close to the machine.

- *Noise immission or noise exposure measurements* where the purpose is to measure the noise to which the receiver is exposed. Even if the exposure is due mainly to one machine, there is a change in emphasis in comparison with the first category, and the measurement position is selected relative to the receiver. It is also necessary to make a distinction between measurements taken in the workplace with the aim of estimating personal daily noise exposure level and protecting employees from hearing damage, and noise immission measurements taken in the environment surrounding the workplace, with the aim of preventing annoyance to neighbours. In the former case, measurements are taken at employee's ear position, exposure time has also to be estimated, and the noise index to be measured and $L_{Ep,d}$ clearly defined. In the latter case, measurements are taken at the receiver's dwelling (usually outside, but sometimes inside) or at the boundary of the premises containing the noise source, and the measurement parameters are governed by standards and codes such as BS 4142, BS 7445 and PPG 24.

- *Diagnostic measurements aimed at determining the cause of the noise problem* whether occupational or environmental, i.e. identifying the main source or sources of the noise and/or in the case of machinery the noise-producing mechanisms and main noise-radiating areas.

Noise emission from machinery — sound pressure level and sound power level

In principle the sound pressure level produced by a sound source at any distance can be predicted from its sound power level, although in practice the usual calculations are based on simple models of free or reverberant sound fields.

Therefore the output from a sound source may be described either by its sound power level, or by specifying the sound pressure level at a certain distance from the source. There are advantages and disadvantages to each method.

The main advantage of using sound power levels is simplicity — the L_W is a single-figure number which depends only on the sound source and not on any other factor such as distance or details of the acoustic environment. This is the idea behind various European Community noise directives which require certain classes of machinery to be labelled with their L_W values, so that users and purchasers can easily compare the noise produced by different types of machine.

There are, however, a number of disadvantages. The measurement of sound power level requires specialist test rooms or equipment, as described below. Also, the L_W value itself has no significance subjectively, unlike the sound pressure level, which can be related to what is actually heard. Although in principle the sound pressure level in any situation may be predicted from the L_W value, it is in practice only possible to predict far-field values and not those in the near field close to the source.

The main disadvantage of specifying the sound pressure level at a particular distance from the source is that it can lead to ambiguity and confusion for users when trying to compare the noise outputs from machines that are described in different ways, for example if different distances are used or if the tests are carried out in different acoustic environments. This method does, however, have the advantage that sound pressure levels may be easily measured and can be related to what is heard.

Measurement of sound pressure levels emitted by machines

Measurement decisions which have to be made include: type of sound level meter, microphone position (relative to the machine), the machine operating conditions (such as load, speed, working material), details of the measurement environment (including presence of nearby reflecting and absorbing surfaces, wind speed and background noise levels).

There are many different standards and codes of practice, including those relating to sound power measurement, giving advice about how to measure noise emission from various types of machinery. Typical measurement positions which are specified include: on a measurement surface (a parallelepiped or hemisphere, for example) surrounding the machine, at fixed distances at various positions around the machine (typically at 1 metre) and including the position where the noise level is a maximum, and at the operator's position. The machine operating conditions should be easily reproducible so that measurements can be repeated, and should relate to typical in-use conditions and also to those that give rise to maximum noise levels. As far as possible the measurement position should not be too close to sound-reflecting surfaces (a minimum distance of 1 metre is recommended in some measurement codes) unless there is some overriding reason such as the need to measure at the operator's ear position.

In the absence of any specific test code the operator will have to make measurement decisions based on his/her experience and training, and upon knowledge and principles introduced in Chapter 3 (including, for example, the concepts of near and far fields and of direct and reverberant sound). The objectives of the measurement and the practicalities of the measurement situation must also be taken into account.

Measurement of sound power levels

There are, in principle, four different test methods:

- *Free-field method* This requires that measurement of sound radiated from the source is not affected by reflected sound. Such an acoustic environment may sometimes be achieved by performing tests outdoors, or in an anechoic or semi-anechoic test room.

- *Sound intensity method* The use of a sound intensity meter, which is sensitive to the direction of flow of sound energy, can be used to measure sound power levels in nonanechoic environments.

- *Reverberant method* This requires the specialist test environment of a reverberant room.
- *Substitution method* This requires a calibrated sound power source.

Free-field method

An anechoic room is a specially constructed chamber in which the walls, floor and ceiling are covered with sound-absorbing material, usually in the form of wedges, which is effective in eliminating reflected sound. Thus measurements of sound pressure levels produced by a noise source in such a room are of direct sound only and can be used to compute the sound power level of the source. The directivity of the source can also be measured. The method is convenient for portable machines, but the size of the anechoic room limits the size of machines which can be tested since measurements should be made in the far field of the sound source.

A semi-anechoic room has sound-absorbing walls and ceiling but a hard, sound-reflecting floor.

The sound power level L_W is related to the average sound pressure level measured over a test surface surrounding the source, L_p, and the area of that surface, S, by the formula:

$$L_W = L_p + 10\log S$$

If the test surface is a sphere of radius r, then $S = 4\pi r^2$, or if, in the case of a semi-anechoic room, it is a hemisphere, then $S = 2\pi r^2$.

Sound intensity method

The sound intensity method is similar in principle to the free-field method outlined above. The average sound intensity, L_I, is measured over a test surface, usually a hemisphere or parallelepiped, surrounding the source. The sound power level is given by:

$$L_W = L_I + 10\log S$$

A necessary requirement of the free-field method, in which measurements are taken using a sound level meter, is that sound energy from the source only travels outwards from the source through the test surface. The great advantage of the sound intensity meter is that it allows measurements to be carried out in an ordinary, i.e. nonanechoic, room, where the presence of reflecting surfaces means that some reflected sound energy will pass through the test surface in the opposite, inwards direction. However, provided that there is no acoustic absorption inside the test surface all of this reflected sound energy will eventually pass out through the test surface again, either directly or maybe after reflection or scattering by the surface of the noise source. Since the sound intensity meter indicates the net flow of acoustic energy through the test surface, the value of the average sound intensity measured over the entire surface will correspond only to that provided by the outward flow of energy from the source. The reflected sound energy passing through the surface cancels out, making a net zero contribution to the flow of acoustic energy through the surface.

For similar reasons measurements can also be taken in the presence of background noise from another source, provided that it produces a constant, steady level and is located outside the test surface so that it also produces a net zero flow of sound energy through the test surface.

BS7703 gives details of the measurement method, including recommendations for the size and shape of the test surface, number of measurement points to be used, and checks on the adequacy of the equipment and the measurement procedures.

Reverberant room method

A truly reverberant room is one in which, as a result of reflection, diffraction and scattering by the surfaces in the room, the sound energy from a source in the room is diffused completely throughout the room so that the sound pressure level is the same everywhere in the room. In practice, measurements are taken at several points in the room and the average sound pressure level, L_p, is obtained. This is related to the sound power level of the source, L_W, and to the amount of absorption in the room, via the reverberation time, T, and the room volume V:

$$L_W = L_p + 10\log V - 10\log T - 14$$

A modified and more accurate version of this formula is given in ISO3741. Only sound power levels can be obtained from reverberant room methods — information about the directivity of the source can only be obtained from free-field methods.

Substitution method
In the substitution method a reference sound source of known sound power level is used. Comparisons are made of the sound pressure levels produced in a room by the machine under test and the standard source. This type of test may be carried out in a reverberant room, in which case it will not be necessary to know room details such as volume and reverberation time, or, with much less accuracy, in an ordinary room or in the in-situ location of the noise source. The reference sound source should be capable of being calibrated and should be omnidirectional, as far as possible, over the frequency range of interest.

Draft noise test code — CEN Standard *Noise Measurement Methods for Printing, Paper Converting, Papermaking Machines and Equipment*
The standard specifies noise measurement methods that are allowed, operating and mounting conditions that shall be used for the test, and the information to be included in the test report. It applies to those types of machine listed in the annexes to the standard. The measurement methods specified are those for the determination of sound power levels or emission sound pressure levels.

Sound power levels shall be determined in accordance with standards EN23744, EN29614/1 (with accuracy grade 2) or EN29614/2 (with accuracy grade 2). Where these standards are not applicable EN23746 (with accuracy grade 3) or EN29614/2 (with accuracy grade 3) shall be used. The test report shall state the reasons why it was not possible to apply a grade 2 method for determining sound power level.

For the determination of emission sound pressure levels, the measurement points are the operator's workstation and those defined in the annexes for the different types of machine. Typically they are either 0.5m or 1m from some specified point on the machine, such as the control desk, charge or discharge points, or feed or delivery points. Where the operator's work position cannot be defined, the point with the highest sound pressure level measured at a distance of 1m from the machine surface at a height of 1.6m above the floor or access platform should also be measured. For machines with dimensions greater than 15m the emission sound pressure level is determined as the mean value of a number of sound pressure levels measured along a path around the machine at a height of 1.6m above the floor or access platform and at a distance of 1m from the machine. The measuring points shall be spaced so that the difference in emission sound pressure levels between adjacent points does not exceed 5dB(A).

The conditions under which the machine is installed and mounted shall be specified in the test report. These shall usually be in accordance with the manufacturer's instructions. Care should be taken to prevent any electrical connections, pipes or air ducts connected to the machine from making significant contributions to the noise emission.

For machines with variable operating conditions it will be necessary to define either typical operating conditions or characteristic work cycles such as the time required for converting and finishing a product such as a printed sheet, folded box, book block etc. Where work cycles are used for measuring and fluctuations of the A-weighted sound pressure level occurring during such cycles exceed 5dB(A), cycles should be divided into subcycles during which the specified operating conditions exist, for example operation under no load or full load conditions. If subdividing the work cycle into subcycles is not possible then the average level over the whole work cycle shall be measured and reported. For machines with varying applications, such as combined machines or production lines, separate measurements shall be taken for each specific application.

The machine operating conditions, noise measurement positions and any required additional technical data about the machine are specified in the annexes for 68 different types of machine, grouped into nine categories (A–H, J): machines for processing raw material, machines for the preparation of wood pulp, machines for the preparation of cellulose, machines for the preparation of stock, paper, board and dewatering machines, finishing and packaging machines, machines for the production of printing forms, printing presses, paper converting machines.

BS7445 (ISO 1996) 1991 Description and measurement of environmental noise

The aim of this international standard is to provide authorities with the methods for describing noise in community environments. Often environmental noise is a composite of the sounds from many sources, and the distribution of the different kinds of noise is likely to change from moment to moment. The methods and procedures described in the standard are intended to be applicable to sounds from all sources, individually and in combination, which contribute to the total noise at a site. At present this requirement seems to be best met by adopting the equivalent continuous A-weighted sound pressure level as the basic quantity, supplemented if necessary by corrections or other descriptors. Based upon the principles described in the standard, acceptable limits of noise can be specified, and compliance with these limits can be controlled, although such limits are not specified in the standard.

The information below is taken from Part 1 of the standard: *Guide to quantities and procedures.* It is assumed that the reader is familiar with the terminology and general principles of the standard relating to the rating of noise; the extracts below relate only to measurement and instrumentation details.

Measurement equipment may comprise integrating/averaging meters, sound exposure level meters, sound level meters (i.e. non-integrating) set to slow, data loggers or statistical distribution analysers which sample the running dB(A) value set to fast. Equipment should preferably be of IEC 651 type 1, but at least of type 2 accuracy.

Integrating/averaging meters are preferred for noise of impulsive, fluctuating or cyclic character and special care should be taken to ensure that the dynamic range of equipment is large enough and that the inherent electrical noise and overload capacity of the instrument is suitable for the application. Magnetic tape recorders may have a lower, inadequate dynamic range.

Calibration should be carried out in accordance with manufacturer's instructions. Field checks should be carried out at least before and after each series of measurements. Comprehensive recalibration should be carried out at certain time intervals, for example annually.

It is important that pertinent details of the measurement instrumentation, measurement procedure and conditions prevailing during the measurements are carefully recorded and kept for reference purposes.

In some circumstances the A-weighting may be inadequate for filtering out high-level infrasound which occurs near some industrial locations and some forms of transport as well as near buildings owing to wind turbulence. This may cause overload and, if not detected, distortion produced at higher frequencies may be inaccurately attributed to audible sound.

The choice of the actual measurement position will depend on the purpose of the measurement. When it is desired to minimize the influence of reflections then the measurement should, whenever possible, be carried out at least 3.5 m from any reflecting structure other than the ground. When not otherwise specified the preferred measurement height is 1.2–1.5 m above the ground. The preferred positions for outdoor measurements near buildings are 1–2 m from the facade, and 1.2–1.5 m above each floor level of interest, unless otherwise specified. Measurement positions inside buildings should, unless otherwise specified, be at least 1 m from the walls or other major reflecting surface, 1.2–1.5 m above the floor and about 1.5 m from windows.

When the sound transmission distance between source and receiver is large the sound levels measured at the reception point may be affected by meteorological conditions. The standard recommends either taking an average of measurements over a range of meteorological conditions found at the measurement position(s), or choosing to take measurements only under specific weather conditions, usually those that result in the most stable sound propagation, that is with a significant positive wind component from source to the measurement position(s).

Recommended equipment and procedures are described for measuring L_{Aeq} for four different types of noise: fluctuating noise, steady noise, steady noise with stepwise variations of level, and noise consisting of separate events. If equipment is used that calculates the L_{Aeq} from samples of the running sound pressure level then the interval between samples must be less than the time constant of the instrumentation if the result is to be a good approximation to that obtained using an integrating sound level meter.

Information to be recorded is listed under the headings of: results of the acoustic measurements, measurement technique, conditions prevailing during measurements, and qualitative data (origin, identification of the source of the noise, and the nature, character and connotation of the sound).

The following additional information is taken from Part 2 of the standard: *Guide to the Acquisition of Data Pertinent to Land Use.*

If possible, information on the prevailing meteorological conditions should include statistical information on wind speed and direction, on precipitation and temperature, including the occurrence of temperature inversions for any time interval (such as a year) over which a long-term average sound level is to be estimated.

The standard enables a rating level to be obtained by making adjustments to the measured level for tonal and impulsive characteristics of the noise. The existence of a prominent tonal component may be clearly audible and may be confirmed if the results of a one-third octave band analysis show that the level of one of the one-third octave bands exceeds the level of the adjacent bands by 5 dB or more, but a less prominent tone may require narrowband analysis. The impulsive character of the sound may be described by the difference between the average dB(A) level measured using the impulse time response and the L_{Aeq} value measured over the same time interval, and also by measuring the peak level. For large amplitude noise, such as that generated by sonic booms or mining or quarrying blasts, measurements with C-weighting are used in some countries to determine the rating level.

The height of the microphone shall be chosen according to the actual or expected height of the receiver. In potentially built-up areas the preferred measurement height shall be 3–11 m. In all other cases it shall be as specified in Part 1 of the standard. The influence of ground effects and low barriers is reduced by choosing a greater measurement height, but the measured level will generally be higher than that measured closer to the ground. The height of the microphone positions shall be stated in the measurement report. If it is desired to minimize the influence of reflections, measurements should be made, whenever possible, at least 0.5 m away from open windows. The microphone should be orientated to be most uniformly sensitive to the incident sound.

Suggested meteorological conditions that give rise to stable sound propagation conditions are: wind direction within ±45° of the direction connecting source to receiver, with the wind blowing from source to receiver at a speed of between 1 and 5 $\mathrm{ms^{-1}}$, measured at a height of 3–11 m above the ground, with no strong temperature inversions near to the ground, and no heavy precipitation.

Part 3 of the standard is a guide to the application of noise limits.

_BS4142: 1997_ Method for Rating Industrial Noise Affecting Mixed Residential and Industrial Areas

This standard was revised in 1990 in order to bring it into line with BS7445 (ISO 1996), although it is much more limited in scope than the international standard. It is assumed that the reader is familiar with the general principles and terminology of BS4142, and the extracts given below relate to measurement aspects only.

Measurement equipment of type 2 accuracy or better is required (BS5969 or BS6698), with type 1 preferred.

Operational calibration using a calibrator which complies with class 2 of BS7189 or better is required before and after each series of measurements, and at least twice daily if measurements are made over a prolonged period of time. In addition, more complete calibration of the measurement equipment, including calibrator, by a NAMAS approved laboratory is required at least every two years.

Measurements should be made outside buildings where people are affected by the noise. The preferred measurement height is 1.2–1.5 m above the ground, and, in order to minimize the influence of reflections, at least 3.5 m from any reflecting surface other than the ground. Where it is necessary to make measurements above ground floor level they should be at a distance of 1 m from the facade at each relevant floor of the building.

The weather conditions prevailing during the measurements should be recorded. Noise measurements should not be carried out in extreme weather conditions, i.e. high winds (greater than 5 ms^{-1}), low temperatures (less than 3°C), or rain. Precautions should be taken to minimize the influence on the noise level readings of wind, rain and electrical interference. The measured levels should be at least 10 dB above readings due to any of these influences.

Advice is given on how to proceed if the measured value of the specific noise is less than 10 dB above the background noise level.

If the level of the residual noise varies, then, if possible, measure the specific noise at times when the level of the residual noise is at least 10 dB less than that of the specific noise, or, if this is not possible, then either correct the measured specific noise level by using a decibel subtraction chart, or take measurements closer to the source, so that they are at least 10 dB above background, and then calculate a distance correction.

Advice is given on the selection of an appropriate measurement time interval for the various types of specific noise which may be encountered, for example continuous, intermittent, cyclic, randomly fluctuating.

Advice is given about strategies for measuring the background noise level in the presence of the specific noise. Background noise measurements should be made under similar conditions (i.e. weather, times of day and week) to those prevailing when the specific noise was measured and will be operating. The background noise level should be measured over a time interval which is long enough for a representative value to be obtained — this should usually be at least five minutes.

The background noise level, L_{A90} should be measured with the measuring instrument set to fast. If a non-integrating meter is used to measure the specific noise, for example if it is steady, then it should be set to slow.

A list is given of information, including measurement information, which should be reported.

Assessment of noise exposure levels

One of the duties of an employer in a noisy workplace is to make sure that an assessment of the noise exposure of employees is carried out by a competent person.

The emphasis here is on the noise energy received by the person rather than the noise level emitted by a machine. Noise exposure depends on both the sound pressure level at the person's ear and the time for which the person is exposed to that level.

Since every workplace situation is different, there is no single method for carrying such assessments. There are a number of possible techniques that may be used. These are described below.

- *Noise level grids and contour plots* If the noise levels are fairly constant throughout the workplace it may be possible to measure at different positions and to plot contours of sound pressure levels which may be used to estimate exposure levels depending upon how long individuals work in different parts of the workplace.

- *Static samples* If the noise level varies with time it is possible to measure samples of L_{Aeq} at various positions in the workplace, for example in gangways or where employees may dwell, such as at stores or drinks vending machines.

- *Activity samples* These are samples of L_{Aeq} taken with a sound level meter held close to an employee's ear while he/she carries out some routine and repetitive cycle of work. The personal daily noise exposure level may be calculated from measurements of all such activities and their durations.

- *Use of dosemeters* Personal noise exposure meters or dosemeters may be carried around by the subject.

Diagnostic measurements

Some diagnostic techniques were introduced in Chapter 4, and are briefly reviewed here.

- *Listening* It is often possible to identify which machine, or which part of a machine is causing the problem simply by listening.

- *Switching off and on in turn* Where this is possible this is the best way of ranking the contribution of several different sources to the noise at the receiver position. Ideally all the sources should be switched off and then each source, on its own, switched on in turn and the noise levels listened to, and measured. This is more effective than turning off each source in turn, with all other sources remaining on, although this quicker and more convenient test may be effective if it is suspected that there is one dominant noise source, but it will be inconclusive if there are several sources that contribute more-or-less equally.

Although these tests are simple in principle they can be complicated in practice, and need to be carried out with care and thoroughness. This can be the case, for example, when trying to identify which of a bank of several different extract fans on a factory roof is responsible for an environmental noise problem.

- *Selective operation of different parts of a machine* This method exploits the operator's expert knowledge of how the machine works. Investigation of how the noise varies with changes in operating conditions such as load, speed, type of working material, can sometimes provide insight into how the noise is generated and where it is radiated from.

- *Wrapping/unwrapping tests* This is a procedure for identifying and ranking different noise-radiating surfaces of a machine. Each part of the machine is fitted with a close-fitting sound insulating cover made of acoustic lagging material. Noise levels are measured with each cover removed in turn, with all the others remaining in place. The covers should be of a sandwich construction with a resilient layer (mineral fibre or foam) fitted next to the noise-radiating surface backed with a sheet of massive impervious material (lead or steel sheet, plasterboard etc.). The technique is only suitable for medium and high frequencies, above about 250 Hz, because the lagging will not be effective at lower frequencies. An extension of the idea is to fit temporary enclosures over small ancillary noise sources such as motors, gearboxes or feed pumps, in order to establish the contribution which they make to the total noise from the machine.

- *Comparison of measurement with theory.*

Sometimes the source of a noise is known but there are two or more transmission paths and it is necessary to determine which is the most important one. A good example is the transmission of fan or pump noise from a plant room through a wall or ceiling to an adjacent space such as an office. The source of the noise in the office is obvious but it is not clear whether airborne or structure-borne sound is the main transmission path. The noise level close to the plant can be measured and the sound level transmitted through the wall or ceiling may be calculated using the theory outlined in Chapter 3, making reasonable estimates for the sound reduction index of the separating partition and amount of absorption in the receiving room. Although there is no simple way of calculating the structure-borne sound level, a comparison of the calculated airborne sound level with the actual measured level in the office can sometimes be useful. If the measured level is much higher than that predicted by airborne sound transmission alone this is a good indication that it is structure-borne sound that is the main cause of the problem.

In another example consider a situation where there are two rooftop extract fans which appear to be prime candidates for the cause of a noise problem from a factory at a nearby house. Both noise sources are clearly visible from the bedroom, both operate 24 hours every day and it is not possible to switch either of them off. In this case it may be possible to determine which is the major contributor by measuring the received noise level outside the bedroom window, and comparing with predictions based on measurements made close to each of the sources. Suppose, for example, that the noise level at the bedroom window is 55 dB(A) and the two sources are 50 m and 200 m away from the window. The noise levels are measured 2.5 m from each source and are 90 dB(A) for the more distant source and 70 dB(A) for the closer source. By assuming that both sources obey the 6 dB per doubling of distance (or 20 dB per decade of distance) rule explained in Chapter 3, the noise level expected at the window from each source can be predicted: 52 dB(A) from the more powerful, distant source, and 49 dB(A) from the closer source. Combining these two predicted levels using the methods described in Chapter 1 gives a predicted level of 54dB(A), which agrees well with the measured value of 55dB(A) — the difference is within measurement uncertainty, or could possibly indicate that a third source, maybe the background noise level, is also contributing. It is clear, however, that the first priority is to reduce the noise from the more distant fan, after which it may or may not be necessary to treat the closer one. In practice it is very likely that the above procedure would have to be carried out in octave bands, as well as in dB(A).

- *Narrowband frequency analysis* Sometimes it is possible to identify the source of a tonal component in a noise spectrum by measuring the frequency using a narrowband frequency analyser such as fast Fourier transform (FFT) analyser, and then linking that frequency to some noise-producing cyclic event, usually associated with rotating machinery, such as the blade-passing frequency of a fan or the tooth-meshing frequency of a set of gears. FFT analysers have also been used successfully in identifying sources of low level, low frequency tonal noise from industrial plant at nighttime. This type of problem can be notoriously difficult to solve. The noise being complained of only becomes clearly audible late at night when all other sources of noise have ceased and the background noise level is low. Noise at low frequencies travels long distances with very little attenuation, and because of the long wavelengths involved it is not possible to detect the direction from which it is coming. Because the sound insulation of buildings is poor at these frequencies and because of the possibility of exciting resonances within rooms, there is sometimes very little difference between the level of noise heard inside and outside the dwelling. To add to the difficulty it is sometimes the case that the investigator is unable to hear the noise although it can be heard by the complainant, and in some cases, but not all, the complainant may be suffering from tinnitus or from some psychological condition, and there is no source of noise. The great advantage of the FFT analyser in these cases, particularly if it is portable, is that it is possible to see the peak or peaks in the narrowband spectrum at the same time as listening to it. Usually there is some variation in the amplitude of the noise, often in the form of a regular modulation, and often it is the ability to correlate these fluctuations as seen on the screen with what is heard which clinches the identification of the source.

The next three techniques are more specialized but are also used occasionally by noise consultants to help diagnose the source of a noise or to identify its transmission path.

- *Use of sound intensity measurements.*

- *Use of vibration measurements* Sometimes it is difficult to take measurements of the noise radiated from a machine or part of a machine because of contributions from nearby sources, but it is possible to measure the vibration level of a surface and from this to estimate the sound pressure level being radiated by the surface. It is then possible to compare the predicted noise levels from different surfaces with each other and with the measured noise level in order to decide which surfaces are the most important radiators of noise.

- *Advanced signal processing techniques — correlation and coherence* There are a number of signal processing techniques that are designed to extract meaningful information from a signal which has been mixed with other unwanted signals, i.e. with 'noise'. These techniques would, for example, be useful for identifying and separating out the sound from a particular machine from the 'noise' from all the other machines. In correlation measurements, for example, two signals are compared, or correlated in order to decide the extent to which they are coherent, i.e. that they are causally related. The two signals could be the signal from a microphone at the reception point in a workshop and that from a second microphone close to a particular machine. Both microphone signals will contain contributions from the noise from all the other machines. The parts of the two signals that originate from the machine under test will be coherent, but the other parts will not be. The correlation process will identify the extent to which the two signals 'match each other', and the extent to which the signal at the receiver position is due to radiation from the test machine. The vibration signal from the surface of the machine could also have been used as an alternative to the microphone close to the surface.

The accuracy of sound level measurements

All measurements contain some degree of uncertainty or experimental error. A measured sound pressure level of 74 ±2 dB indicates that the best estimated value of the level is 74 dB but that because of error or uncertainties it could be anywhere in the range from 72 to 76 dB. Sometimes the statement of uncertainty is expressed statistically, for example as a confidence level. If in the above case the uncertainty was a 90% confidence level then this would mean that there was a 90% chance that the measured value lay between 72 and 76 dB, with a 10% chance of it lying outside the limits.

A measured value of 74 ±1 dB would indicate a smaller uncertainty and would be more accurate. A stated value of 74.3 ±1 dB would imply a greater precision of measures, i.e. that changes of 0.1 dB can be detected, but it would have the same uncertainty, i.e. the same accuracy.

Since important decisions about noise control or relating to planning permission conditions or infringements of regulations often depend on the value of measured sound levels it is important to have some indication of their accuracy.

The measurement of the sound pressure level produced by a machine will involve measurement uncertainties produced by:

- the sound level meter;
- the operator of the sound level meter;
- the machine;
- the acoustic environment in which the measurements are taken.

The accuracy of sound level meters has already been mentioned when typical figures were suggested, for example ±2 dB for a type 2 meter. A closer examination of BS 5969, however, indicates that the allowed tolerance, i.e. degree of departure from the defined A-weighted values, varies from ±2 dB in the middle frequency range (500–2000 Hz) to ±5 dB at 8000 Hz. Therefore, it is likely that the meter will be less accurate when used for measuring high frequency noise than for lower frequencies. Some other aspects relating to the accuracy of high frequency measurements are discussed later.

The operator may introduce uncertainties arising from the way in which the meter is used, i.e. set up, calibrated, positioned and read, indicating that because of small variations in all these a slightly different result would be obtained if the measurement were repeated on another occasion.

Slight variations in the way the machine is being operated, for example its speed, load and temperature, and in environmental conditions such as background noise and reflected and absorbed sound, also give rise to uncertainties.

The ultimate attempts to control and define a standard environment for acoustic measurements are the anechoic or the reverberant room. It is interesting to note that the stated accuracy of sound power level measurements resulting from sound level measurements carried out in these ideal test environments are given in BS 2740 Part 2 as ±5 dB for the 125 Hz octave band, ±3 dB for the 250 Hz band and ±1 dB for all higher bands. The reason is that it is much more difficult to produce perfect anechoic or reverberant test measurements at low frequencies, because of sound reflections giving rise to standing waves, than at higher frequencies where wavelengths are smaller and absorption coefficients (in the case of anechoic rooms) are higher.

At high frequencies uncertainties are introduced by the reflection and scattering of sound by the microphone itself. Remember that, ideally, the microphone will have been calibrated either for free-field use (at normal incidence) or pressure response (at grazing incidence) or random incidence. These differences in calibration only become important at high frequencies, and uncertainties arise from the way in which the microphone is orientated with respect to the sound field and from the fact that the sound field itself will be neither perfectly free-field nor perfectly diffuse.

As a result of all of these factors it can be seen that the measured value will be subject to some overall level of uncertainty. One way of estimating this, which is a good measurement practice, is by repeating the measurement several times and looking at the scatter of the results. This scatter, expressed perhaps as a standard deviation, will give an estimate of the random uncertainties in measurement but will fail to detect any systematic errors, such as a calibrator consistently reading 0.5 dB too high.

It is impossible to give likely figures for the overall accuracy of sound level readings because these will vary with all the factors discussed above. It can be seen, however, that the accuracy of the sound level meter is only one of the factors, and probably, in the case of field measurements, not the main one in determining the overall accuracy of the measurement. Only under the most carefully controlled measurement conditions will an accuracy of ±1 dB be achieved and usually the uncertainty will be ±2 dB or higher. Some allowance for measurement uncertainty should be built into noise policy decisions as a factor of safety. It would be foolish, for example, to consider that estimates of personal daily noise exposure of 84 dB(A) meant that actions required at the First Action Level of the Noise at Work Regulations were not necessary.

If the uncertainties in the measurement are truly random then the well known normal or Gaussian distribution (explained in any statistics textbook) will apply. Under these circumstances there is a 68% chance that a particular measurement will be within ±1 standard deviation of the mean value and a 98% chance that it lies within ±2 standard deviations. This approach is used in the selection of ear protectors. The same protector, an ear muff for example, will produce a different amount of attenuation for different wearers because of differences in how well the seals fit over the ears. Therefore, the British standard test (BSEN24869-1, formerly BS5108) requires manufacturers to specify a standard deviation as well as a mean value of attenuation. When calculating the degree of attenuation provided in any particular case it is the mean minus one standard deviation figure, called the 'assumed protection', that should be used. The calculated figure will then be the amount of protection afforded to 68% of the population who wear the protector and 32% will receive a lower degree of protection. A calculation based on 'mean minus two' standard deviations would give a lower figure for the amount of protection, but one enjoyed by 98% of the population, with only 2% receiving less protection.

Measurement reports

Although, depending on the circumstances, many different report formats may be appropriate, they should contain some or all of the following information:

- Summary of main points including conclusions and recommendations.

- Aims and/or objectives, stating the purpose of the measurements.

- Information about the noise source, for example information about machinery or processes being measured: machine type, load, speed, type of material being processed and so on. These details should be sufficient to enable the noise measurements to be repeated under similar conditions at some later date.

- Information about the acoustic environment in which the measurements are made, for example a plan showing layout of workplace, measurement positions, hard reflecting or sound-absorbing surfaces and so on.

- Information about the measurement equipment: type and serial number of sound level meter and calibrator.

- Details of the noise measurement programme, i.e. what was measured, how, when and where.
- Results of the measurements (tables, graphs and so on).
- Analysis and discussion of results.
- Conclusions and recommendations.

Summary

1 The minimum requirement for noise measurement is a hand-held sound level meter with microphone, calibrator and wind-shield.

2 The main factors to be considered when selecting a sound level meter from the large number of types available are: what parameters it will measure (instantaneous sound pressure level only, or L_{Aeq}, peak sound pressure level, octave band levels), how accurate it is (usually type 1 or type 2 accuracy), cost and ease of use.

3 Other measurement equipment which may sometimes be useful include:

- noise dosemeters — for assessment of noise exposure levels;
- tape recorders — for permanent record, evidence, subjective impressions, further analysis;
- narrowband frequency analysers — for identifying tonal noise;
- sound intensity meters — for in-situ sound power measurements;

- building acoustics analysers — for sound insulation measurements of offices; enclosures and havens.

4 The advent of digital signal processing has meant that increasing use is being made of virtual sound level meters consisting of a microphone linked to a laptop computer.

5 When using a sound level meter it is important to carry out a series of simple checks and precautions in order to minimize unwanted influences on the measurement, and to ensure an accurate result. Good training and a checklist approach are essential.

6 Noise measurements may be taken for many different reasons, and the starting point for making all measurement decisions, such as where, what, how and when to measure, is to decide on the purpose of the measurement.

7 Noise emissions from machinery can be measured either as a sound power level or as a sound pressure level at a specified distance. Sound pressure levels are easier to measure and interpret, but the values will depend upon the test conditions under which the measurements are made. Sound power level values relate only to the machine but they are more difficult to measure.

8 There are four methods for measuring the sound power levels of machines. Two of these require the machine to be located in the specialist test environment of either an anechoic or reverberant room. The other two methods may be carried out with the machine in-situ (but with lower accuracy), but require the use of specialist equipment — a sound intensity meter or calibrated sound power source.

9 A draft noise test code for measuring noise from printing and papermaking machinery and equipment specifies measurement positions and machine operating conditions for various types of machine.

10 Detailed procedures for the measurement of environmental noise are specified by the standards BS4142 and ISO1996/BS7445.

11 A number of different techniques and strategies may be used to assess the noise exposure levels of employees. Because of the immense variety of workplace situations there is no one procedure that is suitable for all situations.

12 A wide range of measurement methods may be used to diagnose which are the most important noise sources.

13 All noise measurements are subject to some uncertainties which determine the accuracy of the result. Typically this could be at least ±2 dB for sound level measurements. Noise policy decisions based on such measurements should recognize the limitations of measurement accuracy.

14 Measurement reports should contain all relevant information about the measurement procedures and equipment, the noise sources and the environment in which the measurements were taken, in addition to the results of the measurements and conclusions drawn from them.

Appendix 1
Glossary

absorption The process whereby sound energy is converted into heat by frictional processes within a material. Also, the property possessed by materials of absorbing sound energy.

absorption coefficient The fraction of the total sound energy incident upon a surface that is absorbed or transmitted (i.e. not reflected) by the surface. The value of the coefficient varies from 0 (for very poor absorbers and good reflectors) to 1 (for very good absorbers and poor reflectors).

acoustics The science of sound.

acoustic calibrator A device used for the calibration of sound level meters which produces an accurately known sound pressure level when fitted over the microphone of a sound level meter.

acoustic enclosure A commonly used and versatile method of noise control in which the noise source, for example a noisy machine, is completely enclosed. The enclosure should be constructed of materials with suitable sound insulation properties, and is often lined on the inside with sound-absorbing material. Careful design and construction is necessary to overcome problems of access, ventilation and safety, and to reduce the effect of sound escaping through holes and gaps in the enclosure.

acoustic lagging A method of covering pipes, ducts and other surfaces in order to reduce the amount of noise radiated from them. The essential elements are a resilient layer such as foam or mineral fibre, applied next to the noise-radiating surface, and then an additional heavy layer, for example, of metal or timber on top of this. Acoustic lagging should not be confused with thermal lagging, which will not be effective at reducing noise.

Action Level A noise exposure level in the workplace defined in the Noise at Work Regulations 1989.

active noise control Reduction in noise levels achieved using a system of microphones, loudspeakers and signal processing equipment whereby the noise is cancelled out by an equal and opposite sound from the loudspeakers.

airborne sound Sound or noise radiated directly from a source, such as a loudspeaker or machine, into the surrounding air in contrast to structure-borne sound that is transmitted from source to receiver via the building structure.

ambient noise The totally encompassing noise in a given situation at a given time, which is usually composed of noise from many sources, near and far. Defined in BS4142.

analogue to digital converter A to D converter, or ADC. A device used in digital sound level meters which samples and digitizes analogue signals from the microphone.

anti-vibration (AV) mounts Springs or other resilient materials used to reduce the transmission of vibration or structure-borne sound by isolating the source from the receiver.

APL *see* assumed protected level.

assumed protection The value of attenuation provided by a hearing protector recommended for use in calculating the A-weighted sound level at the wearer's ear, usually obtained by subtracting the standard deviation from the mean value of attenuation.

assumed protected level (APL) The notional sound level at the protected ear, based upon the assumed protection provided by the hearing protector.

attenuation A measure, in decibels, of the amount by which the level of noise is reduced, by whatever means.

attenuator A device introduced into an exhaust or extract system in order to reduce noise. Absorptive or dissipative types exploit the properties of sound-absorbing materials. Reactive types are designed to use reflected sound to 'cancel out' noise at particular frequencies. Also called silencer, muffler.

audiogram A chart or graph showing variation of hearing level with frequency.

AV mounts *see* antivibration mounts.

a-weighting The most commonly used method of weighting a broadband noise according to its frequency spectrum in order to produce a single-figure measurement. It was devised in an attempt to take into account the fact that human response to sound is not equally sensitive to all frequencies.

⌑ ⌑ ⌑

background noise level The relatively steady average minimum base level of residual noise at a location, underlying any fluctuations in noise level. Background noise level is defined in BS4142 as the L_{A90} value of the residual noise. *See also* residual noise.

broadband noise Noise containing a wide range of frequencies.

⌑ ⌑ ⌑

c-weighting One of the frequency weightings defined in BS5969 (IEC 651), which is closest to the linear or unweighted value. Sometimes used for the measurement of low frequency noise and for peak measurements of impulsive noises.

⌑ ⌑ ⌑

damping A process whereby vibrational energy is converted into heat through some frictional mechanism, thus causing the level of vibration to decrease.

DAT *see* digital audiotape recorder.

dB(A) The A-weighted sound pressure level. *See also* A-weighting.

decibel (dB) A logarithmic scale for measuring sound powers, sound pressures and sound intensities. The decibel scale may be used to measure absolute levels of quantities by specifying reference values which fix one point in the scale (0 dB) in absolute terms.

diffraction The process whereby an acoustic wave is disturbed and its energy redistributed in space as a result of an obstacle in its path.

diffuse sound field A sound field in which, as a result of multiple reflections, sound energy flows equally in all directions, and there is a uniform sound pressure.

digital audio tape recorder (DAT) A tape recorder that records acoustic signals on tape in coded digital form.

direct sound Sound which travels directly from source to receiver without reflection.

directivity factor and directivity index Terms used to describe the directionality of noise sources.

⌑ ⌑ ⌑

emission the total noise output from a noise source, measured either as a sound power level, or as the sound pressure level at a specified distance from the source.

environmental impact assessment (EIA) An assessment of environmental effects likely to result from a proposed development, required in connection with planning applications.

EIA *see* environmental impact assessment.

equivalent continuous noise level, $L_{Aeq,T}$ Of a time-varying noise: the steady noise level which, over the period of time, T, under consideration, contains the same amount of (A-weighted) sound energy as the time-varying noise, over the same period of time.

⌑ ⌑ ⌑

F, fast time weighting An averaging time used in sound level meters, and defined in BS 5969 (IEC 651).

flanking transmissions, flanking paths Any transmission path between source and receiver other than the direct one, which is usually through the partition (wall, floor or ceiling) separating them.

fractional dose A fractional component of a total noise exposure, defined in Noise Guide No. 3 of the Noise at Work Regulations.

frequency The number of cycles per second of a pure tone sound, measured in hertz (Hz).

frequency analysis The separation and measurement of a noise into frequency bands.

frequency spectrum A graph resulting from a frequency analysis, showing the different levels of the noise in the various frequency bands.

frequency weighting An electronic filter built into a sound level meter according to BS 5969. *See also* A-weighting and C-weighting.

⌑ ⌑ ⌑

hearing level A measured threshold of hearing, expressed in decibels relative to a specified standard threshold for normal hearing.

hearing loss Any increase of the hearing levels of an individual above the specified standard of normal hearing.

hertz (Hz) The unit of frequency. The number of cycles per second.

HML method High-medium-low method for estimating the A-weighted sound pressure level at the ear when a hearing protector is worn.

¤ ¤ ¤

immission the noise exposure level, or noise dose, received at a reception point such as a site boundary or a domestic premises, incorporating both the level and duration of the exposure, and measured for example, as an $L_{\mathrm{Aeq,24h}}$.

inertia base A concrete slab used as part of a vibration isolation system to provide additional mass, rigidity and stability.

insertion loss The insertion loss of a noise control device such as a silencer or enclosure is the difference, in dB, between the noise level with and without the device present.

insulation The reduction or attenuation of airborne sound by a solid partition between source and receiver, such as a building partition (e.g. a floor, wall or ceiling), a screen or barrier, or an acoustic enclosure.

integrating sound level meter A sound level meter that electrically integrates sound pressure signals to measure the equivalent continuous sound level, L_{Aeq}.

isolation (or vibration isolation) The reduction of vibration and structure-borne sound by the use of resilient materials inserted in the transmission path between source and receiver.

¤ ¤ ¤

level, L A value on a decibel scale.

L_{A} *see also* A-weighting and dB(A).

LAE *see* sound exposure level, SEL.

$L_{\mathrm{Aeq,T}}$ *see* equivalent continuous noise level.

L_{Amax} The maximum RMS A-weighted sound pressure level occurring within a specified time period. The time weighting, fast or slow, is usually specified.

$L_{\mathrm{AN,T}}$ Percentile level, i.e. the sound pressure level, in dB(A) which is exceeded for N% of the time interval T, as, for example in $L_{\mathrm{A,18h}}$ and $L_{\mathrm{A,90}}$.

$L_{\mathrm{EP,d}}$ *see* personal daily noise exposure level.

L_{W} *see* sound power level.

long-term sound level, long-term average rating level, long-term time interval Terms used in connection with the description and measurement of environmental noise, and defined in BS7445.

loudness The measure of the subjective impression of the magnitude, or strength, of a sound.

¤ ¤ ¤

masking The process whereby the threshold of hearing for one sound is raised owing to the presence of another, thus rendering the first sound inaudible.

mass law An approximate relationship for predicting the sound reduction index of panels and partitions, based only on the surface density of the panel and the frequency of the sound.

measurement time interval A term used in standards on the measurement and rating of environmental noise (BS4142 and BS7445).

⌑ ⌑ ⌑

NAMAS National Accreditation and Measurement Service.

narrowband analysis Frequency analysis using band pass filters with a narrow bandwidth, i.e. less than one-third octave.

NC *see* noise criteria and noise rating.

near field Of a sound source: the region of space surrounding the source where the sound pressure varies with position in a complex way and does not obey the inverse square law.

NEC *see* noise exposure category.

NIPTS Noise-induced permanent threshold shift. Permanent hearing loss resulting from exposure to noise.

noise (1) Unwanted sound. (2) Unwanted signal (usually electrical) in a measurement or instrumentation system.

noise abatement zones Zones that a local authority may set up under provisions in the Control of Pollution Act (1994) in order to prevent or control any future increase in noise levels.

noise criteria (NC) and noise rating (NR) These are methods of rating a steady, i.e. non-time-varying noise, according to its frequency spectrum. The octave band spectrum is compared, band by band, with an empirically determined set of spectra which define the various NC values. This is usually done by plotting the noise spectrum against a set of NC curves. The NC value should not be exceeded in any band and so each band may be assigned an NC value, and the NC value of the noise is that of its highest band value. The NR system is very similar. NC and NR are used, as an alternative to dB(A), as a method for specifying acceptable levels of background noise levels for various types of internal environment (libraries, office, etc.).

noise dose An amount of noise energy, usually A-weighted, received by a person, resulting from a combination of sound pressure level and exposure time. *See also* personal daily noise exposure level, $L_{EP,d}$.

noise emission A measure of the sound energy radiated by a noise source.

noise exposure category (NEC) A term used in Planning Policy Guidance Note No. 24 *Planning and Noise* for appraising proposals for development which might be affected by exposure to noise from transport and other sources. Four noise exposure categories are recommended, ranging from category A, where noise is unlikely to be a significant factor, to category D, where noise is such an important factor that planning permission should normally be refused.

noise immission A measure of the sound energy received at a certain point.

noise index A method of evaluating or rating a noise, usually by assigning a single number to it, based on some combination of its physical characteristics (sound pressure level, frequency and duration) and other factors, such as time of day, or tonal or impulsive characteristics.

noise test codes Documents giving guidance on how noise emission from various types of machine is to be tested, issued in connection with the EC Directive 83/392/EEC.

⌑ ⌑ ⌑

octave and one-third octave bands An internationally standardized system of frequency bands widely used in noise measurement. In the octave band system each band is designated by its centre frequency that is double that of the adjacent lower band. The audio frequency range is covered by measurements in 10 bands centred on the frequencies (in hertz): 31.5, 63, 125, 250, 500, 1000, 2000, 4000, 8000 and 16000. One-third octave band analysis involves splitting the same range into 30 bands, three in each octave.

⌑ ⌑ ⌑

pascal (Pa) Unit of sound pressure. $1\,\mathrm{Pa} = 1\,\mathrm{Nm}^{-2}$

peak sound pressure The maximum deviation of a signal from its mean value within a specified time interval.

percentile level, $L_{AN,T}$ The sound level, in dB(A), which is exceeded for *N*% of the time interval *T*, as, for example, in L_{A18h} and L_{A90}.

permanent threshold shift The component of threshold shift that shows no progressive reduction with the passage of time when the apparent cause has been removed.

personal daily noise exposure level, $L_{Ep,d}$ That steady or constant level that, over 8 hours, contains the same amount of A-weighted sound energy as is received by the subject during the working day.

plane wave A wave in which the wavefronts are plane and parallel everywhere, and so the sound energy does not diverge with increasing distance from the source.

PPG24 Department of Environment Planning Policy Guidance Note 24: *Planning and Noise.*

plenum A chamber or space used to collect air prior to its distribution via a duct system, which, when lined with sound-absorbing material, can be used to reduce noise.

point source An idealized concept of an acoustic source which radiates spherical waves.

PNR Predicted noise level reduction of a hearing protector, as determined by the HML method.

pure tone A sound of single frequency for which the sound pressure varies sinusoidally with time.

pure tone audiometer An instrument for measuring hearing acuity to pure tones by determination of hearing levels.

⌑ ⌑ ⌑

rating level A noise index defined in BS4142 and BS7445. It is the equivalent continuous A-weighted sound pressure level during a specified time period, adjusted for tonal and impulsive characteristics of the sound.

ray A straight line representing the direction in which a sound is travelling, used in situations where the size of reflecting surfaces is large compared with the sound wavelength.

reactive silencer One that uses cancellation of sound by reflections to reduce sound levels rather than sound-absorbing materials.

reference time interval The time interval over which a noise index is measured or calculated for assessment purposes in BS4142 and BS7445.

reflection The redirection of waves that occurs at a boundary between media when the size of the boundary interface is large compared with the wavelength.

refraction The change in direction of travel of sound waves caused by changes in the speed of sound with height above ground in the atmosphere.

residual noise The ambient noise remaining when the specific noise is suppressed. Defined in BS4142 and BS7445. *See also* specific noise, ambient noise.

resonance The situation whereby a maximum amplitude of vibration occurs in a system when the exciting or driving frequency coincides with one of the natural frequencies of the system.

reverberant room A standard acoustic test environment designed to produce diffuse sound conditions throughout the space.

reverberant sound/reverberation The sound in an enclosed space that results from repeated reflections at the boundaries.

reverberant sound field The region in an enclosed space where the reverberant sound is the major contributor to the total sound pressure level.

reverberation time The time required for the steady sound pressure level in an enclosed space to decay by 60 dB, measured from the moment the sound source is switched off.

ringing Transient free vibration of bodies caused by impact.

room constant *Rc* A measure of the amount of sound absorption in a room, used in the calculation of reverberant sound pressure level in a room.

root mean square (RMS) The value of sound pressure usually measured by a sound level meter: it is the square root of the average of the 'pressure squared' values measured over a given time interval.

¤ ¤ ¤

S, slow time weighting One of the standard averaging times for sound level meter displays, defined in BS5969.

Sabine's formula A formula for predicting reverberation times of rooms.

silencer A device for reducing noise in ducts, exhausts and extract systems, either of the absorptive or reactive type. Also called attenuators or mufflers.

snubber A device used to restrict the relative displacement of a vibrating system.

sound exposure level SEL or L_{AE} A measure of A-weighted sound energy, used to describe noise 'events' such as the passing of a train or aircraft. It is the A-weighted sound pressure level that, if occurring over a period of one second, would contain the same amount of A-weighted sound energy as the event.

sound intensity The sound power flowing per unit area, in a given direction, measured over an area perpendicular to the direction of flow. Sound intensity is measured in Wm^{-2}.

sound level meter An instrument for measuring sound pressure levels.

sound power The sound energy radiated per unit time by a sound source, measured in watts (W).

sound power level, L_W Sound power measured on a decibel scale: $L_W = 10\log(W/W_0)$, where W_0 is the reference value of sound power, 10^{-12} W.

sound pressure The fluctuations in air pressure, from the steady atmospheric pressure, created by sound, measured in pascals (Pa).

sound pressure level, SPL or *Lp* sound Pressure measured on a decibel scale: $L_p = 20\log(p/p_0)$ where p_0 is the reference sound pressure, 20×10^{-6} Pa.

sound reduction index, *R* A measure of the airborne sound-insulating properties of a material in the form of a panel or partition, or of a building element such as a wall, window or floor, measured in decibels. Also known as transmission loss.

sound wave A pressure wave in a fluid that transmits sound energy through the medium by virtue of the inertial, elastic and damping properties of the medium.

specific noise The particular component of the ambient noise that is under consideration or investigation, e.g. in connection with a planning application or noise complaint. Defined in BS4142.

speech interference level A measure of the ambient noise level in offices that gives an indication of the degree to which speech will be intelligible. It is based on the arithmetic mean of the octave band sound pressure levels 500 Hz, 1000 Hz and 2000 Hz, which are most significant for good speech intelligibility.

spherical waves An idealized model of how sound propagates in free-field conditions, and used as the basis of certain sound level prediction methods.

standard deviation A measure of the deviation or scatter of a set of values (e.g. sound pressure level measurements) from the mean value.

standing waves A wave system characterized by a stationary pattern of amplitude distribution in space arising from the interference of progressive waves. Also called stationary waves.

stationary waves *see* standing waves.

static deflection The deflection produced in an antivibration mount when placed under a machine by the weight of the machine. It is related to the natural frequency of the machine-isolator system, and is used for specifying isolators of appropriate stiffness.

steady noise Noise for which the fluctuations in time are small enough to permit measurement of average sound pressure level to be made satisfactorily without the need to measure L_{Aeq} using an integrating sound level meter. Defined in BS4142.

structure-borne sound Sound which reaches the receiver after travelling from the source via a building or machine structure. Structure-borne sound travels very efficiently in buildings and is more difficult to predict than airborne sound.

⌑ ⌑ ⌑

threshold of hearing For a given listener, the lowest sound pressure level of a particular sound that, under specified measurement conditions, can be heard, assuming that the sound reaching the ears from other sources is negligible.

threshold shift The deviation, in decibels, of a measured hearing level from one previously established.

time weighting One of the standard averaging times (F, S, I) used for the measurement of RMS sound pressure level in sound level meters, specified in BS5969.

transmission loss *see* sound reduction index.

transmissibility A measure of the performance of a vibration isolation system, the ratio of vibration amplitude on either side of antivibration mounts.

⌑ ⌑ ⌑

vibration A to-and-fro motion which oscillates about a fixed, equilibrium position.

⌑ ⌑ ⌑

wavelength The minimum distance between two points in the medium transmitting a progressive wave which are in phase.

Appendix 2
Additional information

Further reading

Books

Anderson J S and Bratos-Anderson M, *Noise: Its measurement, analysis, rating and control*, Avebury Technical (1993)

Bies D A and Hansen C H, *Engineering Noise Control*, Unwin Hyman (1996)

Beranek L L, *Noise Reduction*, Peninsula Publishing, (1988)

Beranek L L and Ver I L (Eds), *Noise and Vibration Control Engineering*, John Wiley and Sons (1992)

Beranek L L, *Noise and Vibration Control*, Revised Edition, Institute of Noise and Vibration Control (1988)

(the three books by Beranek listed above give both theoretical and practical details)

Elvhammar H and Landstrom L, *Fight the Noise — Examples of methods and solutions within companies and institutions in Sweden*, Swedish Work Environment Fund (1990) (A book of practical case studies, with sections on the printing and papermaking industries)

Harris C M (Ed), *Shock and Vibration Handbook*, 3rd Edition, McGraw-Hill (1988)

Hassall J R and Zaveri K, *Acoustic Noise Measurements*, Bruel and Kjaer (1979)

Norton M P, *Fundamentals of Noise and Vibration Analysis for Engineers*, Cambridge University Press (1989)

Owen S, Peters R J and Smith B J, *Acoustics and Noise Control*, Addison Wesley Longman (1996) (Textbook style, chapter on vibration and comprehensive chapter on the law, with references to legal cases)

Pelton H K, *Noise Control Management*, Van Nostrand Reinhold (1993) (Emphasis on management but contains many practical examples and case studies of noise control)

Penn C, *Noise Control*, Shaw and Sons (1995) (Concerned mainly with legal and administrative aspects of noise control)

Sharland I J, *Woods Practical Guide to Noise Control*, Woods of Colchester (1972) (An engineer's guide, with emphasis on noise from air- and gas-flow systems)

Webb (Ed), *Noise Control in Industry*, Faber (1991) (Contains many practical examples and details of engineering noise control methods)

Noise Control Principles and Practice, Bruel and Kjaer (1982) (Simple but effective illustrations of noise reduction principles and methods)

HSE publications

100 Practical Applications of Noise Reduction Methods (1983) (Out of print, emphasis on enclosures, but still useful with examples relating to printing and packaging)

Damage to Hearing Arising from Leisure Noise: a Review of the Literature (1985)

Noise in the Workplace: a Selective Bibliography (1990)

Hearing Protection (An interactive learning package on CD ROM) (1996)

Protection of Hearing in the Paper and Board Industry (1988)

Noise Reduction at Buckle Folding Machines (1986)

Noise Reduction at Web-fed Presses (1988)

Noise Control in the Rubber Industry (1990)

Noise Control at Foundry Shakeouts (1995)

Noise at Work: the Noise at Work Regulations (1989)

Guide No 1: *Legal Duties of Employers to Prevent Damage to Hearing*

Guide No 2: *Legal Duties of Designers, Manufacturers, Importers and Suppliers to Prevent Damage to Hearing*

HS(G)56 *Noise at Work: Noise Assessment, Information and Control.* Noise Guides 3–8 (1990)

HS(G)88 *Hand/Arm Vibration* (1994)

HS(G)109 *Control of Noise in Quarries* (1993)

HS(G)138 *Sound Solutions: Techniques to Reduce Noise at Work* (1995) (Follow-up of the earlier *100 Practical Applications*, with 60 case studies)

Guidance Note MS26 *A Guide to Audiometric Testing Programmes* (1995)

Guidance Note PM56 *Noise from Pneumatic Systems* (1985)

Contract Research Report 3 *A Small Scale Survey into the Use of Audiometry in Practice* (1988)

Contract Research Report 4 *A Review of Active Attenuation and Development of an Active Attenuator 'Open Refuge'* (1988)

Contract Research Report 14 *The Effects Upon Hearing of Noise in Combination with Other Agents: A Critical Review of the Literature* (1989)

Contract Research Report 24 *The 'Real World' Attenuation of Hearing Protectors* (1990)

Contract Research Report 28 *Investigation of Machinery Noise Reduction at Source* (1991)

Contract Research Report 29 *Tables for the Estimation of Hearing Impairment Due to Noise for Otologically Normal and Typical Unscreened Populations of Males and Females* (1991)

Contract Research Report 54 *Attitudes Towards Noise as an Occupational Hazard, Volume 1: Summary and Volume 2: Detailed Report of the Study* (1993)

Contract Research Report 55 *Attitudes Towards Noise as an Occupational Hazard, Volume 3: Literature Survey and Review of Public Awareness Campaigns* (1993)

Contract Research Report 63 *Noise and the Foetus: a Critical Review of the Literature* (1994)

Contract Research Report 68 *Occupational Hearing Loss from Low Level Noise* (1995)

Contract Research Report 73 *Dust and Noise in the Construction Process* (1995)

Contract Research Report 116 *Cost Benefit Analysis of Noise at Work* (1996)

Research Paper 36 *Assessment of Compliance with the Noise at Work Regulations 1989* (1994)

HSE leaflets

Protection of hearing in paper and board mills

IND(G)75 *Introducing the Noise at Work Regulations: A brief guide to the requirements for controlling noise at work*

IND(G)99L *Noise at Work: A guide for employees*

IND(G)122 *Listen up!*

IND(G)193 *Health Surveillance in Noisy Industries* (1995)

IND(G)200 *Ear Protection in Noisy Firms: Employers' Duties Explained* (1995)

IND(G)201 *Hear This: A Pocket Card for Employees in Noisy Working environments* (1995)

Other reports

Berglund B and Lindvall T, *Community Noise,* document prepared for the World Health Organisation, Center for Sensory Research, Stockholm University and Karolinska Institute (1995)

CEC, *Future Noise Policy,* Commission of the European Communities Green Paper (1996)

Department of the Environment, Planning Policy Guidance 24 *Planning and Noise,* HMSO (1994)

Department of the Environment, *Report of the Noise Review Working Party* (Batho Report) HMSO (1990)

Department of the Environment, *The Health of the Nation*, Consultative Document, HMSO (Nov 1996)

Department of the Environment, *The United Kingdom National Environmental Health Action Plan*, HMSO (1996)

Lambert J and Vallet M, *Study related to the Preparation of a Communication on a Future EC Noise Policy*, INRETS (1994)

Noise. Final Report for the Committee on the Problem of Noise, (Wilson Report) Cmnd 2056: HMSO (1963)

OECD, Fighting Noise in the 1990s, OECD Report, Paris (1991)

Wright F B and Powell J A, *The IRS Guide to the Noise at Work Regulations*, Industrial Relations Services (1991)

Journals

Acoustics Bulletin, Institute of Acoustics

Noise News International, International Institute of Noise Control Engineering

Applied Acoustics, Elsevier Applied Science

Noise and Vibration Worldwide, Institute of Physics

Organizations

The Association of Noise Consultants
6 Trap Road
Guilden Morden (Nr. Royston)
Hertfordshire SG8 OJE
UK

Chartered Institute of Environmental Health
Chadwick Court
15 Hatfields
London SE1 8DJ
UK

Institute of Acoustics
77A St Peter's Street
St Albans
Hertfordshire AL1 3BN
UK

(The Institute of Acoustics publishes an annual register of members, with lists of noise consultants and suppliers of acoustics and noise control products and materials)

National Society for Clean Air and Environmental Protection
136 North Street
Brighton
East Sussex BN1 1RG
UK

Standards

BS British standard; ISO international standard; EN European normalized standard

BS4142: 1997	*Method for Rating Industrial Noise Affecting Mixed Residential and Industrial Areas*
BS5228: 1997	*Noise and Vibration Control on Construction and Open Sites*
BS5969: 1981/ IEC651	*Specification for Sound Level Meters*
BS6655: 1986/ ISO6189: 1983/ EN26189: 1991	*Specification for Pure Tone Air Conduction Threshold Audiometry for Hearing Conservation Purposes*
BS6698: 1986/ IEC804: 1984	*Specification for Integrating-Averaging Meters*

A new international standard IEC 1672 covering the performance and verification of both integrating and non-integrating sound level meters is in the course of preparation to replace IEC651 and IEC804.

BS7445: 1991/ ISO1996: 1982	*Description and Measurement of Environmental Noise*
BS7580: 1997	*Specification for the Verification of Sound Level Meters*
BS8233: 1999	*Sound Insulation and Noise Reduction for Buildings. Code of practice*
BSEN352: 1993	*Part 1: Ear Muffs. Part 2: Ear Plugs* (formerly BS6344)
BSEN458: 1994	*Hearing Protectors: recommendations for selection, use, care and maintenance. Guidance to suppliers, purchasers, safety authorities and wearers*
BSEN24869-1: 1993/ISO 4869	*Sound Attenuation of Hearing Protectors. Part 1: Subjective Methods of Measurements* (formerly BS5108)

BSEN 60942: 1998	*Specification for Sound Calibrators*
BSEN 61252: 1997	*Specification for Personal Sound Exposure Meters*
BSEN ISO 11654: 1997	*Acoustics — Sound Absorbers for Use in Buildings. Rating of Sound Absorption*
BSEN ISO 11688-1: 1998	*Acoustics — Recommended Practice for the Design of Low-noise Machinery and Equipment. Part 1: Planning*
BSEN ISO 1689: 1997	*Acoustics — Procedure for the Comparison of Noise-emmission Data for Machinery and Equipment*
BSEN ISO 11690: 1993	*Acoustics — Recommended Practice for the Design of Low-noise Workplaces Containing Machinery. Part 1: Noise Control Strategies. Part 2: Examples of Noise Control Measures. Part 3: Sound Propagation and Noise Prediction in Work Rooms*
BSEN ISO 12001: 1997	*Acoustics — Noise emitted by Machinery and Equipment. Rules for the Drafting and Presentation of a Noise Test Code.*
BSEN ISO 14163: 1998	*Acoustics — Guidelines for Noise Control by Silencers*
EN 23740	*Acoustics: Determination of Sound Power Levels of Noise Sources. Guidance for the Use of Basic Standards for the Preparation of Noise Test Codes.* See also ISO 3740: 1980
EN 23744	*Acoustics: Determination of Sound Power Levels of Noise Sources. Engineering Method Employing an Enveloping Measurement Surface Over a Reflecting Plane (grade 2 accuracy).* See also ISO 3744: 1994
EN 23746	*Acoustics: Determination of Sound Power Levels of Noise Sources. Survey Method Employing an Enveloping Measurement Surface (Grade 3 Accuracy).* See also ISO 3746: 1995

ISO 1999: 1990	*Acoustics: Determination of Occupational Noise Exposure and Estimation of Noise-induced Hearing Impairment*
ISO 4871: 1996	*Acoustics: Declaration and Verification of Noise Emission Values of Machinery and Equipment*
ISO 9613: 1993	*Acoustics — Attenuation of Sound During Propagation Outdoors. Part 1: Calculation of the Absorption of Sound by the Atmosphere, Part 2: A General Method of Calculation*
ISO 9614/1: 1993	*Acoustics: Determination of Sound Power Levels Using Sound Intensity. Measurement at Discrete Points*
ISO 9614/2: 1996	*Acoustics: Determination of Sound Power Levels Using Sound Intensity. Scanning Method*
ISO 11200: 1995	*Acoustics — Noise emitted by Machinery and Equipment. Guidelines for the Use of Basic Standards for the Determination of Emission Sound Pressure Levels at a Work Station and at Other Specified Positions.* See also BSEN 11200: 1996 and EN 31200
ISO 11201: 1995	*Acoustics — Noise Emitted by Machinery and Equipment. Measurement of Emission Sound Pressure Levels at a Work Station and at Other Specified Positions. Engineering Method in an Essentially Free Field over a Reflecting Plane*
ISO 11202: 1995	*Acoustics — Noise Emitted by Machinery and Equipment. Measurement of Emission Sound Pressure Levels at a Work Station and at Other Specified Positions. Survey Method In Situ*

ISO 11203: 1995	*Acoustics — Noise emitted by machinery and equipment. Measurement of emission sound pressure levels at a work station and at other specified positions*
ISO 11204: 1995	*Acoustics — Noise emitted by machinery and equipment. Measurement of emission sound pressure levels at a work station and at other specified positions. Method requiring environmental corrections*

Index

folios set in italic type refer to figures or tables

A

absorption 349
absorption coefficient 115, 349
acoustic attenuators 152–155
acoustic calibrator 349
acoustic design
  of a new paper board machine 215–217
acoustic enclosure 349
acoustic enclosures 149–152
acoustic energy 16–18
acoustic intensity 16–18
acoustic lagging 156–158, *159*, 349
acoustic power 16–18
  calculate 17
acoustic shielding 221
acoustics 349
Act
  Control of Pollution 1974 268, 288
  Disability Discrimination 259
  Environmental Protection 1990 268, 269, 272–273, 303
  Health and Safety at Work 1974 291
  Health and Safety of Work 1974 289
  Land Compensation 1973 268
  Local Government 1972 272
  Single European (1987) 301
  Town and Country Planning 1990 274
Action Level 40, 42, 60, 65, 193, 196, 243, 245, 289, 300, 301–302, 304, 308, 312, 343, 349
Action Programme
  Fifth 82, 302, 305
  Second 302
active noise control 182, *183*, 349
  components *218*
  vacuum pumps 217–221
activity sample 336
air absorption 116, 134
airborne sound 139, 202, 349
ambient noise 350
amplitude 13
analogue to digital converter 350
anechoic 125
angle of incidence 115
annoyance 75–77
  defined as 75
  different noise types *80*
  measuring public response to 77
  noise types in the UK *81*
  threshold for 76
anti-noise signal 182
antivibration mounts 146, *147*, 148, 149, 350
APL *see* assumed protection level
Assessment of Compliance with the Noise at Work Regulations 72
assumed protected level 350
assumed protection 350
atmospheric pressure 3
attenuation 110, 152, 154, 198, 350
attenuator 207, 350
Attitudes Towards Noise as an Occupational Hazard 70
audible acoustic pressures 6–7
audio-frequency range 4–6
audiogram 257, 260, 263, 350
audiometer *263*
audiometric booth *264*
audiometric checks 305

audiometry 56–57, 256, 294–295
benefits of 69
diagnostic 257
monitoring 190, 203, 213, 260
a-weighted decibels 21–25
a-weighted sound energy 36
a-weighted sound pressure level 52
a-weighting 350

B

background noise
effect of on sound level measurements, example 28
background noise level 350
Bekesy 64, 263
British Society for Audiology 265
British Standard
BS 2740 342
BS 4142 44, 268, 271, 277, 279–286, 304, 308, 323, 334–335, 347, 350, 353, 355, 356, 357
BS 5108 193, 344
BS 5228 132, 268
BS 5969 309, 312, 334, 342, 350, 351, 355, 357
BS 6402 313
BS 6698 334
BS 7189 334
BS 7445 271, 281, 286–287, 304, 323, 330–333, 347, 352, 353, 355
BS7445 334
British Standard/European normalized standard
BSEN 24869-1 193, 344
broadband noise 3, 164, 350
building acoustics analysers 315
Burns 61

C

calibrator 309
canal cap 192
cavity resonator 119
Chartered Institute of Environmental Health 83
close shielding 156–158, 159
common environmental policy 302
community noise
cyclone and ancillary equipment 229–230
constructive interference 91
continuous equivalent noise level 61
calculation *39*
contour plot 336
Contract Research Report 116 66, 68
Contract Research Report 54 65, 70
Control of Noise (Measurement and Registers) Regulations 1976 288
c-weighting 350

D

Damage Risk Criteria 62
damping 138, 155–156, *157*, 350
DAT *see* digital audiotape recorder 350
dB(A) 351
decibel 351
combining *26*
decibel arithmetic
consequences of 27–30
decibel scale 18–19
reasons for using 19–20
Department of Employment
Code of Practice 61, 190
Reducing the Exposure of Employed Persons to Noise 296
Department of Health 84
Department of the Environment 84, 278
Circular 10/73 *Planning and Noise* 268, 275
Circular 15/88 287
Planning Policy Guidance Note 24 43, *276*
Preparation of Environmental Statements for Planning Projects that Require Environmental Assessment 288
destructive interference 91, 182
diagnostic measurement 336–341

diffraction 351
diffuse sound field 351
digital audio tape recorder 351
direct sound 121, 351
  pressure level 122
directionality 134
Directive 83/392/EEC 354
Directive 85/337/EEC 287
Directive 86/188/EEC 289, 294, 298, 301
Directive 89/392/EEC 298
directivity factor 104, 134, 351
directivity index 104, 134, 351
disablement benefit 66
dosemeter 238, *239*, 312–313, 336, 345
dosimeter 312–313
double-leaf construction
  design features of *145*
Draft noise test code — CEN Standard *Noise Measurement Methods for Printing, Paper Converting, Papermaking Machines and Equipment* 328–330

E

ear
  basilar membrane 55, *56*, 64
  cochlea 55, *56*, 64
    damage to 59
  cochlear fluid 55
  control of sense of balance 55
  ear canal 55
  Eustachian tube 54, 56
  hearing 53–65
  how it works 53–56
  incus 54
  inner *54*, 55
    infections of 59
  malleus 54
  middle 53, *54*
    ossicles 55
    stapediary reflex 55
  Organ of Corti 55, *56*
  ossicles 54
  outer 53, *54*
  oval window 55
  pressure equalization 54
  stapes 54, 55
ear muffs 68, 182, 192, 196, 231, 343
ear plugs 68, 191, 196, 231
ear protection 203, 209
  factors found to be important 71
ear protectors 42, 68, 71, 190–201, 240
  information, instruction and training 199–201
  performance of 192–197
  selection of 197–199, 343
  types of 191–192
effects of noise 72–79
  effects on social behaviour 79
EIA *see* environmental impact assessment 351
emission 351
Environment — Towards Sustainability, The 82, 302
environmental impact assessment 351
equal loudness contour *23*
equivalent continuous noise level 351
European Commission regulations 298–303
European normalized standard
  EN 23744 328
  EN 23746 328
  EN 29614/1 328
  EN 29614/2 328
exhaust silencer 168, *169*

F

fan
  modifications 225
fans 224, 231
fast Fourier transform analyser 33, 314, 339
fast time weighting 351
field incidence 115

flanking path 127, 130, 134
flanking transmissions, flanking paths 351
flow-induced acoustic resonance 223, *223*
Fourier analysis 9
Fourier synthesis 9
fractional dose 351
frequency 351
frequency analysis 31–36, 351
  instrumentation 9
frequency and wavelength
  significance of 7
frequency content of sound 8
frequency spectrum 351
frequency weighting 351
  A, B and C 22
  network 21

G

ground attenuation 134

H

Health and Safety Executive 173, 193, 205, 214, 265, 291
  100 Practical Applications of Noise Reduction Methods 205
  A Guide to Audiometric Testing Programmes and Health Surveillance in Noisy Industries — Advice for Employers 263
  Draft code of Practice and Guidance Notes *62*
  Guidance Note (MS 26) *A Guide to Audiometric Testing Programmes* 295
  Health Surveillance in Noisy Industries 295
  Health Surveillance in Noisy Industries — Advice for Employers 256
  Noise Reduction at Web-fed Presses 173
  Protection of Hearing in the Paper and Board Industry 184
  Sound Solutions 206
hearing conservation policies 188–190, 203
hearing conservation programme 71, 291
  factors influencing *73*
hearing levels 352
  conductive deafness 57
  factors affecting 57–59
  presbycusis 57, *58*, 63
hearing loss 59–64, 213, 352
hearing protection
  calculation of *194*
  using industrial audiometry 256–265
    cost of failure 261–262
    financial and medical reasons 256–261
    legal reasons 256
    setting up an audiometric programme 263–265
Helmholtz resonator 119, 154
HML method 195–197, 352
HSE 65, 70, 72
  Protection of Hearing in the Paper and Board Industry 179
HSE *see* Health and Safety Executive

I

immission 352
inertia base 352
infrasonic wave 6
insertion loss 352
Institute of Acoustics 288
Institute of Environmental Assessment 288
instrumentation and equipment 307–312
insulation 352
integrating sound level meter 352
interference
  constructive 91
  constructive and destructive *92*
  destructive 91
International Institute for Noise Control Engineering 66

International Standard
ISO 1996 281, 286–287, 304, 330–333, 334, 347
ISO 1999 62
ISO 4869-2 195
ISO 8253 56
ISO 90631 132
ISO 9613 106

J

jet *167*
nozzle *171*

L

L_{A10} 52
L_{A90} 52, 335
L_{Aeq} 36–49, 52, 308
calculate 38
$L_{Aeq,T}$ 42
Lambert J 80
L_{AN} 36–49
Lancet 65
legal case
AG v. *PYA Quarries* (1957) 272
Gillingham Borough Council v. *Medway (Chatham) Dock Co. Ltd. and Others* (1992) 275
Hunter, McPoland and Williams v. *Robinson Wiley Ltd* (1992) 262
Parish v. Stepney Borough Council (1952) 259
Rushmer v. *Polsue and Alfieri Ltd* (1907) 270, 271
Sturges v. *Bridgeman* (1879) 270
Vanderpant v. *Mayfair Hotel Company Limited* (1930 270
Walter v. *Selfe* (1851) 271
$L_{Ep,d}$ 43
nomogram for calculation of 41
local authority environmental health departments
complaints about noise made to 83
long-term average rating level 352
long-term sound level 352
long-term time interval 352
loudness 352
loudness recruitment 60
loudspeaker 95
low frequency noise 22–25

M

machinery noise
specification 183–184
Maekawa 110
Management of the Health and Safety at Work Regulations 256, 305
masking 72, 352
mass law 353
measurement time interval 353
microphones 310–311

N

NAMAS 353
narrowband analysis 353
narrowband frequency analysers 314, 345
narrowband frequency analysis 33, 188, 339–340
narrowband spectrum *220*
near field 353
NIPTS 59, 62
noise 353
at source
machinery 202
change relative to speed *175*
defined as 1, 49
measurement
aims 320–322
from machinery 322–323
reports 344–345
press room dose reductions *180*
produced by traffic 11
radiation of sound 94–105
directionality of sound radiation 95–96
directionality or directivity 104–105
effect of distance on sound levels 96–98
effect of ground reflections

98–100
line and plane sources 100
point sources and plane waves 95
real noise sources 100–104
range of levels at web-fed presses *181*
reel room dose reductions *180*
transmission *140*
variation of level with position in press hall and reel room *178*
noise abatement zones 353
noise at work 289–297
attitudes of employers and employess to the control of 70–72
health surveillance in noisy industries 294–295
noise exposure assessments 291–294
Noise at Work Regulations 40, 60, 62, 65, 68, 72, 190, 193, 200, 201, 203, 208, 214, 243, 289–291, *292*, 294, 300, 301, 304, 308, 312, 343, 349, 351
noise control
active 182–183, 202
at source 139, 161–181, 221–227
boiler air supply fans 224–225
cyclone separators 222–224
dryer oven 225–227
fans and blowers 164–166
jets and exhausts 166–170
machinery noise 161–164
mechanical handling of materials 173
paper making 179–181
printing presses 173–177, 221–222
punch presses 170
estimated cost *177*
examples of treatments *248*
in a paper mill 206–214
newspaper presses
using acoustic enclosures, havens and partitions 246–248
sheet plastic film production 233
single facers 231–232
terminology 158
the corrugated board industry 228–232
noise control materials 158–160
noise control programme 30
noise criteria 34, 52, 230, 353
curves *35*
noise dose 353
noise emissions 353
from machinery 298–301, 323–324
noise enclosure
features of *151*
noise exposure
assessment 240
at work 301–303
factors important in determining 81
in the workplace 65–66
of employees 189
Noise exposure assessment
large printing press 241–245
small print works 236–241
noise exposure categories 275–276, 353
noise exposure level 46–48
assessment 335–336
personal daily 40
noise generation and control 135–203
mechanisms of 136–138
planning, management and housekeeping 135–136
noise immission 354
noise in the community 79–84
noise exposure in the community, extent of 79–81
public plans and programmes to reduce community noise 82–84
noise in the environment 268–288
environmental assessments 287–288

noise abatement zones 288
noise complaints 273–274
noise nuisance 268–272
planning and noise 274–278
noise in the workplace
costs and benefits 66–70
noise index 354
Noise Insulation Regulations 1975 268
noise level
grids 336
noise levels 270
regional newspapers and commercial printers 174
noise map 233, *235*
noise monitoring positon *242*
noise nuisance
printing works 252–255
noise rating 34, 52
noise reduction *222*, *225*, *227*
measured at the exhaust stack *219*
specification of 32
noise refuges 230
Noise Review Working Party 275, 288
noise source 181, *276*
diagnosis of 185–188
directionality 104
near and far fields *103*
noise test codes 354
noise-induced hearing loss
cause of 55
compensation claims 295–298
disablement benefit because of *67*
effects of 63
insurance claims for 66
understanding speech 63
noise-induced permanent threshold shift *see also* NIPTS 59
noise-producing mechanisms
diagnosis of 185–188
noise-radiating panel *159*
normal incidence 115
nosocusis 62
nuisance
at common law 271
private 268, 269
public 268
statutory 268

O

octave band
analysis 31–33
calculation of dB(A) from *31*
octave band barrier attenuations *112*
one-third octave analysis 33
one-third octave band 354
oto-acoustic emission 64–65

P

peak sound pressure 354
percentile level 354
performance of tasks
effect of noise on 77–78
permanent threshold shift 354
personal daily noise exposure level 336, 354
personal daily noise exposure level *see also* $L_{Ep,d}$ 40
PHONS 36
place theory
Bekesy 64
plane wave 95, 354
plane waves 95
Planning Policy Guidance Note 24 *see also* Department of the Environment 268, 275, 304, 323
plenum 354
PNdB 36
PNR *see also* predicted noise level reduction
point source 133, 354
point sources 95
predicted noise level reduction 195–196
pressure, units of 3
punch press 161
pure tone 8, 354
audiometer 354
frequency 3–6

  sound pressure 3–6
  wavelength 3–6

R

random incidence 115
rating level 355
reactive attenuator 155
reactive silencer 355
reel room 176
reference time interval 355
reflection 355
reflection coefficient 114
refraction 355
residual noise 355
resonance 355
reverberant component 139
reverberant room 355
reverberant sound 355
  field 355
reverberation 91, 355
reverberation time 355
RMS *see also* root mean square
Robinson 61
root mean square 13, *14*, 51, 316, 355

S

Sabine 121, 134, 355
SEL
  example 46
  used in the calculation of environmental noise, example 48
SEL *see also* single exposure level
sensorineural deafness 59
signal processing technique 188, 340
silencer 216, 356
  absorptive 154, 182
  dissipative 154
silencers 152–155
sine wave 11
single exposure level 308
sleep disturbance 75
sociocusis 62
sonar 6
sound
  absorption 139, 202
  frequency and wavelength of *5*
  frequency spectrum 9–11
  insulation 139
  intensity 16
  logarithmic human response to 19
  produced in the ear 1
  reduction
    calculation 145
  reduction index 141
  reflection of 92
  refraction of *109*
  transmission
    between rooms 128
  wavelength of 8
sound absorption 114, 143–146
  calculation 118
  values of *119*
  variation of *120*
sound attenuation 158
  calculating *111*
  in thick forests 113
sound exposure level 356
sound insulation 18, 112, 140–143
  arrangements *249*
sound intensity 356
sound intensity level 20–21
sound intensity measurement 340
sound intensity meter 188, 314, 345
sound level
  against distance *99*
  measurement accuracy 341–344
  meter 356
    analogue and digital signal processing 315–317
    components *316*
    computers, data loggers and virtual meters 317–318
    correct use 318–320
    function *316*
  meter and calibrator 307–312
  meter, selection 310
  meters, performance 309
  press hall *175*
  typical 25

variation across press hall and reel stand room *179*
variation of *102*
sound paths
diagnosis of 185–188
sound power 356
human voice 16
jet airliner 16
pneumatic drill 16
sound power level 20–21, 323–324, 346, 356
disadvantage 324
main advantage 126, 324
measurement 325–330
free-field method 326
reverberant room method 327–328
sound intensity method 326–327
substitution method 328
sound pressure 2–3, 356
magnitude of 13–15
variation of with time
for a pure tone *4*
sound pressure level 20–21, 134, 323–324, 346, 356
combining 25–27
emitted by machines 324–325
variation of *124*
sound pressure levels
disadvantage of 127
sound propagation 105–130
acoustic properties of panels and partitions 114–116
air absorption 106
barriers 110–112
example 111–112
ground attenuation 107
sound absorption by surfaces 116
porous absorbers 116–118
reverberation time 121
tuned or resonant absorbers 118–121
sound distribution in rooms 121–127
example 123–124
nonstandard rooms 124–125
special acoustic test rooms 125
specification of machinery noise 126–127
sound velocity gradients 108–110
transmission of sound in buildings 127–130
calculation of airborne sound transmission between rooms 129
example 129–130
sound reduction
predicting *142*
sound reduction index 356
values of *144*
variation of *143*
sound reflection
reduction of 91
sound transmission *138*
airborne and structure-borne 134
control 138–160
sound velocity gradient 134
sound velocity gradients *109*
sound waves 356
behaviour of 88–94
diffraction 88–89
interference 91–93
reflection 89–91
refraction 93
sound absorption 94
in air 1–3
propagated 1
sound-measuring equipment 9
specific noise 356
speech communication
interference with 72–75
speech interference level 34, 356
speed of sound 93
in air 7
spherical waves 356
SPL *see also* sound pressure level
static deflection 357
static sample 336
statistical percentile levels 48–49

stress-related health effects 78–79
structure-borne sound 139, 202, 357
Supply of Machinery (Safety) Regulations 305
Supply of Machinery (Safety) Regulations, The 298–299, 300

T

tape recorder 313–314
temporary threshold shift 259
threshold of hearing 357
threshold of pain 25
threshold shift 357
time weighting 357
tinnitus 60, 63, 74, 261
tone
  frequency of 50
Town and Country Planning (Assessment of Environmental Effects) Regulations 287
transmissibility 357
transmission coefficient 114
transmission loss 357
Treaty of Rome 298
TUC 65

U

ultrasonic frequencies 116
ultrasonic wave 6
Upper Limits for Noise Levels in the Workplace 66

V

Vallet M 80
vibrating panel 137
  damping *157*
vibration 357
  amplitude 137
  damping 202
  isolation 139, 146–149, 202
  measurement 340

W

wave
  plane 95
  spherical 95
waveform
  harmonic 9, *10*
  harmonic wave 12
  impulsive noise 12
  pure tone 12
  random 11
  random noise 12
  transient 11
wavelength 7–9, 50, 357
waves
  standing 93, 356
weighting curves
  A, B and C *24*
Wilson Report 267–268, 303
windshield 312